D0087265

DICTIONARY OF HERBS, SPICES, SEASONINGS, AND NATURAL FLAVORINGS

GARLAND REFERENCE LIBRARY
OF SOCIAL SCIENCE
(VOL. 918)

DICTIONARY OF HERBS, SPICES, SEASONINGS, AND NATURAL FLAVORINGS

by

Carole J. Skelly

GARLAND PUBLISHING, Inc.
New York & London / 1994

ref
TX
406
.S57
1994

Copyright © 1994 by Carole J. Skelly
All rights reserved

Library of Congress Cataloging-in-Publication Data

Skelly, Carole J., 1933–
    Dictionary of herbs, spices, seasonings, and natural flavor-
ings / by Carole J. Skelly.
        p.   cm. — (Garland reference library of social science ;
vol. 918)
    Includes bibliographical references.
    ISBN 0–8153–1465–5 (alk. paper)
    1. Spices—Dictionaries. 2. Herbs—Dictionaries.
3. Cookery (Herbs)—Dictionaries. I. Title. II. Series.
TX406.S57   1994
641.3'382'03—dc20   93–28205
                                                       CIP

Cover design by Patti Hefner

Printed on acid-free, 250-year-life paper
Manufactured in the United States of America

The author would like to extend heartfelt thanks to Sue Gray and Dwight Thomas for the use of books from their extensive botanical libraries and to John Melaugh who started it all when he said, "You should write a book."

Contents

Introduction

Originally, this collection of herb and spice names began as an aid to the ordinary person who had the curiosity to ask, "What is that spice?" or "What is that ingredient listed in the herbal tea on the grocery store shelf?" It soon became evident that no single reference book attempted to list all of the common names by which a plant was known nor to identify those comon names that could refer to two or more different plants, one being safe to use, the other quite toxic. With the increasing public concerns about health, high costs of medical treatment and prescription medicines, and the age-long pursuit of the fountain of youth, more and more people have assumed that "natural is better," "if it is natural, it is safe," and "if it is not safe, the government would not allow it to be sold in stores." This is not always true.

It is not recommended that herbs be used as substitutes for professional medical treatment. Nor is it recommended that any herb or plant extract be used, even in small amounts, without a thorough knowledge of the plant or expert advice. Some herbs and extracts, even in small quantities, may cause allergic reactions, gastric disturbances, or other undesirable reactions in susceptible people. Many plants are extremely toxic, and some have been included here to make the reader aware of the dangers of using these plants.

In the United States commercial use of spices, seasonings, plant extracts, and other flavorings is regulated by the Food and Drug Administration in accordance with the "Federal Food, Drug and Cosmetic Act." This act was first passed in 1938, and almost every year since there have been numerous amendments and additions to it. These changes and additions are published in the Federal Register and yearly in the Code of Federal Regulations. One needs a road map to find one's way through the *Code*. Section 21, Parts 170 to 199, deals with Food and Drugs. The following is taken from

PART 182—SUBSTANCES GENERALLY REGARDED AS SAFE, Subpart A—General Provisions.

182.1 Substances that are generally recognized as safe.
(a) It is impracticable to list all substances that are generally recognized as safe for their intended use. However, by way of illustration, the

Commissioner regards such food ingredients as salt, pepper, sugar, vinegar, baking powder, and monosodium glutamate as safe for their intended use. This part includes additional substances that, when used for the purposes indicated, in accordance with good manufacturing practice, are regarded by the Commissioner as generally recognized as safe for such uses.

(b) For the purpose of this section, good manufacturing practice shall be defined to include the following restrictions:

(1) The quantity of a substance added to a food does not exceed the amount reasonably required to accomplish its intended physical, nutritional, or other technical effect in food; and

(2) The quantity of a substance that becomes a component of a food as a result of its use in the manufacturing, processing, or packaging of food, and which is not intended to accomplish any physical or other technical effect in the food itself, shall be reduced to the extent reasonably possible.

(3) The substance is of appropriate food grade and is prepared and handled as a food ingredient. Upon request the Commissioner will offer an opinion, based on specifications and intended use, as to whether or not a particular grade or lot of the substance is of suitable purity for use in food and would generally be regarded as safe for the purpose intended, by experts qualified to evaluate its safety.

(c) The inclusion of substances in the list of nutrients does not constitute a finding on the part of the Department that the substance is useful as a supplement to the diet for humans.

(d) Substances that are generally recognized as safe for their intended use within the meaning of section 409 of the act are listed in this part. When the status of a substance has been reevaluated, it will be deleted from this part, and will be issued as a new regulation under the appropriate part, e.g., "affirmed as GRAS" under Part 184 or 186 of this chapter; "food additive regulation" under Parts 170 through 180 of this chapter; "interim food additive regulation" under Part 180 of this chapter; or "prohibited from use in food" under Part 189 of this chapter.

This is followed by Part 182.10, which is a listing of the common name (and botanical name of plant source) of "Spices and other natural seasonings and flavorings that are generally recognized as safe for their intended use, within the meaning of section 409 of the Act." For section 409 of the "Federal Food, Drug and Cosmetic Act," I refer you to your public library. There are other lists contained in Section 21 of the *Code* such as essential oils and extracts of plants, plants restricted for use in alcoholic beverages only, and plants banned from use in foods. In this book, "GRAS" has been used to denote those items "generally recognized as safe," and appropriate notation has been made of any restricted or banned items. This notation is based upon the *Code of Federal Regulations*, Section 21, Parts 170 to 199, April 1, 1991.

It is important to realize that the absence of a plant in the Food and Drug Administration listings does not mean it is safe to use, nor does it mean it is not safe to use. It should be a warning sign to proceed with caution. Travel at your own risk!

In cooking, there is no area that causes more confusion than that of herbs, spices, and seasonings. Especially is this true in the United States where foods and recipes have come from a population of diverse cultural backgrounds. Grandma's recipes have been copied (often incorrectly) from generation to generation; native herbs have been substituted for what was used in the "old country"; immigrants call herbs by names from their native lands; works of the great French chefs as well as other non-English cook books have been incorrectly translated; and cheap ingredient substitutes are sold to the unsuspecting, non-label-reading public. Many times lists of spices and herbs have been copied (often incorrectly and with obvious typographical errors) from one cook book to another with no thought as to the accuracy or appropriateness of the material.

The following listing of common names was compiled from ingredient labels on grocery store items, numerous cook books, either from recipes or from ingredient, herb, seasoning and flavoring listings, herb, spice and health food store products, and numerous herb and spice books. An attempt was made to identify the correct botanical name of the plant, the content of mixtures, the general use, and in particular, to cross-reference the various common names. The detailed use of some of the most common herbs and spices such as garlic, sage, cinnamon, cloves, etc., have not been included. They are found in any good recipe book.

Generally, common fruit extracts or flavorings such as orange, banana, lemon, pineapple, etc., are not included in the list. Imitation fruit flavorings can be compounded from a vast array of ingredients. Fenaroli's *Handbook of Flavor Ingredients* includes an entire section devoted to the compounding of flavorings from both natural and synthetic ingredients.

Some of the plants included in the list should never be used in the kitchen but are included because they were found in cook books. Many are carryovers from the days when great-great-grandma not only ran the kitchen but was responsible for concocting the various home remedies to keep the family free of fevers, dyspepsia, worms, and constipation. Some of the plants are only used commercially for concocting those mysterious "spices" and "natural flavorings" listed on labels.

Legend and tradition have attributed many medical properties to herbs and other plant extracts, some of which have been substantiated by medical science. Many of today's drugs are drawn from herbal remedies. Herbs were also believed to have magical qualities which gave them influence in the mysterious realm of the supernatural. Some of these legendary claims have been included in the descriptions.

The definition of terms is important. Generally, herbs and spices have little food value and are primarily used for flavoring foods and beverages. Botanists define herbs as non-woody plants. Horticulturalists generally state that herbs can be grown in temperate climates, while spices must be imported from the tropics. The American Spice Trade Association avoids this ambiguous division and calls both spices. The legal definition of spices by American trade and tariff regulations is "aromatic vegetable substances (including seeds, leaves, stems, bark, roots, or other relevant plant parts) from which virtually none of the volatile oil or other flavoring principle has been removed." A culinary herb is defined (in the popular sense) as a plant which can be usually grown in temperate regions and is used (or has been used) in minor quantities to flavor foods and beverages. A potherb is defined as a leafy plant (from both temperate and tropical climates) which can be used in minor quantities as an adjunct to salads. (A better name and one sometimes seen in cook books would be salad herb.)

In the simplest terminology, essential oil and volatile oil are used interchangeably. An essential oil is an oil inherent to the plant that has specific properties and qualities. These oils help give plants flavors and aromas. Volatile means easily evaporated, and this quality gives us aroma. A non-volatile oil is called a fixed oil. An essence is a solution of a volatile oil in alcohol. Absolute is a term used when the oil (or other named material) is not combined with anything else, such as rose absolute. Concrete is a term used for a once-liquid material that has been solidified or hardened. The definition of an extract is more complex. Oils or other chemical parts are removed from the plant by dissolving them in a liquid (water, alcohol, ether, or other solvent). This liquid is then evaporated. The resulting solid can then be reconstituted in a liquid in a known concentration. It is the solvents used for making extracts that the Food and Drug Administration is referring to when stating that listed items must be "solvent free."

It is important to know the correct botanical name for a plant. When botanical sources are incompletely or incorrectly known, adulteration and falsification are easy. The science dealing with the describing, naming and classifying of living things is called taxonomy. In the past all things were classified into three kingdoms, animal, plant and mineral. It is now realized that all living things cannot be delineated as either animal or plant, and a five kingdom concept is now used. Four of these kingdoms have traditionally been regarded as plants:

Kingdom *Monera*—bacteria
Kingdom *Protista*—algae and slime molds
Kingdom *Fungi*—fungi (including mushrooms and toadstools) and bread molds
Kingdom *Plantae*

Our concern is primarily with the Kingdom *Plantae*.

In simplest terms, taxonomists use an outline form to categorize plants. Basically, it is as follows.

    I. Kingdom
      A. Division
         1. Class
            a. Order
               (1) Family
                   (a) Genus
                       i) Species

To complicate matters, however, there are thrown in at times, Subdivisions, Subclasses, Suborders, Groups, Subspecies, Hybrids, Cultivars, Variants, etc. Taxonomists not only have problems identifying genus and species of plants but also often disagree as to which plants belong to what family, sometimes creating new family names for a group of plants previously belonging to another family. At times they don't seem to be able to make up their minds. Onions were in the lily family, then they were put in the amaryllis family. Now they are back in the lily family.

In scientifically naming the plants in this book, an attempt was made to use the latest accepted terminology as dictated by the International Code of Botanical Nomenclature or the International Code of Nomenclature for Cultivated Plants—1980 as given in Herbs, Spices and Medicinal Plants, volumes 1 and 2, edited by Craker and Simon, or by *Hortus Third*, compiled by Bailey et al. One cannot, however, guarantee accuracy in a constantly changing field. In this book, older, "out-of-date" terminology has also been included since it is often more familiar and in some instances still used by the Food and Drug Administration in their listings.

There is no claim that this is a complete listing, that the botanical name is in the latest technical terminology, or that the FDA has not changed its mind. This is only an attempt to answer that question, "What is it?"

Note of Explanation

The main section of the book contains an alphabetical listing by common name followed by the genus and species name enclosed in parentheses and the family name enclosed in brackets. These are followed by other common names for the same item. These are in bold print. All common names are cross-referenced.

Example:

COMMON NAME (*Genus species*) [*Family*]

Other common names:

GRAS is the Food and Drug Administration's abbreviation for substances "generally regarded as safe." If there is no mention of a Food and Drug Administration classification, then there is none available.

OTHER COMMON NAME: See COMMON NAME.

In the section "Families" is an alphabetical listing of all the plant families followed by the genus and species and then the common names.

"Genera" lists the genus and species names alphabetically, followed by the family name in brackets, and then the common names by which that genus and species is known.

DICTIONARY OF HERBS, SPICES, SEASONINGS, AND NATURAL FLAVORINGS

A

AARON'S BEARD: See **SAINT JOHN'S-WORT.**

AARON'S ROD: See **HOUSELEEK** and **SWEET GOLDENROD.**

ABATA COLA: See **COLA.**

ABELE: See **POPLAR.**

ABELMOSK (*Abelmoschus moschatus*, formerly *Hibiscus abelmoschus*) [*Malvaceae*]
Abelmusk; Ambrette seed; Musk mallow; Musk seed; Rose mallow; Syrian mallow; Target-leaved hibiscus; Water mallow:

The seeds of this aromatic plant, originating in Martinique, have a very strong flavor of musk. It is used mostly in perfumery, but in India the seeds are mixed with coffee to flavor it and to heighten its stimulating properties. GRAS *Abelmoschus moschatus* is closely related to okra (*Abelmoschus esculentus*).

The common names of Syrian mallow, target-leaved mallow, water mallow, and especially rose mallow can cause considerable confusion since they may refer also to a number of other *Hibiscus* species.

ABSINTHE: See **WORMWOOD.**

ABYSSINIAN TEA (*Catha edulis*) [*Celastraceae*]
Arabian tea; African tea; Cafta; Chat; Kat; Khat; Qat; Somali tea:

This plant is reputed to have antisoporific and antinarcotic properties. The tender shoots are chewed by Moslems as a stimulant or a tea is made from the leaves.

ACACIA (*Acacia senegal*) [*Mimosaceae*, formerly in *Leguminosae*]
Cape gum; Egyptian thorn; Gum-arabic; Sudan gum-arabic:

Gum-arabic is a dry, gummy exudate from the stems and branches of trees of the genus *Acacia*, most commonly *Acacia senegal*. It is used to make mucilage, as a vehicle for various compounds in pharmacy, and in cookery to prevent crystallization of sugar, as a thickener in confections, and to reduce foaming in soft drinks and sometimes beer.

ACHIOTE: See ANNOTTO.

ACONITE: See MONKSHOOD.

ACRID CROWFOOT: See BUTTERCUP.

ADAM-AND-EVE: See ARUM.

ADDER'S FERN: See WALL FERN.

ADDER'S MOUTH: See CHICKWEED.

ADDER'S VIOLET: See RATTLESNAKE PLANTAIN.

ADDER'S-TONGUE (*Erythronium americanum*) [*Liliaceae*]
Amberbell; Dog-tooth violet; Erythronium; Lamb's tongue; Rattlesnake violet; Snake leaf; Trout lily; Yellow adder's-tongue; Yellow erythronium; Yellow snakeleaf; Yellow snowdrop:
This pretty little lily, native to the United States, has been used in herbal remedies. It is an emetic and was supposed to cure scrofula.

ADIMA: See SAINT MARTIN'S-HERB.

AFRICA LILAC: See CHINABERRY.

AFRICAN ELEMI: See OLIBANUM.

AFRICAN MARIGOLD: See MARIGOLD.

AFRICAN TEA: See ABYSSINIAN TEA.

AGAVE (*Agave americana*) [*Agavaceae*]
American aloe; Century plant; Flowering aloe; Maguey; Spiked aloe:
There are over 300 species of *Agave* native to North and South America. The species *Agave americana* is one of the best known. The sap of these plants has been used as an herbal remedy, being both laxative and diuretic. In Mexico the sap is fermented for pulque or distilled for tequila and mescal.

AGRIMONY (*Agrimonia eupatoria*) [*Rosaceae*]
Church steeples; Cockeburr; Cocklebur; Harvest-lice; Sticklewort:
This is an old herbal remedy touted to cure most anything and everything. The seeds have hooked bristles that stick to anything that brushes them. The yellow flowers can be used as a source of yellow dye.

AGUE GRASS: See **STAR GRASS.**

AGUE ROOT: See **STAR GRASS.**

AGUE TREE: See **SASSAFRAS.**

AGUEWEED: See **THOROUGHWORT.**

AIR POTATO: See **WILD YAM.**

AJOWAN (*Trachyspermum copticum*, formerly *Carum ajowan, Carum copticum, Ammi copticum*, and *Trachyspermum ammi*) [*Umbelliferae*]
Ajuan; Omum:
The seed of this plant, native to India, looks somewhat like a large celery seed and has a strong taste of thyme. It is used extensively in Indian cooking. Thyme can be substituted for ajowan in Indian recipes, but the contrary is not recommended because of ajowan's much stronger and cruder taste.

AJUAN: See **AJOWAN.**

ALANT: See **ELECAMPANE.**

ALBERTA SPRUCE: See **SPRUCE.**

ALCANNA: See **HENNA.**

ALDER (*Alnus oregona*, formerly *rubra*) [*Betulaceae*]
Oregon alder; Red alder
(*Alnus rugosa, formerly serrulata*)
Hazel alder; Smooth alder; Speckled alder:
The bark of these North American shrubs has astringent qualities. It is very bitter and is used as a flavoring for vermouth and in certain cordials.

ALDER BUCKTHORN: See **CASCARA.**

ALDER DOGWOOD: See **CASCARA.**

ALECOST: See COSTMARY.

ALEHOOF: See GROUND IVY.

ALEXANDERS (*Smyrnium olusatrum*) [*Umbelliferae*]
Allisanders; Black lovage; Horse parsley
(*Zizia aurea*, formerly *Thaspium aureum*) [*Umbelliferae*]
Golden alexanders; Meadow parsnip:

Alexanders, indigenous to the Mediterranean area, has been naturalized in Great Britain for many years. It grows wild there on waste lands and cliffs near the sea. It has some resemblance to celery in both appearance and flavor and will grow up to four feet in height. Some describe the flavor as being more like parsley. It was used much like celery as both a vegetable and a seasoning. In France where it also grows wild, it is called horse parsley and is used in cooking as a substitute for parsley. The meadow parsnip, *Zizia aurea* [*Umbelliferae*], is called golden alexanders. *Angelica atropurpurea* [*Umbelliferae*] is also called alexanders. See ANGELICA.

ALEXANDRIA SENNA: See CASSIA.

ALFALFA (*Medicago sativa*) [*Leguminosae*]
Buffalo herb; Lucerne; Purple medic:

Alfalfa leaves are a common ingredient in herbal teas. Alfalfa is known as lucerne in Australia. GRAS

ALFILARIA: See STORKSBILL.

ALGARROBA BEAN: See CAROB.

ALL-HEAL: See HERB CARPENTER, MISTLETOE, and VALERIAN.

ALLELUIA: See SORREL.

ALLGOOD: See GOOD-KING-HENRY.

ALLIARIA (*Alliaria petiolata*, formerly *Sisymbrium alliaria*) [*Cruciferae*]
Donkey's foot; Garlic mustard; Jack-by-the-hedge; Onion nettle; Sauce alone:

This is a weed-type plant common in Europe, Asia and the eastern United States and Canada. Its coarsely toothed, nettle-like leaves have a strong smell of garlic when crushed. It was commonly used as a flavoring and a salad herb. It tends to lose its flavor in cooking but is good raw in meat or cheese sandwiches. Its leaves have been used as a pharmaceutical plaster.

ALLISANDERS: See **ALEXANDERS.**

ALLSPICE (*Pimenta dioica*, formerly *officinalis*, a.k.a. *Eugenia pimenta*) [*Myrtaceae*]
Clove pepper; Jamaica pepper; Myrtle pepper; Pimenta; Toute-épice:

Allspice is also known as Jamaica pepper, pimenta (not to be confused with the mild red pepper, *Capsicum annuum* var. *annuum*, Grossum Group), and toute-épice. The *Pimenta* tree is an evergreen native to the West Indies. The berry fruit is gathered when mature but still green. After drying in the sun for six to ten days it turns a dull reddish-brown. The dried berry is easily ground into a powder. It is also used in whole form. The flavor resembles a blend of nutmeg, cinnamon and clove. It is used in pickling, fruit preserving, flavoring fish, meats, sausages, gravies, sauces and stuffings. Pimenta may also be correctly spelled pimento. GRAS

ALMOND (*Prunus dulcis*, var. *dulcis*, formerly *amygdala*, var. *dulcis*) [*Rosaceae*]
Greek nuts; Sweet almond
(*Prunus dulcis*, var. *amara*, formerly *amygdala*, var. *amara*) [*Rosaceae*]
Bitter almond:

Sweet almonds contain a fixed oil, *oleum amygdalae expressum*, with a very mild flavor. Bitter almonds contain amygdalin, a compound which breaks down on extraction to nitrobenzene, "oil of bitter almonds." This is a poisonous compound. Another breakdown product of amygdalin is one very closely related to nitrobenzene, hydrocyanic acid (Prussic acid). This chemical is more commonly known as cyanide and is a deadly poison. It smells identical to nitrobenzene, but there are not sufficient survivors to testify as to the taste. These and related chemicals are present in the seeds of many *Prunus* fruits. Never attempt to make "almond extract" by extracting peach or apricot pits with alcohol. Use of oil of bitter almonds as a flavoring is permitted by the FDA only if it is first rendered free of Prussic acid. It is seldom used. Purified benzaldehyde is used in its place and is labeled artificial almond extract.

In *Classical Cooking the Modern Way* by Eugen Pauli, English translation published in 1978, a book intended to be used as a text for food service instruction, there is the following statement (p. 162): "Mock marzipan—A substitute for marzipan. Apricot, peach, and other fruit kernels are substituted for almonds." I wonder if anyone has survived to tell how it tastes?

TROPICAL ALMONDS (COUNTRY, JAVA, MALAYSIA, OR MALABAR ALMONDS) are all regional tropical nuts with a resemblance to the true almond. The true almond will not grow in the tropics. These nuts may be specified for in Indian,

Malaysian and Vietnamese recipes. The common name for these nuts is BADAM. Sweet almonds can be substituted in the recipes.

CUDDAPAH ALMONDS or CHIRONJI NUTS are also often mentioned in books on Indian cookery, but sweet almonds can be substituted since the Chironji nut itself is considered an almond substitute.

ALOE (*Aloe perryi*) [*Liliaceae*]

Bombay aloe; Socotrine aloe; Turkey aloe; Zanzibar aloe

(*Aloe barbadensis*)

Barbados aloe; Curaçao aloe; Medicinal aloe; Unguentine cactus

(*Aloe ferox*)

Cape aloe:

Extracts of aloe have a very bitter flavor and have been used occasionally in flavor formulations for liqueurs. They also have laxative effects. Traditionally, extracts of aloe were painted on children's fingernails to discourage them from biting their nails. It is best to purchase extract of aloe from a reputable pharmacy rather than to experiment with plants grown in the home, since some species are very poisonous. The above species, along with hybrids of *A. ferox* with *A. africana* and *A. spicata*, are classified by the FDA as GRAS.

ALPINE BASIL THYME: See BASIL THYME.

ALPINE DOCK: See SORREL.

ALPINE LOVAGE: See LOVAGE.

ALPINE STRAWBERRY (*Fragaria vesca*, cultivar Alpine) [*Rosaceae*]:

Alpine strawberry leaves are often an ingredient in commercial herbal teas.

ALPINE VIOLET: See CYCLAMEN.

ALTHAEA (*Althaea officinalis*) [*Malvaceae*]

Marsh mallow; Mortification root; Sweetweed; White mallow; Wymote:

Extracts of the roots and flowers are used in formulations for beverage and liqueur flavorings. This plant should not be confused with cultivars of *Hibiscus syriacus* [*Malvaceae*], commonly called althaea, nor with the genus *Alcea* [*Malvaceae*], the hollyhock. The hollyhock was formerly *Althaea rosea*, and this taxonomic change has caused much confusion. *Althaea officinalis* is GRAS.

ALUMROOT: See GERANIUM.

AMARANTH (*Amaranthus* spp.) [*Amaranthaceae*]

Joseph's-coat; Lady bleeding; Love-lies-bleeding; Lovely bleeding; Pigwort; Pilewort; Prince's feather; Red cockscomb; Spleen amaranth; Wild beet:

The amaranths are usually cultivated for their ornamental colored foliage or their heavy red or green spikes. In Asia some are grown as green vegetables or for their edible seeds. Their astringent properties made them a common ingredient in herbal home remedies.

AMAZONIAN SASSAFRAS: See SASSAFRAS.

AMBER: See AMBERGRIS and SAINT JOHN'S-WORT.

AMBERBELL: See ADDER'S-TONGUE.

AMBERGRIS; AMBER:

Ambergris is a waxy pathological substance obtained from the intestines of the sperm whale (supposedly semi-digested squid), or it can be found floating on the surface of the ocean or washed up on beaches. Lumps ranging from 60 to 225 pounds may be found. There are four qualities of ambergris: (1) soft black, (2) waxy ash-gray, (3) gray, and (4) white. The gray and white are the most highly valued. It is dried and powdered and then used in the form of tinctures, extracts, or as a resinoid prepared from a concentrated tincture. It is described as having a peculiar, sweet, extremely tenacious odor with seaweed, moss-like overtones. It is used primarily in perfumery but is also added to flavor formulations. GRAS

In the late 18th and early 19th centuries, it was thought to have almost magical aphrodisiac and restorative properties. It was made into lozenges and was added to hot chocolate. Brillat-Saverin, a famous French gourmet who lived at that time said,

> . . . when I get one of those days when the weight of age makes itself felt—a painful thought—or when one feels oppressed by an unknown force, I add a knob of ambergris the size of a bean, pounded with sugar, to a strong cup of chocolate, and I always find my condition improving marvelously. The burden of life becomes lighter, thought flows with ease and I do not suffer from insomnia, which would have been the invariable result of a cup of coffee taken for the same purpose. (Montagné p. 32)

AMBRETTE; AMBRETTE SEED: See ABELMOSK.

AMCHUR: See MANGO.

AMERICAN ALOE: See AGAVE.

AMERICAN ANGELICA: See ANGELICA.

AMERICAN CEDAR: See WHITE CEDAR.

AMERICAN CENTAURY: See GENTIAN.

AMERICAN CHESTNUT: See CHESTNUT.

AMERICAN COLUMBO OR CALUMBA: See GENTIAN.

AMERICAN COW PARSNIP: See MASTERWORT.

AMERICAN COWSLIP: See MARIGOLD and COWSLIP.

AMERICAN CRANESBILL: See GERANIUM.

AMERICAN CRESS: See ROCKET.

AMERICAN DITTANY: See DITTANY, COMMON.

AMERICAN ELDER: See ELDER.

AMERICAN FOXGLOVE: See FOXGLOVE and FEVERWEED.

AMERICAN GINSENG: See GINSENG.

AMERICAN GENTIAN: See GENTIAN.

AMERICAN GERMANDER: See GERMANDER.

AMERICAN HELLEBORE: See FALSE HELLEBORE.

AMERICAN INDIGO: See WILD INDIGO.

AMERICAN IVY: See VIRGINIA CREEPER.

AMERICAN LARCH: See LARCH.

AMERICAN LAUREL: See MOUNTAIN LAUREL.

AMERICAN LINDEN TREE: See LINDEN FLOWERS.

AMERICAN MANDRAKE: See MAYAPPLE.

AMERICAN MISTLETOE: See MISTLETOE.

AMERICAN MOUNTAIN ASH: See ROWAN.

AMERICAN NIGHTSHADE: See POKE.

AMERICAN NUTMEG: See CUSTARD APPLE and NUTMEG.

AMERICAN OREGANO: See MARJORAM.

AMERICAN PENNYROYAL: See PENNYROYAL.

AMERICAN RED ELDER: See ELDER.

AMERICAN SAFFRON: See SAFFRON.

AMERICAN SANICLE: See SANICLE.

AMERICAN SARSAPARILLA: See SARSAPARILLA.

AMERICAN SORREL: See SORREL.

AMERICAN SPIKENARD: See SPIKENARD.

AMERICAN STORAX OR STYRAX: See STORAX.

AMERICAN SWEET GUM: See STORAX.

AMERICAN VALERIAN: See NERVEROOT.

AMERICAN VERVAIN: See BLUE VERVAIN.

AMERICAN WHITE HELLEBORE: See FALSE HELLEBORE.

AMERICAN WOODBINE: See VIRGINIA CREEPER.

AMERICAN WORMSEED: See EPAZOTE.

AMOLE: See SOAP PLANT.

AMYRIS (*Amyris balsamifera*) [*Rutaceae*]
West Indian rosewood; West Indian sandalwood:
Extracts of the wood are used in perfumery and also in formulations for liqueur flavorings. GRAS

ANARDANA: See POMEGRANATE.

ANCHOVY PASTE; ANCHOVIES:

Anchovies are small pungent, dark-fleshed fish, available either salted or preserved in oil, as fillets, or ground into a paste. As a seasoning for a sauce, they should be used in the proportion of about one-half a small fillet for each quart. *Lea and Perrins Worcestershire Sauce* is the perfect example of anchovies used for seasoning.

ANET: See DILL.

ANGEL'S-EYE: See VERONICA.

ANGELICA (*Angelica archangelica*, formerly *officinalis*) [*Umbelliferae*]:
   Archangel; Archangelica; European angelica; Wild parsnip
   (*Angelica atropurpurea*)
   Alexanders; American angelica; Bellyache root; Great angelica; Masterwort; Purple angelica
   (*Angelica keiskei* and *ursina*)
   Japanese angelica:

Angelica, also known as archangelica, is a member of the same plant family as parsley. It is native to northern Europe and Syria and can be cultivated in certain areas of the United States. It is usually thought of as the candied leaves and stems which are used as decorations on cakes and confections. The flavor has been described as strongly aromatic but somewhat acrid. The leaves and stems can be roasted or boiled and eaten as a salad. It can be used as a flavoring in rhubarb or in orange marmalade. Some use it in combination with other herbs with fish dishes. Others say that it should be used only after boiling in sugar as a sweet. Angelica should be used with discretion, since many violently dislike its strong, penetrating taste. The roots were once widely used as a medicine and are still used as an ingredient in the finest gins. *Angelica atropurpurea* does not have as strong a flavor as *A. archangelica*. GRAS

Chinese angelica, also known as dong quai, dang qui, female ginseng, Japanese angelica, and women's ginseng, has been identified by some "herbalists" as *Angelica sinensis*. This is incorrect. Chinese ginseng is *Aralia elata* [*Araliaceae*], formerly known as *Aralia chinensis*, *Aralia japonica* and *Aralia sinensis*. See ANGELICA TREE.

ANGELICA TREE (*Aralia spinosa*) [*Araliaceae*]
   Devil's-walking-stick; Hercules'-club; Prickly ash; Spikenard tree
   (*Aralia elata*, formerly *Aralia chinensis*, *Aralia japonica*, and *Aralia sinensis*)
   Chinese angelica; Dang qui; Dong quai; Female ginseng; Japanese angelica; Women's ginseng:

Aralia elata is native to Manchuria, Korea, and Japan. It is considered as the Asian counterpart of *Aralia spinosa*, which is found from central Pennsylvania south to Florida and Texas. Both species will grow to over thirty feet tall. The bark and sometimes the fruit have been used in herbal remedies. They have no relationship to either the prickly ash tree nor to angelica and should not be confused with them. See ANGELICA and PRICKLY ASH TREE.

ANGOLA WEED (*Roccella fuciformis*) [*Lichen*]:
The bitter extracts of this lichen are FDA approved for use as a flavoring for alcoholic beverages only.

ANGOSTURA BARK: See ANGOSTURA BITTERS.

ANGOSTURA BITTERS:
Angostura Aromatic Bitters is a registered trade name of a product made by Angostura Bitters (Dr. J. G. B. Siegert & Sons) Ltd. These bitters, named after an old Venezuelan town, are made in Trinidad, West Indies. They do not contain, as many believe, angostura bark, from the tree, *Galipea trifoliata*, formerly *Galipea officinalis*, *Galipea cusparia*, or *Cusparia trifoliata* [*Rutaceae*], which yields an extract containing the intensely bitter angosturin. Angosturin is GRAS. The ingredients listed on the label are "Water, Alcohol, Gentian and harmless vegetable flavoring extractives and vegetable coloring matter." The label clearly states, "Does not contain Angostura Bark." It is 45% alcohol by volume. It has a unique aroma and flavor that is not unpleasantly bitter. Although most commonly thought of as a cocktail ingredient, it is recommended for use in everything from soups to desserts. The finely printed label makes fascinating reading and gives many suggestions for its use. It is supposed to be a good cure for hiccups—sprinkled generously on a slice of lemon which has been covered with sugar.

ANISE (*Pimpinella anisum*) [*Umbelliferae*]
Aniseed; Sweet cumin:
Anise is an annual plant, native to southern Europe and northern Africa, but it will grow in most any garden in a sunny place. In commercial production the plants are harvested when the fruits are just beginning to ripen. The plants are left in stacks in the fields until ripening is completed, and then the seeds are separated by threshing. The seeds are used whole, as in pickling, or powdered, as flavoring for cakes, cookies, and pastries. It is also used in the Far East, like fenugreek, coriander and cumin, as a general purpose seasoning. The liqueur, anisette, and other beverages are flavored with anise. Because the oils from aniseeds are quite volatile, the seeds should be stored in a tight container. Oil of anise is used in cough medicine. The fresh leaves can be used as a salad or a salad garnish. They have a licorice flavor. In India, anise seed, lightly roasted to

give it a nutty flavor, is chewed after meals. It is thought to sweeten the breath and to aid digestion. Legend claims that anise leaves applied externally remove freckles, and anise oil poisons pigeons, catches mice and combats insects. Sweet chervil has also been called anise. GRAS (See CHERVIL).

ANISE CHERVIL: See CHERVIL.

ANISE HYSSOP (*Agastache foeniculum*) [*Labiatae*]

Blue giant hyssop; Fennel giant hyssop; Fragrant giant hyssop; Giant hyssop

(*Agastache mexicana*)

Mexican giant hyssop

(*Agastache rugosa*)

Korean mint; Wrinkled giant hyssop:

Anise hyssop was used by the Plains Indians for making a beverage tea. Extracts of the roots were used to treat coughs and respiratory diseases. Mexican giant hyssop and Korean mint were used similarly in those areas.

ANISE-PEPPER (*Zanthoxylum piperitum*) [*Rutaceae*]

Chinese pepper; Japanese pepper; Prickly ash; Sansho (or san-sho) pepper; Szechuan pepper

(*Zanthoxylum alatum*)

Chinese pepper; Hua-chaio; Szechuan pepper; Tomarseed; Winged prickly ash

(*Zanthoxylum rhetsa*, formerly *bodunga*)

Mulilan (Indian)

(*Zanthoxylum schinifolium*, formerly *mantchuricum*)

Inuzansho (Japanese); **Pepperbush**

(*Zanthoxylum simulans*, formerly *bungei*)

Chinese pepper; Hua-chiao (Chinese); **Szechuan pepper:**

The peppery hot, aromatic spice made from the ground dried red berries of shrubs which grow in Southeast Asia, China and Japan is called by many different names. They are all very closely related botanically and in taste. Sansho pepper has been described as the ground dried leaves as well as the ground berries.

ANISE-SCENTED GOLDENROD: See GOLDENROD.

ANISEED: See ANISE.

ANISEROOT: See CHERVIL.

ANNOTTO (*Bixa orellana*) [*Bixaceae*]
Achiote; Anatto; Annatto; Arnatto; Bija; Bijol; Lipstick tree; Roucou:
The red-orange pulp of the fruit of this small American tree provides a dye used for coloring butter and foods. The dried seeds have a peppery taste and are widely used in Latin American cooking. It is sometimes used as a substitute for saffron. The juices are also used by natives for decorating their bodies. Bija is actually the dried juice from an East Indian tree, *Pterocarpus marsupium* [*Leguminosae*], and it is used in similar ways. It is also called dragon's blood.

APPALACHIAN TEA (*Ilex glabra*) [*Aquifoliaceae*]
Bitter gallberry; Carolina tea; Gallberry; Inkberry; Winterberry
(*Viburnum cassinoides*) [*Caprifoliaceae*]
Carolina tea; Swamp haw; Teaberry; Wild raisin; Withe-rod:
Appalachian or Carolina tea can be made with either of the berries from the above two plants. It should not be made with *Phytolacca americana* [*Phytolaccaceae*], the pokeweed, which is also known as inkberry. See POKE.

APPLE JACK: See EUCALYPTUS.

APPLE SAGE: See SAGE.

APPLE-SCENTED GERANIUM: See GERANIUM.

APPLEMINT: See MINT.

APRICOT VINE: See PASSIONFLOWER.

ARABIAN JASMINE: See JASMINE.

ARABIAN MYRRH: See MYRRH.

ARABIAN TEA: See ABYSSINIAN TEA.

ARAR TREE: See SANDARAC.

ARBERRY: See UVA-URSI.

ARBORVITAE: See WHITE CEDAR.

ARBUTUS BERRY (*Arbutus unedo*) [*Ericaceae*]

Cane apples; Strawberry tree:

This is a small evergreen tree grown primarily as an ornamental in the southern part of the United States or along the Pacific coast. The fruit is sweet when ripe and leaves a faint acid aftertaste. In Italy and Spain a liqueur (crème d'arbouse) is made from the berries. It is reputed to aid digestion. The fruit can also be used in preserves, and the bark is used by the tanning industry.

ARCHANGEL: See **ANGELICA**.

ARCHANGELICA: See **ANGELICA**.

ARECA NUT: See **CATECHU**.

ARNICA (*Arnica montana* and *cordifolia*) [*Compositae*]

Mountain daisy; Mountain tobacco; Wolf's bane:

Extracts from the arnica flowers are sweet, slightly bitter in flavor, somewhat like camomile. They are used in formulating flavors for beverages, confections, and baked goods. In the United States the use of these two species is restricted to use in alcoholic beverages only. Tincture of arnica used to be applied externally for the treatment of sprains and bruises.

ARROWROOT (*Maranta arundinacea*) [*Marantaceae*]

Obedience plant:

The rhizomes of this tropical American plant are the source of arrowroot starch, commonly used as thickener of sauces. The island of Saint Vincent, West Indies, is the primary producer. One and one half teaspoons of arrowroot has the thickening properties of one tablespoon of wheat flour.

ARROWWOOD, ARROW-WOOD: See **CASCARA** and **WAHOO**.

ARTICHOKE (*Cynara scolymus*) [*Compositae*]

French artichoke; Globe artichoke

(*Cynara cardunculus*)

Cardoon

(*Stachys affinis*) [*Labiatae*]

Chinese artichoke; Chorogi; Crosnes-du-Japon; Japanese artichoke; Knotroot

(*Helianthus tuberosus*) [*Compositae*]

Girasole; Jerusalem artichoke

(*Bomerea edulis*) [*Alstroemeriaceae*]

White Jerusalem artichoke:

The flower head (actually the fleshy bases of the bracts) of *Cynara scolymus* is the French or globe artichoke which is eaten as a vegetable. The dried leaves of this plant are used as flavorings in special bitters and liqueurs. In the United States use of the leaves is restricted to alcoholic beverages only. The root and leaf stalks of *Cynara cardunculus* are eaten as a vegetable.

Stachys affinis and *Helianthus tuberosus* are both grown for the edible tubers. Girasole is the Italian word for sunflower.

Bomerea edulis is a tropical vine native to the West Indies, Mexico and south to Brazil. It is grown in this country as a greenhouse ornamental.

ARTIFICIAL SASSAFRAS OIL: See SASSAFRAS.

ARUGULA: See ROCKET.

ARUM (*Arum maculatum*) [*Araceae*]

Adam-and-Eve; Cocky baby; Cuckoopint; Cypress powder; Dragon root; Gaglee; Ladysmock; Portland arrowroot; Starchwort:

The fresh leaves and root (tuber) of this plant are poisonous. It is said that if the tuber is dried or "cooked properly" it is edible. What is "cooked properly?" It has been used in herbal remedies. It should not be confused with arrowroot, used as a thickener, an entirely different plant. See **Arrowroot.**

ASAFOETIDA (*Ferula assa-foetida* and *foetida*) [*Umbelliferae*]

Asafetida; Devil's dung; Food-of-the-gods; Giant fennel; Persian gum; Stinking gum

A fetid gum-resin with an odor described by some as like rotten garlic is extracted from the stems and roots of a plant native to Persia and Afghanistan. It can be purchased in solid wax-like pieces, as a dried powder, or as an extract. It is used in minute quantities in Hindu dishes. The odor disappears with cooking. In some areas the entire plant is used as a vegetable with the center of the large stem regarded as a delicacy. Medicinally it has antispasmodic qualities and was used in olden times as a treatment for chorea and hysteria.

Laserpitium latifolium [*Umbelliferae*], known as **Herb frankincense** and **laserwort**, seems to be the same plant as *Ferula assa-foetida* although this is not definitely verified. *Laserpitium* is found in old Roman recipes and is supposed to be the same as asafetida.

Ferula communis [*Umbelliferae*] is known as **common giant fennel**. This is considered to be a poisonous plant and should not be confused with the cultivated giant fennel, *Foeniculum vulgare*, Var. *dulce*. See **FENNEL.**

Ferula assa-foetida and "related species of *Ferula*" are GRAS.

ASARABACCA: See CANADIAN SNAKEROOT and EUROPEAN SNAKEROOT.

ASARUM: See CANADIAN SNAKEROOT and EUROPEAN SNAKEROOT.

ASH: See EUROPEAN ASH.

ASHANTI PEPPER (*Piper clusii*) [*Piperaceae*]
Guinea pepper:
This is the dried berry of a western African vine. It has the taste of ordinary black pepper (*Piper nigrum*).

ASHWEED: See HERB GERARD.

ASIAN STORAX: See STORAX.

ASIATIC GINSENG: See GINSENG.

ASPIDIUM: See WOOD FERN.

ASPIDOSPERMA: See QUEBRACHO.

ASS'S FOOT: See COLTSFOOT.

ASTHMA WEED: See SPURGE.

ASTRAGAL: See TRAGACANTH.

ASTRAGALUS: See TRAGACANTH.

ATTAR OF ROSES: See ROSE.

AUGUST FLOWER: See GUM PLANT.

AUSTRALIAN MIMOSA: See MIMOSA.

AUSTRALIAN PEPPER TREE: See PEPPER TREE.

AUSTRALIAN SARSAPARILLA: See SARSAPARILLA.

AUSTRALIAN SASSAFRAS: See SASSAFRAS.

AUTUMN CORALROOT: See CORALROOT.

AUTUMN CROCUS: See SAFFRON.

AVENS: See BENNET and WATER AVENS.

Avens root: See **Water avens.**

Ayapana (*Eupatorium triplinerve* ?) [*Compositae*]:

The *triplinerve* species is probably not the currently correct name for this plant, however it is a South American species of *Eupatorium*. The pleasant-smelling leaves were used to make teas which were supposed to stimulate the appetite and aid sleep. Medical sources say that it has stimulating properties similar to coffee and tea. The smell of the leaves is quite strong, and according to Montagné (p. 75) twelve or thirteen leaves are adequate for a six-cup teapot. Montagné also states, "Ayapana blends perfectly with yolks of egg and cream," but no indication is given as to the type of food.

Azedarach: See **Chinaberry.**

Aztec marigold: See **Marigold.**

B

BACHELOR'S-BUTTON: See CORNFLOWER and BUTTERCUP.

BADAM: See ALMONDS.

BADIAN ANISE: See STAR ANISE.

BAKED-APPLE BERRY: See BRAMBLES.

BALACHONG; BALACHAN; BLACHAN; BLACHEN; MALACCA CHEESE;
NUKEMUM; POPPADOM; TRASI:
This seasoning, much used in Southeast Asia, is used by pounding small shrimp with salt to make a thick paste which is then fermented and dried in the sun. The flavor is similar to anchovy paste. It is never eaten raw.

BALM (*Melissa officinalis*) [*Labiatae*]
Balm mint; Bee balm; Blue balm; Cure-all; Dropsy plant; Garden balm; Lemon balm; Melissa; Sweet balm:
The lemon-scented leaves are used fresh as flavoring in fruit salads or dried in teas and other hot beverages. It is a perennial, preferring a not-too-rich soil. Legend claims that lemon balm braces the nerves, stops fainting spells, and is good for headaches and colds. It renews youth, strengthens the brain, and is used for surgical dressings. GRAS

BALM MINT: See BALM.

BALM OF GILEAD: See BALSAM FIR NEEDLE OIL.

BALMONY: See TURTLEHEAD.

BALSAM:

Balsam is a semifluid, resinous, fragrant plant juice obtained from a number of different plants. It is a resin combined with an oil. See PERUVIAN BALSAM, TOLU BALSAM and BALSAM FIR OIL.

Balsam can also refer to any number of plants of the genus *Impatiens* [*Balsaminaceae*] which are grown as ornamentals. *Impatiens balsamina* is known as garden balsam.

BALSAM FIR NEEDLE OIL (*Abies balsamea*) [*Pinaceae*]

Balm of Gilead; Canada balsam:

Oil extracts from the needles and twigs of *Abies balsamea* are used in flavoring formulations for candies and baked goods and for scenting soaps. The resin of *A. balsamea* is called Canada balsam or balm of Gilead and is used as an adhesive in microscopy. The oils of *A. balsamea* are GRAS.

Balm of Gilead can refer to:

1. *Populus x gileadensis* [*Salicaceae*]

The botanical status of this tree is uncertain. Some believe it to be a hybrid of *P. balsamifera* and *P. deltoides*, others believe it to be a clone of a variety of *P. balsamifera*. For safety purposes, it should be treated as *P. balsamifera*.

2. *Populus balsamifera*, formerly *P. candicans* [*Salicaceae*]

See POPLAR for FDA restrictions.

3. *Commiphora opobalsamum* [*Burseraceae*]

See MYRRH.

4. *Cedronella canariensis*, formerly *C. triphylla* [*Labiatae*]

This is also known as Canary balm and false balm of Gilead. It is a three-to-five-foot tall shrub, native to Madeira and the Canary Islands. It has been cultivated as an ornamental in southern California.

Gilead as found in the Book of Genesis refers to a hill. Giliad was a region in ancient Palestine east of the Jordan River. Probably the original balm of Gilead came from *Commiphora* plants, native to this region.

BALSAM POPLAR: See POPLAR.

BALTIC REDWOOD: See SCOTCH PINE.

BAND PLANT: See PERIWINKLE.

BANDA MACE: See MACE.

BANEBERRY: See HERB CHRISTOPHER.

BANILLES:

. . . A French name given to small pods, long and tapering, which have some similarity with vanilla bean. These pods contain a very fragrant, sugary juice which is often used in the manufacture of ordinary chocolate, instead of real vanilla. [Montagné p. 85]

Is this possibly the tonka bean?

BAOBAB (*Adansonia digitata*) [*Bombacaceae*]
Calabash tree; Dead-rat tree; Lalo; Monkey-bread tree:
This tropical African tree will grow to sixty feet tall. It has a relatively short, massive trunk which can grow to thirty feet in diameter. Fiber from the bark is used in making rope and paper. The gourd-like fruit can be from four to sixteen inches long and has a very sweet, slightly acid flavored white pulp. A lemonade-like drink is made from the pulp. Fresh leaves are eaten as a vegetable. Dried leaves, crushed to a powder, are called lalo. These are mixed with other foods.

A calabash is, generally, any vessel made of a dried gourd shell. Calabash tree can also refer to tropical American trees belonging to the genus *Crescentia* [*Bignoniaceae*] whose gourd-like fruits are often made into utensils.

BARBADOS ALOE: See **ALOE**.

BARBE-DE-CAPUCHIN: See **CHICORY**.

BARBERRY (*Berberis vulgaris*) [*Berberidaceae*]
European barberry; Jaundice berry; Pepperidge; Piprage; Sowberry:
There are nearly 500 species of *Berberis*, however *Berberis vulgaris* is the common barberry. It has been used in herbal medicines but is best known for its use as an ornamental hedge. The stem rust of wheat, oats, barley, and rye passes one stage of its development on susceptible kinds of barberry, and many states have adopted a program to eradicate these kinds. The most susceptible is *Berberis vulgaris* and many of its hybrids.

BARDANA: See **BURDOCK**.

BARLEY: See **MALT EXTRACT**.

BASIL (*Ocimum basilicum*) [*Labiatae*]
Sweet basil; Monk's basil; Saint Josephwort
(*Ocimum basilicum*, var. *citriodora*, formerly *Ocimum citriodora*)
Lemon-scented basil
(*Ocimum basilicum*, var. *minimum*, formerly *Ocimum minimum*)
Bush basil; Dwarf basil
(*Ocimum sanctum*)

Indian holy basil

(*Clinopodium vulgare*, formerly *Calamintha clinopodium*) [*Labiatae*]

Basil; Basilweed; Dog mint; Wild basil

(*Pycnanthemum virginicum*) [*Labiatae*]

Prairie hyssop; Virginia mountain mint; Virginia thyme; Wild basil; Wild hyssop:

An annual plant, native to India (where some consider it a sacred household plant), basil will grow in most any sunny well-drained soil. It is often potted and grown on window sills. The leaves are used fresh or dried. The fresh leaves have a taste similar to cloves, but when dried they taste more like curry leaf. The flavor blends well with tomatoes and can be used to excess in some commercial tomato products. It is a good seasoning for soups, stews, sauces, meats and poultry and can be used to flavor vinegar.

In the past, basil was considered to be a royal plant. It could be cut only by the sovereign, as the story goes, using a golden sickle. At one time it was an almost compulsory decoration in cobblers' shops. Basil keeps away witches, and when burned, it disinfects the air! The *Ocimum* species are GRAS.

Pycnanthemum virginicum, like other plants in the mint family, has been used in many herbal remedies.

BASIL THYME (*Acinos arvensis*, formerly *Acinos thymoides*, *Calamintha acinos*, and *Satureja acinos*) [*Labiatae*]

(*Acinos alpinus*, formerly *Calamintha alpina*, *Satureja alpina*, and *Melissa majoranifolia*) [*Labiatae*]

Alpine basil thyme

Although basil thyme seems to be very confusing botanically, it becomes very simply in the kitchen a combination of the flavors of basil and thyme.

BASILWEED: See BASIL.

BASKET WILLOW: See WILLOW.

BASSWOOD: See LINDEN FLOWERS.

BAST TREE: See LINDEN FLOWERS.

BASTARD DITTANY: See DITTANY (*Dictamnus albus*).

BASTARD HEMP: See HEMP NETTLE.

BASTARD PELLITORY: See PELLITORY.

BASTARD PENNYROYAL: See PENNYROYAL.

BASTARD SAFFRON: See SAFFRON.

BATAVIA CASSIA: See CINNAMON.

BATAVIA CINNAMON: See CINNAMON.

BAY: See BAY LEAF and BAYBERRY.

BAY LEAF (*Laurus nobilis*) [*Lauraceae*]
  Grecian laurel; Indian bay; Laurel; Roman bay; Sweet bay; Sweet laurel

(*Persea borbonia*) [*Lauraceae*]
  Red bay; Sweet bay:

   Laurus nobilis is a tree native to Asia Minor and is now grown in Europe and America. This is the sweet bay tree and should not be confused with species of laurel which are poisonous. The leaves are usually dried. The fresh leaves are much stronger in flavor and only about half as much should be used. Bay leaves grown in Europe are from a different variety of *Laurus nobilis* and are usually not as strong as American. It is recommended that when using American bay leaves in a recipe known to have come from Europe, to use only about half or even one-third as much as called for in the recipe. Bay leaves are used in soups, roasts and stews, also as part of the bouquet garni. GRAS. *Persea borbonia* is also known as sweet bay. It is not listed by the FDA and its use is not recommended.

BAY MALAGUETA: See BAYBERRY.

BAY SALT: See SALT.

BAY STAR VINE: See SARSAPARILLA.

BAY-RUM, SPIRITUS MYRCIA:
   Bay-rum is a mixture of oil of myrcia (see Bayberry), oil of orange peel, and oil of pimenta (oil of allspice). It is used for cosmetic purposes, especially in aftershave lotions, and has no use in cooking.

BAY-RUM TREE: See BAYBERRY.

BAYBERRY (*Myrica cerifera*) [*Myricaceae*]
  Candleberry; Tallow shrub; Vegetable tallow; Wax myrtle; Waxberry

(*Myrica pennsylvanica*)

Swamp candleberry:

Bayberry can refer to (1) the fruit of *Laurus nobilis*, the tree from which bay leaves are obtained (GRAS) (see **BAY LEAF**); (2) the wax myrtles (*Myrica cerifera* and *Myrica pennsylvanica*) and their fruit; (3) the trees, *Pimenta acris* and *racemosa*, and their fruit (GRAS); (4) the allspice berry, *Pimenta dioica* (GRAS) (see **ALLSPICE**).

The fruit of the wax myrtle is also called candleberry or in the case of *Myrica pennsylvanica*, swamp candleberry. The berries are covered with a greenish-white wax, popularly called bayberry tallow. The wax is collected by boiling the fruit in water and then skimming the wax off the surface. The wax is then melted, refined, and made into bayberry candles. A bushel of berries will yield four to five pounds of wax.

Oil of bayberry is also called oil of myrcia, bay malagueta, and West Indian bay-leaf oil. It is usually from *Pimenta racemosa* [*Myrtaceae*] but may also be from *Pimenta acris*. The oil is obtained by steam distillation of the leaves. It has a sharp, spicy, pungent, clove-like odor. It is used in making flavoring formulations for beverages, confections, baked goods, condiments, meats and soups. It is also used in flavorings for liqueurs and by the perfume industry. *Pimenta racemosa* is also called the bay-rum tree.

BAYBERRY WAX: See **BAYBERRY**.

BEAD TREE: See **CHINABERRY**.

BEAN CURD: See **SOY PASTES**.

BEAN HERB: See **SAVORY**.

BEAN SAUCE:

Bean sauces, used in Oriental cooking, are soy sauces. See **SOY SAUCE**.

BEAN TREFOIL: See **BUCKBEAN**.

BEAR'S GARLIC: See **GARLIC**.

BEAR'S GRAPE: See **UVA-URSI**.

BEAR'S PAW ROOT: See **WOOD FERN**.

BEAR'S WEED: See **YERBA SANTA**.

BEAR'S-FOOT: See **LADY'S-MANTLE**, **MONKSHOOD** and **HELLEBORE**.

BEARBERRY: See **CASCARA** and **UVA-URSI**.

BEARDED DARNEL (*Lolium temulentum*) [*Gramineae*]
    Cheat; Tare:

This weed, although closely related to perennial ryegrass (*Lolium perenne*), is a toxic plant. It has been listed in herbal remedies, but it should not be used.

BEARSFOOT: See **HELLEBORE** and **MONKSHOOD.**

BEARWOOD: See **CASCARA.**

BEAU MONDE:

This is a proprietary mixture sold with the "Spice Islands" label by Specialty Brands, Inc., San Francisco, California. It contains salt, sugar, onions and celery seed.

BEAUMONT ROOT: See **CULVER'S PHYSIC.**

BEAVER TREE: See **MAGNOLIA.**

BEAVER-POISON: See **HEMLOCK** (*Cicuta maculata*).

BEBEERU: See **SASSAFRAS.**

BECCABUNGA: See **VERONICA.**

BEDSTRAW (*Galium verum*) [*Rubiaceae*]
    Cheese rennet; Curdwort; Lady's bedstraw; Maid's hair; Our Lady's bedstraw; Yellow bedstraw; Yellow cleavers

(*Gallium aparine*)
    Bedstraw; Catchweed; Cleavers; Cleaverwort; Clivers; Coachweed; Goose grass; Gosling weed; Gripgrass; Hedge-burs; Love-man; Stick-a-back; Sticky-willie; Sweethearts:

Although *Galium verum* was most commonly used for making straw mattresses, the flowering tops were used in making Cheshire cheese. Bedstraw has been used in herbal remedies, primarily externally for skin problems.

BEE BALM: See **BALM** AND **BERGAMOT.**

BEE PLANT: See **BORAGE.**

BEE-NETTLE: See **HEMP NETTLE.**

BEEBREAD: See **BORAGE.**

BEECHDROPS: See BLUE COHOSH.

BEEFSTEAK PLANT: See PERILLA.

BEESWAX ABSOLUTE:
   Beeswax absolute is prepared by alcoholic extraction of crude beeswax. It is a light yellow waxy solid with a very mild, sweet odor. It is used in flavoring formulations for candies and baked goods. White beeswax is prepared by bleaching of the light yellow wax with peroxide or, preferably, with sunlight.

BEGGAR'S BASKET: See LUNGMOSS.

BEGGAR'S-BUTTONS: See BURDOCK.

BEGGAR'S-LICE: See HOUND'S-TONGUE.

BEGGARWEED: See KNOTWEED.

BELGIAN ENDIVE: See CHICORY.

BELL PEPPER: See CAPSICUM.

BELLADONNA (*Atropa belladonna*) [*Solanaceae*]
   Black cherry; Deadly nightshade; Dwale; Poison black cherry:
   Although belladonna is found in some areas of the eastern United States, it is a much more common plant in Europe. All parts of the plant are highly toxic, containing the alkaloids atropine and hyoscyamine. These alkaloids do have extensive uses in medicine, but only in controlled dosage and under strict supervision. The fruit of the plant is a shiny black berry about the size of a cherry, giving rise to the names black cherry and poison black cherry.

BELLY ACHE ROOT: See ANGELICA.

BEN TREE: See HORSERADISH TREE.

BENGALI FIVE SPICES; PANCHPHORAN:
   This is a mixture of whole spices in contrast to most mixtures which are ground. It is used in Southeast Asian fried fish or meat dishes and sometimes included in a curry. It should not be confused with Chinese five-spices. The proportions for the mixture are:
   2 teaspoons whole cumin seeds

2 ¾ teaspoons whole fennel seeds
1 teaspoon whole fenugreek seeds
1 ¼ teaspoons whole black mustard seeds
1 to 2 teaspoons whole nigella seeds

BENJAMIN BUSH: See **SPICEBUSH**.

BENNE OR BENNE PLANT: See **SESAME**.

BENNET (*Geum urbanum*) [*Rosaceae*]

Avens; Blessed herb; Cloveroot; Colewort; European avens; Geum; Goldy stone; Herba benedicta; Herb-bennet; Star of the earth; Wood avens; Yellow avens:

This plant is native to Europe and is commonly found growing wild in shady, damp hedgerows in Britain. It does not grow wild in North America. The roots of this plant smell of cloves. They were formerly used for making a tonic with stimulating properties and for flavoring ale. The young leaves can be used in salads. For some obscure reason, poison hemlock and common valerian have also been called bennet. See also **WATER AVENS**.

BENTOO NO TOMO:

This is a Japanese seasoning compound consisting of dried fish, salt, soy sauce, seaweed, and monosodium glutamate.

BENZOIN (*Styrax benzoin* and other spp.) [*Styracaceae*]:

Benzoin is a resin obtained from *Styrax benzoin* and other tropical *Styrax* species of southeastern Asia. It has a sweet, balsamic, pleasant odor and an aromatic, acrid, bittersweet taste. It becomes plastic when chewed and has been used in chewing gums. It is sometimes used commercially to impart a gloss to chocolate. Tincture of benzoin is often painted on the skin to provide an additional adhesive when taping fractured ribs or sprains. GRAS

BERGAMOT (*Monarda didyma* or *fistulosa*) [*Labiatae*]

Bee balm; Blue balm; High balm; Low balm; Mountain balm; Mountain mint; Oswego; Wild bergamot

(*Monarda punctata*)

Dotted mint; Horsemint:

Bergamot can refer to either the fragrant essential oil from the Bergamot orange or to the above *Monarda* plants, members of the mint family, which contain an oil resembling that of the Bergamot orange. Many varieties of the plant are native to America. The flowers and leaves are used, fresh or dried, to make teas, best known of which is "Oswego tea," usually made from *Monarda didyma*. Oswego tea can also be made from *Monarda punctata*, which is also known as horsemint. Actually the terms "wild bergamot" and "horsemint" can refer to any species of the genus *Monarda*. Bergamot may also refer to water mint (*Mentha aquatica*). (See **Mint**.) *Monarda punctata* is GRAS.

BERMUDA BUTTERCUP: See SORREL.

BETEL: See PEPPER.

BETEL NUT PALM: See CATECHU.

BETHROOT: See TRILLIUM.

BETLE PEPPER: See PEPPER.

BETONY:

Betony may refer to a woundwort of the genus *Stachys* (see WOUNDWORT), to wood betony (see WOOD BETONY), or *Teucrium germander* (see GERMANDER).

BIBLE LEAF: See COSTMARY.

BIG MARIGOLD: See MARIGOLD.

BIJA: See ANNOTTO.

BIJOL: See ANNOTTO.

BILBERRY: See BLUEBERRY.

BILSTED: See STORAX.

BINDWEED: See WILD MORNING-GLORY and WILD JALAP.

BINE: See HOPS.

BIRCH: See SWEET BIRCH and WHITE BIRCH.

BIRD CHERRY: See WILD CHERRY.

BIRD KNOTGRASS: See KNOTWEED.

BIRD PEPPER: See CAPSICUM.

BIRD'S FOOT: See FENUGREEK.

BIRD'S TONGUE: See EUROPEAN ASH.

BIRD'S-EYE: See VERONICA.

BIRD'S-FOOT TREFOIL: See SWEET CLOVER.

BIRDLIME: See MISTLETOE.

BIRDNEST: See INDIAN-PIPE.

BIRDWEED: See KNOTGRASS.

BIRTHROOT: See TRILLIUM.

BIRTHWORT: See SERPENTARIA.

BISABOL MYRRH: See OPOPANAX and MYRRH.

BISHOP'S WEED: See HERB GERARD.

BISTORT: See KNOTWEED.

BITTER ALMOND: See ALMOND.

BITTER ASH: See QUASSIA and WAHOO.

BITTER BUTTONS: See TANSY.

BITTER CLOVER: See GENTIAN.

BITTER CRESS: See LADY'S-SMOCK.

BITTER GALLBERRY: See APPALACHIAN TEA.

BITTER GRASS: See STAR GRASS.

BITTER MILKWORT: See MILKWORT.

BITTER ROOT OR BITTERROOT: See GENTIAN and DOGBANE.

BITTER WINTERGREEN: See PIPSISSEWA.

BITTER-BLOOM: See GENTIAN.

BITTERHERB: See MINOR CENTAURY.

BITTERS:

Bitters usually refers to *ANGOSTURA BITTERS*, however it can mean any decoction or infusion made from a bitter tasting plant. According to Montagné (p. 149):

> ... Among the bitter plants used for making infusions or decoctions are the following: wormwood, camomile, chicory, fumitory, gentian, germander, hops, lichen, wild pansy, lesser centaury, quassia amara (bitter ash), cinchona, rhubarb.
>
> According to Foussagrives, infusions or liqueurs made of the bitter plants can be divided into five classes: (i) purgative bitters, based on rhubarb, aloes, etc.; (ii) nauseous bitters, based on camomile; (iii) astringent bitters, which, with the bitter substance content of tannin, include cinchona, knapweed, bark of chestnut tree, etc.; (iv) stimulating bitters (apértifs) based on wormwood, peel of bitter oranges, gentian, germander, hops, etc.; (v) convulsing or toxic bitters which include the nux vomica and other products which belong in the province of medicine and not of distillery.

BITTERSWEET: See NIGHTSHADE.

BITTERSWEET HERB: See NIGHTSHADE.

BITTERSWEET NIGHTSHADE: See NIGHTSHADE.

BITTERSWEET STEMS: See NIGHTSHADE.

BITTERSWEET TWIGS: See NIGHTSHADE.

BITTERWEED: See ERIGERON.

BITTERWOOD: See QUASSIA.

BITTERWORT: See GENTIAN.

BLACHAN; BLACHEN: See BALACHONG.

BLACK ALDER DOGWOOD: See CASCARA.

BLACK ALDER TREE: See CASCARA.

BLACK BIRCH: See SWEET BIRCH.

BLACK CARAWAY: See NIGELLA.

BLACK CATECHU: See CATECHU.

BLACK CHERRY: See WILD CHERRY and BELLADONNA.

BLACK CHOKE: See WILD CHERRY.

BLACK COHOSH (*Cimicifuga racemosa*) [*Ranunculaceae*]
Black snakeroot; Bugbane; Bugwort; Rattleroot; Rattletop; Rattleweed; Richweed; Squawroot:

This is a perennial plant native to the damp, woody areas of the Appalachians. The small, white, foul-smelling flowers grow in long racemes. The roots have been used medicinally for their sedative properties, but they also act as a cardiac stimulant. Large amounts of the root are poisonous.

BLACK CUMIN: See NIGELLA.

BLACK CURRANT (*Ribes nigrum*) [*Saxafragaceae*]
European black currant; Niribine oil; Quinsy berry:

Besides being used as fruit, extracts of the buds and leaves are used in flavoring formulations for various beverages and foods. Black currant oil is also known as niribine oil. A tea made from the leaves was thought to be beneficial for throat ailments. GRAS

BLACK DOGWOOD: See CASCARA.

BLACK DRINK: See CASSINA.

BLACK ELDER: See ELDER.

BLACK FUNGUS: See DRIED MUSHROOMS.

BLACK HAW (*Viburnum prunifolium*) [*Caprifoliaceae*]
Nannyberry; Sheepberry; Stagbush; Sweet haw; Sweet viburnum:

Bitter, aromatic extracts of the bark are used in flavoring pastries and beverages. In olden days it was used to treat "menstrual colic" and other uterine disorders. GRAS

BLACK HELLEBORE: See HELLEBORE.

BLACK HENBANE: See HENBANE.

BLACK HILLS SPRUCE: See SPRUCE.

Black knapweed: See **Knapweed.**

Black larch: See **Larch.**

Black lovage: See **Alexanders.**

Black malt: See **Malt.**

Black mustard: See **Mustard.**

Black nightshade: See **Nightshade.**

Black pepper: See **Pepper.**

Black poplar: See **Poplar.**

Black Samson: See **Purple coneflower.**

Black sanicle: See **Sanicle.**

Black snakeroot: See **Black cohosh, Canadian snakeroot** and **Sanicle.**

Black spruce: See **Spruce.**

Black walnut: See **Walnut.**

Black wattle: See **Mimosa.**

Black willow: See **Willow.**

Black-berried European elder: See **Elder.**

Blackberry: See **Brambles.**

Blackbutt peppermint: See **Eucalyptus.**

Blackcap: See **Brambles.**

Blackthorn: See **Sloe.**

Blackroot: See **Culver's physic.**

Blackwort: See **Comfrey.**

BLADDERWORT: See LOBELIA.

BLADDERWRACK (*Fucus vesiculosus*) [*Fucaceae*]
Kelp:
This seaweed has long been used in herbal remedies. Its iodine content made it a treatment for hypothyroidism, especially in the days when iodized salt was not available.

BLAZING-STAR (*Liatris scariosa*) [*Compositae*]
Blue blazing-star; Button snakeroot; Gay-feather; Large button snakeroot; Tall blazing-star
(*Liatris spicata*)
Button snakeroot; Colic root; Dense button snakeroot; Devil's bit; Devil's bite; Gay-feather; Marsh blazing-star
(*Liatris squarrosa*)
Button snakeroot; Gay-feather; Rattlesnake-master; Scaly blazing-star
(*Chamaelirium luteum*) [*Liliaceae*]
Devil's-bit; Fairy-wand; False unicorn root; Rattlesnake root:
These two different genera, along with a third, *Veratrum viride* (see FALSE HELLEBORE), are known as blazing-star. This gives rise to considerable confusion.
The *Liatris* plants are most familiar as wild flowers, however because of the diuretic properties of the roots, they have been used in herbal remedies.
Chamaelirium luteum was used in old herbal remedies to treat infertility in women and impotence in men.

BLEEDING HEART: See FUMITORY.

BLESSED HERB: See BENNET.

BLESSED THISTLE (*Cnicus benedictus*, formerly *Carduus benedictus*) [*Compositae*]
Cardin; Holy thistle; Saint Benedict's thistle; Spotted thistle:
This plant was once believed to be an antidote for a large number of poisons and was used in treating liver diseases. Its use in the United States is restricted to alcoholic beverages only.

BLISTERWEED: See BUTTERCUP.

BLOOD ELDER: See ELDER.

BLOODROOT: See **YARROW.**

BLOODSTAUNCH: See **ERIGERON.**

BLOODWOOD TREE: See **CAMPEACHY WOOD.**

BLOWBALL: See **DANDELION.**

BLUE AFRICAN LOTUS: See **LOTUS.**

BLUE BALM: See **BALM** and **BERGAMOT.**

BLUE BARBERRY: See **OREGON GRAPE.**

BLUE BLAZING-STAR: See **BLAZING-STAR.**

BLUE CENTAURY: See **CORNFLOWER.**

BLUE COHOSH (*Caulophyllum thalictroides*) [*Berberidaceae*]
Beechdrops; Blue ginseng; Papoose root; Squaw root; Yellow ginseng:

Extracts of the roots of this plant were used by the Indians to induce labor. It is very irritating to the mucous membranes and can cause a contact dermatitis. The blue berries are very poisonous. Why some call this plant beechdrops is unknown. Beechdrops is actually *Epifagus virginiana* [*Orobranchaceae*], which is a parasitic plant that grows on the roots of beech trees.

BLUE CURLS: See **HERB CARPENTER.**

BLUE ELDER: See **ELDER.**

BLUE FLAG: See **IRIS.**

BLUE GENTIAN: See **GENTIAN.**

BLUE GIANT HYSSOP: See **ANISE HYSSOP.**

BLUE GINSENG: See **BLUE COHOSH.**

BLUE GUM: See **EUCALYPTUS.**

BLUE LUNGWORT: See **LUNGMOSS.**

BLUE MALLOW: See **MALLOW.**

BLUE MELILOT: See SWEET CLOVER.

BLUE MOUNTAIN TEA: See SWEET GOLDENROD.

BLUE NIGHTSHADE: See NIGHTSHADE.

BLUE PEPPERMINT: See EUCALYPTUS.

BLUE PIMPERNEL: See SKULLCAP.

BLUE SAGE: See SAGE.

BLUE SKULLCAP: See SKULLCAP.

BLUE VERVAIN (*Verbena hastata*) [*Verbenaceae*]

American vervain; False vervain; Indian hyssop; Purvain; Simpler's joy; Traveler's joy; Wild hyssop:

Extracts from blue vervain were an old treatment for epilepsy. It is not used in cooking. See also **Vervain.**

BLUE-BUTTONS: See PERIWINKLE.

BLUE-DEVIL: See VIPER'S BUGLOSS.

BLUE-LEAVED MALLEE: See EUCALYPTUS.

BLUE-SAILORS: See CHICORY.

BLUEBEARD SAGE: See SAGE.

BLUEBELLS: See COWSLIP.

BLUEBERRY (*Vaccinium* spp.) [*Ericaceae*]

There are about 150 species of *Vaccinium*, some cultivated for their edible fruit, some cultivated as ornamentals, and others growing wild. The following list of common names is given so that the reader can associate them with the *Vaccinium* species. For further identification of the particular species, consult *Hortus Third*.

> bilberry—related to common blueberry
> cowberry—related to common cranberry
> cranberry
> deerberry—related to common blueberry
> foxberry—related to common cranberry
> grouseberry—related to common blueberry

huckleberry—related to common blueberry
lingberry, lingen- or lingonberry—related to cranberry
moorberry—related to common blueberry
whinberry—related to common blueberry
whortleberry—related to common blueberry

BLUEBONNET: See CORNFLOWER.

BLUEBOTTLE: See CORNFLOWER.

BLUEWEED: See VIPER'S BUGLOSS.

BOFAREIRA: See CASTOR OIL PLANT.

BOG BEAN: See BUCKBEAN.

BOG MYRTLE (*Myrica gale*) [*Myricaceae*]
Meadow fern; Sweet gale:
Bog myrtle is a common plant in boggy areas in the northern part
of the Northern Hemisphere. The leaves are pleasantly aromatic and were
used in northern Europe to flavor beer. In China, the leaves were dried and
used to make a tea. In Sweden and some other countries, both the leaves
and the fruit are used to flavor soups. The leaves and fruit have a high wax
content which is extracted by boiling in water and used to make fragrant
candles.
Buckbean is also called bog myrtle. See BUCKBEAN.

BOG ONION, BOG-ONION: See HERB CHRISTOPHER and INDIAN TURNIP.

BOG SPRUCE: See SPRUCE.

BOHEA-TEA: See SWEET GOLDENROD.

BOIS DE ROSE (*Aniba roseodora, parviflora,* and *duckei*) [*Lauraceae*]
Brazilian rosewood
(*Ocotea caudata*) [*Lauraceae*]
Cayenne rosewood; Linaloe cayenne bois de rose:
Bois de rose oil is obtained by steam distillation of wood chips from
Aniba roseodora, and the other species listed above. It has a sweet, floral,
woodsy odor and is used in perfumes and the formulation of flavorings for
confections and baked goods. It is not derived from the rosewood trees.
Rosewood trees belong to the genus *Dalbergia* of the *Leguminosae* family.

Only bois de rose from *Aniba roseodora* is listed by the FDA as GRAS. The other species are not mentioned.

BOLDO (*Peumus boldus*) [*Monimiaceae*]
   Boldus:
   Derivatives of the leaves of this evergreen tree from Chile have an odor reminiscent of lemon balm (*Melissa officinalis*) and coriander (*Coriandrum sativum*). Flavoring use is restricted to alcoholic beverages only by the FDA.

BOLDUS: See **BOLDO.**

BOLETUS MUSHROOMS: See **DRIED MUSHROOMS.**

BOMBAY ALOE: See **ALOE.**

BOMBAY DUCK:
   Bombay duck is the dried, salted bummalo fish (*Harpodon negerus*), a small gelatinous fish. It is soaked for about an hour to remove some of the salt and then fried or baked until crisp. It is crumbled and sprinkled over the dish it is to season.

BOMBAY MACE: See **MACE.**

BONESET: See **COMFREY** and **THOROUGHWORT.**

BOOKOO: See **BUCHU.**

BOOR TREE: See **ELDER.**

BORAGE (*Borago officinalis*) [*Boraginaceae*]
   Bee plant; Beebread; Burridge; Cool-tankard; Talewort:
   This annual plant, native to the Middle East, is common in southern Europe and southern England, and grows well in dry, sunny places. It is a small herb with bright blue flowers and with a taste reminiscent of cucumber. The young leaves are eaten in mixed salads, the larger ones are cooked as greens; flowers and leafy tips are used in summer beverages; flowers are candied. The flowers and leaves are also dried. Finely chopped leaves can be simmered with cabbage as a seasoning or used to flavor cream cheese and yogurt. The blue flowers have been used to color vinegar. Because of its mild laxative and diaphoretic effects, it has been used as an herbal medicine. It is supposed to fight fevers and act as a stimulant, driving away melancholy. Even though borage is sometimes called beebread, beebread is actually a brown, bitter mixture of pollen and honey, made and eaten by some bees.

BORE TREE: See **ELDER.**

BORONIA (*Boronia megastigma*) [*Rutaceae*]:
Derivatives of this plant have a fruity odor. It is used in perfumery and in flavor formulations for confections, beverages and baked goods. GRAS

BOTTLEBRUSH: See **SHAVE GRASS.**

BOUILLON CUBES, STOCK CUBES:
These are dehydrated meat, yeast, or vegetable extracts used as seasonings in sauces and soups.

BOUNCING BET: See **SOAPWORT.**

BOUNTY: See **ELDER.**

BOUQUET GARNI:

A *bouquet garni* is a mixture of parsley, thyme and bay leaf, which, fresh and in sprigs, is tied together. If the herbs are dried, they are wrapped and tied in a piece of clean cheesecloth. This is done so that the herbs will not be dispersed throughout the liquid and can be easily removed at the end of cooking. Celery, garlic, fennel, or other items may be included in the package but are always specified, such as "a small bouquet garni with a stalk of celery and one clove garlic." A small herb package should contain 2 sprigs of parsley, 1/8 to 1/6 of an American bay leaf, and 1 sprig fresh or 1/8 teaspoon dried thyme.

BOURBON TEA (*Angraecum fragrans*) [*Orchidaceae*]
Faham tea:
The fragrant leaves of this tropical orchid are used to make a tea.

BOURBON VANILLA: See **VANILLA.**

BOURMAN'S ROOT: An incorrect spelling of Bowman's root. See **CULVER'S-PHYSIC.**

BOVRIL:
Bovril is a concentrated meat stock, evaporated to a thick dark brown, salty paste. It was first made in Quebec in 1874 and was known as *Johnston's Fluid Beef*. The name was changed to *Bovril* when Johnston combined the Latin word "bo," meaning ox, with "Vrilya," the name given to the life force in Bulwyer-Lytton's novel, *The Coming Race*.

BOWLES MINT: See MINT.

BOWMAN'S-ROOT: See CULVER'S PHYSIC.

BOX: See BOXWOOD.

BOX HOLLY: See BUTCHER'S BROOM.

BOXWOOD (*Buxus sempervirens*) [*Buxaceae*]
   Box; Bush tree:
      This is the common hedge plant, and although it has been used in herbal remedies, it should be considered a toxic plant. It has been said that animals have died from eating the leaves. It has extreme purgative properties. Some people incorrectly call the dogwood boxwood. See DOGWOOD.

BOYSENBERRY: See BRAMBLES.

BRAKE FERN: See WALL FERN.

BRAKE ROCK: See WALL FERN.

BRAKEROOT: See WALL FERN.

BRAMBLES (*Rubus* spp.) [*Rosaceae*]
   Blackberry; Raspberry; Baked-apple berry; Blackcap; Boysenberry; Cloudberry; Dewberry; Framboise; Himalaya berry; Kneshenka; Loganberry; Malka; Nagoonberry; Salmonberry; Thimbleberry; Wineberry; Yellowberry; Youngberry:
      There are more than 250 species of *Rubus*, all known as brambles. There are many, many variants and cultivars, each one known by at least one common name, some by several. No attempt will be made to list them all. Bark and fruit juices are used in commercial flavoring formulations and the leaves are a common ingredient in herbal teas. *Rubus* species are GRAS.

BRANCHING LARKSPUR: See LARKSPUR.

BRANDY MINT: See MINT.

BRAZILIAN NUTMEG: See NUTMEG.

BRAZILIAN PEPPER TREE: See PEPPER TREE.

BRAZILIAN RHATANY: See RHATANY.

BRAZILIAN ROSEWOOD: See BOIS DE ROSE.

BRAZILIAN SASSAFRAS: See SASSAFRAS.

BRAZILIAN SASSAFRAS OIL: See SASSAFRAS.

BRAZILIAN TEA (*Lippia pseudo-thea*) [*Verbenaceae*]
 Gervao:
 The leaves of this small tropical American shrub of the *Verbenaceae* family are sold in Austria and possibly elsewhere as Brazilian tea.

BRIDEWORT: See HERB CHRISTOPHER.

BRIGHAM YOUNG WEED: See EPHEDRA.

BRITISH HONDURAN SAGE: See SAGE.

BRITISH MYRRH: See CHERVIL.

BRITISH TOBACCO: See COLTSFOOT.

BROAD-LEAVED DOCK: See SORREL.

BROAD-LEAVED PARSLEY: See PARSLEY.

BROAD-LEAVED PEPPERMINT: See EUCALYPTUS.

BROAD-LEAVED PLANTAIN: See PLANTAIN.

BROOK BEAN: See BUCKBEAN.

BROOKLIME: See VERONICA.

BROOM (*Genista* spp.) [*Leguminosae*]
 Broom buds
 (*Genista tinctoria*)
 Dyer's broom; Dyer's greenweed; Dyer's greenwood; Dyer's whin; Furze; Green broom; Waxen woad; Woadwaxen; Woodwaxen
 (*Cytisus scoparius*) [*Leguminosae*]
 Irish broom; Link; Scotch broom:
 There is much confusion among the plants of these two genera. The primary difference between them botanically is that *Cytisus* has a small callus-

like protuberance near the hilum of the seed and *Genista* does not. Most brooms are grown for the showy ornamental flowers, however, *Genista tinctoria* is grown as a source of yellow dye. The buds of a number of species of the genus *Genista* have been pickled and used as a substitute for capers, but it is not a wise thing to do. *Genista* species contain both a central nervous system stimulant and a vasoconstrictor. *Cytisus* species are cathartic, diuretic, emetic, and hallucinogenic. Both of these species are very toxic. Furze usually refers to plants of the *Ulex* genus [*Leguminosae*], a spiny, ornamental shrub.

BROOM BUDS: See **BROOM.**

BROWN BETH: See **TRILLIUM.**

BROWN MUSTARD: See **MUSTARD.**

BROWN SARSAPARILLA: See **SARSAPARILLA.**

BROWN'S PEPPER: See **CAPSICUM.**

BROWNWORT: See **HERB CARPENTER.**

BRUISEWORT: See **COMFREY** and **SOAPWORT.**

BRYONY (*Bryonia alba*) [*Curcurbitaceae*]
   Tetterberry; White bryony; Wild bryony; Wild hops; Wild vine; Wild white vine:
   (*Bryonia dioica*)
   Devil's turnip; Red bryony; Wild hops; Wild vine; Wild white vine:
      Derivatives of the aromatic roots of *Bryonia alba* are restricted to use as alcoholic beverage flavoring by the FDA. *Bryonia dioica* is not listed by the FDA, but in general, it is considered more toxic than *Bryonia alba*. Both have been used in herbal remedies but should be considered poisonous plants. The berries are extremely poisonous and as few as fifteen of the one-fourth inch berries can be fatal.

BUCCO: See **BUCHU.**

BUCHU (*Agathosma betulina*, formerly *Barosma betulina*) [*Rutaceae*]
   Bookoo; Bucco; Bucku; Mountain buchu; Round buchu; Short buchu
   (*Agathosma crenulata*, formerly *Barosma crenulata*)
   Crenate buchu; Long buchu; Oval buchu:

The leaves have a strong, sweet odor with a bitter flavor. They are used in perfumery and in flavor formulations for confections. In the past they were used for treatment of stomach and kidney disorders. Leaves of both of the above species are GRAS.

BUCKBEAN (*Menyanthes trifoliata*) [*Gentianaceae*]
Bean trefoil; Bog bean; Bog myrtle; Brook bean; Marsh clover; Marsh trefoil; Moonflower; Trefoil; Water shamrock; Water trefoil:
The bitter, aromatic leaves are restricted for use in alcoholic beverages only by the FDA. They have also been used in some herbal remedies.

John Lust lists moonflower as a common name for buckbean. However, the moonflower commonly grown for its fragrant nocturnal large white flowers is *Ipomoea alba* [*Convolvulaceae*], closely related to the sweet potato.

BUCKEYE: See HORSE CHESTNUT.

BUCKHORN: See HERB CHRISTOPHER and PLANTAIN.

BUCKHORN BRAKE: See HERB CHRISTOPHER.

BUCKHORN MALE FERN: See HERB CHRISTOPHER.

BUCKLER-LEAF SORREL: See SORREL.

BUCKRAMS: See GARLIC.

BUCKTHORN: See CASCARA.

BUCKU: See BUCHU.

BUDWOOD: See DOGWOOD.

BUFFALO HERB: See ALFALFA.

BUGBANE: See BLACK COHOSH and FALSE HELLEBORE.

BUGWORT: See BLACK COHOSH.

BUKHARA CLOVER: See SWEET CLOVER.

BULBOUS BUTTERCUP: See BUTTERCUP.

BULBOUS CROWFOOT: See BUTTERCUP.

Bull's eyes: See Marigold.

Bullock's eye: See Houseleek.

Bullock's heart: See Custard apple.

Bullsfoot: See Coltsfoot.

Bullweed: See Knapweed.

Bundy: See Eucalyptus.

Burdock (*Arctium lappa*) [*Compositae*]
> Bardana; Beggar's-buttons; Burr seed; Clotbur; Cockle buttons; Cocklebur; Cuckold; Edible burdock; Gobo; Grass burdock; Great bur; Great burdock; Hardock; Hareburr; Harlock; Hurrburr; Lappa; Turkey burrseed

(*Arctium minus*)

Common burdock:

Arctium lappa is the one species of burdock that is grown for its edible roots. It is much cultivated in Japan as a vegetable, known as gobo. The long slender roots are eaten when about two feet (or less) in length.
Arctium minus has been used in herbal remedies.

Burma cinnamon: See Cinnamon.

Burnet (*Sanguisorba officinalis*) [*Rosaceae*]
> **Burnet bloodwort; Great burnet; Italian burnet; Italian pimpernel**

(*Poterium sanguisorba* [*Rosaceae*], formerly *Sanguisorba minor*)

Garden burnet; Pimpinella; Pimpinelle; Salad burnet:

Native to Europe, the leaves are used fresh or dried as seasoning. It smells and tastes strongly of fresh cucumbers, like borage. The fresh young leaves can be used in salads. The dried leaves can be used for seasoning in soups, sauces, and vegetable and fish dishes. Legend claims that it will heal wounds and infections and also cure gout and rheumatism.

Burnet bloodwort: See Burnet.

Burnet saxifrage: See Pimpernel.

Burning bush, Burning-bush: See **Dittany** (*Dictamnus albus*) and **Wahoo.**

BURR SEED: See BURDOCK.

BURRIDGE: See BORAGE.

BURRWORT: See BUTTERCUP.

BURSTING-HEART: See WAHOO.

BUSH BASIL: See BASIL.

BUSH TEA PLANT: See SPIKENARD.

BUSH TREE: See BOXWOOD.

BUSHY GERARDIA: See FEVERWEED.

BUTCHER'S BROOM (*Ruscus aculeatus*) [*Liliaceae*]
Box holly; Hornet holly; Jew's myrtle; Knee holly; Little holly:
The stiff, pointed, leaf-like twigs of this plant were used for making brooms. Tender young shoots were sometimes eaten like asparagus.

BUTTER AND EGGS: See TOADFLAX.

BUTTER ROSE: See COWSLIP.

BUTTERBUR: See COLTSFOOT.

BUTTERCUP (*Ranunculus* spp.) [*Ranunculaceae*]
Crowfoot
(*Ranunculus acris*)
Bachelor's buttons; Blisterweed; Burrwort; Buttercup; Globe amaranth; Gold cup; Meadow crowfoot; Meadowbloom; Tall buttercup; Tall crowfoot; Tall field buttercup; Yellows; Yellowweed
(*Ranunculus bulbosus*)
Acrid crowfoot; Bulbous buttercup; Bulbous crowfoot; Buttercup; Crowfoot; Crowfoot buttercup; Cuckoo buds; Frogwort; King's cup; Meadowbloom; Pilewort; Saint Anthony's turnip
(*Ranunculus sceleratus*)
Buttercup; Celery-leaved buttercup; Crowfoot; Cursed crowfoot; Marsh crowfoot; Water crowfoot:
There are about 250 species of *Ranunculus* all known as buttercup or crowfoot. Although these plants have been used in homeopathic medicine

and herbal remedies, they are almost all very toxic plants and should not be used in home remedies. Some species will cause blistering of the skin on contact.

Butterfly weed: See Indian paintbrush.

Butterweed: See Erigeron.

Button snake-root or **snakeroot:** See Blazing-star and Erigeron.

C

CACAO: See CHOCOLATE.

CADE OIL (*Juniperus oxycedrus*) [*Pinaceae*]
Oil of cadeberry; Juniper tar; Prickly juniper:
Oil derived from the berries or the wood of this species of juniper has a smoky, acrid odor and a bitter taste. It is used in perfumery and occasionally to give a smoky note to canned meats and fish. It formerly was used in the treatment of skin disorders. Of passing interest, a cade is also a barrel or cask and became a unit of measure containing 500 herrings or 1000 sprats.

CAFFEINE NUT: See COLA.

CAFTA: See ABYSSINIAN TEA.

CAJEPUT (*Melaleuca leucadendron*) [*Myrtaceae*]
River tea tree; Weeping tea tree
(*Melaleuca cajaputi*)
Cajeput; Cajuput
(*Melaleuca linariifolia*)
Tea tree
(*Melaleuca minor*)
Cajeput; Cajuput
(*Melaleuca viridiflora*)
Cajeput; Cajuput; Niaouli:
Oils from this plant have a bitter, burning taste and a camphor-like odor. They are used in perfumery and in flavoring formulations for confections and baked goods. The oil was also an old treatment for worms

and was used as an antiseptic, pain reliever, and laxative. *Melaleuca leucadendron* and other *Melaleuca* species are GRAS.

CALABASH TREE: See BAOBAB.

CALAMINT (*Satureja glabella*, formerly *Calamintha glabella*) [*Labiatae*]:
Technically, calamint may refer to any plant of the *Satureja* or *Calamintha* genera, but the above plant is the one used for making herbal tea or occasionally as a spicy addition to a salad.

CALAMUS (*Acorus calamus*) [*Araceae*]
Flagroot; Grass myrtle; Myrtle flag; Sweet calamus; Sweet flag; Sweet grass; Sweet myrtle; Sweet rush:
Sweet flag was once used for flavoring of vermouth and liqueurs. It has a cinnamon-like aroma and flavor. Its use has not been permitted in the United States since 1968. It has appeared in lists of herbs and spices in cook books published as late as 1985 and is sometimes seen listed as a cinnamon substitute. It has often been erroneously identified as belonging to the iris family (*Iridaceae*). The *Araceae*, or arum family, contains plants such as the taro and others with a starchy tuberous root often used for food.

CALENDULA: See MARIGOLD.

CALICO FLOWER: See SERPENTARIA.

CALICO BUSH: See MOUNTAIN LAUREL.

CALIFORNIA BARBERRY: See OREGON GRAPE.

CALIFORNIA BAY: See SASSAFRAS.

CALIFORNIA BUCKTHORN: See CASCARA.

CALIFORNIA FERN: See HEMLOCK (*Conium maculatum*).

CALIFORNIA LAUREL: See SASSAFRAS.

CALIFORNIA NUTMEG: See NUTMEG.

CALIFORNIA OLIVE: See SASSAFRAS.

CALIFORNIA PEPPER TREE: See PEPPER TREE.

CALIFORNIA POPPY: See FUMITORY.

CALIFORNIA SASSAFRAS: See SASSAFRAS.

CALUMBA (*Jateorhiza calumba* or *palmata*) [*Menispermaceae*]
Columba; Columbo:

Extracts of the bitter roots of this plant, native to Mozambique, are permitted for use in alcoholic beverages only. Closely related to this plant is *Chondrodendron tormentosum*, one of the chief sources of curare. American columbo or calumba belongs to the gentian family. (See GENTIAN.) *Columba* is the genus name for the common pigeon.

CAMBRIC TEA:

Cambric tea is usually described as weak tea with milk and sugar but can also be just hot water with milk and sugar.

CAMDEN WOOLLYBUT: See EUCALYPTUS.

CAMMOCK: See REST-HARROW.

CAMOMILE (*Chamaemelum nobile*, formerly *Anthemis nobilis*) [*Compositae*]
Chamomile; English camomile; Garden camomile; Ground apple; Lawn camomile; Little apple; Manzanilla; May-then; Roman camomile; Scotch camomile; True camomile; Whig plant

(*Chamomilla recutita*, formerly *Matricaria recutita*, *Tripleurospermum recutita*, or *Matricaria chamomilla*)

German camomile; Hungarian camomile; Sweet false camomile; Wild camomile

These herbs have strongly scented foliage and flowers. They are daisy-like plants, belonging to the sunflower or aster family. The dried flower heads and leaves are used to make strong-scented, bitter teas and tonics touted as cure-alls in old-wives' tales. It is said that camomile cures insomnia, calms nerves, and repels biting insects. Compresses soaked in camomile are supposed to ease sore muscles. Used as a hair rinse, it is supposed to lighten the color. GRAS

The following list of plants are ones that are or have been used as adulterants of true camomile.

Chamomilla suaveolens, formerly *Matricaria matricarioides*
Pineapple weed; Rayless mayweed
Ormensis mixta and *multicaulis* [*Compositae*]
Moroccan camomile
Anthemis arvensis

Corn camomile

Anthemis cotula

Dog fennel; Stinking camomile; Stinking mayweed; Wild camomile

Anthemis montana

Anthemis tinctoria

Golden Marguerite; Ox-eye camomile; Yellow camomile

Chrysanthemum leucanthemum

Matricaria perforata, formerly *Matricaria inodora* or *Tripleurospermum inodorum*

Corn feverfew; Scentless camomile; Scentless mayweed; Wild camomile

CAMPEACHY WOOD (*Haematoxylon campechianum*) [*Leguminosae*]

Bloodwood tree; Logwood:

The heartwood of this tree, which grows in the West Indies and the Yucatan Peninsula, is the source of hematoxylin dye. This dye is used as a tissue stain in microscopy and occasionally as a Ph indicator. At one time extracts of campeachy wood were used in some liqueurs and wines to improve the color. It should be considered a toxic substance, and its use is not recommended.

CAMPHOR TREE: See SASSAFRAS.

CANADA BALSAM: See BALSAM FIR NEEDLE OIL.

CANADA ROOT: See INDIAN PAINTBRUSH.

CANADA TEA: See WINTERGREEN.

CANADA-PITCH TREE: See HEMLOCK (*Tsuga canadensis*).

CANADIAN BLACK PINE: See SPRUCE.

CANADIAN HEMLOCK: See HEMLOCK (*Tsuga canadensis*).

CANADIAN SNAKEROOT (*Asarum canadense*) [*Aristolochiaceae*]

Asarabacca; Asarum; Black snakeroot; Coltsfoot snakeroot; False coltsfoot; Heart snakeroot; Indian ginger; Southern snakeroot; Vermont snakeroot; Wild ginger:

The rhizomes of this plant have a strong spicy odor and flavor reminiscent of ginger. It is used in flavoring formulations for beverages, confections, baked goods, and condiments. As with any snakeroot plant, it is supposed to cure snake bites. GRAS

Do not confuse this plant with European snakeroot, *Asarum europaeum.* See EUROPEAN SNAKEROOT.

CANADIAN SPRUCE: See SPRUCE.

CANADIAN WHITE PINE: See WHITE PINE.

CANAIGRE: See GINSENG.

CANANGA: See YLANG-YLANG.

CANARY BALM: See BALSAM FIR NEEDLE OIL.

CANCERWEED: See SAGE.

CANDELILLA WAX (*Euphorbia antisyphilitica*) [*Euphorbiaceae*]:

Candelilla wax is obtained by boiling the stems and branches of the almost leafless candelilla plant in a mixture of water and sulfuric acid. The wax is skimmed from the hot solution. It is used as a lubricant and as an ingredient in chewing gums and hard candies. GRAS

CANDLEBERRY: See BAYBERRY.

CANDLEBERRY TREE: See CANDLENUT.

CANDLENUT (*Aleurites moluccana*) [*Euphorbiaceae*]

Candleberry tree; Candlenut tree; Country walnut; Indian walnut; Otaheite walnut; Varnish tree:

Candlenuts, so called because the oily nuts were threaded onto the rib of a palm leaf and burned as candles, are native to Malaysia and many Pacific islands. The nuts are now cultivated in many tropical areas for their oil, which is used for making paints, soaps, and other products. The fresh nuts and the residue left after the oil is expressed are poisonous. It is said that "after some time the poison disappears," but how long is "some time"? Candlenuts are used in Indonesian cooking in some curries, but it is much better to use macadamia nuts or blanched almonds, which evidently, the local people prefer but do not always have available.

CANE APPLES: See ARBUTUS BERRY.

CANELA:

Canela is the Spanish and Portuguese word for cinnamon. See **CINNAMON**.

CANELLA (*Canella winterana*, formerly *Canellaceum alba*) [*Canellaceae*]:
   Canella bark; Wild cinnamon:

This is the bark of a West Indian tree which yields an oil used in the making of perfumes. It has been used as a tonic, stimulant, or stomachic. The tree will grow in parts of Florida. Jamaica canella is the bark of *Cinnamodendron corticosum* or *C. macranthum*, which is often substituted for canella bark. The term canella occurs in cooking only as a translator's error for cinnamon. *Cannelle* is the French word for cinnamon and *cannella* is the Italian.

CANKERROOT: See **GOLDTHREAD** and **LION'S-FOOT**.

CANKERWEED: See **LION'S-FOOT**.

CANKERWORT: See **DANDELION**.

CANNELLA:

Cannella is the Italian word for cinnamon. See **CINNAMON**.

CANNELLE:

Cannelle is the French word for cinnamon. See **CINNAMON**.

CANOE BIRCH: See **WHITE BIRCH**.

CANTON GINGER: See **GINGER**.

CAPE ALOE: See **ALOE**.

CAPE COWSLIP: See **COWSLIP**.

CAPE GUM: See **ACACIA**.

CAPE JASMINE: See **JASMINE**.

CAPER BUSH: See **CAPERS**.

CAPER SPURGE (*Euphorbia lathyris*) [*Euphorbiaceae*]
   Garden spurge; Myrtle spurge; Mole plant:

Caper spurge is most definitely a poisonous plant. Its green seeds look like capers, and some hardy souls say that the pickled seeds are quite good.

It is better to refer to caper spurge as mole plant and use it to keep away moles as folklore says it will do. Also see SPURGE.

CAPERS (*Capparis spinosa*) [*Capparidaceae*]

Mountain pepper:

These are the unopened buds of a spiny shrub growing wild on the rocky shores of the Mediterranean and are used only in their pickled form. The buds, which burst into flower for only one day, must be gathered between dusk and dawn and form a source of pocket money for many children. Families accumulate collections in a cask of brine and then sell them to a dealer who washes out the salt and pickles the buds in little jars of vinegar. The pickled buds are graded according to size, the smallest being the most valuable, and designated by various names such as "capote," "capuchine" (large), "nonpareil" (small), "surfines" (medium), and others. These names are not controlled by any regulations in the United States, so it is difficult to find any capers not labeled "nonpareil" (the most valuable grade), no matter what the size they are. They are pungent and slightly bitter in taste and are used in salads, sauces, for seasoning veal and beef, and as garnishes. Capers should not be cooked with the food but added to the finished product. When cooked they become very bitter. GRAS

Nasturtium buds and immature seeds (*Tropaeolum majus* [*Tropaeolaceae*]) are sometimes sold as capers, but although they make a pleasant substitute, they cannot really be compared to the genuine caper. To add to the confusion, the French word for nasturtium is *capucine*. Nasturtium buds and seeds are not in the FDA listing.

Another plant whose flowering buds have been pickled and eaten like capers is *Larrea tridentata* [*Zygophyllaceae*], also known as creosote bush, chaparral and greasewood. The branches of this bush were boiled to extract Sonora gum which contains high concentrations of phenols. Creosote is a distilled mixture of phenols from wood tars or coal tars. Sonora gum, because of its high concentrations of phenols, was used to make creosote. Creosote is best known as a wood preservative, however it has been used as an antiseptic and, in very small quantities, as an expectorant.

CAPUCINE: See CAPERS and NASTURTIUM.

CAPIVI: See COPAIBA.

CAPSICUM (*Capsicum*, various species) [*Solanaceae*]:

Capsicum annuum, variety *annuum* is divided into five different groups each with many cultivars or subvarieties.

(1)   *Cerasiforme* Group. **Cherry pepper:** This is a yellow or purplish, globose, very pungent pepper.

(2) *Conoides* Group. **Cone pepper**: This pepper is conical in shape, growing to about two inches in length.

(3) *Fasciculatum* Group. **Red cluster pepper** and **cluster pepper**: These are very slender and grow to about three inches in length. They are very pungent.

(4) *Grossum* Group. **Bell pepper, sweet pepper, green pepper, pimento (pimiento)**: These are bell-shaped with a thick flesh, red or yellow when mature, with a nonpungent, mild flavor—the ordinary vegetable or salad pepper and the source of pimento.

(5) *Longum* Group. **Capsicum pepper, cayenne pepper, chili pepper, long pepper, red pepper**: These peppers may grow to a foot in length with a diameter of two inches. They are the principal source of condiment red pepper and the source of medicinal capsicum.

Capsicum annuum, variety *glabriusculum*: **Bird pepper** and other non-cultivated wild forms of capsicum belong with this variety grouping.

Capsicum frutescens: **Tabasco pepper, Tabasco-sauce pepper**: This species is not widely cultivated, but it is the one used in the commercial production of hot pepper sauces. It grows principally in the Gulf states. The Spanish name for the Tabasco pepper is *malagueta* and should not be confused with melegueta pepper. (See **TABASCO SAUCE.**)

Capsicum chinense: **Chinese pepper.**

Capsicum pubescens: **Rocoto** and **chile manzana** (Spanish).

Capsicum baccatum: **Brown's pepper.**

A discussion of the classification of the numerous species and varieties of *Capsicum* would be a book unto itself, and no attempt will be made to include the names of the many varieties or of the varying degrees of "hotness" or "heat."

The hot and pungent varieties of *Capsicum* are known as chilies. Chilies may refer to any number of subvarieties such as *pasilla* pepper, *mulato* pepper, *ancho*, and *jalapeño* pepper. The fruit pod may be fresh, pickled, or dried and then converted into flakes or powder. All are very hot and spicy. Chili heat is measured by the Scoville Organoleptic Heat Test, a method of high pressure liquid chomatography developed by a pharmacologist, Wilbur Scoville, in 1912. This test measures the amount of capsaicin, a colorless, flavorless chemical, found in the papery tissue on the pod's inner wall and is reported in "Scoville units." The common *jalapeños* measure about 6,000 Scoville units while *habenero* and Scotch bonnet chilies can measure 300,000 units. Research is being done to develop even hotter chilies, known as "Super Hots," which measure 400,000 to 500,000 Scoville units.

The common names of some chili peppers have been included just to let the reader know they belong to the *Capsicum* genus.

Pequin is a small, very hot pepper, the name deriving from the Spanish word *pequeño*, meaning small.

Petines are very small (1/8 to 1/4 inch diameter) round peppers, probably belonging to the Cerasiforme Group. The name is possibly a corruption of the French *petit un*, meaning little one. **Creole pepper** is a yellow pepper made from ground yellow chilies. **Nepal pepper**, from India, is similar to Creole pepper.

Cayenne pepper, as sold today, is a ground dried chili. Originally, however, it was prepared by baking a cake from a mixture of wheat flour and ground chilies. This cake was then ground to a coarse powder that was scarcely as potent as black pepper. For this reason recipes of the 19th century specifying large quantities of cayenne pepper must be interpreted with considerable caution. Cayenne is the name of a town in French Guiana. GRAS. See also **PAPRIKA**.

CARAWAY (*Carum carvi*) [*Umbelliferae*]:

Caraway is the sickle-shaped seed of a plant native to Asia, and is considered to be a noxious weed everywhere else it has been introduced. Dutch caraway has a reputation for superior quality, Holland having ideal growing conditions. The seeds have a characteristic pungent taste somewhat like anise. They are cooked with foods and used in rye bread, sauerkraut, beef stews, soups and candies. Caraway seed, along with cumin and anise, gives kümmel, a liqueur, its distinctive flavor. Although cumin (*Cuminum cyminum*) and caraway are both members of the same family, there is a distinct difference in the flavor. The Germans call both caraway and cumin Kümmel, although the correct German botanical name for cumin is Kreuzkümmel. The Spanish call caraway carvi, and cumin is called comino. In France cumin may refer either to cumin or caraway, although more correctly caraway is called carvi or cumin de près. If caraway is listed in a book on Eastern cooking as an ingredient in curry, it is probably a translation error and should be cumin. Caraway is best known as used in baked goods, but it is also used, according to Peter Gray, author of *The Mistress Cook*, "in some Oriental cheeses where it serves to mitigate the overwhelming odor of goat." Legend claims that it will cure colic and gout as well as protect objects from theft. GRAS

CARAWAY THYME: See THYME.

CARDAMINE: See LADY'S-SMOCK.

CARDAMOM; CARDAMON:

There are so many seeds of plants of the ginger family [*Zingiberaceae*] sold under this name that there is considerable confusion as to what is "true cardamom." But whatever you buy, it will be expensive. Most (but not all) dealers distinguish between the small or round cardamom (seeds of *Amomum compactum*, formerly *Amomum cardamomum*) and Malabar, Ceylon, or the large cardamom (seeds of *Elettaria cardamomum*). The small seeds, about the size of a mustard seed, are called "true cardamom" by the pickling and bottled sauce trades, while the confectionery and baking trades call the larger *Elettaria* seeds "true cardamon." The seeds of *Elettaria granum-paradise*, properly called grains of paradise or Guinea grains, occasionally are sold as "false cardamom." They are also called paradise nuts. The seeds of *Elettaria melegueta* are sometimes known as grains of paradise (which they are not) and sometimes as Melegueta pepper.

The fruit of *Elettaria cardamomum* is a pale green pod, picked by hand when ripe. The pods are then either treated by sulphur bleaching or by green curing. In the sulphur bleaching process the pods are subjected to sulphur fumigation with alternate periods of soaking and drying. After four stages there is a final sun drying. The entire process takes ten to twelve days to complete. Green curing is accomplished either drying in a heated oven with forced hot air or by drying in slow burning charcoal ovens for thirty-six hours. After curing the stalks and calices are removed and the pods are sorted into longs, mediums, and shorts. Damaged pods are used only for the seeds.

All of the above mentioned seeds combine the hotness of black pepper with a spicy aroma which is faint in Melegueta pepper, ginger-like in grains of paradise, and strongly reminiscent of allspice in the large cardamom. The small cardamom combines something of the aroma of allspice with a tang, like a cross between juniper and coriander. The cardamoms are used universally in pickles, are the principal flavoring in most spicy German and Scandinavian pastries, are widely used for seasoning in the Far East, and are an ingredient in French mixed spices. In the Near East, Bedouin coffee is flavored with cardamom. A few opened pods of *Elettaria cardamomum* are stuffed into the spout of the pot so that just the right amount of cardamom flavor is imparted to the coffee as it is poured out. *Elettaria cardamomum* is listed by the FDA as GRAS.

CARDIN: See **BLESSED THISTLE**.

CARDOON: See **ARTICHOKE**.

CARLINE THISTLE (*Carlina acaulis*) [*Compositae*]
   Dwarf carline; Ground thistle; Southernwood root:
   Carlina acaulis is native to Europe. Its roots have been used in herbal remedies. It is emetic and purgative. It should not be confused with southernwood which is *Artemisia abrotanum*. See **SOUTHERNWOOD**.

CARMINE: See **COCHINEAL**.

CARNATION (*Dianthus caryophyllus*) [*Caryophyllaceae*]

Clove pink; Divine flower; Gillyflower; Picotee:

The flower of the old-fashioned carnation has an aromatic scent rather like cloves. It was used widely in the seventeenth and eighteenth centuries as a flavoring, the petals often floated in wine or in soups or sauces.

CARNAUBA WAX (*Copernicia prunifera*, formerly *cerifera*) [*Palmae*]

Carnauba palm:

Carnauba wax is prepared from the leaves and buds of the Brazilian carnauba palm. It is used in the commercial preparation of baked goods, chewing gum, frostings, fruits and fruit juices, gravies and sauces, and candies. It is more often used in the home as an ingredient in shoe polishes, leather creams, and furniture, floor and car waxes. Carnauba wax is GRAS as a direct human food ingredient when used according to good manufacturing practice. The FDA has specified maximum amounts that can be used in specific foods. These can be found in the *Code of Federal Regulations*.

CAROB (*Ceratonia siliqua*) [*Leguminosae*]

Algarroba bean; Locust bean; Saint John's-bread:

The fruit of this Mediterranean tree is a long, dry pod containing hard seeds in a sweet pulp. It is used primarily for animal food. The pulp is roasted and finely ground into a powder with the appearance of cocoa. It is sometimes used as a poor substitute for cocoa or chocolate. It has its own distinctive flavor and is used in soft drinks, baked goods and confections. It is also an ingredient in herbal teas. GRAS

CAROLINA JASMINE: See JASMINE.

CAROLINA JESSAMINE: See JASMINE.

CAROLINA PINK: See PINKROOT.

CAROLINA TEA: See APPALACHIAN TEA.

CARPATHIAN WALNUT: See WALNUT.

CARPENTER'S HERB: See HERB CARPENTER.

CARPENTER'S SQUARE: See FIGWORT.

CARPENTER'S WEED: See HERB CARPENTER.

CARRAGEEN; CARRAGHEEN (*Chondrus crispus*) [*Rhodophyceae*]
Irish moss; Pearl moss:

This is a purplish edible seaweed that is found on the western coast of Ireland, England, and Europe and the eastern coast of the United States. It has been used as a food and in medicines by the Irish peasants from time immemorial. When dried, it is called Irish moss. Carrageen is used as a gelling and thickening agent in many food products such as ice cream and other confections. The Food and Drug Administration has defined the amounts of carrageen that can be used in various food products. These can be found in the *Code of Federal Regulations*.

CARROT: See DAUCUS.

CART-TRACK PLANTAIN: See PLANTAIN.

CASCARA (*Rhamnus purshiana*) [*Rhamnaceae*]
Bearberry; Bearwood; Cascara sagrada; California buckthorn; Cascara buckthorn; Chittambark; Sacred bark

(*Rhamnus frangula*)
Alder buckthorn; Alder dogwood; Black alder dogwood; Black alder tree; Black dogwood; Buckthorn; European black alder; European buckthorn; Persian berries

(*Rhamnus cathartica*)
Common buckthorn; Purging buckthorn; Waythorn:

Extracts of the bark of *Rhamnus purshiana* are bitter tasting and have laxative effects. They are used in flavoring formulations and as an ingredient in proprietary laxatives. GRAS

Rhamnus frangula and *Rhamnus cathartica* bark and berries have been used in herbal remedies. They have very, very strong purgative properties and are extremely dangerous to use. They are not listed by the FDA.

Bearberry may also refer to *Arctostaphylos uva-ursi* [*Ericaceae*]. (See UVA-URSI.) The name chittambark should not be confused with chittamwood, the smoke tree, a small ornamental tree of the southern United States, which is *Crotinus obovatus*, formerly *Rhus cotinoides* [*Anacardiaceae*].

CASCARA BUCKTHORN: See CASCARA.

CASCARA SAGRADA: See CASCARA.

CASCARILLA BARK (*Croton eluteria*) [*Euphorbiaceae*]
Sweetwood bark:

The bark of this tree was used as an unofficial substitute for cinchona bark, the source of quinine. Extracts of the bark are occasionally used in flavoring liqueurs. Some references state that cascarilla bark is the same as angostura bark. It is not. GRAS

Croton monanthogynus is called prairie tea and was used as an old herbal tea with questionable medicinal properties. *Croton tiglium* is the source of croton oil, an extremely strong cathartic and a vesicant. It is considered unsafe for use, and numerous deaths have resulted from its consumption.

CASSENA, CASSENE: See CASSINA.

CASSIA (*Cinnamomum cassia*) [*Lauraceae*]

Cassia-bark tree; Chinese cinnamon

(*Cinnamomum cecidodaphne*)

Nepalese tejpat

(*Cinnamomum culiliban*)

Lawang (Indonesian)

(*Cinnamomum tamala*)

Indian cassia; Tejpat:

Cinnamomum cassia is a near relative of cinnamon and often confused with it. It is the dried bark of an evergreen tree native to Burma. It has the pungency but little of the aroma of cinnamon and often is used as an adulterant in cheap ground cinnamon. GRAS

An unfortunate mistake in early pharmacy confused the cassia tree (*Cassia acutifolia*) [*Leguminosae*], also known as senna, Indian senna and Alexandria senna, with the cassia-bark tree (*Cinnamomum cassia*). The cassia tree and related *Cassia* plants yield senna pods, long used as a strong purgative. The two should not be confused. *Cassia acutifolia* is GRAS.

The other *Cinnamomum* species listed above are also closely related to cinnamon and are used as seasonings. They are not included in the FDA listings.

CASSIA BUDS:

Cassia buds are the unripe fruit of a number of different species of Cinnamomum. They are sometimes used in pickling.

CASSIA TREE: See CASSIA.

CASSIA-BARK TREE: See CASSIA.

CASSIA-FLOWER TREE: See CINNAMON.

CASSIE (*Acacia farnesiana*) [*Mimosaceae*, formerly in *Leguminosae*]

Huisache; Opopanax; Popinac; Sponge tree; Sweet acacia; West Indian blackthorn

(*Acacia caven*)

Roman cassie:

Extracts of the flowers are used to enhance fruity flavors, however they are mostly used in perfumery. For some strange reason, this shrub is also call opopanax. See OPOPANAX. *Acacia farnesiana* is GRAS.

CASSINA (*Ilex vomitoria*) [*Aquifoliaceae*]

Black drink; Cassena; Cassene; Cassine; Indian black drink; Yaupon:

The Indians of the southeastern United States made a tea from the dried leaves of this holly to use during tribal ceremonies. Besides being strongly emetic, it is also narcotic.

CASSINE: See CASSINA.

CASTER: See CASTOREUM.

CASTOR: See CASTOREUM.

CASTOR BEAN: See CASTOR OIL PLANT.

CASTOR OIL PLANT (*Ricinus communis*) [*Euphorbiaceae*]

Bofareira; Castor bean; Mexico seed; Oil plant; Palma Christi; Wonder tree:

Oil from the seeds of this tropical plant is occasionally used in flavoring formulations for confections. It is best known for its laxative effects. The seeds contain ricin and are poisonous if eaten. The oil is extracted from the bean at low temperatures leaving the oil ricin free. The oil is listed GRAS for use in flavorings.

CASTOREUM; CASTOR; CASTER:

Castoreum is the dried preputial follicles and glandular secretions from *Castor fiber* and *Castor canadensis* [*Castoridae*], the ordinary beaver. The material is removed during the skinning process and is dried in the sun or over burning wood. The fresh pouch contains a yellowish, butter-like mass with a sharp, fetid aromatic odor. The dried product is dark brown, hard, and resinous. Canadian pouches are wrinkled, pear-shaped, almost flat, from two to six inches long and two to three inches wide. Siberian pouches are ovoid and smooth, slightly larger in size but of less value commercially. It is supposed to have a warm, animal, sweet odor, becoming more pleasant on dilution. Sometimes it has a birch, tar-like, musky odor. It is used in perfumery, and since it blends well with vanilla aromas, in confectionery flavor formulations. GRAS

CAT SPRUCE: See SPRUCE.

CAT THYME (*Teucrium marum*) [*Labiatae*]:
Cat thyme is not related to other thymes (genus *Thymus*) but is a germander. Cats are attracted to its aroma, and it was used in many old medicinal remedies. Like the other species of *Teucrium*, its use in the United States is restricted to flavoring formulations used for alcoholic beverages. See **Germander**.

CAT'S FOOT: SEE EVERLASTING AND GROUND IVY.

CAT'S VALERIAN: See VALERIAN.

CAT'S-PAW: See GROUND IVY.

CATALONIAN JASMINE: See JASMINE.

CATARRH ROOT: See GALANGAL.

CATBRIER: See SARSAPARILLA.

CATCHFLY: See DOGBANE.

CATCHWEED: See BEDSTRAW.

CATECHU (*Uncaria* or *Ourouparia gambir* or *gambier*) [*Rubiaceae*]
Gambier; Gambir; Pale catechu:
Catechu is a powerful astringent made from extracts of the leaves and twigs of *Uncaria gambir*. This is known as pale catechu. Medically it was used in the treatment of diarrhea and as a local application for sore throats. It is not made, as commonly thought, from the betel nut tree, *Areca catechu* [*Palmae*]. The betel nut (also called areca nut) is also highly astringent and when rolled with lime in a betel leaf, it was chewed by the natives for its stimulating properties.
Black catechu is *Acacia catechu* [*Mimosaceae*]. It is used primarily for the khaki brown dye, black cutch, obtained from the heartwood, however, at times, its bitter, astringent bark extracts are used in confectionery and liqueur flavoring formulations. Black catechu is also known as cutch, khair, and Wadalee gum tree. None of these should be confused with cachou, a

pill or lozenge used to sweeten the breath. Both *Uncaria gambir* and *Acacia catechu* are listed as GRAS.

CATESBY'S GENTIAN: See GENTIAN.

CATMINT: See CATNIP.

CATNEP: See CATNIP.

CATNIP (*Nepeta cataria*) [*Labiatae*]
Catmint; Catnep; Catrup; Catswort; Field balm:
Catnip is a strongly aromatic member of the mint family. Cats are supposed to be attracted by it. It has been used in teas and is attributed to be a mild nerve stimulant. Legend claims that it will keep away rats.

CATRUP: See CATNIP.

CATSHAIR: See SPURGE.

CATSUP; CATCHUP: See KETCHUP.

CATSWORT: See CATNIP.

CAUCASIAN WALNUT: See WALNUT.

CAYENNE PEPPER: See CAPSICUM.

CAYENNE ROSEWOOD: See BOIS DE ROSE.

CAYENNE SASSAFRAS: See SASSAFRAS.

CEDAR, WHITE: See WHITE CEDAR.

CEDAR LEAF OIL: See WHITE CEDAR.

CELANDINE (*Chelidonium majus*) [*Papaveraceae*]
Garden celandine; Great celandine; Tetterwort:
This plant, native to Europe and Asia, has become naturalized in the eastern United Sates. The plant juices are very caustic, and although it has been used in herbal remedies, it is a dangerously toxic plant.

CELERY SALT: See CELERY SEED.

CELERY SEED (*Apium graveolens*) [*Umbelliferae*]
Smallage:
These are the seeds from which ordinary celery is grown. Most of the seed sold for seasoning is left over from that sold for growing and has often lost much of its pungency along with its viability. Smallage usually refers to the seed of the wild celery plant, native to Italy. Celery seed has little use, except in pickling spice mixtures, as long as fresh celery is available. Celery salt is crushed celery seeds mixed with salt. Dried celery leaves will usually give more celery flavor (when substituting for fresh celery) than will the celery seeds. GRAS

CELERY-LEAVED BUTTERCUP: See **BUTTERCUP**.

CELTIC NARD: See **SPIKENARD**.

CENTAURY: See **MINOR CENTAURY**.

CENTAURY GENTIAN: See **MINOR CENTAURY**.

CENTURY PLANT: See **AGAVE**.

CEYLON CARDAMOM: See **CARDAMOM**.

CEYLON CINNAMON: See **CINNAMON**.

CHAFEWEED: See **EVERLASTING**.

CHAMOMILE: See **CAMOMILE**.

CHANTARELLES: See **DRIED MUSHROOMS**.

CHAPARRAL: See **CAPERS**.

CHARITY: See **GREEK VALERIAN**.

CHARTREUSE:
Chartreuse is a liqueur made by monks in Chartreux, France, that is flavored with balm, hyssop, angelica leaves, cinnamon bark, mace and saffron.

CHASTE TREE: See **SAGE TREE**.

CHASTEBERRY: See **SAGE TREE**.

CHAT: See **ABYSSINIAN TEA**.

CHEAT: See BEARDED DARNEL.

CHECKERBERRY: See WINTERGREEN and PARTRIDGEBERRY.

CHEESE FLOWER: See MALLOW.

CHEESE PLANT: See MALLOW.

CHEESE RENNET: See BEDSTRAW.

CHEESES: See MALLOW.

CHERRY BIRCH: See SWEET BIRCH.

CHERRY LAUREL (*Prunus laurocerasus*) [*Rosaceae*]
Cherry-bay; English laurel:
The leaves of the cherry laurel contain large quantities of cyanide-related compounds and are extremely poisonous. They should not be confused with other members of the genus *Prunus*. The leaves smell like bitter almond. Extracts of the leaves are FDA approved for use in flavorings only if the Prussic acid content is less than 25 parts per million.

CHERRY PEPPER: See CAPSICUM.

CHERRY-BAY: See CHERRY LAUREL.

CHERVIL (*Anthriscus cerefolium*) [*Umbelliferae*]
Cicely; French parsley; Garden chervil
(*Myrrhis odorata*) [*Umbelliferae*]
Anise; Anise chervil; British myrrh; European sweet cicely; Fern-leaved chervil; Garden myrrh; Giant sweet chervil; Myrrh; Spanish chervil; Sweet chervil; Sweet scented myrrh
(*Osmorhiza claytonii*) [*Umbelliferae*]
Hairy sweet cicely; Sweet jarvil; Sweet javril; Woolly sweet cicely
(*Osmorhiza longistylis*) [*Umbelliferae*]
Aniseroot; New England sweet cicely; Smooth sweet cicely; Sweet chervil; Sweet cicely
(*Chaerophyllum sylvestre*) [*Umbelliferae*]
European wild cicely
(*Cryptotaenia canadensis*, formerly *C. japonica*) [*Umbelliferae*]

Honewort; Japanese parsley; Japanese wild chervil; Mitsuba; White chervil:

The leaves of chervil, *Anthriscus cerefolium*, an annual, parsley-like plant, native to southern Russia, have a pleasant, fresh taste reminiscent of, but not as strong as, tarragon. Some say the aroma and taste of dried chervil is reminiscent of a blend of caraway and anise. It is widely used as a salad herb in Russia and in France. Apart from its use in salads, it goes very well with fish and eggs. Dried leaves are available, but fresh are best. It should not be cooked for very long. It is best used raw or added just before the hot dish is served. It is easily grown as an annual most anywhere in the United States. *Myrrhis odorata* has a more anise-like flavor. The tap root is boiled and is eaten in salads. The tap root of *Anthriscus cerefolium* is said to be poisonous. Wild chervil and the cicely herbs are of very closely related genera to chervil, and their flavors and uses are the same. *Anthriscus sylvestris* is known as cow chervil. *Chaerophyllum bulbosum* is known as turnip-rooted chervil or parsnip chervil, a hardy biennial with a carrot-like edible root. *Cryptotaenia canadensis* is cultivated in Japan where the tips are used as greens and to flavor soups. Only *Anthriscus cerefolium* is contained in the FDA listing as GRAS.

CHESTNUT (*Castanea dentata*) [*Fagaceae*]

American chestnut:

The American chestnut is almost extinct because of the chestnut bark disease or blight. It persists mostly as sprouts coming up from the old stumps in the native forest areas. The leaves are used in flavoring formulations. Occasionally one will find a small tree that has escaped the blight long enough to bear a few of the delicious, sweet nuts. GRAS

CHICKEN-TOES: See CORALROOT.

CHICKWEED (*Stellaria media*) [*Caryophyllaceae*]

Adder's mouth; Indian chickweed; Satin flower; Starwort; Stitchwort; Tongue-grass; Winterweed:

This common pesky weed has been used in herbal remedies for the relief of "serious constipation." Some say chickweed can be eaten as a cooked vegetable like spinach or in salads. Also see **Whitlow grass.**

CHICORY (*Cichorium intybus*) [*Compositae*]

Barbe-de-capuchin; Belgian endive; Blue-sailors; Coffeeweed; Succory; Witloof

(*Cichorium endivia*)

Endive:

Chicory root is dug, washed, cut into pieces and dried in gentle heat. It is then roasted and ground and used as an adulterant in or a substitute for coffee. It varies considerably in quality. The best is not bitter; poor quality can be very bitter. Although *Cichorium endivia* is the species preferred for use as a salad green, *Cichorium intybus* is also used as a salad green and is grown for witloof, the crown of uncolored leaves forced in winter or spring from stored roots. At the end of the growing season the roots are lifted, the tops cut off above the crown, and the roots stored in a cellar the same way as other root crops. For the production of witloof, the roots are trimmed on the lower end to eight or nine inches in length, then placed upright in soil or sand in a box and the crown covered with about eight inches of sand. Temperature is kept at about 60° F. and in about two weeks, the white salad witloof should be ready, being about six inches high. Sometimes leaves of chicory are blanched in the field late in the season the same as celery. The same treatment may be given in the spring to new leaves coming up from roots left in the ground over winter. Some force the stored roots in darkness to obtain the blanched leaves. GRAS

CHIGGER FLOWER: See INDIAN PAINTBRUSH.

CHILE MANZANA: See CAPSICUM.

CHILEAN SASSAFRAS: See NUTMEG and SASSAFRAS.

CHILGHOZA PINE: See PINE NUTS.

CHILI: See CAPSICUM.

CHILI POWDER: See MIXED SEASONINGS.

CHILI SAUCE:

This a mild but spicy sauce, similar to tomato ketchup, made from red peppers, tomatoes and spices. A recipe for homemade:

1 ½ teaspoons ground allspice
1 to 2 tablespoons cinnamon
1 ½ teaspoons cloves
1 gallon chopped peeled tomatoes
1 cup chopped onions
1 ½ cups chopped green peppers
1 ½ cups chopped sweet red peppers
½ to 2 cups vinegar (according to taste)
1 cup sugar
3 tablespoons salt

Tie spices loosely in a cheesecloth bag and boil with the vegetables until the mixture is reduced to half its original volume. Stir well while cooking to prevent scorching. Add vinegar, sugar, and salt. Boil rapidly 5 minutes, stirring constantly. Pour immediately into sterile jars and seal. Makes about 2 ¼ quarts.

CHIMNEY-SWEEPS: See PLANTAIN.

CHINA ROOT: See WILD YAM.

CHINA TREE: See CHINABERRY.

CHINABERRY (*Melia azedarach*) [*Meliaceae*]
Azedarach; Africa lilac; Bead tree; China tree; Hagbush; Hoptree; Indian lilac; Japanese bead tree; Paradise tree; Persian lilac; Pride tree; Pride-of-China; Pride-of-India; Syrian bead tree; Texas umbrella tree:

This ornamental member of the mahogany family is a spreading deciduous tree, growing to forty feet or more. It will only withstand a few degrees of frost. The fruit and root bark have been used in herbal remedies. The root bark is bitter and astringent and has been used in India as a tonic, although large doses are emetic and cathartic. Oils from the seeds are said to be anthelmintic. It is better known for its wood used in cabinet making and for the seeds used to make rosaries. The Texas umbrella tree is a cultivar with drooping foliage and radiating branches which give an umbrella-like effect.

CHINESE ANGELICA: See ANGELICA TREE.

CHINESE ANISE: See STAR ANISE.

CHINESE ARTICHOKE: See ARTICHOKE.

CHINESE BEAN CURD: See SOY PASTE.

CHINESE CHIVES: See CHIVES.

CHINESE CINNAMON: See CASSIA.

CHINESE FIVE-SPICE POWDER:
This is a Chinese spice mixture consisting of finely ground anise-pepper, star anise, cassia or cinnamon, cloves and fennel seed. It has a fragrant, slightly sweet, very pungent taste and can be used in any beef or pork dish. It should be used sparingly. A licorice flavor predominates. Some say the

mixture should contain equal parts of the five spices, but another mixture is as follows:

> 1 teaspoon ground anise-pepper
> ¹/₂ teaspoon ground cassia or cinnamon
> ¹/₂ teaspoon ground cloves
> 1 ¹/₄ teaspoons ground fennel seeds
> 1 teaspoon ground star anise

Whole spices can be mixed together before grinding so that the flavors mingle more during the grinding process.

CHINESE GINGER: See GALANGAL and also GINGER.

CHINESE GINSENG: See GINSENG.

CHINESE PARSLEY: See CORIANDER.

CHINESE PEPPER: See ANISE-PEPPER and CAPSICUM.

CHINESE RADISH: See DAIKON.

CHINESE RED BERRIES (? ?):
This is described in a list of Chinese seasonings as "an herb considered to be a nutrient tonic. It is used in soups." This is not an herb, nor is it a berry as we usually think of berries. It is a type of "red date" which I have not been able to botanically identify as yet. It could be the date plum, the lotusberry or the jujube. See **Lotus**. Besides being used in soups, it is also used in desserts.

CHINESE RHUBARB: See RHUBARB.

CHINESE SASSAFRAS: See SASSAFRAS.

CHINESE SEVEN-SPICE MIXTURE:
This is supposed to be a blend of powdered chili and sansho peppers, mandarin orange rind, black hemp,* white poppy seeds, dried seaweed, and sesame seeds. [Anderson and Hanna, p. 49]

CHINESE SPIKENARD: See SPIKENARD.

CHINESE SWEET ROOT:
This is described in a list of Chinese seasonings as "an herb considered to be a nutrient tonic. It is used in seasoning soups and other dishes. It has

---

*I have not been able to botanically identify "black hemp."

a licorice-like flavor." Actually this is licorice (*Glycyrrhiza glabra*) [*Leguminosae*]. See LICORICE.

CHINESE YAM: See WILD YAM.

CHINWOOD: See YEW.

CHIOS MASTIC TREE: See MASTIC.

CHIRATA (*Swertia* or *Ophelia chirata* or *chirayita*) [*Gentianaceae*]
    Chiretta; Chirayita:
    Extracts of this bitter plant from northern India may be used in alcoholic beverage flavoring formulations only. It was prescribed in olden medicine as an aid in emptying the gall bladder.

CHIRONJI NUTS: See ALMOND.

CHITTAMBARK: See CASCARA.

CHIVES (*Allium schoenoprasum*) [*Liliaceae*]:
    Cive; Schnittlauch:
    The green leaves and stalks of this grass-like onion are very well known. They do not dry well but will flourish all winter in a pot on the kitchen window sill. They should be used whenever a fresh, light suggestion of onion is required. Chives contain a large amount of mustard oil which gives them their peculiar and delicate taste. They cannot withstand heat and should be added after a dish is cooked. It is claimed that they stimulate the appetite, and help gastric juice secretion by stimulating the digestive organs. The French call this herb "The beneficial ciboulette (chive) which cleans the blood."
    Chinese chives (*Allium tuberosum*) have larger leaves and the flowers are said to "smell of roses and taste of garlic." See GARLIC. GRAS

CHOCOLATE (*Theobroma cacao*) [*Byttneriaceae*]
    Cacao; Cocoa:
    Chocolate and cocoa are products of the cacao bean. Cacao nibs are the cleaned, roasted cacao bean from which the outer shell has been removed. The cocoa butter content is about 50%. Nibs are ground by a process warm enough to melt the cocoa butter thus producing a chocolate liquor. Cocoa butter is removed from the chocolate liquor by a high-pressure process, leaving the pure cocoa powder. (This is the American method.) Dutch-process cocoa is made by removing the cocoa butter from the chocolate liquor by treating the liquor with alkali.

Unsweetened chocolate is the ground cacao bean, nothing added. Unsweetened cocoa powder is pure chocolate with almost all of the cocoa butter removed. Semi-sweet chocolate is unsweetened chocolate with sugar and usually additional cocoa butter added. It must contain 35% chocolate liquor. German sweet chocolate is a semi-sweet chocolate with additional cocoa butter and sugar added. It is sweeter than semi-sweet. It must contain 15% chocolate liquor. Milk chocolate contains, in addition to sugar and cocoa butter, milk solids. It must contain 10% chocolate liquor. Pre-melted unsweetened chocolate product is made of cocoa powder and vegetable oil. Substitute a one-ounce envelope for a one-ounce square of unsweetened chocolate. The pre-melted unsweetened type cannot be used for dipping since it will not harden at room temperature. GRAS

CHOCOLATE ROOT: See WATER AVENS.

CHOICE DIELYTRA: See CORYDALIS.

CHOKEBERRY (*Aronia arbutifolia*) [*Rosaceae*]:
This shrub is closely related to the pear genus, *Pyrus*, and is even considered a subspecies by some. It has very showy flowers and the red fruit is attractive in the fall. The very small (3/16 inch) berry-like pome is very astringent. Consider chokeberry as an ornamental.

CHOKECHERRY (*Prunus virginiana*) [*Rosaceae*]:
Extracts of the bark of the chokecherry have sedative qualities and the fruit is highly astringent. Chokecherry can also refer to *Prunus serotina*. See WILD CHERRY.

CHOP SUEY GREEN: See SHUNGIKU.

CHOROGI: See ARTICHOKE.

CHRISTMAS ROSE: See HELLEBORE.

CHRISTMASBERRY TREE: See PEPPER TREE.

CHRYSANTHEMUM, COOKING: See SHUNGIKU.

CHUFU: See GALINGALE.

CHULCO: See SORREL.

CHURCH STEEPLES: See AGRIMONY.

CICELY: See CHERVIL.

CILANTRO: See CORIANDER and ERYNGO.

CINCHONA: See QUININE.

CINNAMON (*Cinnamomum zeylanicum*) [*Lauraceae*]

Ceylon cinnamon; Madagascar cinnamon; Seychelles cinnamon; Sri Lanka cinnamon; Sweetwood; *Cannelle* (French); *Zimt* (German); *Cannella* (Italian); *Canela* (Spanish and Portuguese); *Seiron-nikkei* (Japanese); *Koritsa* (Russian); *Jou-kuei* (Chinese)

(*Cinnamomum burmanii*) [*Lauraceae*]

Batavia cassia; Batavia cinnamon; Burma cinnamon; Indonesian cassia; Java cassia; Korintje cassia; Pedang cinnamon

(*Cinnamomum loureirii*) [*Lauraceae*]

Cassia-flower tree; Cinnamon, U.S. Pharmacopeia; Saigon cinnamon:

The *Cinnamomum* trees will grow to a height of thirty feet, however, when commercially grown, they are kept pruned back to a height of six feet. This produces a very bushy plant with many shoots coming up from the roots. The shoots are allowed to grow for two years and then cut off close to the ground. The yellowish-brown outer bark is cut off in two strips. The outer skin of the bark is scraped off, and the remaining pale brown strips are placed concentrically inside one another and slowly dried into quills. The thinnest varieties are the best. The quality diminishes with increased thickness. Quillings are broken pieces of quills. Featherings are shavings and small pieces left over from processing quills. Chips are trimmings from the shoots.

The flavor of *Cinnamomum zeylanicum* is milder and the color lighter than the barks of *Cinnamomum cassia* (see CASSIA) and *loureirii*. *Cinnamomum loureirii*, Saigon cinnamon, has a higher oil content than the other species. The higher the oil content, the stronger the aroma and flavor. This is the cinnamon in greatest demand in the United States. Most Europeans prefer the milder Ceylon cinnamon. Cinnamon may be ground for use in pastries, breads, puddings, cakes, candies, and cookies. Stick cinnamon is used for preserved fruits, pickles, fruit soups, and hot beverages. Oil of cinnamon, distilled from broken bark, is used for flavoring and for medicinal purposes.

In earliest Colonial days cinnamon and sugar were mixed, put in a special big shaker called an "oomah" and used on waffles, pancakes, coffee cake, and hot buttered toast. "Oomah" may be a variation of the German word *Oma*, which means grandma or granny. GRAS

CINNAMON FERN: See HERB CHRISTOPHER.

CINNAMON VINE: See WILD YAM.

CINNAMON WOOD: See SASSAFRAS.

CINNAMON-COLORED FERN: See HERB CHRISTOPHER.

CINQUEFOIL (*Potentilla anserina*) [*Rosaceae*]
> **Crampweed; Goose tansy; Goosegrass; Moor grass; Silver cinquefoil; Silverweed**
>
> (*Potentilla canadensis*)
>
> **Finger leaf; Five fingers; Five-finger grass**
>
> (*Potentilla erecta*)
>
> **Red root; Shepherd's knot; Tormentil; Upright septfoil**
>
> (*Potentilla reptans*)
>
> **European five-finger grass**
>
> (*Potentilla rupestris*)
>
> **Prairie tea; Rock cinquefoil:**

Potentilla roots and leaves have been used in herbal remedies primarily for the treatment of diarrhea.

CIRCASSIAN WALNUT: See WALNUT.

CITRON-SCENTED GUM: See EUCALYPTUS.

CITRONELLA: SEE LEMONGRASS.
Montagné says that citronella is *Collinsonia canadensis* [*Labiatae*]. The leaves are used for seasoning and the flowers for making "digestive" liqueurs. The U.S. Food and Drug Administration, Fenaroli, and several dictionaries say citronella is *Cymbopogon nardus* [*Gramineae*]. It is used in perfumery and in beverage, candy, and baked goods flavoring formulations. *Collinsonia canadensis* [*Labiatae*] is also known as hardback, hardhack, heal-all, horse balm, horse weed, knob grass, knob root, richweed, and stoneroot. It has been used in many herbal remedies.

CITRONELLA GRASS: See LEMONGRASS.

CIVE: See CHIVES.

CIVET:

Civet is the odorous glandular secretion of both male and female civet cats (*Viverra civetta*). The largest quantities come from Africa, where the animals are kept captive on farms. The animal glands are drained of secretion about once a week. Civet is a yellowish to brownish, honey-like paste with a very strong, putrid odor, becoming sweet on dilution. It is blended with perfumes having honey, fruity aromas and is used in flavoring formulations for beverages, candy, and baked goods. GRAS

CLARY OR CLARY SAGE: See SAGE.

CLEAVERS: See BEDSTRAW.

CLEAVERWORT: See BEDSTRAW.

CLIVERS: See BEDSTRAW.

CLOTBUR: See BURDOCK.

CLOUD EAR MUSHROOM: See DRIED MUSHROOMS.

CLOUD PLANT: See MARIGOLD.

CLOUDBERRY: See BRAMBLES.

CLOVE PEPPER: See ALLSPICE.

CLOVE PINK: See CARNATION.

CLOVER:

Clover usually refers to any of the plants of the genus *Trifolium* [*Leguminosae*], most of which are cultivated as forage plants. The dried blossoms of red clover, *Trifolium pratense*, have been used in herbal remedies. The FDA lists *Trifolium* spp. as GRAS. Sweet clover, lotus, and melilot belong to the very closely related genus, *Melilotus*. See SWEET CLOVER.

CLOVEROOT: See BENNET.

CLOVES (*Syzygium aromaticum*) [*Myrtaceae*]:

The clove tree, botanically, has been called several different names, *Eugenia caryophyllata*, *Eugenia aromatica*, *Caryophyllus aromaticus* and *Jambosa caryophyllus*, and now has been placed in a separate genus, *Syzygium*. Clusters of flower buds are picked by hand when the base of the buds turns a reddish color. Buds are separated from stems and spread out on drying floors for four to five days. Too rapid drying can cause the cloves to become shrivelled and brittle. Under bad drying and storage conditions the color becomes darker, the cloves turn musty, and the head of the clove becomes pale and wrinkled. A good quality clove should be ¹/₂ to ³/₄ inch in length, reddish-brown in color and complete with base and head that is not too wrinkled appearing. United States government standards do not permit more than 5% stems in a sample. The stems are used for distilling oil of cloves. Cloves are used whole or the central head of the bud can be ground into a powder. The name comes from the Latin word *clavus*, meaning "nail." Cloves have a natural affinity for onions and should be used in all dishes containing onions in the proportion of about ¹/₃₂ of a teaspoon of ground cloves or 3 or 4 whole cloves per pound of onions. French housewives eliminate cooking odors by sprinkling a bit of clove on the stove or by placing a little burning clove on a special copper container and carrying it from room to room. Oil of clove is used in medicines, perfumes, and cordials. It is famous for alleviating toothache. Wild clove is *Syzygium* (formerly *Eugenia*) *acris*. GRAS

CLUB MOSS: See HERB-IVY.

CLUSTER PEPPER: See CAPSICUM.

COACHWEED: See BEDSTRAW.

COAKUM: See POKE.

COCA (*Erythroxylum coca*) [*Erythroxylaceae*]:
    The leaves of this South American shrub or tree are the source of coca from which cocaine is extracted. It should not be confused with the cacao bean, the source of chocolate, nor with cocoa, the powder left after cocoa butter is extracted from chocolate. Coca leaves may be used as a flavoring agent only if they are totally free of cocaine.

COCAINE PLANT: See COCA.

COCHINEAL; CARMINE:
    Cochineal (also called carmine) is a red dye prepared from the cochineal insect. This small, bright red, scale-type insect (*Coccus cacti* or *Dactylopius coccus*) lives on cacti in tropical America. The dye is prepared by drying the larva containing female insects, and then extracting the color with an alcohol-aqueous solution. The alcohol is then removed leaving a concentrated color solution. Carmine has the same insect sources but is prepared by aqueous

extraction of the color. The coloring principle for both is chiefly carminic acid. It is used mostly as a biological stain and a pH indicator but also as a food coloring. Cochineal and carmine may be used to color foods if they conform to the specifications pertaining to lead, arsenic, and other impurity content as stipulated in §73.100 Section 21 *Code of Federal Regulations*. Carmine and cochineal extracts must be pasteurized or otherwise treated to destroy all viable Salmonella organisms.

COCKEBURR: See AGRIMONY.

COCKLE BUTTONS: See BURDOCK.

COCKLEBUR: See AGRIMONY and BURDOCK.

COCKSPUR: See HAWTHORN BERRIES.

COCKSPUR THORN: See HAWTHORN BERRIES.

COCKUP HAT: See QUEEN'S DELIGHT.

COCKY BABY: See ARUM.

COCOA: See CHOCOLATE.

COCOA BUTTER: See CHOCOLATE.

COCONUT (*Cocos nucifera*) [*Palmae*]

To most Americans coconut conjures up a picture of white, sweet, dried shreds used in cookies, cakes, desserts and candies that don't have much flavor and tend to stick in the teeth, and the mention of coconut milk in a recipe means an automatic dismissal of any attempt at making the dish. There are primarily four types of products obtained from the coconut palm: (1) fermented beverages made from the sap obtained from incising flower clusters, (2) coir, the fiber from the husk of the nut, used to make rope, mats, etc., (3) copra, the dried meat of the nut, the source of coconut oil, and (4) the mature edible nut.

Coconut milk is the term which produces the most confusion and has led to inaccurate statements in many cookbooks. The green (unripe) coconut contains a milky juice which is used as a tropical drink. The ripe coconut available in grocery stores contains a watery liquid with little flavor. Coconut milk or cream, as called for in Far Eastern recipes, is made by shredding the coconut meat into a bowl, covering it with boiling water, allowing it to stand over night, or at least for several hours, and then draining off the "milk," pressing firmly to squeeze it all out. If this milk is allowed to stand for an hour or so, the fattier "cream" will rise to the top and can be skimmed off. Some cookbooks give instructions for preparing coconut milk using cow's milk instead of water. This gives an excellent flavor to the cow's milk which can be used in cakes and custards. Coconut milk can also be made with an electric blender using about ½ cup of diced fresh coconut and 1 cup of water and blending on high speed for about 30 seconds. Then strain, pressing out all the milk. Do not overload your blender by trying to do larger quantities but repeat with the small quantity until all the coconut is used. A whole coconut will make about one quart of coconut milk. One quart of coconut milk will separate, upon standing, into about 2 ½ cups of cream and 1 ½ cups of milk. Do not use sweetened dried shredded coconut to make coconut milk. The end product will contain too much sugar and will be useful only in sweet dessert-type dishes.

COCONUT MILK: See COCONUT.

COCOWORT: See SHEPHERD'S PURSE.

COFFEEWEED: See CHICORY.

COGNAC OIL:

Cognac oil is obtained by steam distilling of wine lees or dregs or from residual cakes after wine expression. It is green to bluish-green with the aroma of cognac. Green cognac oil is purified yielding a pale-yellow oily liquid called white cognac oil which has a more fruity aroma. It is used in formulations to provide fruity aromas for liqueurs, beverages, candies and baked goods. GRAS

COHOSH: See HERB CHRISTOPHER, BLACK COHOSH, and BLUE COHOSH.

COLA (*Cola nitida* and *acuminata*) [*Sterculiaceae*]
   Abata cola; Caffeine nut; Cola nut; Goora nut; Guru nut; Kola:
   Extracts from cola nuts, which contain both caffeine and theobromine, are used to make cola drinks and other flavoring formulations. *Cola nitida* grows wild and has a large nut while *Cola acuminata* is a cultivated species with a small nut. GRAS

COLA NUT: See COLA.

COLEUS (*Coleus amboinicus*, formerly *aromaticus*) [*Labiatae*]
   Cuban oregano; Indian borage; Oregano; Spanish thyme:

Coleus is best known as an ornamental plant grown for its showy leaves. The above species with its aromatic leaves has been used as a seasoning, but for a good "oregano" flavor, plants of the *Origanum* genus are far superior.

COLEWORT: See BENNET.

COLIC ROOT; COLICROOT: See BLAZING-STAR, STAR GRASS, and WILD YAM.

COLOPHONY: See ROSIN.

COLT'S TAIL: See ERIGERON.

COLTSFOOT (*Tussilago farfara*) [*Compositae*]
   Ass's foot; British tobacco; Bullsfoot; Butterbur; Coughwort; Flower velure; Foal's-foot; Hallfoot; Horsefoot; Horsehoof; The-son-before-the-fathers
(*Petasites*, various species) [*Compositae*]
   Butterbur; Sweet coltsfoot
(*Petasites japonicus*) [*Compositae*]
   Fuki:
   Coltsfoot and sweet coltsfoot have both been used in old remedies for pulmonary ailments, sore throats, and coughs, however *Tussilago farfara* is the one most commonly used. The fresh leaves have sometimes been eaten as a vegetable. There is controversy concerning the use of *Tussilago farfara*, some authorities saying it causes liver damage. The petioles of the very closely related *Petasites japonicus*, called fuki, are cooked as a vegetable in Japan.

COLTSFOOT SNAKEROOT: See CANADIAN SNAKEROOT.

COLUMBA; COLUMBO: See CALUMBA.

COLUMBINE (*Aquilegia vulgaris*) [*Ranunculaceae*]
   European crowfoot; Garden columbine:
   Although there are about seventy different species of *Aquilegia* and numerous varieties and cultivars, they are all known as columbine. *Aquilegia vulgaris* is known by the strongly hooked spurs on the flowers. It has been used in herbal remedies but is best left in the flower garden.

COLZA: See RAPESEED.

COMFREY (*Symphytum officinale*) [*Boraginaceae*]
   Blackwort; Boneset; Bruisewort; Consormol; Gum plant; Healing herb; Knitback; Knitbone; Salsify; Slippery root; Wallwort
(*Symphytum asperum*)
   Prickly comfrey
(*Symphytum uplandicum*)
   Russian comfrey:
   A relative of borage, the leaves have been used either fresh in salads or dried in teas. The dried root is used as flavoring in country wines. As an ingredient in homeopathic medicines, it was used as an aid in the healing of wounds. It is sometimes called salsify because of its thick roots. See SALSIFY. The derivation of the name "consormol" is obscure.
   Rinzler, p. 183, questions the safety of the use of comfrey saying that it has been shown to cause cancer in laboratory rats.
   Wild comfrey is *Cynoglossum virginicum* [*Boraginaceae*], more closely related to hound's tongue. See HOUND'S TONGUE.

COMINO: See CUMIN.

COMMON BETONY: See WOOD BETONY.

COMMON GOLDENROD: See SWEET GOLDENROD.

COMMON NIGHTSHADE: See NIGHTSHADE.

COMMON THORN APPLE: See JIMSONWEED.

COMPASS PLANT: See CUP PLANT.

CONCH APPLE: See PASSIONFLOWER.

CONE PEPPER: See CAPSICUM.

CONEHEAD THYME: See THYME and ZA'ATAR.

CONGOO MALLEE: See EUCALYPTUS.

CONSORMOL: See COMFREY.

CONSUMPTIVE'S WEED: See YERBA SANTA.

CONTINENTAL PARSLEY: See PURSLANE.

CONVULSION ROOT: See INDIAN-PIPE.

COOL-TANKARD: See BORAGE.

COPAIBA (*Copaifera*, various species) [*Leguminosae*]
   Capivi; Copaiva; Copayva:
   The resin from these plants has an agreeable smell but a bitter, somewhat pungent taste, said to be similar to guarana. It is used in flavoring formulations. It has stimulant and diuretic properties and formerly was used to treat gonorrhea. GRAS

COPAIVA: See COPAIBA.

COPALM: See STORAX.

COPAYVA: See COPAIBA.

CORAL PEA: See SARSAPARILLA.

CORAL-BEAD PLANT: See LICORICE.

CORALROOT (*Corallorhiza odontorhiza*) [*Orchidaceae*]
   Autumn coralroot; Chicken-toes; Crawley-root; Dragon's-claw; Fever root; Late coralroot; Scaly dragon's-claw; Small coralroot; Turkey-claw:
   This is a saprophytic terrestrial plant, without chlorophyll, with masses of much-branched coral-like rhizomes. It is found in temperate areas of eastern North America, Mexico, and Guatemala around the roots of trees in dry woodland areas. In summer to early fall, it sends up stalks with clusters of small (¹/₂ inch) purplish flowers. Tea, made from the rhizomes, is used as an herbal remedy. It has diaphoretic and sedative properties.

CORIANDER (*Coriandrum sativum*) [*Umbelliferae*]
   Chinese parsley; Cilantro:
   This annual plant is native to southern Europe and the Middle East but grows world wide. The fresh leaves and the seeds are both used. The leaves and seeds have entirely different flavors. The leaves have a fresh taste somewhat like orange peel and are often sold as cilantro or Chinese parsley. The seeds have a hot, harsh flavor and are used in many of the same ways as cardamom seeds. Resembling small white peppercorns, they are sold in both whole and ground forms. Ground, they are used in gingerbreads, cakes, pastries, and are an important ingredient in curry. In India, the seeds are usually roasted lightly before grinding to bring out a more curry-like flavor.

Fresh leaves are added to curries and other spicy dishes toward the end of cooking or used as a garnish. The whole seeds are used in pickling mixtures and to flavor gin. The roots also have been used in curries. GRAS

CORIDO THYME: See THYME and ZA'ATAR.

CORK OAK (*Quercus suber*) [*Fagaceae*]
    The bark of this tree is the source of ordinary cork. It is native to southern Europe and northern Africa. In the United States it is permitted to be used in flavoring formulations for alcoholic beverages only.

CORN CAMOMILE: See CAMOMILE.

CORN FEVERFEW: See CAMOMILE.

CORN MINT (*Mentha canadensis*, formerly *Mentha arvensis*) [*Labiatae*]
    Field mint; Hakka; Japanese mint; Wild pennyroyal:
    This species of mint is cultivated widely in China, Japan, Brazil, and South Africa. Its use in foods was not permitted in the United States according to the 1967 Code of Federal Regulations. It is not listed in the 1991 Code. [What the exact reason for this is, I have not been able to determine.]

CORN SNAKEROOT: See ERYNGO.

CORNEL: See KINNIKINICK and DOGWOOD.

CORNELIAN TREE: See DOGWOOD.

CORNFLOWER (*Centaurea cyanus* [*Compositae*]
    Bachelor's-button; Blue centaury; Bluebonnet; Bluebottle; Cyani:
    The blue flowers were pounded with sugar and added to pastries and confections when a blue color was desired. It is rarely used today.

CORPSE PLANT: See INDIAN-PIPE.

CORYDALIS (*Corydalis cava*) [*Fumariaceae*]
    Early fumitory
    (*Dicentra eximia*, formerly *Corydalis formosa*) [*Fumariaceae*]
    Choice dielytra; Staggerweed; Turkey corn; Wild turkey pea; Wild bleeding heart:
    There are about 300 species of *Corydalis*. The roots have been used in herbal remedies. They should be considered very dangerous plants, since

they contain poisonous alkaloids the same as the *Fumaria* species. See
Fumitory.

Costa Rica sarsaparilla: See Sarsaparilla.

Costmary (*Balsamita major*, formerly *Chrysanthemum Balsamita majus*
and *Tanacetum balsamita*) [*Compositae*]
    Alecost; Bible leaf; Mint geranium; Sweet Mary; Tansy:
    Costmary is a spicy, slightly bitter herb. Native to the Far East, the
leaves were traditionally used in Britain and America as flavoring for beer—
hence the name alecost. It is used with game and veal and in soups. It is
mostly available dried. In the United States it is restricted to use in alcoholic
beverages only. The costmary referred to in some old recipes (especially as
a cheese flavoring) may be an entirely different plant. It may be Swiss melilot
which is also occasionally called costmary. See Sweet clover. According
to one British author, costmary is called Bible leaf in the United States
because the long leaves were used as Bible markers by the early colonists.

Costus (*Saussurea costus*, formerly *lappa*) [*Compositae*]:
    Extracts of the roots of this Himalayan plant have an odor of orris,
violets, and a little lemon. It is used mostly in perfumery but also in flavoring
formulations. GRAS

Cottonweed: See Everlasting and Milkweed.

Couch grass (*Agropyrum repens*) [*Gramineae*]
    **Cutch; Dog grass; Durfa grass; Durfee grass; Quack grass; Quick
grass; Quitch grass; Scutch; Twitch grass; Witchgrass:**
    Infusions of the roots of couch grass were used to treat bladder
infections. It has diuretic effects. GRAS
    Use of the name triticum as another common name for couch grass
(as is in *The New Age Herbalist*, Richard Mabey, Ed., p. 60) is incorrect. The
Triticum species are wheat.

Coughroot: See Trillium.

Coughwort: See Coltsfoot.

Country mallow: See Mallow.

Country walnut: See Candlenut.

Cow cabbage: See Masterwort and Lotus.

COW CHERVIL: See CHERVIL.

COW GRASS: See KNOTWEED.

COW PARSLEY: See CHERVIL.

COW-ITCH: See SUMAC.

COWBERRY: See BLUEBERRY.

COWSLIP:

Cowslip is another one of those terms that can refer to a large number of plants. It can refer to:

(1) *Caltha palustris* [*Ranunculaceae*]. See MARIGOLD.

(2) *Pulmonaria officinalis* [*Boraginaceae*]. See LUNGMOSS.

(3) *Mertensia virginica* [*Boraginaceae*], also known as bluebells, Roanoke-bells, Virginia bluebells, and Virginia cowslip. It is also called a lungwort. It is grown as an ornamental.

(4) *Lachenalia*, various species [*Liliaceae*], the cape cowslip, grown as an ornamental.

(5) *Dodecatheon*, various species [*Primulaceae*], also known as American cowslip and shooting-star. These are also ornamentals.

(6) *Primula veris*, formerly *officinalis* [*Primulaceae*], known as butter rose, cowslip, English cowslip, keyflower, palsywort, and primrose. The flowers of this plant were used in England for making wine and tea. They were used in salads and also candied. The English primrose (*Primula vulgaris*) was used in similar manners. Its young leaves were also used in salads, however many people are allergic to them, and this use is not recommended.

COYOTE MINT: See PENNYROYAL.

CRAB'S EYE: See LICORICE.

CRAMPBARK (*Viburnum opulus*) [*Caprifoliaceae*]

Cranberry bush; European cranberry bush; Guelder rose; High bush cranberry; Snowball bush; Whitten tree

(*Viburnum trilobum*)

Cranberry bush; Cranberry tree; Grouseberry; High bush cranberry, Pimbina; Squawbush; Summerberry; Tree cranberry:

Viburnum opulus is native to Europe and *Viburnum trilobum* to North America. Not all authorities segregate the two species but consider them as one, *V. opulus*.

Extracts of the bark were used in herbal remedies for the treating of menstrual cramps. Some sources say the berries are edible; other sources say they are poisonous. The well-known ornamental snowball bush is actually a sterile cultivar of *V. opulus*. Guelderland is a province of the eastern Netherlands, hence the name guelder rose.

CRAMPWEED: See **CINQUEFOIL.**

CRANBERRY: See **BLUEBERRY.**

CRANBERRY BUSH: See **CRAMPBARK.**

CRANBERRY TREE: See **CRAMPBARK.**

CRANESBILL: See **GERANIUM.**

CRAWLEY-ROOT: See **CORALROOT.**

CRAWLGRASS: See **KNOTWEED.**

CREASHAK: See **UVA-URSI.**

CREEPER: See **VIRGINIA CREEPER.**

CREEPING CHARLIE: See **GROUND IVY.**

CREEPING OXALIS: See **SORREL.**

CREEPING SAINT JOHN'S-WORT: See **SAINT JOHN'S-WORT.**

CREEPING THYME: See **THYME.**

CREEPING WOOD SORREL: See **SORREL.**

CRÈME DE NOYEAU: See **NOYAU.**

CRENATE BUCHU: See **BUCHU.**

CREOLE PEPPER: See **CAPSICUM.**

CREOSOTE BUSH: See **CAPERS.**

CRESS: See **WATERCRESS.**

CRETAN ROCKROSE: See **LABDANUM.**

CRETAN THYME: See THYME and ZA'ATAR.

CRISP-LEAVED MINT: See MINT.

CROSNES-DU-JAPON: See ARTICHOKE.

CROSS MINT: See MINT.

CROSSWORT: See THOROUGHWORT.

CROTON OIL: See CASCARILLA BARK.

CROW CORN: See STAR GRASS.

CROWFOOT: See BUTTERCUP and GERANIUM.

CROWFOOT BUTTERCUP: See BUTTERCUP.

CROWN DAISY: See SHUNGIKU.

CRYSTAL TEA: See WILD ROSEMARY.

CUBAN OREGANO: See COLEUS.

CUBEB (*Piper cubeba*) [*Piperaceae*]:
Java pepper; Tailed cubebs; Tailed pepper
   Extracts from the unripe berry have a peppery taste. Small amounts are used in flavor formulations. In Java, the unripe berries are made into cigarettes and smoked. It is a stimulant and a diuretic having been used in the treatment of urinary problems, catarrh, and bronchial diseases. Large amounts have a toxic effect and the medical condition, cubebism, describes these effects. GRAS

CUCKOLD: See BURDOCK.

CUCKOO BREAD: See SORREL.

CUCKOO BUDS: See BUTTERCUP.

CUCKOOFLOWER: See LADY'S-SMOCK.

CUCKOOPINT: See ARUM.

CUDDAPAH ALMONDS: See ALMOND.

CUDWEED: See EVERLASTING.

CULANTRO: See ERYNGO.

CULVER'S-PHYSIC (*Veronicastrum virginicum,* formerly *Veronica virginica* and *Leptandra virginica*) [*Scrophulariaceae*]
Beaumont root; Blackroot; Bowman's-root; Culver's-root; Hini; Leptandra; Oxadoddy; Physic root; Purple leptandra; Tall speedwell; Tall veronica; Whorlywort:

The root of this plant contains a glycoside, leptandrin. It has long been known to the medical profession as a violent emetic and cathartic. Its use can be extremely dangerous.

CULVER'S-ROOT: See CULVER'S-PHYSIC.

CUMIN (*Cuminum cyminum*) [*Umbelliferae*]
Comino:

Cumin is the dried seed of an annual plant belonging to the parsley family. It has a pungent, hot, and somewhat bitter taste and is one of the principal ingredients of commercial chili and curry powders. Commercially, it is used most often in sausages, pickles, cheeses, and meats. It has the interesting property of being able to kill the flavor of garlic but to have no effect upon the exuded and exhaled aftaroma after garlic is eaten. In olden times, cumin mixed with honey was applied to black-and-blue marks. There was a superstition that cumin was a "vexatious plant" and that the farmer had to curse and abuse it while sowing the seeds if he wanted his crop to prosper and be abundant. Wild cumin is *Lagaecia cuminoides* [*Umbelliferae*], a European plant. It is sometimes used as a flavoring in Münster cheese. Also see CARAWAY for an explanation of name confusion. GRAS

CUP PLANT (*Silphium perfoliatum*) [*Compositae*]
Compass plant; Indian cup; Indian gum; Prairie dock; Ragged cup; Rosinweed:

The resinous sap of this plant has been used in herbal remedies, supposedly helpful for most everything from fevers to ulcers.

CURAÇAO ALOE: See ALOE.

CURCUMA:

Curcuma may refer to any plant belonging to the genus *Curcuma* [*Zingiberaceae*] which includes turmeric and zedoary. See TURMERIC and ZEDOARY.

CURDWORT: See BEDSTRAW.

CURE-ALL: See BALM and WATER AVENS.

CURLED DOCK: See SORREL.

CURLED MINT: See MINT.

CURRANT: See BLACK CURRANT and RED CURRANT.

CURRY LEAF (*Murraya koenigii,* formerly *Chalcas koenigii*) [*Rutaceae*]
Curry-leaf tree:

Native to southwest Asia, the leaves of this tree, fresh or dried, are a curry ingredient. Fresh leaves are preferred, as the dried leaves do not retain their flavor very long. They are described as being pungent and aromatic. The fresh leaves are usually chopped and fried in oil at the start of making a curry.

CURRY POWDER:

Commercial curry powder is a blend of any number of different spices and can range from mild to very hot depending upon the spices and amounts included. In India, the home of curries, every family has its own formula. The golden color of curry powder is due to turmeric. Generally, there are three different types of curry powder: North Indian (Bombay), South Indian (Madras), and the oriental (Malay). Bombay curry is less pungent than Madras and Malay is considered mild. In India, preparation of a curry usually begins with garam masala (see GARAM MASALA) and proceeds according to the whims of the cook. There are mixtures available for specific dishes, but these are known by the name of the dish. A pre-mixed curry powder was most likely invented for Europeans who wanted to take it home with them. The formula for the curry powder, then, was determined by the area of India from which it originated.

Some curry seasoning mixtures are made into pastes by grinding the spices with vinegar. (See VINDALOO MIXTURE.) Those who are really interested in Eastern foods should be prepared to roast and grind their own spices. This one can do with nothing more elaborate than a heavy frying pan, a coffee mill (used for spices only), and a fine sieve. For a small quantity, a peppermill works quite well.

As an example of how many different variations of curry powder there can be, a number of examples from a variety of sources have been compiled in a chart. This gives an idea of the range of ingredients and their proportions. (See chart on pages 90 and 91.)

CURSED CROWFOOT: See BUTTERCUP.

CUSCUS OIL: See VETIVER.

CUSH-CUSH: See WILD YAM.

CUSPARIA BARK (*Galipea trifoliata*, formerly *Galipea officinalis*, *Galipea cusparia* and *Cusparia trifoliata*) [*Rutaceae*]:
Cusparia bark is another name for angostura bark. See *Angostura Bitters*. GRAS

CUSSO: See KOUSSO.

CUSTARD APPLE (*Annona*, various species) [*Annonaceae*]
(*Annona muricata*)
Guanabana; Prickly custard apple; Soursop
(*Annona reticulata*)
American nutmeg; Bullock's heart
(*Annona squamosa*)
Jamaica nutmeg; Sugar apple; Sweetsop:
The fruit of the *Annona* genera are only called nutmegs because of a similarity of the seed to the true nutmeg. *Annona muricata* is used to flavor sherbets and drinks. *Annona squamosa* is considered to be the best flavored and is used mostly as a dessert fruit.

CUTCH: See CATECHU and COUCH GRASS.

CYANI: See CORNFLOWER.

CYCLAMEN (*Cyclamen* spp.) [*Primulaceae*]
Alpine violet; Groundbread; Persian violet; Sowbread; Swinebread:
There are about fifteen species of *Cyclamen* all native to central Europe and the Mediterranean region. Some species are popular as florist plants, others as houseplants, others as outdoor ornamentals. All are extremely toxic plants. Pliny the Elder, a Roman naturalist who lived between 23 and 79 A.D., reported its use as a poison for arrowheads.

CYPRESS: See SANTOLINA.

CYPRESS POWDER: See ARUM.

Curry Powder Mixtures

Ingredient	1	2	3	4	5	6	7	8	9	10	11
Black pepper	1	4	-	1	1	4	1	1	1.3	2	2
Chili pepper	1	2	4	1	2	-	1	8	1	3	2
Cloves	1	1	1	1	1	4	-	-	-	-	-
Cinnamon	2	-	1	-	2	1	-	-	-	-	-
Cardamom	-	2	8	1	1	1	-	-	-	-	-
Coriander	8	8	-	8	6	-	8	6	8	8	8
Cumin	-	8	-	-	2	4	2	1	-	1	1
Curry leaves	-	-	-	-	-	0.5	-	0.5	-	-	-
Fenugreek	4	2	-	-	0.5	-	2	1	-	1	-
Ginger	2	4	16	1	-	-	1	-	2	-	1
Mace	1	2	-	-	1	1	0	-	-	-	-
Nutmeg	-	-	-	-	1	1	0	-	-	-	-
Allspice	-	-	-	-	1	1	-	-	-	-	-
Mustard seed	2	1	-	-	-	-	0.5	1	-	-	2
Poppy seed	-	-	-	-	-	-	1	-	-	-	-
Turmeric	8	8	24	10	-	-	5	-	10	4	2
Fennel	-	-	-	-	-	-	-	-	-	-	-
Garlic powder	-	-	-	-	-	-	-	-	-	-	-
Anise-pepper	-	-	-	-	-	-	-	-	-	-	-
Star anise	-	-	-	-	-	-	-	-	-	-	-

The numbers in 1 through 16 all represent parts by weight

1—Bombay—Peter Gray
2—Madras—Peter Gray
3—Malay—Peter Gray
4 through 16—Tom Stobart

12	13	14	15	16	17	18	19	20	21
0.5	1	1.25	8	4	-	1 t.	-	-	1 t.
6	8	4	-	-	1 t.	1 to 3 t.	1 t.	-	1 t.
-	-	-	-	-	-	-	$3/4$ t. whole	1 T. whole	-
-	-	-	-	- 1" to 2"		-	1" to 2"	6 sticks	-
-	-	-	-	-	-	-	-	$1/3$ c.	-
8	8	8	8	8	4.5 T.	8.5 T.	6 $2/3$ T.	1 $1/2$ T.	$1/2$ c.
1.5	4	2	6	4	1 t.	3 T.	-	-	2 T.
-	-	-	-	- 2 leaves		-	-	-	-
1.5	-	1	-	-	$2/3$ t.	1 t.	-	-	-
-	-	-	-	-	-	$1/8$ t.	-	-	1 - 1" piece
-	-	-	-	-	-	-	-	1 pinch	-
-	-	-	-	-	-	-	1 $1/2$ t.	1 pinch	-
-	-	-	-	-	-	-	-	-	-
-	-	-	-	-	-	1 t.	-	-	1 t.
-	-	-	-	-	-	-	-	-	-
2	3	2.5	-	-	2 $2/3$ t.	1 $2/3$ t.	2 $1/2$ t.	-	1 t.
-	-	-	-	-	$1/2$ t.	-	3 $1/2$ t.	-	-
-	-	-	-	-	-	-	-	-	3 cloves fresh
-	-	-	-	-	$1/2$ t.	-	1 $1/2$ t.	-	-
-	-	-	-	-	-	-	2 t.	-	-

17—Bombay—Arabella Boxer et al.
18—Madras—Arabella Boxer et al.
19—Malay—Arabella Boxer et al.
20—Margaret Fulton
21—Madras—Margaret Fulton

D

DAIKON (*Raphanus sativus*, Cv. *Longipinnatus*) [*Cruciferae*]
   Chinese radish:
   This is a large, white radish commonly grown in Japan. It is eaten both raw and cooked. It is also grated and the expressed juice is used as a flavoring for bean curd dishes.

DAILY-DEW: See SUNDEW.

DALMATIA PYRETHRUM: See PYRETHRUM.

DALMATIAN INSECT FLOWER: See PYRETHRUM.

DALMATIAN INSECT POWDER: See PYRETHRUM.

DAMASCENE NIGELLA: See NIGELLA.

DAMASK VIOLET: See ROCKET.

DAME'S ROCKET: See ROCKET.

DAME'S VIOLET: See ROCKET.

DAMIANA (*Turnera diffusa*) [*Turneraceae*]
   Hierba de la pastora:
   The bitter leaves of this plant are used in flavor formulations for liqueurs. In Mexico it is known as *hierba de la pastora* and is attributed with aphrodisiac, diuretic, and stimulant properties. GRAS

DANDELION (*Taraxacum officinale*) [*Compositae*]:

93

Blowball; Cankerwort; Fairy clock; Lion's tooth; Pee-in-the-bed; Priest's crown; Puffball; Swine snout; White endive; Wild endive:

In addition to dandelion's use as vegetable greens, the bitter, aromatic extracts of its roots are used in commercial flavoring formulations. Wine can be made from the flowers. Dandelion leaves have a diuretic effect. GRAS

DANEWORT: See ELDER.

DANG QUI: See ANGELICA TREE.

DAPHNE (*Daphne mezereum*) [*Thymelaeaceae*]

February daphne; Mezereon; Mezereum; Spurge flax; Spurge laurel; Spurge olive; Wild pepper:

This is a small European and Asian shrub that has escaped cultivation and now grows wild in the northeastern United States and Canada. All parts of the plant are extremely toxic. Three or four of its red berries can kill a person, and it is said that people have been poisoned from eating birds that have eaten the berries. The plant has been used to make a fine quality handcrafted paper.

DATE PLUM: See LOTUS.

DAUCUS (*Daucus carota*, Var. *carota*) [*Umbelliferae*]

Devil's-plague; Queen-Anne's-lace; Queen's-lace; Wild carrot

(*Daucus carota*, Var. *sativus*)

Carrot:

Daucus can be any plant of the genus *Daucus*. Montagné (p. 341) describes daucus as "an umbrella plant whose aromatic seeds, used medicinally in former times, are now used in the preparation of some liqueurs." In my opinion, wild carrot or Queen-Anne's-lace really can be a devil's-plague. I never could get the flowers to soak up food dye and turn pretty colors like everybody said they would. GRAS

DAVANA (*Artemisia pallens*) [*Compositae*]:

Oil from the flowers is used for compounding flavorings for beverages, confections and baked goods. Although in the FDA listing of natural flavoring agents there is no restriction listed for this species of *Artemisia*, there is a general statement that with all *Artemisia* species, the finished food must be thujone-free.

DEAD MEN'S BELLS: See FOXGLOVE.

Dead nettle: See **White dead nettle.**

Dead-rat tree: See **Baobab.**

Deadly nightshade: See **Belladonna** and **Nightshade.**

Deal pine: See **White pine.**

Deer's-tongue: See **Vanilla.**

Deerberry: See **Blueberry, Wintergreen,** and **Partridgeberry.**

Delphinium: See **Larkspur.**

Dense button snakeroot: See **Blazing-star.**

Desert herb: See **Ephedra.**

Desert tea: See **Ephedra.**

Devil's apple: See **Jimsonweed.**

Devil's bit: See **Blazing-star.**

Devil's bite: See **Blazing-star** and **False hellebore.**

Devil's bones: See **Wild yam.**

Devil's dung: See **Asafoetida.**

Devil's eye: See **Henbane.**

Devil's fuge: See **Mistletoe.**

Devil's root: See **Peyote.**

Devil's trumpet: See **Jimsonweed.**

Devil's turnip: See **Bryony.**

DEVIL'S VINE: See WILD MORNING-GLORY.

DEVIL'S-DARNING-NEEDLE: See VIRGIN'S BOWER.

DEVIL'S-PLAGUE: See DAUCUS.

DEVIL'S-WALKINGSTICK: See ANGELICA TREE.

DEVIL-IN-THE-BUSH: See NIGELLA.

DEW PLANT: See SUNDEW.

DEWBERRY: See BRAMBLES.

DIGITALIS: See FOXGLOVE.

DILL (*Anethum graveolens*) [*Umbelliferae*]
Dill weed; Anet:

Aromatic and pungent, dill is Russia's best-known contribution to the art of seasoning. The leaves are used fresh or dried, also the seeds. Dill weed usually refers to the fresh or dried leaves. The seeds have a more pungent and bitter flavor, a little like caraway. Famous as a flavoring for pickles, fresh dill can be added to vinegar for salads. It goes well with all members of the cabbage family as well as with fish and lamb. The best flavor is obtained if the dill is not cooked with the food but added after cooking is finished. Fresh dill is best since it loses some of its flavor with drying. It freezes well. Both the seeds and leaves are used to obtain, by steam distillation, the essential oils which are used for commercial flavorings, particularly commercial dill pickles. It is an annual plant which, if sown in late spring, will grow in any ordinary garden soil in a sunny location. Legend claims that dill stops hiccoughs and strengthens the brain. GRAS

DILL, INDIAN: See INDIAN DILL.

DIPTAM: See DITTANY (*Dictamnus albus*).

DITTANY (*Dictamnus albus*) [*Rutaceae*]
Bastard dittany; Burning-bush; Diptam; False dittany; Fraxinella; Gas-plant:

This is a perennial plant native to Crete and southern Europe. Use of extracts of the aromatic roots and bark are allowed only in alcoholic beverage flavor formulations. The plant has thick foliage and white flowers. It is called burning-bush or gas-plant because on hot nights it gives off inflammable vapors. Contact with the plant and subsequent exposure to sunlight may cause a dermatitis.

DITTANY, COMMON (*Cunila origanoides*) [*Labiatae*]

American dittany; Maryland dittany; Stone mint; Sweet horsemint:

This plant is closely related to the genus *Origanum* and the leaves have an aroma similar to wild marjoram. It is used to make a mild tea, as a substitute for oregano, and formerly in herbal medicines to treat headaches and snakebite.

DITTANY OF CRETE: See **MARJORAM.**

DIVINE FLOWER: See **CARNATION.**

DOCK: See **SORREL.**

DOG CLOVES: See **SOAPWORT.**

DOG FENNEL: See **CAMOMILE.**

DOG GRASS: See **COUCH GRASS.**

DOG MINT: See **BASIL.**

DOG POISON: See **FOOL'S PARSLEY.**

DOG-BUR: See **HOUND'S-TONGUE.**

DOG-NETTLE: See **HEMP NETTLE.**

DOG-TOOTH VIOLET: See **ADDER'S TONGUE.**

DOG'S COLE: See **MERCURY.**

DOG'S FINGER: See **FOXGLOVE.**

DOG'S MERCURY: See **MERCURY.**

DOG'S TONGUE: See **HOUND'S-TONGUE.**

DOGBANE (*Apocynum androsaemifolium*) [*Apocynaceae*]

Bitterroot; Catchfly; Flytrap; Honeybloom; Milk ipecac; Milkweed; Mountain hemp; Spreading dogbane; Wallflower; Wandering milkweed; Western wallflower:

Although used in herbal medicine, this should be treated as a very toxic plant. Livestock die from eating the leaves.

DOGBERRY: See ROWAN.

DOGTREE: See DOGWOOD.

DOGWOOD (*Cornus florida*) [*Cornaceae*]

Boxwood; Budwood; Cornel; Cornelian tree; Dogtree; False box; Florida cornel; Florida dogwood; Flowering cornel; Flowering dogwood; Green ozier; Virginia dogwood:

Although there are about forty-five species of *Cornus*, all known as dogwood or cornel, *Cornus florida* is the ornamental dogwood familiar to all. Numerous cultivars have been developed. The bark has been used in herbal remedies as a tonic, in ointments for "ague," and even as a rather dubious substitute for quinine.

DOLL'S-EYES: See HERB CHRISTOPHER.

DOLLOFF: See HERB CHRISTOPHER.

DONG QUAI: See ANGELICA TREE.

DONKEY'S FOOT: See ALLIARIA.

DOORWEED: See KNOTGRASS.

DOORYARD PLANTAIN: See PLANTAIN.

DOTTED MINT: See BERGAMOT.

DOUBLE SPRUCE: See SPRUCE.

DOWNY RATTLESNAKE ORCHID: See RATTLESNAKE PLANTAIN.

DOWNY RATTLESNAKE PLANTAIN: See RATTLESNAKE PLANTAIN.

DRAGON ROOT: See ARUM and INDIAN TURNIP.

DRAGON TREE: See DRAGON'S BLOOD.

DRAGON'S BLOOD:

Dragon's blood may refer to (1) *Dracaena draco* [*Agavaceae*, formerly *Liliaceae*], the dragon tree, (2) *Daemonorops draco* [*Palmae*] GRAS, or (3) *Pterocarpus draco* [*Leguminosae*] (commonly called bija). The resin exudate from the cherry-sized fruit of *Daemonorops draco* is red in color with astringent properties. It is used in flavoring formulations for beverages. In medicine it was used for treatment of dysentery and as an astringent in tooth powders. See also ANNOTTO and HERB ROBERT.

DRAGON'S-CLAW: See CORALROOT.

DRAGONROOT: See ARUM and INDIAN TURNIP.

DRAGONWORT: See KNOTWEED.

DRIED MUSHROOMS:

Dried mushrooms have a highly concentrated flavor and will keep for over a year. They should always be soaked for thirty minutes or more in warm water before using. The soaking water can be added to the dish or to a stock. The main types of dried mushrooms are as follows:

(1) **Shiitake** and **matsutake**. These are also called Japanese tree mushrooms. They are cultivated in Japan and China on tree logs, shiitake usually on oak logs, matsutake on pine. They have a delicate flavor and are used extensively in Oriental cooking. Shiitake mushrooms are now cultivated in the United States and are available fresh.

(2) **Padistraw** or **paddy straw mushrooms**. The padistraw mushroom is a Chinese mushroom cultivated on wet rice straw and dried over charcoal. They should be stored in an airtight jar since they tend to smell if allowed to become damp. The smell usually disappears with cooking. They are used with steamed or fried chicken and with vegetables.

(3) **Wood** or **cloud ear mushrooms**. These are a Chinese mushroom cultivated on wood. They have an earthy flavor and are used in chicken and fish dishes as well as soups.

(4) **Morels**. These mushrooms grow wild throughout the world and a few species are cultivated. They have a delicate flavor and are used extensively in French cooking.

(5) **Chantarelles** or **girolles**. These are from the Alps and southern Germany. They are a spindly, golden mushroom with a good flavor.

(6) **Boletus mushrooms**. These are a popular European mushroom with a strong, meaty taste.

Black fungus in an oriental recipe can be either the shiitake or the cloud ear mushroom.

DROPBERRY: See SOLOMON'S-SEAL.

Dropsy plant: See Balm.

Dropwort: See Herb Christopher.

Drumstick: See Horseradish tree.

Duck's foot: See Mayapple.

Dudder grass: See Maidenhair fern.

Dukkah:

This is a spice mixture from the Middle East. In Egypt, bread is dipped into olive oil and then into this mixture and eaten as a snack.

    10 tablespoons whole coriander seeds
    8 tablespoons whole cumin seeds
    1 ounce (25 grams) whole hazel or other nuts
    9 tablespoons brown sesame seeds

The ingredients are lightly crushed together and salt and pepper are added to taste. Mint or other herbs can be used instead of cumin, and cinnamon can also be added.

Dulse (*Rhodymenia palmata*):

This is a red seaweed with very little nutritional value. It is used for its gelatinous properties as a gelling agent and thickener and not for its flavor.

Dumb nettle: See White dead nettle.

Dumpling cactus: See Peyote.

Durfa grass: See Couch grass.

Durfee grass: See Couch grass.

Dutch tonka bean: See Tonka beans.

Dutchman's breeches: See Fumitory.

Dutchman's laudanum: See Passionflower.

Dutchman's-pipe: See Serpentaria.

DUXELLES:

Montagné (p. 364) describes duxelles as a kind of mushroom hash, its name coming from the Marquis d'Uxelles. It was supposedly created by La Varenne, an official in the Marquis' household. Others have called it a mushroom paste. It can be added to soups, stews, and other dishes when a mushroom flavor is desired. It can also be added to other ingredients for a filling for omelettes and crepes.

To make duxelles, cook 2 tablespoons of finely chopped shallots in 2 tablespoons of butter until soft. Add 2 cups (8 ounces) of finely chopped mushrooms (can include stems and trimmings) and cook gently 5 minutes. Increase heat and cook briskly, stirring, until almost dry. Season with salt and pepper and stir in 1 tablespoon chopped parsley. Spoon into a jar, press down firmly and cover. Store in refrigerator. If it is to be kept longer than one week, pour melted butter over the top to seal before refrigerating. Duxelles may also be frozen for longer storage.

If the chopped mushrooms are placed in a cloth and twisted tightly to extract as much liquid as possible before cooking, cooking time is greatly reduced. Half an onion, finely chopped, can be substituted for the shallots. Some add a dash of ground nutmeg.

DWALE: See **BELLADONNA.**

DWARF BASIL: See **BASIL.**

DWARF CARLINE: See **CARLINE THISTLE.**

DWARF ELDER: See **ELDER.**

DWARF MALLOW: See **MALLOW.**

DWARF MILKWORT: See **MILKWORT.**

DWARF MYRTLE: See **MYRTLE.**

DWARF PINE (*Pinus mugo*) [*Pinaceae*]

Mountain pine; Mugo pine; Swiss mountain pine:

Extracts of the needles and twigs have a pine-like aroma. They are used in flavoring formulations for beverages, confections and baked goods. GRAS

DWARF SUMAC: See **SUMAC.**

DYER'S BROOM: See **BROOM.**

DYER'S GREENWEED: See BROOM.

DYER'S GREENWOOD: See BROOM.

DYER'S SAFFRON: See SAFFRON.

DYER'S WEED: See SWEET GOLDENROD.

DYER'S WHIN: See BROOM.

DYSENTERY WEED: See EVERLASTING.

E

EARLY FUMITORY: See CORYDALIS.

EARTH ALMOND: See GALINGALE.

EARTH GALL: See FALSE HELLEBORE.

EARTH SMOKE: See FUMITORY.

EARTH-NUTS (*Carum bulbocastanum* ?) [*Umbelliferae*]:
    Montagné (p. 365) describes an earth-nut in the following manner: "Tuberous root about the size of a nut, black outside and white inside, of a plant whose scientific name is *Carum bulbocastanum*. It tastes like chestnut and is prepared in the same ways. The seeds of the plant are sometimes used in place of caraway."
    This could be a plant now belonging to either the *Perederidia* or *Petroselinum* genera since both are closely related to the *Carum* genus and many have a tuberous root.

EAST INDIA ROOT: See GALANGAL.

EAST INDIAN GERANIUM: See GERANIUM and LEMONGRASS.

EAST INDIAN LEMONGRASS: See LEMONGRASS.

EAST INDIAN LOTUS: See LOTUS.

EAST INDIAN SANDALWOOD: See SANDALWOOD.

EASTER FLOWER: See PASQUE FLOWER.

EASTER GIANT: See KNOTWEED.

EASTERN ARBORVITAE: See WHITE CEDAR.

EASTERN ROCKET: See ROCKET.

EASTERN WHITE PINE: See WHITE PINE.

EAU DE COLOGNE MINT: See MINT.

ECHINACEA: See PURPLE CONEFLOWER.

EDELWEISS: See LION'S-FOOT.

EDIBLE BURDOCK: See BURDOCK.

EGYPTIAN PRIVET: See HENNA.

EGYPTIAN THORN: See ACACIA.

ELDER; ELDERBERRY (*Sambucus canadensis*) [*Caprifoliaceae*]
American elder; Black elder; Rob elder; Sweet elder
(*Sambucus caerulea*)
Blue elder
(*Sambucus nigra*)
Black elder; Black-berried European elder; Boor tree; Bore tree; Bounty; Elfhorn; Ellanwood; European elder; German elder
(*Sambucus pubens*)
American red elder; Red-berried elder; Stinking elder
(*Sambucus racemosa*)
European red elder
(*Sambucus ebulus*)
Blood elder; Danewort; Dwarf elder; Walewort; Wallwort; Wild elder:

Sambucus canadensis, caerulea and nigra, according to *Hortus Third*, all have edible berries. All parts of *Sambucus pubens* are considered to be poisonous. The flowers of *Sambucus canadensis* and *nigra* are included in the FDA list of GRAS items. Oil extracted from the flowers has a bitter flavor and is used in flavoring formulations. Use of the leaves of *Sambucus nigra* is restricted by the FDA to flavoring for alcoholic beverages, and only then if the Prussic acid does not exceed twenty-five parts per million in the flavoring. John Lust (p. 178) states that fresh parts of *Sambucus canadensis* are poisonous, especially the bark, but that the cooked berries are safe.

Cooked berries are made into pies and jams. The flowers were used in the past for dressing wounds and burns. They were also thought to have diuretic effects.

The seeds inside the berries of *Sambucus racemosa* are poisonous. In Europe the seedless berries are made into a jam. *Sambucus ebulus* is native to Europe, North Africa and Asia. A blue dye is made from its poisonous berries.

ELECAMPANE (*Inula helenium*) [*Compositae*]

Alant; Elfdock; Elfwort; Horse-elder; Horsehead; Horseheal; Inula; Scabwort; Yellow starwort; Wild sunflower:

This plant is native to Europe, Asia and Africa. In the United States the bitter root extracts are allowed to be used in alcoholic beverage flavoring formulations only. Elsewhere a candy is made from the root called elecampane. It is attributed with numerous medical properties and is used in cough medicines and in the treatment of menstrual problems.

ELEMI (*Canarium commune* or *luzonicum*) [*Burseraceae*]

The resin has a lemon-like, balsamic odor, which is used primarily in perfumery but is also used in flavoring formulations for confections. Medically it is used externally only in ointments for treating ulcers. It is also an ingredient in some varnishes. Pili nuts come from a tree of the genus *Canarium*. These are an edible almond-like nut from the Philippine Islands. GRAS

ELEMI FRANKINCENSE: See OLIBANUM.

ELEPHANT'S-FOOT: See WILD YAM.

ELEQUEME: See LINALOE.

ELFDOCK: See ELECAMPANE.

ELFHORN: See ELDER.

ELFWORT: See ELECAMPANE.

ELLANWOOD: See ELDER.

ELM-LEAVED SUMAC: See SUMAC.

EMETIC HERB: See LOBELIA.

EMETIC WEED: See LOBELIA.

ENCHANTER'S PLANT: See VERVAIN.

ENDIVE: See CHICORY.

ENGLISH CAMOMILE: See CAMOMILE.

ENGLISH COWSLIP: See COWSLIP.

ENGLISH DAISY (*Bellis perennis*) [*Compositae*]
   Although English daisies have been used in all sorts of herbal remedies, they are nicest in the flower garden.

ENGLISH HAWTHORN: See HAWTHORN BERRIES.

ENGLISH IVY (*Hedera helix*) [*Araliaceae*]
   Gum ivy; True ivy:
   Extracts of English ivy leaves have been used in herbal remedies. However, it is a dangerous plant in that it causes a contact allergic dermatitis in some people and, if taken internally, will cause a break down of red blood cells.

ENGLISH LAUREL: See CHERRY LAUREL.

ENGLISH OAK (*Quercus robur*) [*Fagaceae*]
   Bitter extracts of the wood are permitted in flavoring of alcoholic beverages only. This is the wood used to make barrels in which alcoholic beverages are aged.

ENGLISH PLANTAIN: See PLANTAIN.

ENGLISH PRIMROSE: See COWSLIP.

ENGLISH VALERIAN: See VALERIAN.

ENGLISH VIOLET: See VIOLET.

ENGLISH WALNUT: See WALNUT.

ENGLISH YEW: See YEW.

EPAZOTE (*Chenopodium ambrosiodes*) [*Chenopodiaceae*]
   American wormseed; Goosefoot; Jesuits' tea; Mexican tea; Spanish tea; Wormseed

(*Chenopodium botrys*)

Feather geranium; Jerusalem oak:

Epazote can be found growing wild all over the Americas and in many parts of Europe. It is widely used as a green herb in Mexican cooking and as an herbal tea in Europe. It contains an oil with anthelmintic properties which is used in the treatment of roundworms and hookworms. It is claimed to take the "gas" out of cooked dried bean dishes! Levant or Russian wormseed, cina, or santonica is the dried flower heads of Artemisia maritima. This plant contains santonin, a chemical also used as a vermifuge.

EPHEDRA (*Ephedra* spp.) [*Ephedraceae*]

Brigham Young weed; Desert herb; Desert tea; Joint fir; Mormon tea; Squaw tea; Teamster's tea

(*Ephedra sinica*)

Ma huang:

The *Ephedra* plants are scraggly shrubs native to dry or desert regions. In the southwestern United States they have long been used as an herbal tea with tonic and diuretic properties. The Asian species, known commonly as ma huang, has been used medically for over 5000 years. It contains concentrated amounts of ephedrine, a sympathetic nervous system stimulant. The North American species contains only trace amounts of ephedrine.

ERIGERON (*Conyza canadensis*, formerly *Erigeron canadensis*) [*Compositae*]

Bitterweed; Bloodstaunch; Butterweed; Colt's tail; Fleabane; Herb Christopher; Horseweed; Mare's tail:

Oils from this plant have a fresh, slightly pungent, herbaceous odor and a burning, unpleasant bitter aftertaste. They are used in condiment flavoring formulations and in perfumery. The plant is supposed to repel fleas. GRAS

ERINGO: See ERYNGO.

ERYNGO (*Eryngium maritimum*) [*Umbelliferae*]

Eringo; Sea eryngium; Sea holly; Sea holm

(*Eryngium campestre*)

Field eryngo; Snakeroot

(*Eryngium foetidum*)

Cilantro; Culantro; Oregano de Cartegena

(*Eryngium aquaticum*)

Water eryngo

(*Eryngium yuccifolium*)

Button snakeroot; Corn snakeroot; Rattlesnake weed; Rattlesnake-master:

In Europe the root of *Eryngium maritimum* is candied. It is believed to be a strong aphrodisiac. In the United States it is propagated as an ornamental plant for borders and rock gardens.

Eryngium foetidum has been used at times as an oregano substitute.

Eryngium aquaticum and *Eryngium yuccifolium* have been used in cure-all type herbal remedies. They have emetic properties. Many plants cultivated under the name of *Eryngium aquaticum* are really *Eryngium yuccifolium*.

ERYNGO-LEAVED LIVERWORT: See ICELAND MOSS.

ERYTHRONIUM: See ADDER'S-TONGUE.

ESCHALOTTE OR ÉSCHALOTE: See SHALLOT.

ESTRAGON: See TARRAGON.

EUCALYPTUS (*Eucalyptus globulus*) [*Myrtaceae*]

Blue gum; Fever tree; Southern blue gum; Tasmanian blue gum
(*Eucalyptus citriodora*)

Citron-scented gum; Lemon-scented gum; Spotted gum
(*Eucalyptus cneorifolia*)

Kangaroo Island narrow-leaved mallee
(*Eucalyptus dives*)

Blue peppermint; Broad-leaved peppermint; Peppermint
(*Eucalyptus dumosa*)

Congoo mallee; Mallee
(*Eucalyptus elata*)

River peppermint; River white gum
(*Eucalyptus goniocalyx*)

Apple jack; Bundy; Long-leaved box; Olive-barked box
(*Eucalyptus leucoxylon*)

White gum; White ironbark; Yellow gum
(*Eucalyptus macarthurii*)

Camden woollybut; Paddy's river box

(*Eucalyptus oleosa*)

Glossy-leaved red mallee; Red mallee

(*Eucalyptus polybractea*)

Blue-leaved mallee

(*Eucalyptus radiata*)

Gray peppermint; Narrow-leaved peppermint

(*Eucalyptus sideroxylon*)

Ironbark; Mugga; Red ironbark

(*Eucalyptus smithii*)

Blackbutt peppermint; Gully gum; Gully peppermint

(*Eucalyptus viridis*)

Green mallee:

The volatile oil from the eucalyptus leaves has numerous medical uses especially in salves and ointments. It is used in small amounts in flavoring formulations for confections. It should not be used in any large amount because of various toxic effects. Only *Eucalyptus globulus* leaves are listed as GRAS.

EUPATORIUM: See HEMP AGRIMONY, JOE-PYE WEED, and THOROUGHWORT.

EUPHRASY: See RED EYEBRIGHT.

EUROPEAN ANGELICA: See ANGELICA.

EUROPEAN ASH (*Fraximus excelsior*) [*Oleaceae*]

Bird's tongue:

In the United Sates, the ash is thought of as a shade tree, a source of wood, and many times, as a nuisance because of the winged seeds that make a mess on a perfectly groomed lawn. In France, the leaves are sometimes used to make a fermented drink called frenette. The winged seeds (keyes) are boiled until tender in large quantities of water to remove the bitterness and then made into a pickle with salted, spiced vinegar. In Italy, the leaves and seeds are used to make a tea which is said to be refreshing, diuretic, and mildly laxative. Tender young shoots and also young, tender keyes have been used in salads.

EUROPEAN AVENS: See BENNET.

EUROPEAN BARBERRY: See BARBERRY.

EUROPEAN BITTER POLYGALA: See MILKWEED.

EUROPEAN BLACK CURRANT: See BLACK CURRANT.

EUROPEAN BLACK ALDER: See CASCARA.

EUROPEAN BROOKLIME: See VERONICA.

EUROPEAN BUCKTHORN: See CASCARA.

EUROPEAN CENTAURY: See MINOR CENTAURY.

EUROPEAN CRANBERRY BUSH: See CRAMPBARK.

EUROPEAN CROWFOOT: See COLUMBINE.

EUROPEAN ELDER: See ELDER.

EUROPEAN FIR: See PINE FIR.

EUROPEAN FIVE-FINGER GRASS: See CINQUEFOIL.

EUROPEAN GERMANDER: See GERMANDER.

EUROPEAN GOLDENROD: See SWEET GOLDENROD.

EUROPEAN HOP: See HOPS.

EUROPEAN HORSEMINT: See MINT.

EUROPEAN LARCH: See LARCH.

EUROPEAN LIME TREE: See LINDEN FLOWERS.

EUROPEAN LINDEN: See LINDEN FLOWERS.

EUROPEAN LOTUS: See LOTUS.

EUROPEAN LOVAGE: See LOVAGE.

EUROPEAN MILKWORT: See MILKWORT.

EUROPEAN MISTLETOE: See MISTLETOE.

European mountain ash: See Rowan.

European pennyroyal: See Pennyroyal.

European polypody: See Wall fern.

European ragwort: See Ragwort.

European red elder: See Elder.

European sanicle: See Sanicle.

European senega snakeroot: See Milkwort.

European seneka: See Milkwort.

European snakeroot (*Asarum europaeum*) [*Aristolochiaceae*]
   Asarabacca; Asarum; Hazelwort; Public house plant; Wild nard:
   European snakeroot, although belonging to the same genus as Canadian snakeroot, should not be confused with it. Both are known as asarabacca and asarum. While Canadian snakeroot is considered to be safe for use, European snakeroot is dangerously emetic and is not safe to use. Canadian snakeroot is a deciduous plant; European snakeroot is an evergreen. See Canadian snakeroot.

European sorrel: See Sorrel.

European sweet cicely: See Chervil.

European tansy: See Tansy.

European vervain: See Vervain.

European white birch: See White birch.

European wild cicely: See Chervil.

European wild pansy: See Pansy.

European wood sorrel: See Sorrel.

Eve's cup: See Pitcher plant.

Evening primrose (*Oenothera biennis*) [*Onagraceae*]

Fever plant; Field primrose; German rampion; King's cureall; Night willow-herb; Primrose; Scabish; Scurvish; Tree primrose:

This is a rather weedy species of the evening primroses native to eastern North America. The roots may be eaten as a vegetable and the shoots in salads. It has been used in numerous herbal remedies.

Evening trumpet flower: See Jasmine.

Evergreen snakeroot: See Milkwort.

Everlasting: See Immortelle.

Adding to the confusion, as is discussed under Immortelle, there are a number of other plants known as everlasting. Some have been used in old herbal remedies, others for making dried flowers. They all belong to the *Compositae* family and are listed here with the other common names by which they are known.

Ammobium alatum

Winged everlasting

Anaphalis, about 35 species

Cottonweed; Cudweed; Everlasting; Indian posey; Ladies' tobacco; Large-flowered everlasting; Life everlasting; Pearly everlasting

Antennaria, variously estimated to be between 15 and 75 species

Cat's foot; Everlasting; Ladies' tobacco; Mountain everlasting; Pussy-toes

Gnaphalium, about 120 species

Chafeweed; Cudweed; Dysentery weed; Everlasting; Field balsam; Indian posey; Life everlasting; Low cudweed; Marsh cudweed; Mouse ear; Old field balsam; Sweet balsam; Sweet-scented life everlasting; Wartwort; White balsam

Helipterum, between 60 and 90 species

Everlasting; Strawflower

Eye balm: See Goldenseal.

Eye root: See Goldenseal.

Eye-bright or Eyebright: See Red eyebright and Gentian.

F

FAHAM TEA: See BOURBON TEA.

FAIRY CLOCK: See DANDELION.

FAIRY FINGERS: See FOXGLOVE.

FAIRY GLOVE: See FOXGLOVE.

FAIRY SMOKE: See INDIAN-PIPE.

FAIRY-WAND: See BLAZING-STAR.

FALL CROCUS: See SAFFRON.

FALSE BALM OF GILEAD: See BALSAM FIR NEEDLE OIL.

FALSE CARDAMOM: See CARDAMOM.

FALSE COLTSFOOT: See CANADIAN SNAKEROOT.

FALSE DITTANY: See DITTANY (*Dictamnus albus*).

FALSE FOXGLOVE: See FEVERWEED.

FALSE GRAPES: See VIRGINIA CREEPER.

FALSE HELLEBORE (*Veratrum viride*) [*Liliaceae*]
American hellebore; American white hellebore; Blazing-star; Bugbane; Devil's bite; Earth gall; Green hellebore; Indian poke; Itchweed; Swamp hellebore; Tickleweed; White hellebore:

Although the roots of this plant have been used in herbal remedies, it is extremely dangerous. The plant roots or leaves if ingested will cause severe allergic reactions and severe cardiac depression which may be fatal. See also BLAZING-STAR.

FALSE INDIGO: See WILD INDIGO.

FALSE PIMPERNEL: See PIMPERNEL.

FALSE SAFFRON: See SAFFRON.

FALSE SPIKENARD: See SPIKENARD.

FALSE UNICORN ROOT: See BLAZING-STAR.

FALSE VERVAIN: See BLUE VERVAIN.

FAT-HEN: See GOOD-KING-HENRY.

FEATHER GERANIUM: See EPAZOTE.

FEBRIFUGE PLANT: See FEVERFEW.

FEBRUARY DAPHNE: See DAPHNE.

FELON HERB: See MUGWORT and MOUSE EAR.

FELONWOOD: See NIGHTSHADE.

FELONWORT: See NIGHTSHADE.

FEMALE FERN: See WALL FERN.

FEMALE GINSENG: See ANGELICA TREE.

FENNEL (*Foeniculum vulgare*) [*Umbelliferae*]:
Common fennel grows wild throughout the world and is also grown commercially. The cultivated fennel is *Foeniculum vulgare*, subspecies *vulgare*. There are two varieties in this subspecies: *azoricum*, Florence fennel, cultivated as a vegetable, and *dulce* which is cultivated for extraction of essential oils used commercially. It is a tall, feathery-leaved perennial plant, but it is treated as an annual in the United States. The anise-tasting leaves, fresh or dried, seeds, and dried root are all used. The leaves do not dry very well and if fresh leaves are not available, the seed is better as a seasoning. Fennel seeds are an essential ingredient of Italian sausage. Florence fennel, also

known as giant fennel, is a variety of fennel developed in Italy. It has thick stems and is used as a vegetable. The stalks can be eaten raw, like celery stalks. They add flavor to sauces. Italians traditionally eat a stalk of fennel after heavy meals to clear the palate. Oil of fennel is used in cordials, liqueurs, perfumery, and in old medicine as a carminative and emmenagogue. Legend claims that fennel sharpens sight, wards off evil spirits and promotes longevity. GRAS

FENNEL FLOWER: See NIGELLA.

FENUGREEK (*Trigonella foenum-graecum*) [*Leguminosae*]
   Bird's foot; Greek hay; Methi:
   The rock-hard seeds of Greek hay are dried, ground into a powder, and used as a seasoning in curries. The seeds should be lightly roasted before they are ground. If roasted too long a bitter flavor will develop. The faintly bitter-tasting leaves are used fresh or dried. Very young, tender leaves are sometimes put in salads. Fenugreek sprouts are also used in salads in the same manner as alfalfa sprouts. Peter Gray, with his wonderful British sense of humor, described fenugreek in the following manner (p. 306):

> This is a wholly delightful legume, the pronounced flavor of which has led people, from remotest antiquity, to attribute to it those powers which they wished a seasoning would possess. The trainer of horses believes that it produces a shiny coat and fleetness of foot: the stockman, smelling it in a patented food additive, is convinced that it induces hunger and thirst: the Egyptian householder has no doubt that it insures plumpness and concupiscence in his women: and so the tale has gone on since the dawn of history. The flavor, though not the name, is known to all cooks since it is the outstanding constituent of curry powder. As such, it demands garlic as a diluent and coconut milk as an antidote. As a seasoning for any dish except curry, or egg-laying mash, it is too harsh and rank for consideration.

GRAS

FERMENTED SOYBEAN PURÉE:
   Fermented soybean purée is used in Chinese and Japanese dishes. It is made from soybeans, water, and sea salt and may be red, yellow, or black depending upon the variety of soybean used.

FERN: See HERB CHRISTOPHER, MAIDENHAIR FERN; WALL FERN, and WOOD FERN.

FERN BRAKE: See WALL FERN.

FERN BUSH: See SWEET FERN.

FERN GALE: See SWEET FERN.

FERN ROOT: See WALL FERN.

FERN-LEAVED FALSE FOXGLOVE: See FEVERWEED.

FETID HELLEBORE: See HELLEBORE.

FETID NIGHTSHADE: See HENBANE.

FEVER BARK TREE: See QUININE.

FEVER GRASS: See LEMONGRASS.

FEVER PLANT: See EVENING PRIMROSE.

FEVER ROOT: See CORALROOT.

FEVER TREE: See EUCALYPTUS.

FEVER TWIG: See NIGHTSHADE.

FEVERBUSH: See SPICEBUSH.

FEVERFEW (*Chrysanthemum parthenium*) [*Compositae*]
Febrifuge plant; Pellitory:
Feverfew is native to southeast Europe to the Caucasus and has been introduced in both North and South America. The dried flowers are purgative and are used in herbal remedies. Also see PELLITORY and PYRETHRUM.

FEVERWEED (*Aureolaria pedicularia*, formerly *Agalinus pedicularia* and *Gerardia pedicularia*) [*Scrophulariaceae*]
American foxglove; Bushy gerardia; False foxglove; Fern-leaved false foxglove; Lousewort:
This is a parasitic plant that grows on the roots of oaks. It has been used in herbal remedies for its diaphoretic and sedative properties.

FEVERWORT: See THOROUGHWORT.

FIDDLEHEADS: See HERB CHRISTOPHER.

FIELD BALM: See GROUND IVY and CATNIP.

FIELD BALSAM: See EVERLASTING.

FIELD ERYNGO: See ERYNGO.

FIELD GOLDENROD: See SWEET GOLDENROD.

FIELD LADY'S-MANTLE: See LADY'S-MANTLE.

FIELD MINT: See CORN MINT.

FIELD PANSY: See PANSY.

FIELD PRIMROSE: See EVENING PRIMROSE.

FIGWORT (*Scrophularia* spp.) [*Scrophulariaceae*]
(*Scrophularia marilandica*)
Carpenter's square; Heal-all; Kernelwort; Knotty-rooted figwort; Scrofula plant:
There are about 200 species of *Scrophularia*, all known as figworts. *Scrophularia marilandica* is native to the eastern United States. As an herbal remedy, it was used primarily as a skin medication, and like almost all of the plants of the *Scrophulariaceae* family, it was used to treat the repulsive lesions of scrofula.

FILÉ: See SASSAFRAS.

FINES HERBES:
Fines herbes is a French mixture of fresh herbs including parsley, chives, tarragon, and chervil. The Mediterranean region of France adds basil, fennel, oregano, sage and saffron to the mixture. Some American cook books inaccurately describe *fines herbes* as what is really a *bouquet garni*.

FINGER FLOWER: See FOXGLOVE.

FINGER LEAF: See CINQUEFOIL.

FIR NEEDLES OIL: See PINE FIR and HEMLOCK (*Tsuga canadensis*).

FIRE CHERRY: See WILD CHERRY.

FISH FUDDLE: See JAMAICAN DOGWOOD.

FISH-POISON TREE: See JAMAICAN DOGWOOD.

FIT PLANT: See INDIAN-PIPE.

FITSROOT: See INDIAN-PIPE.

FIVE FINGERS: See GINSENG and CINQUEFOIL.

FIVE LEAVES: See VIRGINIA CREEPER.

FIVE-FINGER GRASS: See CINQUEFOIL.

FIVE-FINGERS: See GINSENG and CINQUEFOIL.

FIVE-LEAFED GINSENG: See GINSENG.

FIVE-LEAVED IVY: See VIRGINIA CREEPER.

FIVE-SPICE POWDER: See CHINESE FIVE-SPICE POWDER and BENGALI FIVE SPICES.

FLAG: See ORRIS and IRIS.

FLAGROOT: See CALAMUS.

FLANNEL PLANT: See MULLEIN.

FLAX (*Linum usitatissimum*) [*Linaceae*]
   Flax seed; Linseed; Lint bells; Winterlien:
   This is the common flax plant. Linen is made from the plant fibers and linseed oil is obtained from the seeds. Flax seeds and linseed oil, because of their purgative properties, have been used in herbal remedies. Unripe flax seeds are considered toxic.

FLAX SEED: See FLAX.

FLAXWEED: See TOADFLAX.

FLEABANE: See ERIGERON.

FLEAWORT: See PLANTAIN.

FLEECE FLOWER: See KNOTWEED.

FLEUR-DE-LIS: See IRIS.

FLOR DE JAMAICA: See ROSELLA.

FLORENTINE IRIS: See ORRIS.

FLORIDA CORNEL: See DOGWOOD.

FLORIDA DOGWOOD: See DOGWOOD.

FLORIDA PEPPER TREE: See PEPPER TREE.

FLORIST'S VIOLET: See VIOLET.

FLORIST'S WILLOW: See WILLOW.

FLOWER VELURE: See COLTSFOOT.

FLOWER-DE-LUCE: See IRIS.

FLOWERING ALOE: See AGAVE.

FLOWERING BRAKE: See HERB CHRISTOPHER.

FLOWERING CORNEL: See DOGWOOD.

FLOWERING DOGWOOD: See DOGWOOD.

FLOWERING FERN: See HERB CHRISTOPHER.

FLOWERING WINTERGREEN: See MILKWORT.

FLUELLEN: See VERONICA.

FLUX ROOT: See INDIAN PAINTBRUSH.

FLYTRAP: See DOGBANE and PITCHER PLANT.

FO-TI: See KNOTWEED.

FOAL'S-FOOT: See COLTSFOOT.

FOLKS' GLOVE: See FOXGLOVE.

FOOD-OF-THE-GODS: See ASAFOETIDA.

FOOL'S CICELY: See FOOL'S PARSLEY.

FOOL'S PARSLEY (*Aethusa cynapium*) [*Umbelliferae*]
Dog poison; Fool's cicely; Small hemlock:

This is a common European weed which looks very much like a smooth-leaved parsley. It is quite poisonous.

FOUR SPICES; *QUATRE ÉPICES*:

All references seem to agree that the four spices are pepper, cloves, nutmeg and ginger; however, none seems to agree as to the proportions of the spices.

Margaret Fulton (p. 128) states that it is a mixture of almost equal parts of pepper, cloves, nutmeg, and ginger. To make, grind 1 tablespoon white peppercorns and 1 tablespoon whole cloves to a fine powder in a blender. Mix with 1 tablespoon freshly grated nutmeg and 1 scant tablespoon ground ginger.

Montagné (p. 428) gives the proportions as: 1 ¹/₈ cups (125 grams) white pepper, 1 ¹/₂ tablespoons (10 grams) powdered cloves, 3 ¹/₂ tablespoons (30 grams) ginger, and 4 tablespoons (35 grams) grated nutmeg.

Arabella Boxer et al. (p. 22) give similar proportions to those given by Montagné but in a smaller amount: 4 tablespoons ground white pepper, 1 teaspoon ground cloves, 3 ¹/₂ teaspoons ground ginger, and 3 ¹/₄ teaspoons grated nutmeg.

FOXBERRY: See **BLUEBERRY.**

FOXGLOVE (*Digitalis*, various species) [*Scrophulariaceae*]

(*Digitalis lanata*)

Grecian foxglove

(*Digitalis purpurea*)

American foxglove; Common foxglove; Dead men's bells; Digitalis; Dog's finger; Fairy fingers; Fairy gloves; Finger flower; Folks' glove; Ladies' glove; Lion's mouth; Purple foxglove:

Foxglove is contained in many lists of herbs, but it is not one that belongs in the kitchen, nor should it ever be used as a home remedy. Use of foxglove as medicine has been recorded as early as 1250 in writings of Welsh physicians, but it was in 1785 that William Withering, a master physician and botanist from Birmingham, England, published his famous book, *An Account of the Foxglove and Some of Its Medical Uses: with Practical Remarks on Dropsy and Other Diseases.* Since that time, the active ingredient, digitalis, has been refined and purified and has become a valuable drug in the treatment of heart failure. Self-treatment should never be attempted since improper use can be fatal. Medical digitalis is obtained from *Digitalis lanata* and *Digitalis purpurea.*

FOXTAIL: See **HERB-IVY.**

FRAGRANT GIANT HYSSOP: See **ANISE HYSSOP.**

FRAGRANT WATER LILY: See LOTUS.

FRAMBOISE: See BRAMBLES.

FRANGIPANI: See JASMINE.

FRANKINCENSE: See OLIBANUM.

FRAXINELLA: See DITTANY (*Dictamnus albus*).

FRENCH ARTICHOKE: See ARTICHOKE.

FRENCH LAVENDER: See LAVENDER.

FRENCH MARIGOLD: See MARIGOLD.

FRENCH PARSLEY: See CHERVIL.

FRENCH SORREL: See SORREL.

FRENCH TARRAGON: See TARRAGON.

FRIAR'S-CAP: See MONKSHOOD.

FRIJOLITO: See PEYOTE.

FRINGE TREE (*Chionanthus virginicus*) [*Oleaceae*]
Gray beard tree; Old man's beard; Poison ash tree; Snowdrop tree; Snowflower; White fringe:
   The fringe tree is considered an ornamental by most because of its fragrant white blossoms, but its bark has been used in herbal remedies.

FRINGED GENTIAN: See GENTIAN.

FRINGED POLYGALA: See MILKWORT.

FROGWORT: See BUTTERCUP.

FROST PLANT: See ROCK ROSE.

FROSTWORT: See ROCK ROSE.

FUKI: See COLTSFOOT.

FULLER'S HERB: See SOAPWORT.

FUMITORY (*Fumaria officinalis*) [*Fumariaceae*]

Earth smoke; Hedge fumitory; Smoke-of-the-earth:

Fumitory is listed in old cookbooks as a bitter. It is sometimes called smoke-of-the-earth because of its smell. It should not be used in any form. The *Fumaria* plants are a source of fumarine, also called protopine, a poisonous alkaloid, $C_{20}H_{19}NO_5$.

Fumarine is also found in:

Eschscholtzia californica [*Papaveraceae*]

California poppy

Dicentra cuculleria [*Fumariaceae*]

Dutchman's breeches

Dicentra spectabilis

Bleeding heart

Dicentra canadensis

Squirrel corn

Dicentra eximia, formerly *Corydalis formosa*

Choice dielytra; Staggerweed; Turkey corn; Wild bleeding heart; Wild turkey pea

FURZE: See BROOM.

G

GAGLEE: See ARUM.

GAGROOT: See LOBELIA.

GALANGAL, GREATER (*Alpinea galanga*) [*Zingiberaceae*]
Catarrh root; Laos; Lengkuas

GALANGAL, LESSER (*Alpinea officinarum*)
Chinese ginger; East India root; Galingal; Kencur
(*Kaempferia galangal*) [*Zingiberaceae*]
Galangal; Kentjur:
The dried tubers of these Chinese plants, related to ginger, are ground into a powder used to season curries and to flavor liqueurs. It has a gingery-peppery taste with a hint of camphor. Use of greater galangal (*Alpinea galanga*) in the United States is limited to alcoholic beverage flavoring formulations. Lesser galangal (*Alpinea officinalis*) is GRAS. *Kaempferia galangal* has a sweeter taste than the *Alpinea* species.
The dried galangal root found in Oriental markets in this country comes in small packages of slices. It is very hard and must be soaked in warm water for about an hour if it is to be minced. It is used in Thai cooking.

GALANGALE: See GALINGALE.

GALBAN: See GALBANUM.

GALBANUM (*Ferula galbaniflua* and *rubricaulis*) [*Umbelliferae*]
Galban

Ferula diversivittata and *moschata*)

Muskroot; Sumbul:

Dried resinous exudates of these plants have a spicy, balsamic odor. They are used in perfumery and in compounding flavorings for baked goods and confections. The resin was also compounded with myrrh, asafoetida and syrup to use as an expectorant, antispasmodic, and stimulant and for the treatment of chronic catarrh and amenorrhea. GRAS

GALINGAL: See GALANGAL.

GALINGALE (*Cyperus longus*) [*Cyperaceae*]

Galangale; Sweet sedge

(*Cyperus esculentis*)

Nut grass; Nut sedge; Yellow nut grass; Yellow nut sedge

(*Cyperus esculentis*, Var. *sativus*)

Chufa; Earth almond; Rush nut; Tiger nut; Zulu nut:

Galingale actually can refer to any member of the genus *Cyperus*, however, it is usually thought of as the *longus* species which is native to England. This English sedge has aromatic roots similar to galangal in flavor and aroma. The *esculentis* species is usually thought of as a troublesome weed. The *sativus* variety of *esculentis* is widely cultivated abroad. The edible, nutty-flavored tubers are rich in starch, sugar, and fat. They are eaten cooked or roasted or are made into flour.

GALLBERRY: See APPALACHIAN TEA.

GALLWEED: See GENTIAN.

GAMBIR; GAMBIER: See CATECHU.

GANG FLOWER: See MILKWORT.

GARAM MASALA:

This is a fragrant blend of spices used in curries. There are dry masalas in powder form and wet masalas ground into a paste with water, oil, or vinegar. The spices are roasted to bring out the flavor and make it easier to grind to a fine powder. There are many versions, some using hot spices such as pepper, while others use only the fragrant, aromatic spices.

Two basic mixtures from Margaret Fulton (pp. 139-140) are given below. The individual spice is roasted in a small pan over medium heat until it begins to smell fragrant. It can be cooled on a saucer while the next spice is roasted. Put all the cooled spices into a blender and blend to a fine powder or pound using a mortar and pestle. The nutmeg is not roasted but is grated and added to the other spices after they have been ground to a powder. Store in an airtight jar in a cool, dry place.

Hot mixture	Fragrant mixture
4 tablespoons coriander seeds	3 3-inch cinnamon sticks
2 tablespoons cumin seeds	2 teaspoons cardamom seeds
1 tablespoon black peppercorns	1 teaspoon whole cloves
2 teaspoons cardamom seeds	1/2 nutmeg, grated
4 3-inch cinnamon sticks	
1 teaspoon whole cloves	Makes 1 ounce (1/4 cup)
1 whole nutmeg, finely grated	

Makes 3 ounces (3/4 cup)

The following two mixtures are from Arabella Boxer et al. (pp. 24–25).

Mixture 1	Mixture 2
3/4 to 2 teaspoons ground cardamom	1 1/2 to 3 teaspoons ground cardamom
1/2 to 1 teaspoon ground cinnamon	1 2-inch piece cinnamon stick, ground
1/2 teaspoon ground cloves	1/2 to 1 teaspoon ground cloves
1 1/2 teaspoons ground black cumin	1 to 1 1/3 teaspoons ground black cumin
1 3/4 teaspoons ground black pepper	1 to 1 1/2 teaspoons ground black pepper
1/2 teaspoon ground bay leaves*	1 teaspoon ground nutmeg, or 2 teaspoons ground pomegranate seeds
1 3/4 teaspoons ground coriander*	
1 1/2 teaspoons ground cumin*	
1/4 teaspoon ground mace*	
1/4 to 1 teaspoon ground nutmeg*	

In mixture 1, items marked with * are optional.
In mixture 2, use of the pomegranate seeds and the lower amounts of the other ingredients will give a sharper, tarter mixture.

GARDEN BALM: See SWEET CLOVER and BALM.

GARDEN BALSAM: See BALSAM.

GARDEN BURNET: See BURNET.

GARDEN CAMOMILE: See CAMOMILE.

GARDEN CELANDINE: See CELANDINE.

GARDEN CHERVIL: See CHERVIL.

GARDEN COLUMBINE: See COLUMBINE.

GARDEN CRESS: See ROCKET.

GARDEN CURRANT: See RED CURRANT.

GARDEN HELIOTROPE: See VALERIAN.

GARDEN LOVAGE: See LOVAGE.

GARDEN MYRRH: See CHERVIL.

GARDEN NASTURTIUM: See NASTURTIUM.

GARDEN NIGHTSHADE: See NIGHTSHADE.

GARDEN PARSLEY: See PARSLEY.

GARDEN PATIENCE: See SORREL.

GARDEN RUE: See RUE.

GARDEN SAGE: See SAGE.

GARDEN SORREL: See SORREL.

GARDEN THYME: See THYME.

GARDEN VALERIAN: See VALERIAN.

GARDEN VIOLET: See VIOLET.

GARGET: See POKE.

GARLAND CHRYSANTHEMUM: See SHUNGIKU.

GARLIC (*Allium sativum*) [*Liliaceae*]
   (*Allium sativum*, var. *ophioscorodon*)
   Giant garlic; Rocambole; Serpent garlic
   (*Allium sativum*. var. *pekinense*)

Peking garlic

(*Allium scorodoprasum*)

Giant garlic; Sand leek; Spanish garlic (incorrectly called rocambole)

(*Allium tuberosum*)

Chinese chive; Garlic chive; Oriental garlic

(*Allium ampeloprasum*)

Great-headed garlic; Levant garlic; Wild leek

(*Allium ursinum*)

Bear's garlic; Buckrams; Gypsy onion; Hog's garlic; Ramsons; Ransoms:

Most everyone is familiar with the flavor of garlic and its use as a flavoring, but as a seasoning it is highly abused and neglected. In dishes not specifically flavored with garlic, it is an adjunct to onions and the correct proportions should be observed. One medium-sized clove of garlic, per medium-sized onion, will give a perceptible garlic savor; one-half medium-sized clove, per medium-sized onion, will allow the real gourmet to know, from the improved flavor, that a seasoning of garlic has been added; half this quantity of garlic will improve the flavor without allowing anyone to be certain of its presence. *Allium tuberosum* has a mild garlic flavor, and *Allium ampeloprasum* has very large bulbs with many cloves. Wild garlic can be most any species of *Allium* that smells or tastes like garlic. *Allium ursinum* is a wild garlic native to Europe and Asia. Louis P. De Gouy describes garlic in the following manner:

> When you think of garlic think of lilies whose relative they are. One of the oldest recorded seasonings, garlic may be eaten raw. For centuries garlic has been employed by superstitious people to ward off evil spirits—especially the legendary vampires. According to the old tales, vampires were the blood-sucking nocturnal reincarnations of the dead that rose from their graves at night and hunted the living by sucking their blood like the South American "vampire" bats of real life. Garlic is widely used in French cuisine, in soups, stews, roasts, poultry, steaks, bread, stuffings, salad dressings, salads, pickles, chutneys, and so forth. Until the middle of the eighteenth century many Siberian villagers paid taxes in garlic: 15 bulbs for a man, 10 for a woman, 5 for a child.

Legend also claims that garlic is useful in treating asthma, hysteria, colds, scurvy, and sun stroke. Crushed on the skin, it cures poison ivy and poison oak.

GARLIC CHIVE: See GARLIC.

GARLIC MUSTARD: See ALLIARIA.

GARNETBERRY: See RED CURRANT.

GAS-PLANT: See DITTANY (*Dictamnus albus*).

GAY-FEATHER: See BLAZING-STAR.

GELSEMIN, GELSEMINE: See JASMINE.

GENET (*Spartium junceum*) [*Leguminosae*]
   Spanish broom; Weavers' broom:
   This is a plant from the Mediterranean region. Extracts of the flowers are used in perfumery and in minute amounts to produce a honey-like aroma and yellow coloring in confectionery flavorings. Genet is the French word for a female donkey, but it is also the French word for broom (botanical). GRAS

GENTIAN (*Gentiana acaulis*) [*Gentianaceae*]
   Stemless gentian
   (*Gentiana catesbaei*)
   American gentian; Blue gentian; Catesby's gentian; Sampson's snakeroot
   (*Gentiana lutea*)
   Bitter root; Bitterwort; Pale gentian; Yellow gentian
   (*Gentianopsis crinita*, formerly *Gentiana crinita*)
   Fringed gentian
   (*Gentianella quinquefolia*, formerly *Gentiana quinquefolia*)
   Gallweed; Stiff gentian
   (*Sabatia angularis*) [*Gentianaceae*]
   Bitter-bloom; Bitter clover; Eyebright; Red centaury; Rose pink; Wild succory
   (*Frasera caroliniensis*) [*Gentianaceae*]
   American gentian; American columbo; Green gentian:
   Gentian can refer to any plant in the genus *Gentiana*. The flowers and the extremely bitter roots of these plants have been used in the past in the preparation of tonics and as a bitter flavoring in apértifs. Stemless gentian is restricted to use in alcoholic beverages only. *Gentiana lutea*, the chief commercial source of gentian root which is used as a medicine and for flavoring vermouth, is GRAS. American gentian can be either *Frasera caroliniensis* [*Gentianaceae*] or *Gentiana catesbaei*. American centaury (*Sabatia*

angularis) [*Gentianaceae*], commonly called rose pink or bitter-bloom, is also a member of the gentian family. It was used as an herbal medicine for the treatment of intermittent fevers and stomach problems. The gentian plants have no connection to gentian violet, a chemical mixture used as a stain in microscopy and as an antiseptic.

GEORGIA PINE: See **PINE OIL.**

GERANIUM:

Geranium may refer to plants in the family *Geraniaceae* of either the genus *Geranium* or the genus *Pelargonium*. Those of the genus *Geranium* are commonly referred to as cranes-bill (named for the shape of the fruit), and the astringent roots have been used in medicine. Those of the genus *Pelargonium* include those cultivated for their showy flowers, such as the scarlet geraniums, or for their fragrant leaves, such as rose, or sweet-scented, geranium (*Pelargonium graveolens*). East Indian geranium is *Cymbopogon martini* [*Gramineae*]. See **LEMONGRASS.**

Oils from the leaves and stems of the genus *Pelargonium* are used in perfumery and in flavoring formulations. Generally they fall into three types: (1) Reunion geranium oil, also known as Bourbon geranium oil, is distilled from fresh plants harvested at the time of initial bloom. It has a rose-like odor with a hint of mint. (2) Algerian geranium oil is distilled from fresh green leaves harvested before blossoming. It has a rose-like odor and is considered superior (less minty) to Reunion (Bourbon) oil. (3) Moroccan geranium oil is distilled from the fresh cut leaves and stems of *Pelargonium roseum* and has a rose-like, herbaceous odor. All have a bitter, rather disagreeable flavor.

Specific species of *Pelargonium* that are used for flavoring are *fragrans* (nutmeg-scented), *crispum* (lemon-scented), *citrosum* orange-scented), *odoratissimum* (apple-scented), and *tomentosum* (peppermint or herb-scented). A flavored sugar syrup can be made by infusing the leaves in a thin syrup for twenty to thirty minutes and then straining.

Wild geranium, also known as American cranesbill, cranesbill, wild cranesbill, spotted cranesbill, spotted geranium, crowfoot, and alumroot, is *Geranium maculatum*. Extracts of the roots were used in the past to control diarrhea, and the powdered root was used as a styptic. See also **HERB ROBERT.**

All *Pelargonium* species are listed as GRAS.

GERMAN CAMOMILE: SEE **CAMOMILE.**

GERMAN ELDER: See **ELDER.**

GERMAN IRIS: See **ORRIS.**

GERMAN MYRTLE: See MYRTLE.

GERMAN RAMPION: See EVENING PRIMROSE.

GERMAN RUE: See RUE.

GERMAN SARSAPARILLA: See RED SEDGE.

GERMAN VALERIAN: See VALERIAN.

GERMANDER (*Teucrium chamaedrys*) [*Labiatae*]
  European germander
  (*Teucrium canadense*)
  American germander; Wood sage
  (*Teucrium germander*) (not an official species)
  Betony
    Germander may refer to any of the above species or to *Veronica chamaedrys* [*Scrophulariaceae*], known as germander speedwell, angel's-eye, or bird's-eye. (See VERONICA.) In the United States use of the bitter flowers of both the *Veronica* and *Teucrium* species is limited to flavoring formulations for alcoholic beverages.

GERMANDER SPEEDWELL: SEE VERONICA.

GERVAO: See BRAZILIAN TEA.

GEUM: See BENNET.

GHOST FLOWER: See INDIAN-PIPE.

GIANT FENNEL: See ASAFOETIDA and FENNEL.

GIANT GARLIC: See GARLIC.

GIANT HYSSOP: See ANISE HYSSOP.

GIANT SWEET CHERVIL: See CHERVIL.

GILL TEA: See GROUND IVY.

GILL-OVER-THE-GROUND: See GROUND IVY.

GILLRUN: See GROUND IVY.

GILLYFLOWER: See CARNATION.

GINGER (*Zingiber officinale*) [*Zingiberaceae*]
True ginger; Canton ginger; *Jamai*can ginger:

Ginger originally came from South China where the ripe roots were boiled in several changes of water to remove the worst of their heat and then preserved in a thick syrup. This is the true Canton ginger used in Chinese recipes and often eaten with cream as a dessert. The dried Canton ginger is also made from roots that have been boiled several times. Jamaican ginger is not boiled before drying and is the peppery-hot ginger to which most are accustomed. Its largest use in cooking is in the flavoring of cakes and cookies, then in beverages, in meat cookery, gravies, preserves, pickles, chutneys, and candies. If dried ginger root is first pounded to separate the fibers, it is easier to grind and sift. Fresh ginger root should be kept in the refrigerator, uncovered and unwrapped. It can be grated as needed. Finely minced homemade candied ginger is a nice addition to baked goods. The length of time boiled and the number of water changes will determine the "hotness" of the ginger. GRAS

GINGERGRASS: See LEMONGRASS.

GINKGO NUT (*Ginkgo biloba*) [*Ginkgoaceae*]
Maidenhair tree:

Ginkgo trees are usually grown in the United States only as street or ornamental trees, and then preferably only the male trees. The fruit of the female tree is a small, foul-smelling (a rancid butter odor from butyric acid) plum-like fruit. The kernel of this fruit, extracted after the fruit has rotted off, is the ginkgo nut. It is used as a flavoring in Chinese and Japanese cooking as well as roasted as a nut.

GINSENG (*Panax ginseng*, formerly *pseudoginseng* or *schinseng*) [*Araliaceae*]
Asiatic ginseng; Chinese ginseng; Eastern Asian ginseng; Korean ginseng; San Qi ginseng; Wonder-of-the-world
(*Panax quinquefolia*)
American ginseng; Five-fingers; Five-leafed ginseng; North American ginseng; Redberry:

The ginseng root is aromatic with a sweet licorice-like taste. It was prized by the ancient Chinese aristocracy as "the root of life." Tradition gave to it the power to cure everything from loss of appetite to heart ailments; from barrenness in women to a decline in masculine virility. Its use is primarily in Chinese cooking and as a medicinal tea. When taken freshly from the fields, washed, peeled, and sun dried, it is called white ginseng. This is used in soups. When steamed and then dried over a fire, it takes on a reddish tint and is known as red ginseng. This is used more as a medicinal tonic. Imported ginseng is very expensive.

The roots of *Eleutherococcus senticosis* [*Araliaceae*], called Siberian ginseng and eleuthero ginseng root, and of *Rumex hymenosepalus* [*Polygonaceae*], commonly called canaigre, tanner's dock or wild rhubarb have been sold (deceptively) as ginseng root. Canaigre is grown primarily for its roots which yield tannin and a yellow dye. Its leaves can be eaten as greens and the stems like rhubarb. It is sometimes called wild pie plant.

GIRASOLE: See ARTICHOKE.

GIROLLES: See DRIED MUSHROOMS.

GLOBE AMARANTH: See BUTTERCUP.

GLOBE ARTICHOKE: See ARTICHOKE.

GLOSSY-LEAVED RED MALLEE: See EUCALYPTUS.

GOAT WILLOW: See WILLOW.

GOAT'S RUE (*Galega officinalis*) [*Leguminosae*]

Found growing wild in southern Europe and western Asia, goat's rue is cultivated as an ornamental in the United States. Although *Hortus Third*, p. 493, states it is used medicinally and as food for livestock, John Lust, p. 208, states that sheep have been poisoned by the fresh plant. It has been used in herbal remedies.

GOATSBEARD (*Tragopogon porrifolius*) [*Compositae*]

Oyster plant; Purple goatsbeard; Salsify; Vegetable-oyster

(*Tragopogon pratensis*)

Jack (or John)-go-to-bed-at-noon; Meadow salsify; Noon flower; Noonday flower; Noontide; Star of Jerusalem; Yellow goatsbeard:

These plants are native to southern Europe, northern Africa, and Asia. Both species have become naturalized in North America and are generally considered weeds. *Tragopogon porrifolius*, however, is widely cultivated for its edible root better known as salsify or oyster plant. Both species have been used in herbal remedies, but *Tragopogon pratensis* seems to be preferred for this purpose. (Is that because it doesn't taste as good?) The yellow flower of *Tragopogon pratensis* opens early in the morning and closes up at midday, hence the name Jack (or John)-go-to-bed-at-noon. Also see HERB CHRISTOPHER.

GOATWEED: See SAINT JOHN'S-WORT.

GOBO: See BURDOCK.

GOLD CUP: See BUTTERCUP.

GOLD FLOWER: See SAINT-JOHN'S-WORT.

GOLDEN ALEXANDERS: See ALEXANDERS.

GOLDEN BOUGH: See MISTLETOE.

GOLDEN DAISY: See HERB MARGARET.

GOLDEN MARGUERITA: See CAMOMILE.

GOLDEN SAGE: See SAGE.

GOLDEN-BUTTONS: See TANSY.

GOLDEN-SLIPPER: See NERVEROOT.

GOLDENROD: See SWEET GOLDENROD.

GOLDENSEAL (*Hydrastis canadensis*) [*Ranunculaceae*]
Eye balm; Eye root; Ground raspberry; Indian plant; Indian tumeric; Jaundice root; Orangeroot; Tumeric root; Yellow puccoon; Yellowroot:
Extracts of the rhizomes contain several alkaloids which were used as an herbal medicine. Although derivatives of the roots were used in eye and mouth washes, eating the fresh plant can cause ulcerations of the mucous membranes. It has been called turmeric and turmeric root because of its yellow color. It should not be confused with nor used in place of true turmeric (*Curcuma longa*) [*Zingiberaceae*]. See **Turmeric.**

GOLDTHREAD (*Coptis trifolia*) [*Ranunculaceae*]
Cankerroot; Mouthroot; Yellowroot:
Goldthread has been used in herbal remedies as a "bitter tonic." It was also thought to cure canker sores of the mouth.

GOLDY STONE: See BENNET.

GOOD-KING-HENRY (*Chenopodium Bonus-Henricus*) [*Chenopodiaceae*]
All-good; Fat-hen; Goosefoot; Mercury; Wild spinach:
Good-King-Henry is used more as a cooked green than as a seasoning. It is cooked like spinach, however it should be cooked in two changes of water, the first being discarded. This is to remove much of the green and very bitter taste.

GOORA NUT: See COLA.

GOOSE GRASS: See BEDSTRAW and CINQUEFOIL.

GOOSE TANSY: See CINQUEFOIL.

GOOSEFOOT:
Goosefoot may refer to any one of a large group of plants belonging to the *Chenopodiaceae* (Goosefoot) family which includes spinach and beets. See EPAZOTE and GOOD-KING-HENRY.

GOOSEGRASS: See BEDSTRAW and CINQUEFOIL.

GOSLING WEED: See BEDSTRAW.

GOTU COLA: See GUTU COLA.

GOURMET POWDER: See MONOSODIUM GLUTAMATE.

GOUTWEED: See HERB GERARD.

GRAINS OF PARADISE (*Elettaria granum-paradise*) [*Zingiberaceae*]
Guinea grains:
See CARDAMOM for a more complete discussion. Guinea grains should not be confused with Guinea pepper. The FDA lists grains of paradise as being *Amomum melegueta*, and they are classified as GRAS. *Amomum melegueta* is most likely now an unused taxonomic classification, however, this has not been verified.

GRANADILLA: See PASSIONFLOWER.

GRASS BURDOCK: See BURDOCK.

GRASS MYRTLE: See CALAMUS.

GRAVEL WEED: See JOE-PYE WEED.

GRAVELROOT: See JOE-PYE WEED.

GRAY BEARD TREE: See FRINGE TREE.

GRAY GOLDENROD: See SWEET GOLDENROD.

GRAY PEPPERMINT: See EUCALYPTUS.

GRAY RIBWORT: See PLANTAIN.

GRAY SAGE: See SAGE.

GRAY SARSAPARILLA: See SARSAPARILLA.

GREASEWOOD: See CAPERS.

GREAT ANGELICA: See ANGELICA.

GREAT BINDWEED: See WILD MORNING-GLORY.

GREAT BUR: See BURDOCK.

GREAT BURDOCK: See BURDOCK.

GREAT BURNET: See BURNET.

GREAT CELANDINE: See CELANDINE.

GREAT WILD VALERIAN: See VALERIAN.

GREAT-HEADED GARLIC: See GARLIC.

GREATER GALANGAL: See GALANGAL.

GREATER PERIWINKLE: See PERIWINKLE.

GREATER PIMPERNEL: See PIMPERNEL.

GREATER PLANTAIN: See PLANTAIN.

GRECIAN FOXGLOVE: See FOXGLOVE.

GRECIAN LAUREL: See BAY LEAF.

GREEK HAY: See FENUGREEK.

GREEK MYRTLE: See MYRTLE.

GREEK NUTS: See ALMOND.

GREEK OREGANO: See MARJORAM.

GREEK SAGE: See SAGE.

GREEK VALERIAN (*Polemonium caeruleum*) [*Polemoniaceae*]
   Charity; Jacob's ladder:
   This plant was applied to ulcers in an attempt to aid healing.

GREEN ALMOND:
   Green almond is another name for the pistachio nut (*Pistacia vera*) [*Anacardiaceae*], also correctly called pistacia nut.

GREEN BROOM: SEE BROOM.

GREEN GENTIAN: See GENTIAN.

GREEN GINGER: See WORMWOOD.

GREEN HELLEBORE: See HELLEBORE and FALSE HELLEBORE.

GREEN MALLEE: See EUCALYPTUS.

GREEN OZIER: See DOGWOOD.

GREEN PEPPER: See CAPSICUM.

GREEN PEPPERCORNS: See PEPPER.

GREEN SAUCE: See SORREL.

GREEN-STEMMED JOE-PYE WEED: See JOE-PYE WEED.

GREENBRIER: See SARSAPARILLA.

GREENHEART TREE: See SASSAFRAS.

GRENADINE:
   This is a syrup made from sugar and pomegranate (*Punica granatum*) [*Punicaceae*] juice, used as a sweetener in cocktails and desserts.

GRIPGRASS: See BEDSTRAW.

GROUND APPLE: See CAMOMILE.

GROUND ASH: See HERB GERARD.

GROUND BERRY: See WINTERGREEN.

GROUND ELDER: See HERB GERARD.

GROUND HOLLY: See PIPSISSEWA.

GROUND IVY (*Glechoma hederacea*) [*Labiatae*]
Alehoof; Cat's-foot; Cat's-paw; Creeping Charlie; Field balm; Gill tea; Gill-over-the-ground; Gillrun; Hay maids; Hedge maids; Runaway robin; Turnhoof:
This is a small creeping plant very common in Britain and Europe. The leaves, when bruised, have a somewhat minty smell. If the plant is dried in the shade at the time of flowering, the dried blossoms and leaves can be made into a medicinal tea said to be good for coughs and colds. It was also used to flavor beer. It has become naturalized in the United States where in some areas it has become a serious lawn and garden weed. Also see HERB-IVY.

GROUND LEMON: See MAYAPPLE.

GROUND LILY: See TRILLIUM.

GROUND PINE: See HERB-IVY.

GROUND RASPBERRY: See GOLDENSEAL.

GROUND SQUIRREL PEA: See TWIN LEAF.

GROUND THISTLE: See CARLINE THISTLE.

GROUNDBREAD: See CYCLAMEN.

GROUNDHELE: See VERONICA.

GROUSEBERRY: See BLUEBERRY and CRAMPBARK.

GUADELOUPE VANILLA: See VANILLA.

Guaiac (*Guaiacum officinale*) [*Zygophyllaceae*]
Guaiacum; Guayacan; Lignum vitae; Pockwood; Tree of life
(*Bulnesia sarmienti*) [*Zygophyllaceae*]
Wild guaiacum:

Oil extracts of the wood and sawdust of these trees are used in perfumery and in aroma formulations. The odor is reminiscent of tea roses. Extracts of the resins were used to treat rheumatism and gout. *Guaiacum officinale* is the cultivated species and *Bulnesia sarmienti* is the wild species which grows in Argentina and Paraguay. GRAS

The term lignum vitae usually refers to the wood, one of the hardest commercial woods. The white cedar has also been called the tree of life. See WHITE CEDAR.

GUAIACUM: See GUAIAC.

GUANABANA: See CUSTARD APPLE.

GUARANA (*Paullinia cupana*) [*Sapindaceae*]

The seeds of this South American shrub are roasted and then mixed with water to make a paste that has a chocolate-like flavor. It is used in South America as a chocolate or coffee substitute in flavoring soft drinks and liqueurs. It is also used to make bread. Guarany Indians used it as a medicine for gastric problems. GRAS

GUAYACAN: See GUAIAC.

GUAYAQUIL SARSAPARILLA: See SARSAPARILLA.

GUELDER ROSE: See CRAMPBARK.

GUINEA GRAINS: See CARDAMOM.

GUINEA PEPPER: See ASHANTI PEPPER.

GUINEA SORREL: See ROSELLA.

GULLY GUM: See EUCALYPTUS.

GULLY PEPPERMINT: See EUCALYPTUS.

GUM IVY: See ENGLISH IVY.

GUM PLANT (*Grindelia robusta*) [*Compositae*]

August flower; Gumweed; Resin-weed; Rosinweed; Sticky-heads; Tarweed:

Sometimes grown as an ornamental, this plant has been used in herbal remedies. The *Grindelia* plants will take up and store selenium compounds from the soil. Selenium poisoning or "alkali disease" of livestock was first described in 1856. Whether acute or chronic, it results in death of both livestock and humans.

Comfrey has also been called gum plant. See COMFREY.

GUM TREE: See STORAX and EUCALYPTUS.

GUM-ARABIC: See ACACIA.

GUMBO FILÉ: See SASSAFRAS.

GUMBO LIMBO: See LINALOE.

GUMDRAGON: See TRAGACANTH.

GUMWEED: See GUM PLANT.

GURU NUT: See COLA.

GUTU KOLA (*Hydrocotyle asiatica*) [*Umbelliferae*]

Gotu cola; Navelwort; Water pennyroyal:

This Asian plant was used for the treatment of syphilis and leprosy in India. It is a highly toxic plant and will cause dizziness, coma, and death. It should not be used.

GYPSY FLOWER: See HOUND'S-TONGUE.

GYPSY ONION: See GARLIC.

GYPSYWEED: See VERONICA.

H

HACKMATACK: See POPLAR and LARCH.

HAGBUSH: See CHINABERRY.

HAIRY SWEET CICELY: See CHERVIL.

HAISEIN SAUCE: See HOISIN SAUCE.

HALLFOOT: See COLTSFOOT.

HARD MAPLE: See SUGAR MAPLE.

HARDBACK: See CITRONELLA.

HARDHACK: See CITRONELLA.

HARDHEADS: See KNAPWEED.

HARDOCK: See BURDOCK.

HAREBURR: See BURDOCK.

HARLOCK: See BURDOCK.

HARTSHORN:

Although this sounds like an herb, avid readers of Gothic romance novels know that when milady fainted someone ran to fetch the hartshorn. Hartshorn is ammonium acid carbonate (NH_4HCO_3). It was obtained from deer antlers and was used as smelling salts. Hartshorn was also used as a leavening agent in the same manner as baking soda ($NaHCO_3$) and can be found listed as a cookie ingredient in *The New Pennsylvania Dutch Cook Book*.

Hartshorn is about four times more soluble in water than baking soda. (Although I have never seen it in substitution listings, I would assume one could substitute baking soda for hartshorn in equal amounts.)

HARTSHORN BUSH: See HERB CHRISTOPHER.

HARTSHORN PLANT: See PASQUE FLOWER.

HARTSHORN PLANTAIN: See HERB-IVY.

HARVEST-LICE: See AGRIMONY.

HARVEY'S SAUCE:

In 1870, English courts decided there was no exclusive commercial right to the name "Harvey's Sauce." There are many different recipes for it, generally based on walnut or mushroom ketchups, anchovies, garlic, soy sauce, and vinegar. The proprietary sauce made in England by Keddie Ltd., can be purchased in the United States. It contains malt vinegar, molasses, black malt, anchovies, salt, acetic acid and spices. It is used as a marinade for meats and as a seasoning sauce for fish, meats, and game. According to the label:

> This celebrated Sauce, regarded as a masterpiece by the London society epicures of the time, was reputedly invented in the latter part of the 18th century by Peter Harvey, mine host of the Black Dog Inn, which until it closed around 1850 stood on the corner of Bedfont Green in the County of Middlesex, a haunt of highwaymen on the main London road to and from the West.

HAWTHORN BERRIES (*Crataegus*, various species) [*Rosaceae*]
Cockspur; Cockspur thorn; English hawthorn; May bush; May tree; Mayblossom; Quick-set thorn; Red haw; Thorn apple; Summer haw; Washington thorn; White thorn; Yellow-fruited thorn:

There are nearly 1000 species of *Crataegus*, all known as hawthorns and having berries. Hawthorn berries are listed as an ingredient in some commercial herbal tea preparations. These teas should be used with extreme caution since they have vasodilatory and sedative properties. The leaves and flowers have also been used in herbal remedies. The name thorn apple as applied to hawthorn berries should not be confused with the true thorn apple which is very poisonous. See JIMSONWEED.

HAY FLOWERS: See SWEET CLOVER.

HAY MAIDS: See GROUND IVY.

HAZEL ALDER: See ALDER.

HAZELWORT: See EUROPEAN SNAKEROOT.

HEADED SAVORY: See THYME and ZA'ATAR.

HEADSMAN: See PLANTAIN.

HEAL-ALL: See HERB CARPENTER, CITRONELLA and FIGWORT.

HEALING HERB: See COMFREY.

HEART SNAKEROOT: See CANADIAN SNAKEROOT.

HEARTEASE: See KNOTWEED and PANSY.

HEARTWEED: See KNOTWEED.

HEATHER (*Calluna vulgaris*, formerly *Erica vulgaris*) [*Ericaceae*]
   Ling; Scotch heather:
   This is the common heather found in Scotland and other parts of
Europe. The flowering shoots were an ingredient in herbal remedies.

HEDGE BINDWEED: See WILD MORNING-GLORY.

HEDGE FUMITORY: See FUMITORY.

HEDGE HYSSOP (*Gratiola officinalis*) [*Scrophulariaceae*]
   *This is a European plant which has been use*d in herbal remedies. It has
very potent cardiac effects and should be regarded as a poisonous plant.

HEDGE LILY: See WILD MORNING-GLORY.

HEDGE MAIDS: See GROUND IVY.

HEDGE MUSTARD: See HERB SOPHIA.

HEDGE-BURS: See BEDSTRAW.

HELLEBORE (*Helleborus foetidus*) [*Ranunculaceae*]
   Bearsfoot; Fetid hellebore; Oxheal; Stinking hellebore
   (*Helleborus niger*)

Black hellebore; Christmas rose

(*Helleborus viridis*)

Green hellebore; Winter hellebore:

All of the hellebores contain digitalis-like glycosides and are extremely poisonous plants. The crushed leaves will cause a dermatitis. Also see FALSE HELLEBORE.

HELMET FLOWER: See MONKSHOOD and SKULLCAP.

HELMET POD: See TWIN LEAF.

HEMLOCK (*Conium maculatum*) [*Umbelliferae*]

California fern; Nebraska fern; Poison hemlock; Poison parsley; Poison root; Poison snakeweed; Spotted hemlock; Winter fern

(*Cicuta maculata*) [*Umbelliferae*]

Beaver-poison; Musquash root; Spotted cowbane

(*Cicuta virosa*)

Water hemlock; Water parsley:

It is hard to believe one would find hemlock listed in a cook book after all the publicity of Socrates' death, but it is contained in *Larousse Gastronomique* by Prosper Montagné. Poison hemlock belongs to the *Umbelliferae* family, the same family as parsley and carrots. In appearance it somewhat resembles parsley, however, the leaves when crushed have an unpleasant smell. As a poison it has wide systemic effects. The dried, unripe fruit is strongly narcotic. All parts of the plant are poisonous, fatally so, if eaten by man or animal. *Cicuta virosa* and *Cicuta maculata* belong to the same family and are also quite toxic. In fact, they are among the most violently poisonous plants (when eaten) of the north temperate region. Musquash is the Algonquin word for muskrat.

HEMLOCK (*Tsuga canadensis*) [*Pinaceae*]

Canada-pitch tree; Canadian hemlock; Eastern hemlock; Hemlock gum tree; Hemlock pitch tree; Hemlock spruce; Weeping spruce:

Extracts of the needles and twigs are used in perfumery and in commercial flavoring formulations. The oil is sold not only as hemlock oil but as fir needle oil and spruce oil. GRAS (See PINE FIR and SPRUCE.)

HEMLOCK GUM TREE: See HEMLOCK (*Tsuga canadensis*).

HEMLOCK PITCH TREE: See HEMLOCK (*Tsuga canadensis*).

HEMLOCK SPRUCE: See HEMLOCK (*Tsuga canadensis*).

HEMP AGRIMONY (*Eupatorium cannabinum*) [*Compositae*]
Sweet-smelling trefoil; Water maudlin:
This plant is native to Europe, North Africa, and western and central Asia. It has been used in a number of herbal remedies, both internal and external. In large doses it is both laxative and emetic.

HEMP DEAD NETTLE: See HEMP NETTLE.

HEMP NETTLE (*Galeopsis tetrahit*) [*Labiatae*]
Bastard hemp; Bee-nettle; Dog-nettle; Hemp dead nettle:
This is a common weed of Canada, Alaska and parts of the northern United States. It has astringent properties and has been used in herbal remedies.

HEMP TREE: See SAGE TREE.

HEN AND CHICKENS; HEN AND CHICKS; HENS AND CHICKENS: See HOUSELEEK.

HENBANE (*Hyoscyamus niger*) [*Solanaceae*]
Black henbane; Devil's eye; Fetid nightshade; Henbell; Hog bean; Jupiter's bean; Poison tobacco; Stinking nightshade:
Henbane contains large quantities of scopolamine as well as atropine and hyoscyamine like belladonna. All parts of the plant are extremely poisonous. It is said that children have died from eating the seeds or seed pods and that uninformed adults, believing the roots to be chicory or parsnips, do not survive to make the same mistake twice.
Henbane is not the same as henbit, that common weed that invades lawns and gardens. Henbit is *Lamium amplexicaule* [*Labiatae*], closely related to the dead nettle.

HENBELL: See HENBANE.

HENNA (*Lawsonia inermis*) [*Lythraceae*]
Alcanna; Egyptian privet; Jamaica mignonette; Mignonette tree; Reseda:
This shrub grows in Arabia, North Africa, Iran and the East Indies. The fragrant red flowers are highly prized. The ground dried leaves yield henna, a very fast orange dye used to color hair. It has astringent properties and has been used in herbal remedies.

Hepatica: See Herb trinity.

Herb Barbara: See Rocket.

Herb carpenter (*Prunella vulgaris*) [*Labiatae*]

All-heal; Blue curls; Brownwort; Carpenter's herb; Carpenter's weed; Heal-all; Hercules woundwort; Hock-heal; Self-heal; Sicklewort; Woundwort:

This herb is reputed to aid in healing wounds inflicted by tools. Whether the herb is applied externally to the wound or taken internally is a debatable question. It does grow nicely in rock gardens and is useful for slightly shady borders. The French call yarrow herb carpenter. See Yarrow.

Herb Christopher:

Herb Christopher may refer to:

(1) (*Actaea*, various species) [*Ranunculaceae*]

Baneberry; Cohosh; Doll's-eyes; Necklaceweed; Red baneberry; Snakeberry; White baneberry; White cohosh:

These plants all have a very poisonous berry.

(2) (*Osmunda regalis*) [*Osmundaceae*]

Bog onion; Buckhorn; Buckhorn brake; Buckhorn male fern; Flowering brake; Flowering fern; Hartshorn bush; King's fern; Royal fern; Royal flowering fern; Saint Christopher's herb; Water fern

(*Osmunda cinnamomea*)

Buckhorn; Cinnamon fern; Cinnamon-colored fern; Fiddleheads:

The roots of both of these species of *Osmunda* have been used in herbal remedies. The young shoots or croziers of *Osmunda cinnamomea* can be eaten like asparagus.

(3) (*Conyza canadensis*, formerly *Erigeron canadensis*) [*Compositae*] (see Erigeron).

(4) (*Filipendula* spp.) [*Rosaceae*]

Meadowsweet

(*Filipendula ulmaria*)

Bridewort; Dolloff; Meadow queen; Meadow-wort; Meadowsweet; Pride-of-the-meadow; Queen-of-the-meadow

(*Filipendula vulgaris*)

Dropwort; Goatsbeard:

Meadowsweet has been used as an herbal medicine and as a tea. The flowers were used to flavor herb beers and country wines. The dried leaves were used to make a tea which was an old-fashioned remedy for rheumatism and kidney problems. The plant does contain salicylic acid.

HERB EVE:

Herb eve is said to be the same as herb-ivy. See **HERB-IVY.**

HERB FRANKINCENSE: See **ASAFOETIDA.**

HERB GERARD (*Aegopodium podagraria*) [*Umbelliferae*]

Ashweed; Bishop's weed; Goutweed; Ground ash; Ground elder:

Reputed to be a cure for gout, this plant, especially a variegated-leaved cultivar, is used as a ground cover. It can become a nasty weed if not controlled.

HERB LILY (*Alstroemeria haemantha*) [*Alstroemeriaceae*]

Herb lily belongs to a genus of plants commonly called lily-of-the-Incas or Peruvian lily. Use other than an ornamental is unknown to me.

HERB LOUISA: See **LEMON VERBENA.**

HERB MARGARET (*Chrysanthemum* spp.) [*Compositae*]

Herb Margaret can refer to any plant that was thought to aid in the healing of bruises—a bruisewort. Most commonly these are members of the *Chrysanthemum* genus and in particular *Chrysanthemum leucanthemum*, known as golden daisy, maudlinwort, Marguerite, oxeye daisy, white daisy and white weed. This is the common daisy found growing as a weed all over the United States. It has been used as a camomile adulterant. See **CAMOMILE.**

HERB MASTIC:

Herb mastic is called a "medicinal plant." It can be *Thymus mastichina* [*Labiatae*], Spanish thyme (see **THYME**), or *Teucrium marum* [*Labiatae*], cat thyme (see **CAT THYME**).

HERB OF THE CROSS: See **VERVAIN.**

HERB PATIENCE: See **SORREL.**

HERB ROBERT (*Geranium robertianum*) [*Geraniaceae*]

Dragon's blood; Red robin; Storkbill; Wild cranesbill:

Herb Robert is said to be so named from being used to cure a disease known as Robert's plague, named after Robert, Duke of Normandy. It is a small plant which grows wild in rocky, moist places. It has red stems, red-stained leaves and purplish-rose flowers. Exactly what Robert's plague was, I have no idea.

HERB SOPHIA (*Sisymbrium*, various species) [*Cruciferae*]
Hedge mustard:
This wild plant belonging to the mustard family was widely used in old medical formulations. Several of the *Sisymbrium* species are used as salad greens. See ROCKET.

HERB TRINITY:
Herb trinity can refer to either *Viola tricolor* [*Violaceae*], the pansy (see PANSY), or to *Hepatica americanus* and *nobilis* [*Ranunculaceae*], plants called liverworts since it was believed they would cure diseases of the liver. All the *Hepatica* plants should be considered toxic. They can produce skin irritation and if taken internally, poisoning.

HERB-BENNET: See BENNET.

HERB-IVY:
Exactly what is being referred to by the term herb-ivy is difficult to determine. It has been described as a ground pine, hartshorn plantain, swine's cress, and a species of chives.
Ground pine is a common name for several different species of plants of the genus *Lycopodium* [*Lycopodiaceae*], the club mosses. These evergreens are often used as Christmas decorations. *Lycopodium clavatum*, known as foxtail, ground pine, lycopod, running pine, staghorn, vegetable sulfur, and wolf claw, is a poisonous plant. The spores, however, are not considered poisonous. The spores have been used in herbal remedies as a hemostatic.
Hartshorn plantain is *Plantago coronopus* [*Plantaginaceae*], a European species of plantain, whose seeds become mucilaginous when moist and are used as a mild laxative. See PLANTAIN.
Swine's cress is described as the herb ivy *Senebiera coronopus* [*Cruciferae*], also known as wart cress. *Sturtevant's Edible Plants of the World*, p. 531, states, "The whole herb is nauseously acrid and fetid and requires much boiling to render it eatable."
Larousse Gastronomique describes herb-ivy as a species of chives used in the flavoring of salads and sauces.

HERB-OF-GRACE:
Herb-of-grace and herb-of-repentance are the same. They can be: (1) common rue (*Ruta graveolens*) [*Rutaceae*] (see RUE), (2) hedge hyssop (*Gratiola officinalis*) [*Scrophulariaceae*] (see HEDGE HYSSOP), or (3) vervain (*Verbena officinalis*) [*Verbenaceae*] (see VERVAIN).

Herb-of-repentance: See Herb-of-grace.

Herb-scented geranium: See Geranium.

Herba benedicta: See Bennet.

Hercules woundwort: See Herb carpenter.

Hercules'-club: See Angelica tree and Prickly ash tree.

Heron's-bill: See Storksbill.

Hibiscus flowers (*Hibiscus*, ? species) [Malvaceae]
Hibiscus flowers are listed as an ingredient in many herbal teas. Exactly what species is used is not listed in the ingredients. It should not be the species *sabdariffa*. See Rosella.

Hickory (*Carya*, various species) [Juglandaceae]
Extracts from the bark of many of the different species are used in commercial flavoring formulations. GRAS

Hierba de la pastora: See Damiana.

Hierba de las nubes: See Marigold.

High balm: See Bergamot.

High bush cranberry: See Crampbark.

High mallow: See Mallow.

Hill berry: See Wintergreen.

Hills-of-snow: See Hydrangea.

Himalaya berry: See Brambles.

Hindheal: See Tansy.

Hini: See Culver's-physic.

Hirabol myrrh: See Myrrh.

Hive vine: See Partridgeberry.

Ho shou wu: See Knotweed.

Hoarhound; Hoarehound: See Horehound.

Hoary plantain: See Plantain.

Hock-heal: See Herb carpenter.

Hog bean: See Henbane.

Hog cranberry: See Uva-ursi.

Hog potato: See Wild jalap.

Hog's fennel: See Imperatoria.

Hog's garlic: See Garlic.

Hogberry: See Uva-ursi.

Hogweed: See Masterwort.

Hoisin sauce; Haisein sauce; Peking sauce; Red seasoning sauce; Red vegetable sauce; Sweet vegetable paste; Sweet vegetable sauce:
This is a Chinese seasoning sauce. It is thick and dark brownish red, sweet and spicy, made from soy beans, various spices, garlic, and chili and used in cooking shellfish, spareribs, and duck. It is sold in cans and bottles.

Holigold: See Marigold.

Holly (*Ilex* spp.) [*Aquifoliaceae*]:
The leaves of hollies are astringent and were used in the past in the treatment of malaria and other diseases with periodic fever. In Corsica a variety of holly berries is roasted, ground and made into a drink similar to coffee. The berries of most of the ornamental and wild species of holly grown in the United States have varying degrees of toxicity, and it is not wise to consume the berries. They can be particularly dangerous to small children. Also see Butcher's broom, Appalachian tea and Maté.

Holly barberry: See Oregon grape.

Holly bay: See Magnolia.

Holly mahonia: See Oregon grape.

HOLY HERB: See YERBA SANTA.

HOLY THISTLE: See BLESSED THISTLE and MILK THISTLE.

HONDURAS SARSAPARILLA: See SARSAPARILLA.

HONEWORT: See CHERVIL.

HONEYBLOOM: See DOGBANE.

HONEYSUCKLE (*Lonicera* spp.) [*Caprifoliaceae*]
There are more than 150 species of *Lonicera*, all known as honeysuckles. They can be erect or climbing shrubs, deciduous or sometimes almost evergreen and are wide-spread in the Northern Hemisphere. Climbing species are often called woodbines. In the past "honeysuckle" was often used in herbal remedies, especially those for the skin. Even today some say that sipping the nectar of honeysuckle in the spring will prevent skin reactions to poison ivy.

HOODWORT: See SKULLCAP.

HOP TREE (*Ptelea trifoliata*) [*Rutaceae*]
Pickaway anise; Prairie grub; Scubby trefoil; Shrubby trefoil; Stinking ash; Stinking prairie bush; Swamp dogwood; Three-leaved hop tree; Wafer ash; Water ash; Wingseed:
This is a very variable species (with numerous subspecies and varieties) of a tree-like shrub, growing up to twenty-five feet tall. It is native to North America and is grown as an ornamental. Root bark and the leaves have been attributed with medicinal "tonic" properties. Also see CHINABERRY.

HOPS (*Humulus lupulus*) [*Moraceae*]
Bine; European hop; Lupulin:
Hops are the dried ripe strobiles, or cones, of the female flowers of the hop vine. They are well-known as a flavoring for beer. In France, Belgium, and Germany the young shoots are used as a vegetable, boiled or steamed like asparagus. In Germany they are also eaten cold as a salad. Pillows stuffed with hops are said to aid insomnia as is hop tea. Lupulin is a yellow, resinous powder of hops which was used as a stomachic and sedative. Japanese hops are *Humulus japonica*. GRAS

HOREHOUND (*Marrubium vulgare*) [*Labiatae*]
Hoarhound; Hoarehound:
The bitter juice of this perennial member of the mint family has long been used as a flavoring for candy and beverages. It was thought to be useful

in the alleviation of coughs, dyspnea, and as a vermifuge. Legend claims that it is useful in combatting snake bites and poisoning. GRAS

HORNET HOLLY: See BUTCHER'S BROOM.

HORSE BALM: See CITRONELLA.

HORSE CHESTNUT (*Aesculus hippocastanum*) [*Hippocastanaceae*]
Buckeye; Common horse chestnut:
The horse chestnut contains substances which, in olden medicine, were used to treat rheumatism and malaria. These are quite toxic, usually producing central nervous system symptoms. Eating of horse chestnuts can be fatal.

HORSE PARSLEY: See ALEXANDERS.

HORSE WEED: See CITRONELLA.

HORSE-ELDER: See ELECAMPANE.

HORSEFLY WEED: See WILD INDIGO.

HORSEFOOT: See COLTSFOOT.

HORSEHEAD: See ELECAMPANE.

HORSEHEAL: See ELECAMPANE.

HORSEHOOF: See COLTSFOOT.

HORSEMINT:
This may refer to either *Mentha longifolia* (see MINT), to *Monarda punctata* (see BERGAMOT), or to *Monardella villosa* (see PENNYROYAL).

HORSERADISH (*Armoracia rusticana*, formerly *Cochlearia armoracia*) [*Cruciferae*]
This pungent root is scraped or grated into vinegar and is used primarily as a condiment. It loses its pungency when cooked, so it should always be added to a sauce or other dish after cooking is completed. GRAS

HORSERADISH TREE (*Moringa pterygosperma*) [*Moringaceae*]
Ben tree; Drumstick:

The root of this tree has the pungent flavor of common horseradish. The name drumstick comes from the pods which may be up to eighteen inches long. These have a meaty taste when cooked and are used in Indian vegetable curries. The small leaves are also used in chutneys and curries. The mature seed is the ben nut, source of oil of ben. Oil of ben is used in perfumery. The tree is cultivated in India and grows wild in the West Indies.

HORSETAIL: See SHAVE GRASS.

HORSETAIL GRASS: See SHAVE GRASS.

HORSETAIL RUSH: See SHAVE GRASS.

HORSEWEED: See ERIGERON.

HOTTENTOT TEA: See IMMORTELLE.

HOTTENTOT-BREAD: See WILD YAM.

HOUND'S-TONGUE (*Cynoglossum officinale*) [*Boraginaceae*]
   Beggar's-lice; Dog-bur; Dog's tongue; Gypsy flower; Sheep-lice; Woolmat:
   Considered by most as a weed, this plant is sometimes grown in the flower garden. The seed nutlets have barbed prickles which stick to everything. It has been used in herbal remedies and is said to be "weakly poisonous." It can cause an allergic dermatitis in some individuals.

HOUSELEEK (*Sempervivum tectorum*) [*Crassulaceae*]
   Aaron's rod; Bullock's eye; Hen and chickens; Jupiter's beard; Jupiter's eye; Live-forever; Old-man-and-woman; Roof houseleek; Thunder plant:
   This is an old-fashioned house and garden plant prized for its durable rosettes and progeny of smaller ones. In European countries it often grows on roofs. The sliced fresh leaves placed on the skin were supposed to remove freckles, warts and other skin blemishes.

HUA-CHIAO: See ANISE-PEPPER.

HUANG QI: See TRAGACANTH.

HUBAM CLOVER: See SWEET CLOVER.

HUCKLEBERRY: See BLUEBERRY.

HUISACHE: See CASSIE.

HUNGARIAN CAMOMILE: See CAMOMILE.

HUNGARIAN PAPRIKA: See PAPRIKA.

HURRBURR: See BURDOCK.

HYACINTH (*Hyacinthus orientalis*) [*Liliaceae*]:
Extracts of the flowers are used in perfumery and rarely, because of the prohibitively high cost, as an ingredient in flavorings. GRAS

HYDRANGEA (*Hydrangea arborescens*) [*Saxifragaceae*]
Hills-of-snow; Sevenbark; Wild hydrangea:
This species of *Hydrangea* has been used in herbal remedies. It is diuretic and was thought to dissolve kidney stones.

HYSSOP (*Hyssopus officinalis*) [*Labiatae*]
(*Origanum syriacum*, var. *syriacum*) [*Labiatae*]
The flowers and leaves of *Hyssopus officinalis*, either fresh or dried, are used. It is described as being minty, pungent and slightly bitter. It is used in flavoring liqueurs such as Bénédictine and Chartreuse. The leaves may be used sparingly in salads and stews. GRAS
Origanum syriacus, var. *syriacus* is supposed to be the hyssop mentioned in the Bible and is used as oregano.

I

ICELAND MOSS (*Cetraria islandica*) [*Parmeliaceae*]
Eryngo-leaved liverwort:
Bitter extracts of this lichen are permitted to be used in the United States in flavor formulations for alcoholic beverages only. It has been said that it is nutritious (?) and useful in treating bowel and lung disorders.

ILANG-ILANG: See YLANG-YLANG.

IMMORTELLE (*Helichrysum orientale*) [*Compositae*]
Everlasting
(*Helichrysum italicum*)
Curry plant; White-leaved everlasting
(*Helichrysum serpyllifolium*)
Hottentot tea:
The Food and Drug Administration has contributed much to the confusion surrounding the identification of immortelle by identifying it as "*Helichrysum augustifolium*" (note spelling "au"). Immortelle is correctly *Helichrysum orientale*. The cultivated curry plant, *Helichrysum italicum*, subspecies *siitalicum*, was formerly known as *Helichrysum angustifolium* (note spelling "an"). Oil extracts of the flowering tops of the cultivated curry plant have a sweet odor with fruity tones. It is used mostly in perfumery but is also used in fruit-type flavor formulations. The FDA lists *Helichrysum augustifolium* as GRAS.

IMPERATORIA (*Peucedanum osthruthium*, formerly *Imperatoria osthruthium*) [*Umbelliferae*]
Hog's fennel; Imperial masterwort; Masterwort; Sulfurwort:

155

This is a perennial plant found growing wild in European mountain meadows. It is occasionally cultivated in Europe but not in the United States. The roots have a sulfurous odor and a bitter, tonic taste. Use in the United States was restricted to alcoholic beverage flavoring formulations (1967), but it is now listed as GRAS.

IMPERIAL MASTERWORT: See IMPERATORIA.

INCENSE TREE: See LINALOE.

INDIAN ANISE: See STAR ANISE.

INDIAN APPLE: See MAYAPPLE.

INDIAN ARROW: See WAHOO.

INDIAN BALM: See TRILLIUM.

INDIAN BARK: See MAGNOLIA.

INDIAN BAY: See BAY LEAF.

INDIAN BLACK DRINK: See CASSINA.

INDIAN BORAGE: See COLEUS.

INDIAN CASSIA: See CASSIA.

INDIAN CHICKWEED: See CHICKWEED.

INDIAN CHOCOLATE: See WATER AVENS.

INDIAN CRESS: See NASTURTIUM.

INDIAN CUP: See CUP PLANT.

INDIAN DILL (*Anethum sowa*) [*Umbelliferae*]

The seeds of this species of dill have a more caraway-like odor and flavor than ordinary dill. It is used in commercial preparation of essential oils for flavorings the same as ordinary dill. GRAS

INDIAN ELM: See SLIPPERY ELM.

INDIAN FRANKINCENSE: See OLIBANUM.

INDIAN GINGER: See CANADIAN SNAKEROOT.

INDIAN HOLY BASIL: See BASIL.

INDIAN HYSSOP: See BLUE VERVAIN.

INDIAN GUM: See CUP PLANT.

INDIAN JASMINE: See JASMINE.

INDIAN LICORICE: See LICORICE.

INDIAN LILAC: See CHINABERRY.

INDIAN LOTUS: See LOTUS.

INDIAN MUSTARD: See MUSTARD.

INDIAN NUTS: See PINE NUTS.

INDIAN OLIBANUM: See OLIBANUM.

INDIAN PAINT: See YARROW.

INDIAN PAINTBRUSH (*Asclepias tuberosa*) [*Asclepiadaceae*]
Butterfly weed; Canada root; Chigger flower; Flux root; Milkweed; Orange swallow-wort; Pleurisy root; Tuberroot; White root; Wind root:
This member of the milkweed family is an old American Indian cure-all. Extracts of the root were used to treat pulmonary disorders, and the dried, powdered root was used on wounds. The young pods have been cooked and eaten as a vegetable, however, animals have been poisoned by feeding on the leaves and stems. The milkweeds should all be considered as dangerous plants.

INDIAN PINK: See PINKROOT.

INDIAN PLANT: See GOLDENSEAL and YARROW.

INDIAN POKE: See FALSE HELLEBORE and POKE.

INDIAN POSEY: See EVERLASTING.

INDIAN RED PAINT: See YARROW.

INDIAN ROOT: See SPIKENARD.

INDIAN SAGE: See THOROUGHWORT.

INDIAN SENNA: See CASSIA.

INDIAN SHAMROCK: See TRILLIUM.

INDIAN SORREL: See ROSELLA.

INDIAN SPIKENARD: See SPIKENARD.

INDIAN TOBACCO: See LOBELIA.

INDIAN TURMERIC: See GOLDENSEAL.

INDIAN TURNIP (*Arisaema triphyllum*) [*Araceae*]

Bog-onion; Dragonroot; Jack-in-the-pulpit; Wakerobin; Wild turnip:

This is a very toxic plant. The Pawnee applied the powdered root to the head to cure headache, and it is said the Hopis drank it in water to produce temporary sterilization, which often turned out to be permanent. Consider it only as an ornamental plant.

INDIAN VALERIAN: SEE VALERIAN.

INDIAN WALNUT: See CANDLENUT.

INDIAN WORMWOOD: See MUGWORT.

INDIAN-CUP: See PITCHER PLANT.

INDIAN-PIPE (*Monotropa uniflora*) [*Pyrolaceae*]

Birdnest; Convulsion root; Corpse plant; Fairy smoke; Fit plant; Fitsroot; Ghost flower; Pine-sap; Pipe plant:

This is a fleshy, saprophytic plant without chlorophyll, native to North America, Japan, and the Himalayas. The four to ten inch high waxy stem is topped by a single white, pipe-bowl-shaped flower which will turn black when bruised. Extracts of the root were used in herbal remedies for the treatment of spasms, fainting spells, and various nervous conditions. It does have some antispasmodic and sedative properties.

INDIAN-SPICE: See SAGE TREE.

INDIGO BROOM: See WILD INDIGO.

INDONESIAN CASSIA: See CINNAMON.

INKBERRY: See APPALACHIAN TEA and POKE.

INULA: See ELECAMPANE.

INUZANSHO: See ANISE-PEPPER.

IRIS *(Iris versicolor)* *[Iridaceae]*
   Blue flag; Flag lily; Fleur-de-lis; Flower-de-luce; Liver lily; Poison flag; Snake lily; Water flag; Wild iris:
   There are 200 or more species of *Iris* and none belongs in the kitchen or in herbal remedies. Iris roots contain substances that are not only cathartic and emetic but can also cause liver and kidney damage. Also see ORRIS.

IRISH BROOM: See BROOM.

IRISH MOSS: See CARRAGEEN.

IRISH SHAMROCK: See SORREL.

IRISH WALNUT KETCHUP: See WALNUT KETCHUP and KETCHUP.

IRONBARK: See EUCALYPTUS.

IRONWEED *(Vernonia* spp.) *[Compositae]*
   There are between 500 and 1000 species of *Vernonia,* all known as ironweed. The roots have been used in herbal remedies as a "bitter tonic."

ITALIAN BURNET: See BURNET.

ITALIAN LOVAGE: See LOVAGE.

ITALIAN OREGANO: See MARJORAM.

ITALIAN PARSLEY: See PARSLEY.

ITALIAN PIMPERNEL: See BURNET.

ITALIAN STONE PINE: See PINE NUTS.

ITCHWEED: See FALSE HELLEBORE.

IVA: See YARROW.

IVRY-LEAVES: See WINTERGREEN.

IVY: See ENGLISH IVY and MOUNTAIN LAUREL.

IVYBUSH: See MOUNTAIN LAUREL.

J

Jack-by-the-hedge: See **Alliaria.**

Jack-in-the-pulpit: See **Indian turnip.**

Jack-go-to-bed-at-noon: See **Goatsbeard.**

Jacob's ladder: See **Greek valerian** and **Sarsaparilla.**

Jalap (*Ipomoea jalapa*) [*Convolvulaceae*]
Extracts of the root of jalap have been used by the medical profession for many years and it is contained in the *National Formulary*. Proper dosage will produce a very rapid and thorough emptying of the bowel with very little intestinal irritation. Needless to say, improper dosage could be very dangerous. It is named for Xalapa, Mexico, where it grows.
Wild jalap can refer to several different plants. See **Wild jalap** and **Mayapple.**

Jamaica canella: See **Canella.**

Jamaican dogwood (*Piscidia piscipula*) [*Leguminosae*]
Fish fuddle; Fish-poison tree; West Indian dogwood:
This tree, which will grow up to fifty feet tall, is native to southern Florida and the West Indies and is sometimes grown as an ornamental. The leaves and tender young branches are the source of a poison used to stupefy fish so they are more easily caught. It has been used in some herbal remedies as a sedative and a pain killer.

Jamaica mignonette: See **Henna.**

Jamaica nutmeg: See **Custard apple** and **Nutmeg.**

161

JAMAICA PEPPER: See ALLSPICE.

JAMAICA SORREL: See ROSELLA.

JAMAICAN GINGER: See GINGER.

JAMAICAN WILD LICORICE: See LICORICE.

JAMESTOWN WEED: See JIMSONWEED.

JAMMU LEMONGRASS: See LEMONGRASS.

JAPANESE ANGELICA: See ANGELICA and ANGELICA TREE.

JAPANESE ANISE TREE: See STAR ANISE.

JAPANESE ARTICHOKE: See ARTICHOKE.

JAPANESE BEAD TREE: See CHINABERRY.

JAPANESE FIR NEEDLE OIL: See PINE FIR.

JAPANESE HOPS: See HOPS.

JAPANESE HORSERADISH: See LADY'S-SMOCK.

JAPANESE MINT: See CORN MINT.

JAPANESE PARSLEY: See CHERVIL.

JAPANESE PEPPER: See ANISE-PEPPER.

JAPANESE PINE NEEDLE OIL: See PINE FIR.

JAPANESE STAR ANISE: See STAR ANISE.

JAPANESE THYME: See THYME.

JAPANESE TREE MUSHROOMS: See DRIED MUSHROOMS.

JAPANESE VALERIAN: See VALERIAN.

JAPANESE WILD CHERVIL: See CHERVIL.

JASMINE:

Jasmine may refer to any of four totally unrelated groups of plants.

(1) *Jasminum auriculatum* [*Oleaceae*]

Indian jasmine

Jasminum grandiflorum

Catalonian jasmine; Royal jasmine; Spanish jasmine

Jasminum sambac

Arabian jasmine; sambac

The fragrant flowers of these plants belonging to the olive family are used in teas. GRAS

(2) *Gelsemium sempervirens* [*Loganiaceae*]

Carolina jasmine; Carolina jessamine; Evening trumpet flower; Gelsemin; Gelsemine; Wild jessamine; Woodbine; Yellow jasmine; Yellow jessamine:

This is a poisonous plant. It contains a very powerful sedative and can cause respiratory failure. This family also includes the East Indian tree, *Strychnos nux-vomica*, well known for its seeds, which contain extremely large quantities of strychnine.

(3) *Gardenia jasminoides* [*Rubiaceae*]

Cape jasmine:

This plant is cultivated for its fragrant, wax-like, white flowers. Coffee, cinchona, and ipecac also belong to this plant family.

(4) *Plumeria ruba* [*Apocynaceae*]

Frangipani flower; Nosegay; Red jasmine:

Marquis Muzeo Frangipani was a 17th century Italian nobleman who owned a perfumery and was also well known as a gourmet cook. Using flowers from the red jasmine and other ingredients, he invented a perfume widely known as "Frangipani Perfume." He also is said to have invented a dessert which also bears his name, frangipani, a sweetened, thickened cream containing almonds or macaroons, served plain as a pudding or as filling in a cake or pastry.

JAUNDICE BERRY: See **BARBERRY**.

JAUNDICE ROOT: See **GOLDENSEAL**.

JAVA CASSIA: See **CINNAMON**.

JAVA CITRONELLA: See **LEMONGRASS**.

JAVA PEPPER: See CUBEB.

JAVA PLUM: See ROSE APPLE.

JEQUIRITY: See LICORICE.

JERUSALEM ARTICHOKE: See ARTICHOKE.

JERUSALEM COWSLIP: See LUNGMOSS.

JERUSALEM OAK: See EPAZOTE.

JERUSALEM SAGE (*Phlomis fruticosa*) [*Labiatae*]

This plant is often used as an adulterant of common sage, *Salvia officinalis* [*Labiatae*]. Jerusalem sage can also refer to *Pulmonaria officinale* [*Boraginaceae*]. See LUNGMOSS.

JESUITS' BARK: See QUININE.

JESUITS' TEA: See EPAZOTE.

JEW'S-HARP PLANT: See TRILLIUM.

JEW'S MYRTLE: See BUTCHER'S BROOM.

JIMSONWEED (*Datura stramonium*) [*Solanaceae*]

Common thorn apple; Devil's apple; Devil's trumpet; Jamestown weed; Mad-apple; Nightshade; Peru-apple; Stinkweed; Stinkwort; Stramonium; Thorn apple:

Jimsonweed has been cultivated in the past as a source of hyoscyamine, an atropine and scopolamine related alkaloid, for medical usage. It is an extremely toxic plant and ingestion, especially of seeds and leaves, may be fatal. All *Datura* plants are toxic.

JOE-PYE WEED (*Eupatorium purpureum*) [*Compositae*]

Gravelroot; Gravel weed; Green-stemmed Joe-Pye weed; Kidney root; Purple boneset; Queen-of-the-meadow; Sweet Joe-Pye weed; Trumpet weed:

A New England Indian medicine man, named Joe Pye, is said to have cured typhus with this plant. It has diuretic properties. Some American Indian tribes used extracts of the roots as an aphrodisiac.

JOHN-GO-TO-BED-AT-NOON: See GOATSBEARD.

JOHNSWORT: See SAINT JOHN'S-WORT.

JOHNNY JUMPER: See PANSY.

JOHNNY-JUMP-UP: See PANSY.

JOINT FIR: See EPHEDRA.

JOSEPH SAGE: See SAGE.

JOSEPH'S-COAT: See AMARANTH.

JOSHUA TREE: See YUCCA.

JOU-KUEI:
This is a Chinese term for cinnamon. See CINNAMON.

JUJUBE: See LOTUS.

JUNIPER (*Juniperus communis*) [*Pinaceae*]
Juniper berry:
The dark blue berries of an evergreen shrub, which grows in the northern hemisphere, are dried when fully ripened. They are used to flavor gin, game, and other meats. In Germany they are used in sauerkraut. The berries should be cooked with the food. The berries vary considerably in strength, and it is said that the best berries, those with the largest amount of essential oils, grow on Italian hillsides. GRAS

JUNIPER RESIN: SEE SANDARAC.

JUNO'S TEARS: See VERVAIN.

JUPITER'S BEAN: See HENBANE.

JUPITER'S BEARD: See HOUSELEEK.

JUPITER'S EYE: See HOUSELEEK.

K

KALONJI: See **NIGELLA.**

KANGAROO ISLAND NARROW-LEAVED MALLEE: See **EUCALYPTUS.**

KANSAS NIGGERHEAD: See **PURPLE CONEFLOWER.**

KAT: See **ABYSSINIAN TEA.**

KAVA-KAVA: See **PEPPER.**

KELP: See **BLADDERWRACK.**

KENCUR: See **GALANGAL.**

KENTJUR: See **GALANGAL.**

KEORA, ATTAR or ATAR OF: See **KEWRA.**

KERNELWORT: See **FIGWORT.**

KESSO: See **VALERIAN.**

KETCHUP:
    Ketchup (catchup or catsup) does not always mean a thick, red, spicy tomato sauce. The word ketchup most likely came from a number of related Far Eastern words (ketsiap, kitjap, etc.) that meant the brine in which fish have been pickled. Today ketchup means almost any salty extract of fish, fruit, vegetable or mushroom. For specific types of ketchup see **LEMON CATSUP, MUSHROOM KETCHUP, WALNUT KETCHUP, OYSTER KETCHUP, MUSSEL KETCHUP, WINDERMERE KETCHUP, POULAC KETCHUP,** and **WOLFRAM KETCHUP.**

KEWDA, ATTAR OF: See KEWRA.

KEWRA (*Pandanus fascicularis,* formerly *odoratissimus*) [*Pandanaceae*]
   Atar of keora; Attar of kewda; Nicobar breadfruit; Padang; Pandang; Screw pine; Umbrella tree
   (*Pandanus tectorus*)
   Pandanus palm; Thatch screw pine:
      An essential oil derived from the male flowers is used in syrups, cordials, or scented waters that are used, often along with rose water, to flavor Indian sweet dishes. The oil is obtained by macerating the flowers with sesame oil, other flower oils or sometimes sandalwood oil. The leaves are much used as thatch and are woven into baskets and mats. It is not even distantly related to the breadfruit tree, *Artocarpus altilis* [*Moraceae*], whose starchy fruit is cooked like a vegetable.

KEYFLOWER: See COWSLIP.

KHAIR: See CATECHU.

KHAS-KHAS: See VETIVER.

KHAT: See ABYSSINIAN TEA.

KHUS-KHUS: See VETIVER and POPPY SEEDS.

KIDNEY ROOT: See JOE-PYE WEED.

KIDNEY VETCH (*Anthyllis vulneraria*) [*Leguminosae*]
   Ladies' fingers; Lamb's toes; Staunchwort; Woundwort:
      Flowers of this plant have been used as an ingredient in herbal remedies, but it is best known as a forage plant that will grow on poor soils in eastern Europe and western Asia.

KING'S CLOVER: See SWEET CLOVER.

KING'S CUP: See BUTTERCUP.

KING'S CURE: See PIPSISSEWA.

KING'S CUREALL: See EVENING PRIMROSE.

KING'S FERN: See HERB CHRISTOPHER.

KING-SOLOMON'S-SEAL: See **SOLOMON'S-SEAL.**

KINGCUP: See **MARIGOLD.**

KINNIKINICK:

Kinnikinick can refer to the dried bark or leaves of the sumac smoked by the American Indians, to the dried bark of *Cornus amomum* [*Cornaceae*] (known as silky dogwood, cornel and red willow) also smoked by the Indians, or to *Arctostaphylos uva-ursi* [*Ericaceae*]. See **UVA-URSI.**

KITCHEN-GARDEN PURSLANE: See **PURSLANE.**

KLAMATH WEED: See **SAINT JOHN'S-WORT.**

KNAPWEED (*Centaurea nigra*) [*Compositae*]

Black knapweed; Bullweed; Hardheads; Knobweed; Spanish-buttons:

Knapweed, which appears in lists of bitters, actually can refer to any plant belonging to the genus *Centaurea*. This would include the cornflower, which is not usually used in this manner. See **CORNFLOWER.**

KNEE HOLLY: See **BUTCHER'S BROOM.**

KNESHENKA: See **BRAMBLES.**

KNIGHT'S SPUR: See **LARKSPUR.**

KNITBACK: See **COMFREY.**

KNITBONE: See **COMFREY.**

KNOB GRASS: See **CITRONELLA.**

KNOB ROOT: See **CITRONELLA.**

KNOBWEED: See **KNAPWEED.**

KNOTROOT: See **ARTICHOKE.**

KNOTTED MARJORAM: See **MARJORAM.**

KNOTTY BRAKE: See **WOOD FERN.**

KNOTTY-ROOTED FIGWORT: See **FIGWORT.**

KNOTWEED (*Polygonum aviculare*) [*Polygonaceae*]
Beggarweed; Bird knotgrass; Birdweed; Cow grass; Crawlgrass; Doorweed; Fleece flower; Ninety-knot; Pigweed; Smartweed
(*Polygonum bistorta*)
Bistort; Dragonwort; Easter giant; Patience dock; Poor-man's cabbage; Red leg; Snakeroot; Snakeweed; Sweet dock
(*Polygonum hydropiper*)
Smartweed; Water pepper
(*Polygonum multiflorum*)
Fo-ti; Ho shou wu
(*Polygonum persicaria*)
Doorweed; Heartease; Heartweed; Lady's thumb; Pinkweed; Red leg; Spotted knotweed
(*Polygonum punctatum*)
Water smartweed:
There are about 150 species of *Polygonum* all called knotweed, smartweed, or fleece flower. Probably all have been used in herbal remedies of some sort. Generally, the plant juices can be quite irritating to the skin and mucous membranes and can be hazardous when used as an herbal remedy.

Polygonum bistorta has been called patience dock and sweet dock. It should not be eaten like the *Rumex* species. See SORREL.

The tuberous roots of *Polygonum multiflorum* are used in a number of Chinese herbal remedies.

KOKUM (*Garcinia indica*) [*Guttiferae*]
The kokum tree bears a purplish, plum-like fruit. When the skin is stripped from the fruit, flattened and dried, it turns a dark black-brown. It is this sour-tasting skin that is used, like tamarind, as a souring agent in Indian cooking.

KOLA: See COLA.

KOREAN GINSENG: See GINSENG.

KOREAN MINT: See ANISE HYSSOP.

KORINTJE CASSIA: See CINNAMON.

KORITSA:
This is the Russian word for cinnamon. See CINNAMON.

KORMA MIXED SPICE:

Korma is an Indian braised meat dish using yogurt, cream or stock as the liquid. It is milder than a curry. The basic spice mixture can be made as follows.

2 teaspoons ground almonds or 4 teaspoons dried coconut
1 $^1/_2$ teaspoons ground cardamom
$^1/_2$ to $^3/_4$ teaspoon ground dried chili
$^1/_2$ teaspoon ground cinnamon
$^1/_2$ teaspoon ground cloves
3 to 4 garlic cloves, chopped
$^3/_4$ teaspoon ground ginger or 2 $^1/_2$-inch piece fresh ginger, finely chopped
1 $^1/_4$ teaspoons ground turmeric
1 to 2 teaspoons ground coriander

KOSHER SALT: See **SALT.**

KOUSSO (*Brayera anthelminica*, formerly *Hagenia abyssinica*) [*Rosaceae*]

Cusso:

This is a northeastern Ethiopian tree. Preparations made from the flowers have been used to eliminate tapeworms. They will also cause nausea and vomiting.

KRAMERIA: See **RHATANY.**

L

LA KAMA:

La kama is a spice mixture used to season and flavor Moroccan soups and stews. It can be made as follows.

1 ¹/₂ teaspoons ground cinnamon
4 teaspoons ground ginger
¹/₃ teaspoon ground nutmeg
3 ¹/₂ teaspoons ground black pepper
4 ¹/₃ teaspoons ground turmeric

LABDANUM (*Cistus incanus* subspecies *creticus*, formerly *Cistus creticus*) [*Cistaceae*]

Cretan rockrose; Ladanum:

Labdanum is the resin-like secretion of the glandular hairs on the undersurface of the leaves. It is collected in the spring and summer. The leaves are placed in boiling water and the resin is skimmed off. In the past plants were flogged with a special multi-thonged leather whip. The leather would become impregnated with the resin, which was then shaved off with a special knife. The resin has a sweet, herbaceous, balsamic odor reminiscent of ambergris. It is used in perfumery and in flavoring formulations for confections. Medically, it is "little used as medicine in civilized countries." (Dorland) GRAS

LABRADOR TEA (*Ledum groenlandicum*) [*Ericaceae*]

This plant, closely related to wild rosemary, is a native of northern North America and Greenland. A tea is made from the leaves.

LAD'S LOVE: See **SOUTHERNWOOD**.

LADANUM: See **LABDANUM**.

LADIES' FINGERS: See KIDNEY VETCH.

LADIES' GLOVE: See FOXGLOVE.

LADIES' TOBACCO: See EVERLASTING.

LADY BLEEDING: See AMARANTH.

LADY'S BEDSTRAW: See BEDSTRAW.

LADY'S NIGHTCAP: See WILD MORNING-GLORY.

LADY'S THUMB: See KNOTWEED.

LADY'S-MANTLE (*Alchemilla vulgaris*) [*Rosaceae*]
Bear's-foot; Lion's-foot
(*Alchemilla arvensis*, formerly *Aphanes arvensis*)
Field lady's-mantle
(*Alchemilla microcarpa*)
Parsley piert:
The *Alchemilla* species are all known as lady's-mantle. Extracts of leaves and roots are highly astringent and were used in the past to control external bleeding and excessive menstrual flow. Parsley piert was used for kidney problems.

LADY'S-SLIPPER: See NERVEROOT.

LADY'S-SMOCK (*Cardamine pratensis*) [*Cruciferae*]
Bitter cress; Cardamine; Cuckooflower; Mayflower; Meadow cress
(*Cardamine amara*)
Bitter cress; Large bitter cress
(*Cardamine pennsylvanica*)
Bitter cress
(*Cardamine yezoensis*)
Japanese horseradish; Wasabi (Japanese):
These are common wild plants which grow in moist meadow areas. In some areas of Europe and Japan they are used early in the spring as a salad plant.

LADY-SLIPPER: See NERVEROOT.

LADYSMOCK: See ARUM. Do not confuse with Lady's-smock. See LADY'S-SMOCK.

LALO: See BAOBAB.

LAMB MINT: See MINT.

LAMB'S QUARTER: See TRILLIUM and LAMB'S-QUARTERS.

LAMB'S TOES: See KIDNEY VETCH.

LAMB'S TONGUE: See ADDER'S-TONGUE.

LAMB'S-EARS (Stachys byzantina) [Labiatae]
   Woolly betony:
      Besides being used as a woundwort in the past, the leaves of this plant have been used to make a mild tea. The fresh leaves have a mild, aromatic taste, whereas upon drying, they take on an apple-like flavor. Because its velvety-soft, thick leaves were used to cover wounds during the American Revolution, some like to call it the "Colonial Band-Aid."

LAMB'S-QUARTERS (Chenopodium album) [Chenopodiaceae]
   Pigweed; White goosefoot:
      The leaves of this plant are sometimes eaten as greens. Also see TRILLIUM.

LAMBKILL: See MOUNTAIN LAUREL.

LAMPWICK PLANT (Phlomis lychnitis) [Labiatae]
      This plant has been used as an adulterant in common sage, Salvia officinalis [Labiatae]. It is called lampwick plant because its leaves were said to have been used as lampwicks. It is an evergreen native to Southern Europe.

LANCE-LEAF PLANTAIN: See PLANTAIN.

LAOS: See GALANGAL.

LAPPA: See BURDOCK.

LARCH (Larix decidua, formerly europaea) [Pinaceae]
   European larch; Venice turpentine
   (Larix laricina)

American larch; Black larch; Hackamatack; Tamarack:

Extracts of the bark, young shoots, and needles of the European larch have been used in various herbal remedies. Venice turpentine, made from the sap of the European larch, has also been used, especially in Europe, in numerous external and internal remedies. It is extremely dangerous. It can cause kidney damage and skin blisters.

American larch is another tree known as hackamatack (See **POPLAR**), an Algonquian Indian word which refers to a natural bend in the larch tree used in boat building for the stem or framing of a boat.

LARGE BITTER CRESS: See LADY'S-SMOCK.

LARGE BUTTON SNAKEROOT: See BLAZING-STAR.

LARGE-FLOWERED EVERLASTING: See EVERLASTING.

LARK HEEL: See LARKSPUR.

LARK'S CLAW: See LARKSPUR.

LARKSPUR (*Consolida regalis*, formerly *Delphinium consolida*) [*Ranunculaceae*]
Branching larkspur; Knight's spur; Lark heel; Lark's claw; Staggerweed; Stavesacre:

There is considerable confusion between the *Consolida* and *Delphinium* genera, and many species of *Consolida* were formerly placed in the *Delphinium* genus. Both genera should be considered as toxic plants, and although *Consolida regalis* has been used in herbal remedies because of its purgative properties, it should be treated as a toxic plant. Use should be restricted to the flower garden.

LASERWORT: See ASAFOETIDA.

LATE CORALROOT: See CORALROOT.

LATTICELEAF: See RATTLESNAKE PLANTAIN.

LAUREL: See BAY LEAF and MOUNTAIN LAUREL.

LAVENDER (*Lavandula augustifolia*, formerly *officinalis* or *vera*) [*Labiatae*]
English lavender; True lavender
(*Lavandula stoechas*)
French lavender; Spanish lavender:

The aromatic leaves and flower spikes of this plant, belonging to the mint family, are used mostly in perfumery. An oil from the flowers of the true lavender is used occasionally in flavoring formulations for confections, and it has been used in medicine as an antispasmodic. The oil from *Lavandula latifolia* is used in paints. *Lavandula spica*, sometimes called spikenard, is an ambiguous name and may be a variety of *Lavandula augustifolia* or a subspecies of *Lavandula stoechas*. It is the source of spike oil, a not quite as fragrant substitute for the true lavender oil. The oils from some lavenders are not as aromatic as others. Good quality oils end up being called true lavender oil, while less aromatic oils are called spike oil. English lavender is *Lavandula augustifolia*. This plant is grown in France and sold in the United States as French lavender. Legend claims that lavender added to bath water soothes nervousness, relieves rheumatism and gout, and cures head pains. GRAS

LAVENDER COTTON: See SANTOLINA.

LAVOSE: See LOVAGE.

LAWANG: See CASSIA.

LAWN CAMOMILE: See CAMOMILE.

LEAF MUSTARD: See MUSTARD.

LEATHER FLOWER: See VIRGIN'S BOWER.

LEMON BALM: See BALM.

LEMON BERRY (*Rhus integrifolia*) [*Anacardiaceae*]
Lemonade berry; Lemonade sourberry; Sourberry:
  The following is the only reference found in cook books for using lemon berries. I have no information as to their safety. "Lemon berries are the red berries of a shrub often found on hillsides and growing among the sand dunes of southern California. They excrete an acid substance which when soaked in plain or charged water, makes an excellent beverage, as a substitute for lemonade, and for flavoring desserts, hot, cold, and frozen." L. P. De Gouy, *The Gold Cook Book*, p. 1003.

LEMON CATSUP:
  12 large lemons, grated rind and juice
  4 tablespoons white mustard seed
  1 tablespoon turmeric
  1 tablespoon white pepper
  1 teaspoon each cloves and mace

2 tablespoons sugar
2 tablespoons fresh grated horseradish
1 shallot, minced fine
2 tablespoons salt
dash cayenne

Mix ingredients together and let stand in a cool place 3 hours. Heat to boiling and cook 30 minutes. Pour into a crock, cover closely and let stand 2 weeks, stirring well every day. Strain, fill sterile bottles and seal. Makes about 4 pints.

LEMON THYME: See THYME.

LEMON VERBENA (*Aloysia triphylla*, formerly *Lippia citriodora*) [*Verbenaceae*]
   Herb Louisa; Verbena oil:
   The leaves of this common garden and house plant have a strong lemon scent. The leaves have been used fresh or dried as a tea. Oils derived from the plant are used in perfumery. In the United States use as a flavoring is restricted to alcoholic beverage flavoring formulations only.

LEMON WALNUT: See WALNUT.

LEMON-SCENTED BASIL: See BASIL.

LEMON-SCENTED GERANIUM: See GERANIUM.

LEMONADE BERRY: See LEMON BERRY.

LEMONADE SOURBERRY: See LEMON BERRY.

LEMONGRASS (*Cymbopogon citratus*) [*Gramineae*]
   Fever grass; Serah powder; West Indian lemongrass
   (*Cymbopogon nardus*)
   Citronella grass; False spikenard; Nard grass; Oil grass
   (*Cymbopogon flexuosus*)
   East Indian lemongrass
   (*Cymbopogon martinii* var. *martinii*)
   East Indian geranium; Motia; Palmarosa
   (*Cymbopogon martinii* var. *sofia*)
   Gingergrass; Sofia
   (*Cymbopogon pendulus*)

Jammu lemongrass

(Cymbopogon winterianus)

Java citronella:

Lemongrass includes several species of grasses, all containing citric oils which give them a lemony flavor. They are used extensively in Southeast Asian curries and spiced dishes and are useful in flavoring salads, fish dishes and soups. The fresh leaves are chopped, while the dried can be tied in a knot and removed after cooking like a bay leaf. The dried grass is available in powdered form, known as serah powder. This is very strong and should be used sparingly.

Citronella is the aromatic oil from *Cymbopogon nardus*. It is used in perfumery and in liniments. The burning of candles containing citronella oil is supposed to repel mosquitoes. The species *nardus* is also known as false spikenard. East Indian geranium or palmarosa is *Cymbopogon martinii* var. *martinii*. Its oil has a sweet rose-like odor and is used similarly to the geranium oils. Also see CITRONELLA. GRAS

LENKUAS: See GALANGAL.

LEPTANDRA: See CULVER'S-PHYSIC.

LESSER CELANDINE *(Ranunculus ficaria)* *[Ranunculaceae]*

Pilewort; Small celandine:

Lesser celandine has been called pilewort because of the appearance of its tuberous roots and was thought, because of this appearance, to be effective for the treatment of hemorrhoids. It is not and should be treated as a toxic plant like most of the *Ranunculus* species. It should not be confused with celandine, *Chelidonium majus* *[Papaveraceae]*. See CELANDINE.

LESSER CENTAURY: See MINOR CENTAURY.

LESSER GALANGAL: See GALANGAL.

LESSER PERIWINKLE: See PERIWINKLE.

LEVANT GARLIC: See GARLIC.

LEVANT STORAX: See STORAX.

LEVANT WORMSEED: See WORMSEED.

LIBERTY TEA: See NEW JERSEY TEA.

LICORICE (*Glycyrrhiza glabra*) [*Leguminosae*]

Chinese sweet root; Spanish juice; Sweetroot; Sweetwood

(*Abrus precatorius*) [Leguminosae]

Coral-bead plant; Crab's-eye; Indian licorice; Jamaica wild licorice; Jequirity; Licorice vine; Love pea; Prayer-beads; Red-bean vine; Rosary pea; Weather plant; Weather vine; Wild licorice

(*Galium lanceolatum* or *circaezans*) [*Rubiaceae*]

Wild licorice:

Licorice is the ground or sliced root of a small perennial plant, *Glycyrrhiza glabra*, grown in southern Europe and the Middle East. It has a bitter-sweet taste and is used in candies and drinks. Extracts of the roots are called Spanish juice.

Wild licorice, Indian licorice, licorice vine, and Jamaican wild licorice are all the same plant, *Abrus precatorius* [*Leguminosae*]. This plant is known by many different names. Its roots yield a licorice-like substance, but it should not be used as a flavoring. The plant has an extremely toxic seed— a single seed if chewed and swallowed can be fatal. The seeds, glossy red with a black base, were often made into necklaces and sold as costume jewelry, especially during the 1920s. This use of the seed has been banned in the United States.

Galium lanceolatum or *circaezans* [*Rubiaceae*] has also been called wild licorice. This plant is closely related to the bedstraws and to woodruff.

LICORICE VINE: See LICORICE.

LIFE EVERLASTING: See EVERLASTING.

LIFE-OF-MAN: See SPIKENARD.

LIGNUM VITAE: See GUAIAC.

LILY OF THE VALLEY (*Convallaria majalis*) [*Liliaceae*]

May bells; May lily:

The well-known, fragrant lily of the valley has been used in herbal remedies. Since it contains glycosides which act similarly to digitalis, it can produce irregular heart rhythms and should be considered a dangerous plant.

LIMA SARSAPARILLA: See SARSAPARILLA.

LIME FLOWERS: See LINDEN FLOWERS.

LIME TREE: See LINDEN FLOWERS.

LINALOE (*Bursera aloexylon, fagaroides, glabrifolia*, and *penicillata*) [*Burseraceae*]
(*Bursera simaruba*)

Elequeme; Gumbo limbo; Incense tree; Tacamahaca; West Indian birch; West Indian elemi:

Extracts of these woods have a rose-like odor. They are used in soaps and in flavoring formulations. It should not be confused with bois de rose. The gum of *Bursera simaruba* is known as elequeme and tacamahaca in Costa Rica. All of the species are GRAS.

LINALOE CAYENNE BOIS DE ROSE: See BOIS DE ROSE.

LINDEN: See LINDEN FLOWERS.

LINDEN FLOWERS (*Tilia* spp.) [*Tiliaceae*]

Lime flowers

(*Tilia X europaea*)

European lime tree; European linden

(*Tilia americana*)

American linden tree; Basswood; Bast tree; Lime tree; Spoonwood; Whitewood; Wycopy:

In Europe the linden tree is commonly called a lime tree and should not be confused with the citrus fruit. Extracts of the flowers of the European linden tree were attributed with powers to relieve catarrh and headaches. They were also used to prepare "sedative baths" for "irritable conditions." Linden or tilia flowers are often an ingredient in commercial herbal teas. The American linden, or basswood, makes a beautiful shade tree. A tea can be made from its flowers also. Linden flowers are GRAS, however, the use of the leaves is restricted to alcoholic beverage flavoring formulations.

LING: See HEATHER.

LINK: See BROOM.

LINGBERRY; LINGENBERRY; LINGONBERRY: See BLUEBERRY.

LINSEED; LINSEED OIL: See FLAX.

LINT BALLS: See FLAX.

LION'S MOUTH: See FOXGLOVE.

LION'S TOOTH: See DANDELION.

LION'S-BEARD: See PASQUE FLOWER.

LION'S-EAR (*Leonotis leonurus*) [*Labiatae*]

Lion's-ear is grown now primarily as an ornamental border. Formerly, it was used as a remedy for leprosy, epilepsy, heart failure, snakebite, and numerous other disorders. Also see LION'S-TAIL which is also known as lion's-ear.

LION'S-FOOT:

Lion's-foot can refer to *Alchemilla vulgaris* [*Labiatae*] (See LADY'S-MANTLE), to *Leontopodium alpinum* [*Compositae*], the well-known edelweiss of the European Alps, or to Prenanthes alba and serpentaria [*Compositae*], commonly called canker root, cankerweed, rattlesnake root, white cankerweed, and white lettuce, an old folk remedy for cankersores, snakebite, and diarrhea.

LION'S-TAIL (*Leonurus cardiaca*) [*Labiatae*]

Lion's-ear; Motherwort; Roman motherwort; Throw-wort:

Lion's-tail is closely related to lion's-ear and the names are often confused. The bitter extracts were an old herbal remedy for everything from heart problems to snakebite. It can be rather toxic and can cause a contact allergic dermatitis.

LIPSTICK TREE: See ANNOTTO.

LIQUID STORAX: See STORAX.

LIQUIDAMBER: See STORAX.

LITTLE APPLE: See CAMOMILE.

LITTLE HOLLY: See BUTCHER'S BROOM.

LITTLE POLLOM: See MILKWORT.

LIVE-FOREVER: See HOUSELEEK.

LIVER LILY: See IRIS.

LIVERWORT: See HERB TRINITY.

LOBELIA (*Lobelia inflata*) [*Lobeliaceae*]

Bladderpod; Emetic herb; Emetic weed; Gagroot; Indian tobacco; Vomitroot; Vomitwort; Wild tobacco:

Lobelia contains several very toxic alkaloids. Although used in olden medicine for the treatment of many disorders including whooping cough, it is included here only because it is in many herb lists. It should be considered a poisonous plant and kept out of the kitchen. It can be fatal.

LOCO WEED: See TRAGACANTH.

LOCUST BEAN: See CAROB.

LOGANBERRY: See BRAMBLES.

LOGWOOD: See CAMPEACHY WOOD.

LOMBARDY POPLAR: See POPLAR.

LONDON ROCKET: See ROCKET.

LONG BUCHU: See BUCHU.

LONG PEPPER: See CAPSICUM and PEPPER.

LONG PURPLES: See LOOSESTRIFE.

LONG-LEAVED BOX: See EUCALYPTUS.

LONGLEAF PINE and LONGLEAF YELLOW PINE: See PINE OIL.

LOOSESTRIFE (*Lythrum salicaria*) [*Lythraceae*]

Long purples; Milk willow-herb; Purple loosestrife; Purple willow-herb; Rainbow weed; Soldiers; Spiked loosestrife; Spiked willow-herb; Willow sage:

This plant, usually cultivated as an ornamental, has been used in herbal remedies to combat diarrhea. It has astringent properties.

LOTUS:

Lotus may refer to several quite different plants. It may refer to any of several tropical water lilies of the genus *Nymphaea* [*Nymphaeaceae*], especially the blue African lotus (*Nymphaea caerulea*), a similar species from India, or the white lotus of Egypt (*Nymphaea lotus*). East Indian lotus or Indian lotus is *Nymphaea stellata*. The tuberous roots of these are eaten as a vegetable.

Chinese cooking uses water lily leaves, both fresh and dried, to season and flavor foods.

The North American water lilies *Nymphaea odorata* and *Nymphaea tuberosa*, especially the latter, should not be used as a substitute for the tropical species above. *Nymphaea tuberosa*, also known as magnolia water lily and tuberous water lily, is a poisonous plant. The roots of *Nymphaea odorata*, known as cow cabbage, fragrant water lily, pond lily, Saint Joseph's lily, sweet-scented pond lily, sweet-scented water lily, white pond lily, and white water lily, have been used because of their astringent properties in herbal remedies.

European lotus is a species of lotus tree, *Diospyrus lotus* [*Ebenaceae*], which bears a fruit resembling a plum, called the date plum. The *Diospyrus* genus is the persimmon trees. Lotusberry is the edible fruit of the West Indian tree, *Byrsonima coriacea* [*Malpighiaceae*]. The jujube, the edible, date-like fruit of trees of the genus *Zizyphus* [*Rhamnaceae*], has also been called lotus. Lotus may also refer to plants of the genus *Melilotus*. See SWEET CLOVER.

LOTUSBERRY: See LOTUS.

LOUSEWORT:

A lousewort is any plant of the genus *Pedicularis* belonging to the *Scrophulariaceae* family. Formerly these plants were reputed to cause sheep feeding upon them to be subject to infestation with vermin. See also FEVERWEED.

LOVAGE (*Levisticum officinale*) [*Umbelliferae*]
European lovage; Garden lovage; Italian lovage; Lavose; Love parsley; Sea parsley; Wild parsley
(*Ligusticum mutellina*) [*Umbelliferae*]
Alpine lovage
(*Ligusticum scoticum*)
Northern lovage; Scotch lovage; Sea lovage:

Levisticum officinale is a large celery-like plant that contains an essential oil which gives it its strong aromatic flavor. It was grown in the family herb garden primarily for its use as a domestic remedy, but the entire plant can be used: stems and root can be cooked in the manner of celery or candied as for angelica; leaves, roots and seeds are used in salads, soups, and sauces, and seeds can be used in baking. The roots are often an ingredient in herbal teas. *Levisticum officinale* is GRAS. The other species are not listed.

LOVE APPLE: See MAYAPPLE.

LOVE PARSLEY: See LOVAGE.

LOVE PEA: See LICORICE.

LOVE-IN-A-MIST: See NIGELLA.

LOVE-LIES-BLEEDING: See AMARANTH.

LOVE-MAN: See BEDSTRAW.

LOVELY BLEEDING: See AMARANTH.

LOW BALM: See BERGAMOT.

LOW CUDWEED: See EVERLASTING.

LOW MALLOW: See MALLOW.

LOW SPEEDWELL: See VERONICA.

LUCERNE: See ALFALFA.

LUNGMOSS (*Pulmonaria officinalis*) [*Boraginaceae*]
    Beggar's basket; Blue lungwort; Jerusalem cowslip; Jerusalem sage; Lungwort; Maple lungwort; Spotted comfrey; Spotted lungwort
    (*Sticta pulmonacea*) [Lichen group]:
        Extracts of *Pulmonaria officinalis* are used to flavor vermouth, and in Siberia *Pulmonaria officinalis* is used as a substitute for hops. Extracts of *Sticta pulmonacea*, a lichen, are listed by the FDA as GRAS. There is no listing for *Pulmonaria officinalis*. *Pulmonaria officinalis* has been used in herbal remedies.

LUNGWORT: See LUNGMOSS and COWSLIP.

LUPULIN: See HOPS.

LURK-IN-THE-DITCH: See PENNYROYAL.

LUSTWORT: See SUNDEW.

LYCOPOD: See HERB-IVY.

LYRE-LEAVED SAGE: See SAGE.

M

MA HUANG: See EPHEDRA.

MACASSAR MACE: See MACE.

MACE (*Myristica fragrans*) [*Myristicaceae*]
Banda mace; Penang mace
(*Myristica argentica*)
Macassar mace; Papua mace
(*Myristica malabarica*)
Bombay mace; Wild mace:
Mace is the thread-like tendrils (ruminated arils) that are on the surface of the nutmeg, the fruit of *Myristica fragrans*. These arils are similar to those on the surface of a cling peach seed. It is quite expensive, but this is understandable when one realizes that only about a quarter of an ounce of mace is obtained per pound of nutmeg. The arils are pressed flat and dried and sold as "blades" or they are ground. The blades are best when thin and brittle with a reddish-yellow color. Mace is more pungent than nutmeg, and only the smallest pinch is needed to enhance the flavor of a dish. It is rarely used as a flavoring. Ground mace quickly loses its pungency. Inexpensive mace is either old and has lost its pungency, or it has been adulterated. At one time mace was considered to be quite inferior to nutmeg, probably because it was quite old and stale, an inferior adulterated product, or it was used in an excessive quantity and was overpowering. Mace obtained from *Myristica argentica* (from New Guinea) and *malabarica* (from India) is of inferior quality to that from *Myristica fragrans*. *Myristica fragrans* is GRAS.

MAD-APPLE: See JIMSONWEED.

MAD-DOG-WEED: See SKULLCAP.

MADAGASCAR CINNAMON: See CINNAMON.

MADAGASCAR PERIWINKLE: See PERIWINKLE.

MADDER (*Rubia tinctorum*) [*Rubiaceae*]
Madder is a plant native to southern Europe and Asia Minor. It was once cultivated for the yellowish-red root dye, alizarin, used for dying fabrics. Alizarin is now prepared synthetically from anthracene, a product of coal tar distillation. Alizarin is $C_8H_4(CO)_2C_6H_2(OH)_2$.
Madder root has also been used in a number of herbal remedies, purported to be useful in urinary tract problems, problems, rickets, broken bones, lack of appetite, diarrhea, and hectic fever.

MADEIRA NUT: See WALNUT.

MADNEP: See MASTERWORT.

MAGNOLIA (*Magnolia virginiana*, formerly *glauca*) [*Magnoliaeeae*]
Beaver tree; Holly bay; Indian bark; Red bay; Red laurel; Swamp laurel; Swamp sassafras; Sweet bay; Sweet magnolia; White bay:
This is not the southern magnolia. Southern magnolia is *Magnolia grandiflora*. *Magnolia virginiana* is deciduous in the north and evergreen in the south. The bark has been used in numerous herbal remedies. It should not be confused with the bay leaf, sweet bay, *Laurus nobilis*. See BAY LEAF.

MAGNOLIA VINE: See SARSAPARILLA.

MAGNOLIA WATER LILY: See LOTUS.

MAGUEY: See AGAVE.

MAHALEB (*Prunus mahaleb*) [*Rosaceae*]
Mahleb; Mahlepi; Perfumed cherry; Saint Lucie cherry:
This is a small ornamental cherry tree, native to Europe and western Asia, whose blackish fruit is used to make a fermented liquor similar to kirsch. The small seed kernels are sold in specialty spice stores as "mahaleb" or "mahleb." They are used in Indian cookery, and freshly ground, in Middle Eastern and Greek breads. As a substitute, some cookbooks recommend using a little ground fennel, however the flavor is not exactly the same. The FDA has no listing for mahaleb. The FDA permits the use of cherry pits in flavorings only if the prussic acid content is less than twenty-five parts per million.

MAHLEPI: See MAHALEB.

MAHOGANY BIRCH: See SWEET BIRCH.

MAID'S HAIR: See BEDSTRAW.

MAIDENHAIR FERN (*Adiantum capillus-veneris*) [*Polypodiaceae*]

Dudder grass; Southern maidenhair; Venus's-hair-fern:

There are over 200 species of *Adiantum*, all known as maidenhair ferns. The above species is the only one mentioned by the FDA. In the United States extracts of the fronds are permitted to be used only in flavoring formulations for alcoholic beverages. These extracts are sometimes used in hair lotions. Application of the fronds to the chest was supposed to help lung disorders.

MAIDENHAIR TREE: See GINKGO NUT.

MALABAR CARDAMOM: See CARDAMOM.

MALABAR PLUM: See ROSE APPLE.

MALACCO CHEESE: See BALACHONG.

MALDEN SALT: See SALT.

MALE FERN: See WOOD FERN.

MALEGUETA PEPPER: See MELEGUETA PEPPER.

MALKA: See BRAMBLES.

MALLEE: See EUCALYPTUS.

MALLOW (*Malva sylvestris*) [*Malvaceae*]

Cheese flower; Cheese plant; Cheeses; Country mallow; High mallow

(*Malva rotundifolia*)

Blue mallow; Cheese plant; Cheeses; Dwarf mallow; Low mallow:

The leaves of the mallow have been boiled and eaten as a vegetable or brewed in a tea. Shoots, seed pods (known as cheeses), and flowers have been chopped and added to salads. The plant juices are sticky and mucilaginous with astringent properties. Mallow is an ingredient in a number of both external and internal herbal remedies.

MALT (*Hordeum vulgare*) [*Gramineae*]
Barley:

Malt is grain, for the most part barley, which has been soaked, allowed to germinate and then killed by heat and dried. The higher the temperature to which it is heated, the darker the malt. The darkest is known as black malt.

MALT EXTRACT:

Dried malt contains an enzyme, diastase, which converts the carbohydrate of malt to dextrin and maltose. When powdered malt is soaked in water, heated, and then partially evaporated, it produces a sweet, gummy substance. It is used in brewing and distilling, where it is called a "wort," in the manufacture of breakfast cereals, as a coffee substitute, and in baking. If the liquid malt is filtered and completely evaporated to a solid, it is known as malt extract.

MALT VINEGAR: See VINEGAR.

MALTED MILK:

In 1869, William Horlick, an immigrant from England, while working on invalid and infant diets, developed a method of combining powdered malt and dehydrated milk into a soluble powder. This was marketed in 1887 as *Horlick's Malted Milk Powder*, from whence has come the famous drugstore soda fountain item—the "chocolate malt."

MAN ROOT: See WILD JALAP.

MAN-IN-THE-EARTH: See WILD JALAP.

MAN-OF-THE-EARTH: See WILD JALAP.

MAN-IN-THE-GROUND: See WILD JALAP.

MANDRAKE: See MAYAPPLE.

MANGO (*Mangifera indica*) [*Anacardiaceae*]
Amchur:

The unripe mango fruit is sliced and dried in the sun. Known as amchur, it is used as a souring agent in curries and other Southeast Asian dishes. It has a sweet-sour taste with a slightly resinous bouquet. It can be purchased in sliced or powdered form. Double or triple quantities of lemon or lime juice may be used as a substitute, but it does not have the slightly resinous bouquet. The ripe mango is used to make sherbets, jams, and ice creams. It is also available dried in slabs. It is sweet. Dried mango seeds are used in some Eastern dishes. The flowers are eaten in Siam, and in Java the tender leaves are eaten. Mango may also refer to pickled cucumber or muskmelon.

MANGOSTEEN (*Garcinia mangostana*) [*Guttiferae*]

This is considered to be one of the most delicious tropical fruits and is rarely seen outside of the areas where it is grown. It is closely related to the fruit used to make kokum (See **KOKUM**) and should not be confused with the mango.

MANZANILLA: See **CAMOMILE**.

MANZANITA (*Arctostaphylos manzanita*) [*Ericaceae*]

There are about fifty species of *Arctostaphylos* which are all known as manzanita. Most of these are native to the Pacific coastal region of the United States. The berries, the flavor, and dryness of which vary from species to species were used by the Indians for making vinegar and an alcoholic drink. They were used as a flavoring in cooked dishes and breads. The above species is used sometimes for making jelly.

MAPLE: See **MOUNTAIN MAPLE**, **RED MAPLE** and **SUGAR MAPLE**.

MAPLE LUNGWORT: See **LUNGMOSS**.

MAPLELENE:

Maplelene refers to an artificial maple flavoring. Artificial maple flavorings usually contain a blend of fenugreek, vanilla extract, coffee, and other natural or synthetic ingredients.

MARASCHINO; MARASCHINO CHERRIES:

Maraschino is a liqueur made from the crushed fruit (including pits) and leaves of the marasco cherry, a small, black, tart cherry grown in Dalmatia, Yugoslavia. The crushed fruit, pits, and leaves are fermented with honey, distilled, and then mixed with a sugar syrup. The cherry pits give a bitter flavor to the liqueur in contrast to kirsch which is made from only the juice of a different variety of black cherry. Maraschino syrup is used to flavor drinks and confections. Maraschino cherries are usually made from a bleached sweet cherry which is then preserved in maraschino syrup. Most of those sold in grocery stores in the United States are preserved in an imitation maraschino syrup.

MARCORY: See **QUEEN'S DELIGHT**.

MARE'S TAIL: See ERIGERON and SHAVE GRASS.

MARGUERITE: See HERB MARGARET.

MARIGOLD:

Marigold may refer to any one of a number of different plants that have only one thing in common—golden-yellow flowers.

Calendula officinalis [*Compositae*], pot marigold, poet's marigold, holigold, Mary bud, bull's eyes, or calendula is an annual plant native to southern Europe and Asia. It was believed to be a stimulant, as a poultice, to help in the healing of wounds and to be effective in resolving tumors. The petals of the flowers are used today, either fresh or dried, as an herb and a food dye. They are used to color and flavor rice, meat, and fish dishes or in soups and salads. The petals are sold dried. GRAS

Chamaemelum nobile, formerly *Anthemis nobilis* [*Compositae*], common camomile or Roman camomile, and *Chamomilla recutita*, formerly *Matricaria recutita* [*Compositae*], German camomile, are both referred to as marigolds. GRAS

Tagetes erecta [*Compositae*], known as African marigold, Aztec marigold, and big marigold, *Tagetes lucida*, known as sweet-scented marigold, sweet mace, sweet marigold, cloud plant, hierba de las nubes, Mexican marigold mint, Mexican tarragon, mint marigold, Texas tarragon, and winter tarragon, and *Tagetes patula*, French marigold, are some of the most well-known marigolds grown in the United States. The FDA has specific restrictions pertaining to the use and the preparation of the oil extracts of the petals of *Tagetes erecta*. This oil is permitted to be added to chicken feed to enhance the yellow color of chicken skin and eggs. The oil is also permitted to be used in conjunction with other flavoring substances. Use is restricted to the oil extracts only. Oils from the *Tagetes* plants are also used in perfumery. In England *Tagetes lucida* is known as winter tarragon and is used as tarragon. It smells like tarragon and has a strong anise flavor.

The marsh marigold, or American cowslip, is *Caltha palustris* [*Ranunculaceae*]. It is also known as king cup, may-blob, meadow bouts, meadow-bright, palsywort, and water dragon. This plant contains protoanemonin, an extremely irritating substance which will cause blistering of the skin. It is considered a poisonous plant. The plant referred to below in L. P. De Gouy's (*The Gold Cook Book*, p. 1005) description of "marigold" is the marsh marigold, but the uses seem to be confused. The use of the word "marigold" should be reserved for the flower garden.

> Marigold—sometimes known as "American cowslip," it has more than 25 different aliases. The leaves and stems are boiled and served in the same manner as spinach, and many people say that it is the equal of and even superior to spinach. In some parts of the country, the tender flower buds are picked and used as a substitute for capers. The flowers are also used

as a food coloring.

MARJORAM:

The area of marjoram and oregano can lead to mass confusion when attempting to determine what herb to use in recipes having their origin in other countries. Of the aromatic-leaved plants of the genus *Origanum* [*Labiatae*], there are, or have been, primarily four species used to flavor food. These are *Origanum vulgare, Origanum majorana, Origanum onites,* and *Origanum dictamnus* in technical Latin, but what they are called in any other language is almost anyone's guess. It is generally accepted in English-speaking countries that what is referred to as sweet marjoram or knotted marjoram is *Origanum majorana.* This is also the *origane* of French recipes and the *orégano dolce* of Italian recipes. *Origanum vulgare* is beyond doubt the marjoram, pot marjoram, and wild marjoram of English recipes, and the *origane des champs* of French recipes. *Origanum vulgare* has also been called mountain mint, winter marjoram and wintersweet. This leaves the *orégano* of Spanish, Italian, Greek, Mexican, and other Latin American cooking. Italians call it a Greek herb *(Origanum dictamnus* is native to Crete), and the Spanish refer to *orégano d'Italia* (where *Origanum onites* grows wild). *Origanum dictamnus* is also called dittany of Crete and Spanish hops. In the United States the situation becomes almost hopeless since much that is sold as oregano is really a Mexican herb, *Lippia graveolens* [*Verbenaceae*], which has a similar flavor to members of the genus *Origanum.* It is also called Mexican sage. All the marjorams have a flavor that is in between thyme and sage. So . . . take your choice. Legend claims that if marjoram is applied externally, it will heal sprains and bruises. All of the above plants are GRAS.

Origanum vulgare is now divided into six subspecies. They are (with common names):

subsp. *vulgare*: wild marjoram; oregano
subsp. *glandulosum*: oregano
subsp. *gracile*: Russian oregano
subsp. *hirtum*: Greek or Italian oregano
subsp. *virens*: wild marjoram
subsp. *viride*: wild marjoram; orégano

The following is a listing of other plants which are or have been called "oregano" in either English or another language. It is not complete. Some of these may be regarded as safe to use; others may not. Why use a plant that may be unsafe when safe ones are readily available?

Coleus amboinicus [*Labiatae*]
   Cuban oregano, orégano brujo, orégano de Cartagena, orégano de
   España, orégano Frances (See COLEUS)
Eryngium foetidum [*Umbelliferae*]
   orégano de Cartagena

Hedeoma floribundum [*Labiatae*]
Hedeoma patens [*Labiatae*]
Hyptis albida [*Labiatae*]
Hyptis americana [*Labiatae*]
Hyptis capitata [*Labiatae*]
Lantana achyranthifolia [*Verbenaceae*]
Lantana glandulosissima [*Verbenaceae*]
  orégano silvestre; orégano xiu
Lantana hispida [*Verbenaceae*]
  oréganillo del monte
Lantana involucrata [*Verbenaceae*]
Lantana microcephala [*Verbenaceae*]
  orégano xiu
Lantana trifolia [*Verbenaceae*]
Lantana velutina [*Verbenaceae*]
  orégano xiu
Limnophila stolonifera [*Scrophulariaceae*]
Lippia affinis [*Verbenaceae*]
  orégano montes
Lippia formosa [*Verbenaceae*]
Lippia fragrans [*Verbenaceae*]
Lippia micromeria [*Verbenaceae*]
  orégano del pais
Lippia origanoides [*Verbenaceae*]
  orégano del pais
Lippia palmeri [*Verbenaceae*]
Lippia umbellata [*Verbenaceae*]
  orégano montes
Monarda citriodora var. *austromontana* [*Labiatae*]
Origanum syriacum var. *syriacum* [*Labiatae*]
Origanum x *applii* [*Labiatae*]
  orégano; orégano comum; orégano del pais
Origanum x *majoricum* [*Labiatae*]
Plectranthus spp. [*Labiatae*]
  Cuban oregano; prostrate coleus; spur flower; Swedish begonia;
  Swedish ivy; "Vick's" plant
Poliomintha longiflora var. *longiflora* [*Labiatae*]
Thymus capitatus [*Labiatae*]
  Spanish origanum
Thymus mastichina [*Labiatae*]
  Spanish marjoram

Markry: See **Sumac**.

MARMITE:

This is a proprietary yeast paste produced by evaporating yeast cells that have undergone autolysis. (Marmite is also a French name for a large cooking pot, and petite marmite is a clear broth type of soup.)

MARSH BLAZING-STAR: See BLAZING-STAR.

MARSH CISTUS: See WILD ROSEMARY.

MARSH CLOVER: See BUCKBEAN.

MARSH CROWFOOT: See BUTTERCUP.

MARSH CUDWEED: See EVERLASTING.

MARSH MALLOW: See ALTHEA.

MARSH MARIGOLD: See MARIGOLD.

MARSH TREFOIL: See BUCKBEAN.

MARY BUD: See MARIGOLD.

MARYLAND DITTANY: See DITTANY, COMMON.

MARYTHISTLE: See MILK THISTLE.

MASTER OF THE WORLD: See WOODRUFF.

MASTERWORT (*Heracleum sphondylium* subspecies *montanum*, formerly *Heracleum lanatum*) [*Umbelliferae*]

American cow parsnip; Cow cabbage; Cow parsnip; Hogweed; Madnep; Wooly parsnip; Youthwort:

Planted in gardens for bold effects and sometimes as specimen plants, the foliage of masterwort causes an allergic dermatitis in some individuals. It has been used in herbal remedies but should be regarded as a toxic plant. It is said that cattle have died after eating the foliage.

Angelica and imperatoria have both been called masterwort. See ANGELICA and IMPERATORIA.

MASTIC THYME: See THYME.

MASTIC TREE (*Pistacia lentiscus*) [*Anacardiaceae*]

Chios mastic tree:

Mastic is the resinous exudate of *Pistacia lentiscus* which is native to the Greek island of Chios. People of the eastern Mediterranean countries chew it and also use it to flavor bread, pastries and liqueurs. In the United States it is used in microscopy and dentistry.

MATÉ (*Ilex paraguayensis*) [*Aquifoliaceae*]

Paraguayan holly; Paraguayan tea; Yerba maté; Saint Bartholomew's tea:

The dried leaves of this holly are made into a tea which is both diuretic and diaphoretic. Some cook books go into great detail as to the exact methods, steeping times, water temperature, etc., for brewing this tea. GRAS

MATICO (*Piper angustifolium*) [*Piperaceae*]

The dried leaves of this Peruvian shrub have been used medically in the past for their stimulating and hemostatic properties. Peruvians use it as an aphrodisiac. Matico is also an alternative spelling for mataco, a South American three-banded armadillo.

MATSUTAKE MUSHROOMS: See DRIED MUSHROOMS.

MAUDLINWORT: See HERB MARGARET.

MAY BELLS: See LILY OF THE VALLEY.

MAY BUSH: See HAWTHORN BERRIES.

MAY LILY: See LILY OF THE VALLEY.

MAY TREE: See HAWTHORN BERRIES.

MAY-BLOB: See MARIGOLD.

MAY-THEN: See CAMOMILE.

MAYAPPLE (*Podophyllum pelatum*) [*Berberidaceae*]

American mandrake; Duck's foot; Ground lemon; Hog apple; Indian apple; Mandrake; Raccoon berry; Wild lemon; Wild jalap; Wild mandrake:

The fruit of the mayapple is small, lemon-shaped and yellow with a sweet, slightly acid flavor reminiscent of a strawberry. The fruit is edible, but the rest of the plant can be fatally toxic. Some of the refined chemical constituents of the plant have been found useful in medicine, however, others have been shown to be too toxic.

Mayapple has also been called mandrake. The true mandrake, however, is *Mandragora officinarum* [*Solanaceae*], native to the Mediterranean and Himalayan regions. This is another plant attributed with almost magical medical properties. Also known as love apple, Oriental mandrake, and satan's apple, it has properties similar to belladonna and should be treated as a dangerously toxic plant.

MAYBLOSSOM: See HAWTHORN BERRIES.

MAYFLOWER: See LADY'S-SMOCK.

MAYPOP: See PASSIONFLOWER.

MAYR SAKHALIN FIR: See PINE FIR.

MEADOW ANEMONE: See PASQUE FLOWER.

MEADOW BOUTS: See MARIGOLD.

MEADOW CABBAGE: See SKUNK CABBAGE.

MEADOW CRESS: See LADY'S-SMOCK.

MEADOW CROWFOOT: See BUTTERCUP.

MEADOW FERN: See BOG MYRTLE and SWEET FERN.

MEADOW PARSNIP: See ALEXANDERS.

MEADOW QUEEN: See HERB CHRISTOPHER.

MEADOW SAFFRON: See SAFFRON.

MEADOW SALSIFY: See GOATSBEARD.

MEADOW SORREL: See SORREL.

MEADOW-BRIGHT: See MARIGOLD.

MEADOW-WORT: See HERB CHRISTOPHER.

MEADOWBLOOM: See BUTTERCUP.

MEADOWSWEET: See HERB CHRISTOPHER.

MEADSWEET: See HERB CHRISTOPHER.

MEALBERRY: See UVA-URSI.

MEALY STARWORT: See STAR GRASS.

MEDICINAL ALOE: See ALOE.

MEI YEN:

This is a proprietary seasoning mixture with the "Spice Islands" label marketed by Specialty Brands, Inc., San Francisco, California. It contains primarily salt, sugar and monosodium glutamate.

MELEGUETA PEPPER (*Elettaria meleguetta*) [*Zingiberaceae*]

MALEGUETA PEPPER: See CARDAMOM.

This should not be confused with Guinea pepper, which is really Ashanti pepper, the dried berry of an African vine (*Piper clusii*) [*Piperaceae*] with the taste of black pepper. Nor should it be confused with *malagueta*, the Spanish name for the Tabasco pepper, *Capsicum frutescens*. See CAPSICUM.

MELILOT: See SWEET CLOVER.

MELISSA: See BALM.

MELIST: See SWEET CLOVER.

MELON TREE: See PAPAYA.

MENTHOL:

Menthol is a chemical derivative of oil of peppermint or the oils of other mints. GRAS

MERCURY (*Mercurialis annua*) [*Euphorbiaceae*]

Mercury herb

(*Mercurialis perennis*)

Dog's cole; Dog's mercury; Perennial mercury:

These plants are native European plants that have become naturalized to some extent in the eastern United States. They are poisonous plants. The poison is thought to be cumulative in the body. In the past extracts of these plants were used to treat scrofula. See also **Good-King-Henry** and **Sumac**.

Mercury herb: See **Mercury**.

Mescal bean: See **Peyote**.

Mescal button: See **Peyote**.

Methi: See **Fenugreek**.

Mexican bush sage: See **Sage**.

Mexican giant hyssop: See **Anise hyssop**.

Mexican marigold mint: See **Marigold**.

Mexican oregano: See **Marjoram**.

Mexican sage: See **Marjoram**.

Mexican sarsaparilla: See **Sarsaparilla**.

Mexican tea: See **Epazote**.

Mexican vanilla: See **Vanilla**.

Mexico seed: See **Castor oil plant**.

Mezereum; Mezeron: See **Daphne**.

Mignonette; Mignonnette: See **Pepper** and **Henna**.

Mignonette pepper: See **Pepper**.

Mignonette tree: See **Henna**.

Milfoil: See **Yarrow**.

Milk ipecac: See **Dogbane** and **Trillium**.

Milk thistle (*Silybum marianum,* formerly *Carduus marianus*) [*Compositae*]
    Holy thistle; Marythistle; Saint Mary's thistle:

This is a weed, native to the Mediterranean region and naturalized in the United States, that has been used in herbal remedies as a bitter tonic.

Milk vetch: See Tragacanth.

Milk willow-herb: See Loosestrife.

Milkweed (*Asclepias syriaca*) [*Asclepiadaceae*]

Cottonweed; Silkweed; Silky swallow-wort; Swallow-wort; Virginia silk:

This common North American weed has very strong emetic and purgative properties and should be treated as a very dangerous, even poisonous, plant. Dogbane has also been called milkweed. See Dogbane and Indian paintbrush.

Milkwort (*Polygala amara*) [*Polygalaceae*]

Bitter milkwort; Dwarf milkwort; **European bitter polygala; European senega snakeroot; Evergreen snakeroot; Flowering wintergreen; Fringed polygala; Little pollom**

(*Polygala senega*)

Seneca snakeroot

(*Polygala vulgaris*)

European milkwort; European seneka; Gang flower; Rogation flower; Senega snakeroot:

Polygala amara and *Polygala vulgaris* are European plants. *Polygala senega* is the species which grows in eastern North America. The roots of all three species have been used in herbal remedies. Milkwort is supposed to increase the milk supply of nursing mothers.

Mimosa (*Acacia decurrens*) [*Leguminosae*]

Australian mimosa; Black wattle

(*Acacia dealbata*)

Mimosa:

Extracts of the flowers of these Australian trees are used mostly in perfumery, however, at times they are used in flavoring formulations. *Acacia decurrens* is GRAS. *Acacia dealbata* is not listed.

Miniature pansy: See Pansy.

Minor centaury (*Centaurium erythraea*, formerly *Centaurium umbellatum* and *Erythraea centaurium*) [*Gentianaceae*]

Bitterherb; Centaury; Centaury gentian; European centaury; Lesser centaury:

Extracts of the bitter flavored flowering tops are permitted to be used in alcoholic beverage flavorings only. It should not be confused with the genus *Centaurea* of the *Compositae* family which includes the cornflower or bluebottle, nor with American centaury (*Sabbatia angularis*) [*Gentianaceae*], commonly called the rose pink. (See GENTIAN.)

MINT (*Mentha* spp.) [*Labiatae*]

The mints are not quite as bad as the marjorams, but there has been considerable natural cross-breeding producing a large number of varieties. Although there are about 600 named species, these are probably variants of a basic 25 species. Peppermint (*Mentha piperita*) has been said to be the common ancestor, however according to *Hortus Third*, *Mentha piperita* is a cross between *Mentha aquatica* and *Mentha spicata*. *Mentha officinalis* is supposed to be the mint used in juleps and in mint sauces, however technically there is no *officinalis* mint species. Julep mint is probably whatever grows in New Orleans and other southern backyards.

Some of the other mints are: spearmint (*Mentha spicata*); applemint (*Mentha suaveolens*); round-leaved mint (*Mentha rotundifolia*, a cross between *Mentha suaveolens* and *Mentha longifolia*); Bowles mint (*Mentha villosa alopecuroides*); Eau de Cologne mint or orange mint (*Mentha citrata*, a variant of *Mentha piperita*); horsemint (*Mentha longifolia*, formerly *sylvestre*); bergamot or water mint (*Mentha aquatica*) used in perfumery. *Mentha crispa* is a variant of *Mentha aquatica*. *Mentha crispa* is known as curled mint, crisp-leaved mint, and cross mint.

Peppermint is also known as brandy mint and lamb mint. Spearmint is known as lamb mint, Our Lady's mint, and sage of Bethlehem.

Peppermint is used in liqueurs, cordials, candies, and beverages. Spearmint is the preferred mint for use with lamb, vegetables, fruit soups, potatoes, and for mint sauce. If you wish to grow mint in your own garden, it is best to start with root cuttings of a variety you like. It is impossible to tell what kind of mint a seed will produce and most tend to revert to an inferior version of peppermint. Legend claims that mint is useful for stomach disorders. If rubbed on the table, it stimulates appetites. Mint cures mouth and gum sores, whitens teeth, relieves chapped hands, and repels mice. The FDA lists *Mentha piperita* and *Mentha spicata* as GRAS. See also CORN MINT and PENNYROYAL.

MINT GERANIUM: See COSTMARY.

MINT MARIGOLD: See MARIGOLD.

MIRBANE:

Mirbane is nitrobenzene ($C_6H_5NO_2$). This is a poisonous substance. It has been described in cook books as "artificial essence of bitter almonds." It can be used in making dyes or perfumes. It should never be used in cooking.

MIRIN:

Mirin is a sweet rice vinegar. It can be found in some supermarkets or in Japanese markets, or add a little sugar to regular rice-wine vinegar.

MISO:

Miso is a fermented soybean paste. See SOY PASTE.

MISSEY-MOOSEY: See ROWAN.

MISSOURI SNAKEROOT: See PURPLE CONEFLOWER.

MISTLETOE (*Phoradendron serotinum*, formerly *flavescens*) [*Loranthaceae*]
American mistletoe; Birdlime; Golden bough
(*Viscum album*) [*Loranthaceae*]
All-heal; Birdlime; Devil's fuge; European mistletoe:

Both the American and European species of mistletoe are very toxic plants. They are evergreen shrubs, parasitic on other woody plants. From New Jersey to Florida, west to southern Illinois and Texas, it is common to see masses of mistletoe in the tops of various deciduous tree hosts. Extracts of the leaves of both plants have been used in herbal remedies, but these can dangerously increase blood pressure. Death, especially of children, can result from consumption of the berries.

Mistletoe is best for kissing under during the Yuletide season, but kissing under the birdlime seems to spoil the whole idea.

MIXED SEASONINGS:

It seems that there are almost as many herb and spice mixtures as there are cooks. An attempt has been made to identify some of the most common, but many are "secret." Proportions in similar mixtures vary according to the taste of the person compounding the mixture, so instead of using an already prepared mixture, you may prefer to make your own to suit your own taste. Many ready-prepared herb and spice mixtures are available on grocery store shelves. It is always prudent to read the ingredient list before purchasing. One often ends up paying an exorbitant price for something containing primarily salt or sugar. It is surprising, too, that even those who sell herbs and spices in specialty shops often have no idea what a mixture contains, let alone the proportions. Some mixtures are very good and difficult to duplicate. The chart on pages 204–205, taken from *The Mistress Cook* by Peter Gray, gives a clear outline of the proportions of the various herbs and spices that should be used for various mixtures. It can be used as a guide for determining relative proportions when using combinations of the individual items or for preparing your own mixtures. The parts are by weight and if grams are used as a unit, the total weight will not be far from an ounce. Other mixtures will be found under the specific name of the mixture.

There are many variations of mixtures as can be seen by comparing the following with the "chili powder" and the pastry spice mixtures on page 205.

Dry chili mixture
1 to 3 teaspoons ground
dried chilies
1 ¹/₂ to 2 teaspoons ground
coriander seeds
1 teaspoon ground
cumin seeds
¹/₂ teaspoon garlic powder,
or 5 garlic cloves
1 ¹/₂ to 2 teaspoons dried
crushed oregano
³/₄ t. ground cloves (optional)

Wet chili mixture or Salsa cruda
2 tablespoons skinned, seeded
and chopped tomatoes
1 to 2 tablespoons finely
chopped onion
2 teaspoons chopped seeded
fresh chili
Salt to taste
4 tablespoons water,
or 2 tablespoons olive oil plus
2 tablespoons wine vinegar
4 garlic cloves, peeled and crushed
(optional)

British sweet spice mixture
1 teaspoon ground allspice
³/₄ teaspoon ground cinnamon
1 teaspoon ground cloves
1 ¹/₄ teaspoons ground ginger
³/₄ t. grated or ground nutmeg
pinch of black pepper

Gingerbread spice mixture
4 teaspoons ginger
2 teaspoons cinnamon
1 teaspoon ground cloves
1 teaspoon grated nutmeg

MOCCASIN FLOWER: See **NERVEROOT.**

MOCHA:

Mocha may refer to either the choice variety of coffee grown in southern Yemen, a flavoring made from this coffee, or to a flavoring made from combining chocolate and coffee. Mocha (now known as Al Mukha) is a seaport in southern Yemen. Mocha may also refer to a fine glove leather made from Arabian goatskins.

MOCK PENNYROYAL: See **PENNYROYAL.**

Herb mixture for French type sauces

Bay leaf	20
Thyme	10
Tarragon	2
Mint	1

Herb mixture for Russian type sauces

Thyme	15
Rosemary	15
Dill	2
Sage	2

Herb mixture for savory omelettes

Parsley	15
Rosemary	5
Thyme	5
Sweet marjoram	5
Mint	2
Tarragon	1

Spice mixture for game stews

Black pepper	10
Juniper berries	5
Nutmeg	5
Mace	3
Paprika	3
Cloves	1
Cayenne pepper	1
Mustard	1
Ginger	1
Coriander	1

Herb mixture for Italian type sauces

Bay leaf	20
Thyme	12
Basil	4
Sage	2

Herb mixture for heavy stews

Bay leaf	10
Thyme	10
Sage	10
Wild marjoram	2

Herb mixture for fish stuffings

Parsley	10
Thyme	5
Sweet marjoram	5
Chervil	5
Mint	3
Basil	1

Spice mixture for beef stews

Black pepper	15
Nutmeg	5
Juniper berries	3
Mace	3
Cloves	2
Cinnamon	2
Paprika	1

Herb mixture for Spanish type sauces

Sage	10
Oregano	10
Thyme	15

Herb mixture for light stews

Bay leaf	15
Thyme	15
Rosemary	5
Sweet marjoram	1

Herb mixture for poultry stuffings

Thyme	10
Sweet marjoram	10
Wild marjoram	6
Sage	4
Basil	2

Spice mixture for veal and poultry stews

Black pepper	18
Cinnamon	5
Ginger	3
Cardamom	2
Cloves	2
Mace	2
Coriander	1
Saffron	1

Spice mixture for fish

Black pepper	20
Cinnamon	5
Cloves	2
Mace	2

Spice mixture for "chili powder"

Paprika	25
Cumin	8
Cayenne pepper	1

This mixture intended for use with fresh garlic

Spice mixture for French type sauces

Black pepper	10
Cinnamon	5
Nutmeg	5
Cloves	3
Mace	3
Coriander	2
Ginger	2
Cayenne pepper	1

Spice mixture for Italian type sauces

Black pepper	10
Coriander	4
Mace	4
Cardamom	3
Cayenne pepper	3
Cinnamon	2
Nutmeg	2
Cloves	2
Ginger	1

Spice mixture for Spanish type sauces

Black pepper	8
Cumin	5
Ginger	4
Coriander	3
Cardamom	3
Saffron	3
Mace	2
Cloves	2
Cinnamon	1

Spice mixture for spicy pastries, Latin type

Cinnamon	15
Cloves	10
Nutmeg	5
Caraway	2
Allspice	1

Spice mixture for spicy pastries, Scandinavian type

Cinnamon	10
Cardamom	5
Caraway	5
Allspice	5
Coriander	2

MOHAVE YUCCA: See YUCCA.

MOLE or MOLÉ:

Mole is a spicy hot sauce of Spanish or Mexican origin which is served over roast beef or pork. It has many variations and has become better known in the United States as barbecue sauce.

MOLE PLANT: See CAPER SPURGE.

MOLÉ POWDER:

Molé powder is a mixture of spices used to season molé. According to the label of the item found in a "spice store" it contained pepper, flour, sugar, peanuts, garlic, onion, pumpkin seed, chocolate, and monosodium glutamate.

MOLLE: See PEPPER TREE.

MONK'S BASIL: See BASIL.

MONK'S PEPPER TREE: See SAGE TREE.

MONK'S RHUBARB: See SORREL.

MONKEY FLOWERS: See NERVEROOT.

MONKEY-BREAD TREE: See BAOBAB.

MONKSHOOD (*Aconitum napellus*) [*Ranunculus*]

Aconite; Bear's-foot; Friar's-cap; Helmet flower; Mousebane; Soldier's-cap; Turk's-cap; Wolfsbane:

This plant and many others of the *Aconitum* genus are extremely poisonous. It was a source of poison for darts.

MONOSODIUM GLUTAMATE; MSG; GOURMET POWDER; TASTE POWDER; VE-TSIN:

Monosodium glutamate is a tasteless salt of glutamic acid. It is used to "enhance" other flavors. It produces undesirable side effects in a large number of individuals, and there is absolutely no reason for its use other than the economic one of being able to decrease the amount of seasoning needed to produce a desired taste.

MOONFLOWER: See BUCKBEAN.

Moonseed: See Sarsaparilla.

Moor grass: See Cinquefoil.

Moorberry: See Blueberry.

Moose elm: See Slippery elm.

Morels: See Dried mushrooms.

Mormon tea: See Ephedra.

Moroccan camomile: See Camomile.

Mortification root: See Althaea.

Moth herb: See Wild rosemary.

Mother's heart: See Shepherd's-purse.

Motherwort: See Lion's-tail.

Motia: See Lemongrass.

Mountain ash: See Rowan.

Mountain balm: See Bergamot and Yerba santa.

Mountain box: See Uva-ursi.

Mountain buchu: See Buchu.

Mountain cranberry: See Uva-ursi.

Mountain daisy: See Arnica.

Mountain everlasting: See Everlasting.

Mountain hemp: See Dogbane.

Mountain laurel (*Kalmia latifolia*) [*Ericaceae*]
American laurel; Calico bush; Lambkill; Laurel; Ivy; Ivybush;
Mountain ivy; Rose laurel; Sheep laurel; Spoonwood:

The beautiful mountain laurel is an extremely poisonous plant, especially the leaves, twigs, flowers, and pollen grains. It is not related at all to *Laurus nobilis* [*Lauraceae*], the bay leaf, and should never be used in cooking or any herbal remedies. American Indians brewed a suicide drink from the leaves, and children have been poisoned by sucking on the flowers. Rinzler, p. 186, says, "People may be poisoned by honey made from its flowers."

Why it is called ivy, I have no idea. It is a shrub.

MOUNTAIN LICORICE (*Trifolium alpinum*) [*Leguminosae*]

This is a species of clover found in Europe. Its roots taste like licorice.

MOUNTAIN MAHOGANY: See SWEET BIRCH.

MOUNTAIN MAPLE (*Acer spicatum*) [*Aceraceae*]

This is not the same tree as the sugar maple. Extracts of the bark of this maple are used in flavoring tobaccos and in the making of flavoring formulations for confections. GRAS

MOUNTAIN MINT: See BERGAMOT and MARJORAM.

MOUNTAIN PEPPER: See CAPERS.

MOUNTAIN PINE: See DWARF PINE.

MOUNTAIN RHUBARB: See SORREL.

MOUNTAIN SORREL: See SORREL.

MOUNTAIN SUMAC: See SUMAC.

MOUNTAIN SWEET: See NEW JERSEY TEA.

MOUNTAIN TEA: See WINTERGREEN.

MOUNTAIN TOBACCO: See ARNICA.

MOUSE BLOODWORT: See MOUSE EAR.

MOUSE EAR (*Hieracium pilosella*) [*Compositae*]

Felon herb; Hawkweed; Mouse bloodwort; Pilosella:

This plant, native to Europe and western Asia, has been naturalized in the United States. It has become a troublesome weed in the northeastern states and Oregon. It possesses astringent and diuretic properties and has been used in herbal remedies. Also see EVERLASTING.

MOUSEBANE: See MONKSHOOD.

MOUTH-SMART: See VERONICA.

MOUTHROOT: See GOLDTHREAD.

MOXA: See MUGWORT.

MSG: See MONOSODIUM GLUTAMATE.

MUGGA: See EUCALYPTUS.

MUGO PINE: See DWARF PINE.

MUGWORT (*Artemisia vulgaris*) [*Compositae*]

Felon herb; Indian wormwood; Moxa; Sailor's tobacco; Saint John's herb:
    In cookbooks and books listing ingredients there seems to be considerable confusion as to what is called mugwort. Botanically mugwort is *Artemisia vulgaris*, but it has also been described in the following ways: tansy, a plant also called worm herb because of its anthelmintic properties; an aromatic plant used for flavoring cakes; tansy, used in England for flavoring ale; and woodruff, used to flavor wine. See WOODRUFF and TANSY.
    In the United States, if any *Artemisia* plant is used as a flavoring, the finished product must be certified thujone-free.
    Moxa is actually *Artemisia moxa*, a species native to China and Japan. A soft, downy substance was prepared from dried young leaves and was burned on the skin to cauterize wounds or as a counter-irritant. In old medical terminology, moxa refers to any tuft of soft combustible material to be burned upon the skin. This process is called moxibustion.

MULLEIN (*Verbascum phlomoides* and *V. thapsiforme*) [*Scrophulariaceae*]
    Mullen
    (*Verbascum thapsus*)
    Flannel plant; Mullen; Velvet plant:
    Bitter infusions from the flowers are permitted by the FDA to be used in alcoholic beverage flavoring formulations only. They were also used in many old medical formulations.

Mushroom ketchup:

Mushroom ketchup is a ketchup based upon mushrooms. Montagné (p. 555) gives the following recipe.

Put in a salting jar layers of fresh sliced mushrooms (about ¹/₃ inch in depth) and sprinkle each layer with table salt, pepper and allspice. Leave the mushrooms in the salt for 5 or 6 days in a cool place. Press the mushrooms to extract all the juice. Boil the juice. Season with pepper, thyme, bay leaf, ginger, marjoram and a little tomato paste. Cool, filter and bottle.

Another more modern recipe is:

1 peck (8 quarts) mushrooms
1 cup water
2 cups vinegar
2 tablespoons salt
1 tablespoon cinnamon
¹/₂ teaspoon cloves
¹/₂ teaspoon mace
2 tablespoons mustard
¹/₄ teaspoon cayenne pepper

Pick over mushrooms, clean, peel, and slice. Discard any tough portions of stems. Cook mushrooms in the water until tender, stirring frequently. Press through a sieve and add vinegar, salt, and spices. Boil 30 minutes, pour into sterile jars and seal. Makes 12 cups (3 quarts).

Mushrooms:

The subject of edible mushrooms is a book unto itself. The only mushrooms dealt with in this book are truffles and dried mushrooms. See **Truffles** and **Dried mushrooms**.

Musk; Tonquin musk:

Musk is obtained from the adult male musk deer (*Moschus moschiferus*). The musk sacs are removed from under the abdominal skin and dried. The fresh content of the sac is an oily, clotted, reddish-brown substance the consistency of honey with a strong penetrating odor. Infusions and tinctures are made from the dried substance and are used in perfumery and as flavor modifiers. In olden medicine it was used as a sedative in cases of hysteria. GRAS

Musk mallow: See **Abelmosk**.

Musk yarrow: See **Yarrow**.

Muskseed: See **Abelmosk**.

MUSQUASH ROOT: See HEMLOCK (*Cicuta maculata*).

MUSSEL KETCHUP:
This is a poor man's version of oyster ketchup. It is based upon mussels and cider. See KETCHUP and OYSTER KETCHUP.

MUSTARD (*Brassica juncea*) [*Cruciferae*]
Brown mustard; Indian mustard; Russian mustard; Sarepta mustard
(*Brassica juncea* var. *crispifolium*)
Indian mustard; Leaf mustard; Mustard greens
(*Brassica nigra*)
Black mustard
(*Sinapis alba*, formerly *Brassica alba* or *hirta*)
White mustard:
The undisputed British 19th-century mustard king, Jeremiah Colman, is reputed to have said: "My fortune came not from the mustard people eat, but from the amount they leave on the side of their plate." The three plants that yield commercial mustard seed are: *Brassica nigra* (black mustard), *Sinapis alba* formerly *Brassica hirta* or *alba* (white mustard), and *Brassica juncea* (Sarepta or Russian or brown mustard—used almost exclusively in Russia and the Far East). *Brassica juncea*, var. *crispifolium* is cultivated for its leaves also. It is known as mustard greens, leaf mustard, and Indian mustard. [*Brassica alba* and *Sinapis alba* are the same plant, and although *alba* means white, this mustard is sometimes called yellow mustard.] Dry mustard is made by extracting the oils from the mustard seeds and then grinding them into a powder. The hot pungency developed when ground mustard is mixed with water is the result of the interaction of two chemicals found in the mustard seed, myrosin, and sinigrin (in black mustard), or myrosin and sinalbin (in white mustard). This interaction is inhibited by heat. A mustard paste made with boiling water and kept hot over boiling water for fifteen minutes will result in a mild condiment with only a mustard flavor. For this reason, dry mustard should always be mixed with cold water, and if used in cooked sauces, be added at the end of cooking. Vinegar also tends to interfere with this chemical action, making mustards thusly prepared less pungent. Generally, mustards can be categorized as follows:

American—purchased already prepared from a blend of *Brassica nigra* and *Sinapis alba* seeds; it is light-colored and mild.
Chinese—prepared from dry *Brassica juncea* mustard and water or flat beer; it is extremely hot.
English—made of *Brassica nigra* seeds alone or blended with *Sinapis alba* plus a quantity of wheat flour and sometimes a small amount

of turmeric. That made with *nigra* seeds alone, when freshly made, is quite hot.

French—can be divided into four types:

(1) Dijon—made from *Brassica nigra* without the seed husk, it is hotter than the Bordeaux mustard.

(2) Whole seed mustards (Meaux)—Dijon mustards containing whole and crushed seeds so that biting into the seed releases a quantity of the pungent oil.

(3) Bordeaux—contain the seed husk and are darker in color than the Dijon, are prepared with a variety of herbs, vinegar, and sugar, and are milder than the Dijon.

(4) Florida—made with wine from the Champagne region and is mild.

German—similar to but usually more pungent than Bordeaux mustard.

The whole mustard seeds, both black and white, are used in pickling spice mixtures. GRAS

MUSTARD GREENS: See MUSTARD.

MYRCIA OIL: See BAYBERRY.

MYRRH (*Commiphora molmol*) [*Burseraceae*]

Somalian myrrh

(*Commiphora madagascariensis*, formerly *abyssinica*)

Abyssinian myrrh; Arabian myrrh

(*Commiphora myrrha*)

Common myrrh; Hirabol myrrh

(*Commiphora erythraea*)

Bisabol myrrh; Opopanax:

Oils from the gum-resin exudate of these plants have a warm, balsamic, aromatic odor and a bitter, slightly pungent flavor. They are used in pharmacology, perfumery, and in flavoring formulations for beverages, candies, and soups. They have been used in the past to treat numerous illnesses from sore gums and decayed teeth to shortness of breath and amenorrhea. Sweet chervil has also been called myrrh. GRAS. See CHERVIL and OPOPANAX.

MYRTLE (*Myrtus communis*) [*Myrtaceae*]

Dwarf myrtle; German myrtle; Greek myrtle; Polish myrtle; Swedish myrtle:

Extracts from the bitter and astringent leaves of this European tree are permitted to be used in the United States in alcoholic beverages only. In some Mediterranean countries, small birds and pork, after cooking, were wrapped in myrtle leaves while waiting to be served. This gave the meat an aroma of myrtle. Application of the leaves to wounds was thought to aid in healing. This myrtle should not be confused with the wax myrtle. See **BAYBERRY**. The California sassafras and periwinkle are also called myrtle. See **SASSAFRAS** and **PERIWINKLE**.

MYRTLE FLAG: See **CALAMUS**.

MYRTLE PEPPER: See **ALLSPICE**.

MYRTLE SPURGE: See **CAPER SPURGE**.

MYSTERIA: See **SAFFRON**.

N

NAILWORT: See **WHITLOW GRASS.**

NAKED LADY: See **SAFFRON.**

NAM PLA:
This is a Cambodian fish sauce with a richer flavor than nguoc-nam, the Vietnamese fish sauce. See **NGUOC-NAM.** The two sauces can be used interchangeably.

NAGOONBERRY: See **BRAMBLES.**

NANNYBERRY: See **BLACK HAW.**

NARD: See **SPIKENARD.**

NARD GRASS: See **LEMONGRASS.**

NARINGIN:
Naringin is a crystalline carbohydrate (glycoside) found in grapefruit.
GRAS

NARROW DOCK: See **SORREL.**

NARROW-LEAVED LABRADOR TEA: See **WILD ROSEMARY.**

NARROW-LEAVED PEPPERMINT: See **EUCALYPTUS.**

NARROW-LEAVED PLANTAIN.

NASTURTIUM (*Tropaeolum majus*) [*Tropaeolaceae*, formerly *Oxalidaceae*]

Garden nasturtium; Indian cress; Tall nasturtium; Capucine (French):

All parts of the common garden nasturtium are edible. The fresh leaves and flowers have a peppery cress-like taste and can be used in salads. The buds and immature seeds may be preserved in brine, washed, and then pickled in vinegar to be used in the same manner as capers. The leaves may also be dried for use in soups or stews. Nasturtium is not listed by the FDA.

Natto: See Soy paste.

Navelwort: See Gutu cola.

Neapolitan parsley: See Parsley.

Nebraska fern: See Hemlock (*Conium maculatum*).

Necklaceweed: See Herb Christopher.

Neckweed: See Veronica.

Nepal nut pine: See Pine nuts.

Nepal pepper: See Capsicum.

Nepalese tejpat: See Cassia.

Neroli; Neroli oil; Neroli bigarade:

This is an essential oil derived from orange blossoms, *Citrus bigardia* [*Rutaceae*]. It was named after an Italian Princess Neroli. It is used in soft drinks, ice cream, candy and baked goods. GRAS

Nerveroot (*Cypripedium calceolus*) [*Orchidaceae*]

American valerian; Golden-slipper; Lady-slipper; Lady's-slipper; Moccasin flower; Noah's-ark; Slipper root; Umbilroot; Venus'-shoe; Whippoorwill-shoe; Yellow Indian-shoe; Yellow Lady's-slipper; Yellow moccasin flower; Yellows:

The roots of this well known wild flower have been used in herbal remedies. However, it can be quite dangerous since all parts of the fresh plant will cause hallucinations. John Lust incorrectly calls this plant bleeding heart and monkey flower. Bleeding heart is *Dicentra spectabilis* [*Fumariaceae*], a very toxic plant. (See Fumitory.) Monkey flowers belong to the *Mimulus* genus [*Scrophulariaceae*] and are greenhouse and florist plants.

NET-LEAF PLANTAIN: See RATTLESNAKE PLANTAIN.

NETTLE (*Urtica dioica*) [*Urticaceae*]
Stinging nettle:
The nettle is best known for its hairy leaves which release chemicals (histamine and others) when touched. These chemicals produce an urticarial skin reaction (hives). Upon cooking or drying, this chemical activity is lost, making nettles safe to use either as a cooked green or as a seasoning. Early spring shoots are the best for cooking. Dried leaves can be used to season salads, soups, or vegetables. They have a slightly salty flavor. In various forms, the leaves have been used in the past to treat a wide variety of ailments including inhalation of the smoke of burning leaves to treat asthma.

NETWORT: See RATTLESNAKE PLANTAIN.

NEW ENGLAND SWEET CICELY: See CHERVIL.

NEW JERSEY TEA (*Ceanothus americanus*) [*Rhamnaceae*]
Mountain sweet; Wild snowball:
A tea was made from the root-bark. It was used to treat chest problems and was said to help raise the patient's spirits when despondency set in during illness.

NGUOC-NAM; NUOC MAM:
This is a Vietnamese fish sauce. In general, it is made by fermenting small fish in brine for two or three months. The liquid is drained off and used as a sauce. It can vary considerably in flavor and quality. It may be poured over rice or served in a small dish into which other foods are dipped. Flavor of the sauce is adjusted with lemon juice, sugar, garlic, and red pepper according to individual tastes. In Vietnam a few drops are often added to infant feeding formulas.

NIAOULI: See CAJEPUT.

NICOBAR BREADFRUIT: See KEWRA.

NIGELLA (*Nigella sativa*, and various species) [*Ranunculaceae*]
Black caraway; Black cumin; Devil-in-the-bush; Fennel flower; Kalonji; Nutmeg flower; Roman coriander; Wild onion seed
(*Nigella damascena*)
Damascene nigella; Love-in-a-mist; Ragged lady; Saint Catherine's flower; Venus' hair; Wild fennel:

There are various species of *Nigella,* native to the eastern Mediterranean area, that have an aromatic, pungent seed which can be used instead of pepper. It is cultivated as a spice in Egypt. The seeds of Damascene nigella, sometimes known as Venus' hair because of its thread-like leaves, are sprinkled on breads and cakes. Damascene nigella is also known as St. Catherine's flower or ragged lady. Kalonji is the Indian name for nigella. Although called wild onion seed by some, it is totally unrelated to the true wild onion. It should not be confused with the black variety of cumin. GRAS

NIGHT WILLOW-HERB: See EVENING PRIMROSE.

NIGHTSHADE *(Solanum dulcamara)* [*Solanaceae*]

Bittersweet; Bittersweet herb; Bittersweet nightshade; Bittersweet stems; Bittersweet twigs; Blue nightshade; Deadly nightshade; Felonwood; Felonwort; Fever twig; Nightshade vine; Poisonous nightshade; Scarlet berry; Staff vine; Violet bloom; Woody; Woody nightshade

(Solanum nigra)

Black nightshade; Common nightshade; Deadly nightshade; Garden nightshade; Poisonberry:

There are about 1,700 species of *Solanum,* the most common of which is the ordinary white potato, *Solanum tuberosum.* Some of the species are edible, others are deadly.

All parts of *Solanum dulcamara* are considered poisonous. This plant is most familiar by the name of bittersweet, those woody branches of red berries used for decoration. The berries are quite poisonous.

Hortus Third, p. 1055, states that *Solanum nigrum* is "Often reported as a poisonous plant, but cooked locally as a potherb and ripe berries are made into pies and preserves." John Lust comments about *Solanum nigrum,* p. 294, "The berries are poisonous, but boiling apparently destroys the toxic substances and makes them usable for preserves, jams, and pies." Poisonberry jam? No, thank you.

Jimsonweed is also called nightshade. It belongs to the same *Solanaceae* family. See JIMSONWEED.

NIGHTSHADE VINE: See NIGHTSHADE.

NINETY-KNOT: See KNOTWEED.

NIRIBINE OIL: See BLACK CURRANT.

NOAH'S-ARK: See NERVEROOT.

NOBLE YARROW: See YARROW.

NODDING WAKE-ROBIN: See TRILLIUM.

NOON FLOWER: See GOATSBEARD.

NOONDAY FLOWER: See GOATSBEARD.

NOONTIDE: See GOATSBEARD.

NORTHERN LOVAGE: See LOVAGE.

NORTHERN PRICKLY ASH: See PRICKLY ASH TREE.

NORTHERN RED CURRANT: See RED CURRANT.

NORTHERN WHITE CEDAR: See WHITE CEDAR.

NORWAY PINE: See SCOTCH PINE and SPRUCE.

NORWAY SPRUCE: See SPRUCE.

NOSE-BLEED: See YARROW and TRILLIUM.

NOSEGAY: See JASMINE.

NOYAU OR NOYEAU:

Noyau is the French word for the stone or pit of a fruit such as the cherry, peach or apricot. Noyeau or crème de noyeau is a liqueur from the kernels of cherries, peaches, apricots, or bitter almonds. The kernels are crushed in alcohol and the mixture is redistilled, supposedly to get rid of the prussic acid (cyanide). This process does not always do the job, and many of these liqueurs may be very toxic, and almost all are toxic if drunk in large quantities. In the United States any flavoring material made from such pits must be certified to have less than 25 parts per million of Prussic acid before it is added to the alcohol which it is to flavor.

NUKEMUM: See BALACHONG.

NUOC MAM: See NGUOC-NAM.

NUT GRASS: See GALINGALE.

NUT PINE: See PINE NUTS.

NUT SEDGE: See GALINGALE.

NUTMEG (*Myristica fragrans*) [*Myristicaceae*]

Nutmeg is the kernel of the fleshy apricot-like fruit of *Myristica fragrans*. The ripe fruit is picked when the husk begins to split or the fruit is allowed to drop to the ground. The mace is carefully removed, flattened by hand or between boards, and sun dried. It turns from its natural crimson color and becomes brittle and hard. The nutmeg is dried slowly. It is exposed to the sun for limited time periods and turned twice daily. The complete drying process takes six to eight weeks. When they are completely dry the seed will rattle within the seed coat or shell. The shell is then broken off. At one time the nutmeg trade was under the complete control of the Dutch. To prevent the seeds from being planted in other areas not under Dutch control, the nutmegs were treated with quicklime to destroy their viability. For many, many years no nutmeg was accepted as genuine by the housewife unless it was covered with a white powder. The whole nutmeg has the unique advantage of retaining its flavor almost indefinitely, while the ground spice becomes stale quite rapidly. Every kitchen should be equipped with a small nutmeg grater so that one can always have available the best of this fragrant, versatile spice. Nutmeg is used in custards, eggnogs, cream puddings, and other desserts. It is also used in aspics, meat pies, soups, fried brains, shelled vegetables, chicken soups and fricassee, breast of veal, mushroom dishes, and spinach.

Large amounts of nutmeg (such as an entire nutmeg or more) are toxic. Small amounts are said to be soporific. In fact, nutmeg and alcohol are supposed to have synergistic effects. That is why nutmeg was always added to nighttime punches and drinks to help sleep. GRAS

To eliminate confusion about other "nutmegs," so called because they have a nutmeg-like seed, the following ones have been identified. They should not be substituted for the genuine nutmeg. American nutmeg is the custard apple (*Annona reticulata*) [*Annonaceae*]. The Jamaica nutmeg is the sweetsop (*Annona squamosa*) [*Annonaceae*]. Brazilian nutmeg is *Cryptocarya moschata* [*Lauraceae*], which has an aromatic fruit. California nutmeg is *Torreya californica* [*Taxaceae*], which bears a fruit resembling the nutmeg. (*Torreya taxifolia* is called the Florida stinking cedar.) Peruvian nutmeg, also called Chilean sassafras, is *Laurelia sempervirens* [*Monimiaceae*]. It also bears an aromatic fruit.

NUTMEG FLOWER: See NIGELLA.

NUTMEG-SCENTED GERANIUM: See GERANIUM.

O

Oak moss (*Evernia prunastri*) [*Usneaceae*]
   (*Evernia furfuracea*)
   Tree moss
   (*Usnea barbata*) [*Usneaceae*]
   Tree moss:
   Extracts from these mosses, used for their mossy odor, can only be used in flavoring formulations for beverages, confections and condiments if they are certified free of thujone, a very toxic ketone.

Obedience plant: See Arrowroot.

Oil grass: See Lemongrass.

Oil nut: See Walnut.

Oil of bay or bayberry: See Bayberry.

Oil of cadeberry: See Cade oil.

Oil of cajeput: See Cajeput.

Oil of gaultheria: See Wintergreen.

Oil of petit-grain: See Pettigrain.

Oil plant: See Castor oil plant.

Old field balsam: See Everlasting.

OLD MAID'S PINK: See **SOAPWORT**.

OLD MAN'S BEARD: See **FRINGE TREE**.

OLD MAN: See **ROSEMARY** and **SOUTHERNWOOD**.

OLD-MAID: See **PERIWINKLE**.

OLD-MAN-AND-WOMAN: See **HOUSELEEK**.

OLIBANUM (*Boswellia carterii*) [*Burseraceae*]
  Frankincense
  (*Boswellia bhau-dajiana*)
  Frankincense
  (*Boswellia frereana*)
  African elemi; Elemi frankincense
  (*Boswellia papyrifera*)
  Sudanese frankincense
  (*Boswellia sacra*)
  Saudi frankincense
  (*Boswellia serrata*)
  Indian frankincense; Indian olibanum:
    The gum-resin exudate from these African and Arabian trees burns freely and is used as incense. It is also used in pomades, ointments, perfumery, and occasionally in flavoring formulations. In old medicine it was used as treatment for bronchial and laryngeal afflictions. All of the *Boswellia* species are GRAS.

OLIVE-BARKED BOX: See **EUCALYPTUS**.

OMUM: See **AJOWAN**.

ONE-BERRY: See **PARTRIDGEBERRY**.

ONION (*Allium cepa*) [*Liliaceae*]
  (*Allium*, various species)
  Wild onion:
    The mighty (or lowly) onion really belongs in a vegetable listing, but it has been universally used since the dawn of man for seasoning and flavoring. Dehydrated onion powders, flakes, chopped and minced onion are

convenience items, good to have in a pinch and almost as good as fresh onion for some cooking. Add a little onion powder to mashed potatoes, especially instant ones, for a little added interest. Commercial onion salt, like most other flavored salts, is a useless item. Using onion powder and salt separately is much less expensive and gives better control over the amount of each desired, especially the salt. There are many ways to keep from crying when chopping onions, but the best one is to use a sharp knife. A sharp knife minimizes the splattering and spraying of the juices which irritate the eyes. Remember the relationship between cloves and onions, particularly in stews and soups. (See CLOVES) Wild onion can be most any member of the *Allium* genus that has an oniony smell. GRAS

ONION NETTLE: See ALLIARIA.

OPIUM POPPY: See POPPY.

OPOBALSAM: See TOLU BALSAM.

OPOPANAX (*Opopanax chironium*) [*Umbelliferae*]
Bisabol myrrh; Sweet myrrh:

Opopanax chironium is the true opopanax (GRAS). *Commiphora erythaea*, Eng. var. *glabrescens* [*Burseraceae*] is also called bisabol myrrh, sweet myrrh and opopanax (GRAS). *Acacia farnesiana* [*Leguminosae*] is also called opopanax (GRAS). (See CASSIE.) The roots of true opopanax, which comes from Turkey and the East Indies, have a strong smell and an acrid taste. The gum-resin exudate is used in perfumery and to give a warm, spicy note to alcoholic beverages.

OPOSSUM TREE: See STORAX.

ORANGE SWALLOW-WORT: See INDIAN PAINTBRUSH.

ORANGE-SCENTED GERANIUM: See GERANIUM.

ORANGEROOT: See GOLDENSEAL.

OREGANO: See MARJORAM.

ORÉGANO DOLCE: See MARJORAM.

OREGON ALDER: See ALDER.

OREGON GRAPE (*Mahonia aquifolium*) [*Berberidaceae*]

Blue barberry; California barberry; Holly barberry; Holly mahonia; Mountain grape; Rocky Mountain grape; Trailing mahonia; Wild Oregon grape:

This is a thornless, evergreen shrub native to the northwestern United States and western Canada. It is usually grown as an ornamental, a number of cultivars being available. The roots have been used in herbal remedies because of their diuretic and laxative properties.

OREGON MYRTLE: See SASSAFRAS.

ORIENTAL GARLIC: See GARLIC.

ORIENTAL SWEET GUM: See STORAX.

ORIGANE; ORIGANE DES CHAMPS: See MARJORAM.

ORIGANUM: See MARJORAM.

ORRIS (*Iris germanica* var. *florentina*) [*Iridaceae*]

Flag; Florentine iris; German iris; Orris root:

Orris, the peeled rhizome of this species of Iris, has a licorice-like flavor. It is used to flavor candies and baked goods. It was thought to be antitussive and, therefore, a common ingredient in cough medicines and lozenges. It is also used in perfumery and, when pulverized to fine powder, to whiten the hair in stage make-up. GRAS

OSWEGO; OSWEGO TEA: See BERGAMOT.

OTAHEITE WALNUT: See CANDLENUT.

OUR LADY'S BEDSTRAW: See BEDSTRAW.

OUR LADY'S MINT: See MINT.

OVAL BUCHU: See BUCHU.

OX-EYE CAMOMILE: See CAMOMILE.

OXADODDY: See CULVER'S-PHYSIC.

OXEYE DAISY: See HERB MARGARET.

OXHEAL: See HELLEBORE.

OYSTER KETCHUP:

Oyster ketchup is based on oysters, white wine, brandy and/or sherry, shallots, spices and salt. It is similar to but not quite the same as oyster sauce used in Chinese cooking. See OYSTER SAUCE and KETCHUP.

OYSTER PLANT: See GOATSBEARD.

OYSTER SAUCE:

Oyster sauce is a concentrate of oysters cooked in soy sauce and brine. It is used as seasoning in Chinese cooking. It intensifies flavors without imparting its own. It is sold in cans and bottles. In French cooking it means a thick sauce made from puréed oysters.

P

PADANG: See KEWRA.

PADANG CASSIA: See CINNAMON.

PADANG CINNAMON: See CINNAMON.

PADDY STRAW MUSHROOMS: See DRIED MUSHROOMS.

PADDY'S RIVER BOX: See EUCALYPTUS.

PADISTRAW MUSHROOMS: See DRIED MUSHROOMS.

PAINTED DAISY: See PYRETHRUM.

PALE CATECHU: See CATECHU.

PALE GENTIAN: See GENTIAN.

PALMA CHRISTI: See CASTOR OIL PLANT.

PALMAROSA; PALMAROSA OIL: See LEMONGRASS.

PALSYWORT: See MARIGOLD and COWSLIP.

PAN LEAVES: See PEPPER.

PANAMA BARK: See QUILLAJA.

PANCHPHORAN: See BENGALI FIVE SPICES.

PANDANG: See KEWRA.

PANDANUS PALM: See KEWRA.

PANSY (*Viola tricolor*) [*Violaceae*]
European wild pansy; Field pansy; Heartease; Herb trinity; Johnny jumper; Johnny-jump-up; Miniature pansy; Step-mother; Wild pansy:

In the United States extracts of pansy flowers are permitted to be used in alcoholic beverage flavoring formulations only. Pansies contain a very powerful emetic.

PAPAW: See PAPAYA.

PAPAYA (*Carica papaya*) [*Caricaceae*]
Melon tree; Papaw; Pawpaw:

The tropical papaya tree is best known for its edible fruit and the protein-digesting enzyme, papain, derived from the fruit and other plant parts. Papaya leaves are also an ingredient in some commercial herbal teas. The North American pawpaw, which also has edible fruit, is *Asimina triloba* [*Annonaceae*].

PAPER BIRCH: See WHITE BIRCH.

PAPOOSE ROOT: See BLUE COHOSH.

PAPRIKA (*Capsicum annuum* var. ?, formerly *Capsicum tetragonum*) [*Solanaceae*]
Paprika is made from a red sweet pepper. It is identified by the area of its origin, Spain, Portugal, or Hungary.

Spanish paprika is of three types:

1. Dolce or sweet
2. Agridulce or semisweet
3. Picante or pungent

Each of these types can come in three qualities:

1. Extra—made with only the fleshy walls
2. Select—made from the fleshy walls and 10% or less seeds
3. Common—may contain up to 30% seeds

Portuguese paprika is of two types:

1. Doce-Extra—made from the fleshy walls only
2. Doce-Superior—made from the fleshy walls and a percentage of seeds which have first been macerated and soaked in water to remove some of the pungency, and then dried and ground

Hungarian paprika is of five types:

1. First Quality or "Noble Sweet"—made from the fleshy walls and seeds, treated as above, of the finest quality peppers. It has a rich red color and a slightly pungent flavor.
2. Semisweet—similar to Noble Sweet, but it may also contain the fibrous plant parts which contain the seeds in the inside of the pepper. Its color is similar to Noble Sweet but the flavor is not quite as intense.
3. Rose—made from the entire pepper except for stems and calices. Its color is not as rich a red and the flavor is pungent.
4. Pungent—a second-grade Rose paprika. It is made from a lower quality pepper and is brick-red in color.
5. Mercantile—a third-quality paprika made from portions of the peppers left after the making of the better-quality paprikas. It may contain parts of the stems and calices and is brownish-red or brownish-yellow in color.

Unidentified paprika may be made from any sweet red pepper since the FDA lists the botanical source of paprika as *Capsicum annuum*. These paprikas will have a wide range of color and of flavor. GRAS

PAPUA MACE: See MACE.

PARADISE NUTS: See CARDAMOM.

PARADISE TREE: See CHINABERRY.

PARAGUAY PETTIGRAIN: See PETTIGRAIN.

PARAGUAYAN HOLLY: See MATÉ.

PARAGUAYAN TEA: See MATÉ.

PARISWORT: See TRILLIUM.

PARMA VIOLET: See VIOLET.

PARRY PINYON PINE: See PINE NUTS.

PARSLEY (*Petroselinum crispum*, var. *crispum* formerly *Petroselinum sativum*) [*Umbelliferae*]
Garden parsley; Rock parsley:
There are many varieties of parsley. The curly leaved varieties are the best known. Along with the broad-leaved parsleys, there are Neapolitan, or

Italian, parsley (var. *neapolitanum*) grown for its celery-like stems and turnip-rooted parsley (var. *tuberosum*) with its thick, parsnip-like, edible roots. The fresh parsley leaves have more flavor than the dried. Parsley seeds are very slow to germinate, so if growing your own, it is wise to soak them in warm water before sowing. For winter use, roots may be transplanted to pots and kept on a sunny window sill. GRAS

PARSLEY FERN: See TANSY.

PARSLEY PIERT: See LADY'S-MANTLE.

PARSNIP CHERVIL: See CHERVIL.

PARTRIDGEBERRY (*Mitchella repens*) [*Saxifragaceae*]
   Checkerberry; Deerberry; Hive vine; One-berry; Running box; Squaw vine; Squawberry; Twinberry; Two-eyed berry; Winter clover:
   This evergreen vine is native to eastern North America. The fruit is a twin berry, usually red, rarely white, about 3/8 inch in diameter. It is edible but rather insipid. The leaves were used to make teas thought by some Indian tribes to make childbirth easier and more rapid and also to relieve insomnia. See also WINTERGREEN and BLUEBERRY.

PASQUE FLOWER (*Anemone patens*, formerly *Pulsatilla patens*) [*Ranunculaceae*]
   Easter flower; Meadow anemone; Prairie anemone; Pulsatilla; Wild crocus; Wind flower
   (*Anemone pulsatilla*, formerly *Pulsatilla amoena* or *P. vulgaris*)
   Easter flower; Meadow anemone; Prairie anemone; Pulsatilla; Wild crocus; Wind flower
   (*Anemone nuttalliana*)
   Hartshorn plant; Lion's-beard; Prairie-smoke; Wild crocus:
   All of these plants are known as Pasque flower, but *Anemone patens* is the one most commonly used in herbal remedies. All should be considered highly toxic and can be fatal if consumed. They can cause irritation of the skin if touched. The name hartshorn plant should not be confused with hartshorn (see HARTSHORN), hartshorn bush (see HERB CHRISTOPHER), or hartshorn plantain (see HERB-IVY).

PASSIONFLOWER (*Passiflora*, various species) [*Passifloraceae]*
   Passionfruit
   (*Passiflora incarnata*)

Apricot vine; Maypop; Wild passionflower
(*Passiflora maliformis*)
Conch apple; Sweet calabash; Sweetcup
(*Passiflora murucuja*)
Dutchman's laudanum:

The sweet fruit of the passionflower, known as passionfruit, water lemon, or granadilla, is edible with some species being cultivated for the fruit alone. Other species are cultivated as ornamentals for the flowers. *Passiflora incarnata* was so named because parts of the flower are supposed to resemble Jesus' wounds and the crown of thorns. Extracts of the flowers have sedative qualities, some species containing more than others. A narcotic is prepared from the flowers of *Passiflora murucuja*, which is native to Jamaica. Extracts of the leaves and flowers are used in flavoring formulations, and the leaves are found in commercial herbal teas. They were widely used in old medical formulations because of their sedative properties. *Passiflora maliformis* has an apple-like fruit, yellow when ripe, a thick rind, and a grape-flavored, sweetish edible pulp. It is cultivated in the West Indies for the pulp which is used in beverages. The FDA lists only *Passiflora incarnata* as GRAS.

PASSIONFRUIT: See **PASSIONFLOWER.**

PATCHOULI (*Pogostemon cablin, patchouly* or *heyneanus*) [*Labiatae*]
Patchouly:

One of the largest market places for patchouli oil, made from the leaves, is Singapore. The fragrant oil is used extensively in perfumes, especially for soaps. It is also used in flavoring formulations for confections. GRAS

PATIENCE; PATIENCE DOCK: See **SORREL** and **KNOTWEED.**

PAUL'S BETONY: See **VERONICA.**

PAUSON: See **YARROW.**

PAWPAW: See **PAPAYA.**

PEACH LEAVES (*Prunus persica*) [Rosaceae]

The use of extracts of peach leaves is restricted to flavorings for alcoholic beverages, and then only if the Prussic acid content in the flavor does not exceed twenty-five parts per million.

PEARL MOSS: See CARRAGEEN.

PEARLY EVERLASTING: See EVERLASTING.

PEE-IN-THE-BED: See DANDELION.

PEKING GARLIC: See GARLIC.

PEKING SAUCE: See HOISIN SAUCE.

PELICAN FLOWER: See SERPENTARIA.

PELLITORY (*Parietaria officinalis*) [*Urticaceae*]
Pellitory-of-the-wall; Wall plant:

This nettle's botanical name comes from the Latin word *parietis*, meaning "wall." It is often found growing among the ruins of old stone walls. It has been used in old herbal remedies, usually for kidney and bladder problems.

Pellitory can also refer to some plants of the genus *Chrysanthemum* [*Compositae*] which were formerly classified separately as *Pyrethrum* (see PYRETHRUM) and to feverfew, *Chrysanthemum parthenium*. (See FEVERFEW.)

Pellitory of Spain is *Anacyclus pyrethrum* [*Compositae*]. It was used in old herbal remedies as a sedative. This plant has also been called pyrethrum. (See PYRETHRUM.)

Bastard pellitory is *Achillea ptarmica* [*Compositae*] which is also known as sneezewort and sneezeweed. It is closely related to yarrow and has strong smelling flowers. The leaves have been used in snuff. Sneezeweed can also refer to *Helenium autumnale* [*Compositae*], the flowers of which are said to cause sneezing. There are many cultivars of this plant that are grown as ornamentals.

PELLITORY OF SPAIN: See PELLITORY.

PELLITORY-OF-THE-WALL: See PELLITORY.

PELLOTE: See PEYOTE.

PENANG MACE: See MACE.

PENNYROYAL (*Mentha pulegium*) [*Labiatae*]
European pennyroyal; Lurk-in-the-ditch
(*Hedeoma pulegioides*) [*Labiatae*]

American pennyroyal; Mock pennyroyal; Mosquito grass; Pudding grass; Squaw balm; Squaw mint; Stinking balm; Tickweed

(*Trichostema dichotomum*) [*Labiatae*]

Bastard pennyroyal

(*Monardella lanceolata*) [*Labiatae*]

Pennyroyal

(*Monardella odoratissima*)

Western balm; Wild pennyroyal

(*Monardella villosa*)

Coyote mint; Horsemint; Pennyroyal:

Although European and American pennyroyal belong to different genera, they have the same taste and are used in the same manner as an herbal medicine and for making teas. Consumption of pure pennyroyal oil obtained by steam distillation of the leaves has been known to be fatal. Pennyroyal oil is used in commercial flavoring formulations in small quantities. Wild pennyroyal (*Mentha canadensis*) is an entirely different plant and its use in foods was banned in the United States at one time. (See CORN MINT.) Wild pennyroyal (*Monardella odoratissima*) is not listed by the FDA, nor are the other *Monardella* species. Bastard pennyroyal is grown as a rock garden ornamental. It is also called blue curls. *Mentha pulegium* and *Hedeoma pulegioides* are GRAS.

PENNYWORT: See TOADFLAX.

PEONY (*Paeonia officinalis*) [*Paeoniaceae*]

This popular flower garden plant is included in listings of plants used in herbal remedies. Extracts of the roots were used, however, the entire plant is poisonous, especially the flowers. Fatalities have occurred from drinking tea made from the flowers. Extracts of the roots will cause nausea, diarrhea, and renal vasoconstriction which may lead to permanent kidney damage.

PEPPER (*Piper nigrum*) [*Piperaceae*]

Black pepper and white pepper are made from the same berry—black pepper being the sun-dried green berry, while white pepper is the ripe berry with the hull removed. The ripe red berry is allowed to ferment for a period of time and then the skin and fleshy part can be washed off, leaving the corn which is then dried. White pepper is also made by mechanically rubbing off the outer dark layer of black pepper. This is not truly white pepper but decorticated black pepper. Black pepper is hotter than white pepper. Green peppercorns are also preserved in brine. Freshly ground pepper is far superior to that purchased already ground.

There are several different descriptions or definitions of mignonette pepper: a coarsely ground combination of white and black pepper; white pepper which has been crushed and then sifted until there remain only pieces the size of a mignonette seed; coarse-ground pepper; whole pepper. (Mignonette is the diminutive form of the French word, *mignon*, meaning small, delicately formed and pretty. It is also the name of an annual flowering plant, *Reseda odorata* [*Recedaceae*], with very fragrant flowers used in perfumery.) In former times, mignonette was also the name given to a muslin sachet containing red pepper, nutmeg, coriander, cinnamon, ginger, and cloves. The sachet was dipped for a few moments into the cooking pot to season the food. It could be used several times. GRAS

Botanical identification of many peppercorns found in the market is quite difficult since the pepper is often given the name of the area in which it is produced, such as Brazilian pepper, Ceylon pepper, and Lampong pepper. Other times the name comes from the port from which it is shipped, such as Malabar Alleppy pepper and Malabar Tellicherry pepper. Usually the pepper is *Piper nigrum.*

Some other members of the genus *Piper* of interest are:

Piper methysticum, known as kava-kava. Kava-kava is a Fiji Island fermented drink made from the plant roots. It is an intoxicating drink with motor depressant, anesthetic and cardiac stimulant properties. Extracts of the roots were also used in olden medicine as a treatment for cystitis, gout and "wasting diseases."

Piper betle, known as betel, betle pepper, and pan leaves. The leaves of this vine are used with slaked lime to wrap betel nuts before chewing.

Piper longum, known as long pepper and pipel. The berries of this species are fused together and look like small, hard catkins about one-half inch long. The flavor is very much like black pepper, however a little sweeter. It may be listed in curry ingredients by the Indian name of pipel.

PEPPER AND SALT: See SHEPHERD'S-PURSE.

PEPPER BERRIES: See PEPPER TREE.

PEPPER GRASS: See ROCKET.

PEPPER TREE (*Schinus molle*) [*Anacardiaceae*]

Australian pepper; California pepper tree; Molle; Peruvian mastic tree; Peruvian pepper tree; Pink peppercorns; Pirul; Red peppercorns

(*Schinus terebinthifolius*)

Brazilian pepper tree; Christmasberry tree; Florida pepper tree:

These tropical American trees are erroneously called "pepper trees." They yield a resinous substance which is aromatic and a mild purgative. They belong to the same family (*Anacardiaceae*) as the cashew, mango, pistachio, and sumac. The resin is used in slide preparation in microscopy. The pungent red seed has been used as a seasoning called pink or red peppercorns. It should be used with extreme caution since it causes allergic reactions in many people. An interesting sidelight is that the shell of the cashew nut contains a substance that causes allergic skin reactions in persons allergic to poison ivy. Poison ivy also belongs to the *Anacardiaceae* family.

There is also a Tasmanian tree, Drimys lanceolata, formerly Drimys aromatica [*Winteraceae*], the berries of which are used as pepper. The *New Doubleday Cookbook* states, "Pink peppercorns (dried Baies rose berries) imported from Madagascar via France are considered safe by the FDA." There is no botanical source given. Rosé peppercorns (source unknown) are sold by a local spice specialty store. The FDA lists *Schinus molle* as GRAS.

PEPPERBUSH: See **ANISE-PEPPER**.

PEPPERIDGE: See **BARBERRY**.

PEPPERMINT: See **MINT** and **EUCALYPTUS**.

PEPPERMINT-SCENTED GERANIUM: See **GERANIUM**.

PEPPERWOOD: See **SASSAFRAS** and **PRICKLY ASH TREE**.

PEQUIN: See **CAPSICUM**.

PERENNIAL MERCURY: See **MERCURY**.

PERFUMED CHERRY: See **MAHALEB**.

PERILLA (*Perilla frutescens*) [*Labiatae*]
Beefsteak plant; Shiso zoku:

Perilla is widely grown in Japan, primarily for its seeds which contain high concentrations of a quick-drying oil used as a substitute for linseed oil. Although the Japanese use all parts of the plant (leaves, flowers, stems, and seeds) in cooking, and commercially use oil from the leaves to sweeten tobacco, use of this plant is not recommended. Ketones present in the leaves are suspected of causing pulmonary disease.

PERIWINKLE (*Vinca major*) [*Apocynaceae*]
Band plant; Blue-buttons; Greater periwinkle

(*Vinca minor*)
Common periwinkle; Lesser periwinkle; Myrtle; Running myrtle
(*Catharanthus roseus*, formerly *Vinca rosea*) [*Apocynaceae*]
Madagascar periwinkle; Old-maid; Rose periwinkle
The periwinkle used as an evergreen ground cover can be either *Vinca major* or *Vinca minor* but is usually *Vinca minor*. The periwinkle treated by most as an annual flowering plant is *Catharanthus roseus*. All of these plants have been used in herbal remedies. *Vinca major* and *Vinca minor* have sedative properties and were used to treat hysteria and fits. *Catharanthus roseus* is considered a poisonous plant. Cattle have been poisoned by eating its leaves.

PERSIAN BERRIES: See CASCARA.

PERSIAN GUM: See ASAFOETIDA.

PERSIAN INSECT FLOWER: See PYRETHRUM.

PERSIAN INSECT POWDER: See PYRETHRUM.

PERSIAN LILAC: See CHINABERRY.

PERSIAN VIOLET: See CYCLAMEN.

PERSIAN WALNUT: See WALNUT.

PERU-APPLE: See JIMSONWEED.

PERUVIAN BALSAM (*Myroxylon balsamum*, var. *pereirae*) [*Leguminosae*]
This balsam is used in many flavoring formulations. It has a warm, sweet odor and a bitter taste. It has been used as an expectorant and is soothing to the skin. GRAS

PERUVIAN BARK: See QUININE.

PERUVIAN MASTIC TREE: See PEPPER TREE.

PERUVIAN NUTMEG: See NUTMEG and SASSAFRAS.

PERUVIAN PEPPER TREE: See PEPPER TREE.

PERUVIAN RHATANY: See RHATANY.

PETER'S CRESS: See SAMPHIRE.

PETINES: See CAPSICUM.

PETTIGRAIN; OIL OF PETIT-GRAIN; PETITGRAIN BIGARADE; PARAGUAY
PETITGRAIN:

This volatile oil from the leaves, buds and shoots of the lemon tree
and various orange trees goes by many variations of spelling and descriptive
adjectives. Ordinary pettigrain is from *Citrus aurantium* [*Rutaceae*] (the bitter
orange), pettigrain lemon is from *Citrus limon;* and pettigrain mandarin is
from *Citrus reticulata.* Petitgrain bigarade is also from the bitter orange.
GRAS

PETTY MOREL: See SPIKENARD.

PETTY WHIN: See REST-HARROW.

PEWTERWORT: See SHAVE GRASS.

PEYOTE (*Lophophora williamsii*) [*Cactaceae*]
**Devil's root; Dumpling cactus; Mescal button; Pellote; Sacred
mushroom:**

Much has been written about both the medical and religious use of
peyote. It contains mescaline, an alkaloid, that not only produces vivid
hallucinations but also causes changes in the cardiac rhythm. It adversely
affects many who have mental disorders such as schizophrenia. It should
never be used by anyone without a thorough knowledge of its effects. Mescal
buttons are sun dried pieces of the plant.

The mescal bean is *Sophora secundiflora* [*Leguminosae*], also known as
frijolito. This plant is native to Texas, New Mexico and northern Mexico.
It was used in some Indian religious ceremonies. However, because it contains
a highly toxic alkaloid, cytisine or sophorine, the side effects were often
fatal. Its use by the Indians was discontinued when they discovered, according
to Michael A. Weiner (p. 98), that peyote was "safer" and much more
"spectacularly hallucinogenic." Today the seeds are used to make necklaces.

PHOENICIAN JUNIPER: See SAVIN OIL.

PHOENICIAN SAVIN OIL: See SAVIN OIL.

PHYSIC ROOT: See CULVER'S-PHYSIC.

PICHURIM; PICHURIM BEANS: See SASSAFRAS.

PICKAWAY ANISE: See HOP TREE.

Pickled walnuts:

The nuts of *Juglans regia*, the English walnut, are pickled while still green, kept in their shells, and packed in a malt vinegar solution.

Pickling spice:

The content of pickling spice mixtures should be determined by the type of food being pickled, the method by which the pickling is being done, and by the taste preferences of the pickler. One does not want to use the same spices for peaches as one would use for cucumbers. Cinnamon and cloves predominate in fruit pickles, while mustard seed, celery seed, and turmeric predominate in cucumber pickles. Accordingly, the amount of spices needed would be determined by the method used. The same amount of spice would not be used if the spices are packed in the jars as would be used if they are first boiled with the vinegar and then removed before adding the vinegar to the jars. Most good pickle recipes will give the exact proportions of spices needed for the quantity of fruit or vegetable being used and for the method being used. A popular commercial pickling spice mixture contains: allspice, mustard seed, pepper, red pepper, ginger, coriander seed, cloves, dill seed, cinnamon and bay leaves. Peter Gray recommends the following proportions:

Pickling spice mixture

Crushed ginger root	15
Whole black pepper	5
Whole allspice	2
Whole coriander	2
Whole cardamom	2
Whole mustard	2
Chili pods	1

If grams are used as the unit, the total will be about one ounce. Another mixture (enough for one quart of vinegar) is:

Whole allspice berries	15 to 18
Whole fresh green chili	1
Cinnamon stick	1 inch
Whole cloves	10 to 12
Whole coriander seeds	1 teaspoon
Fresh ginger root	$1/4 \times 1$ inch piece
Mace blades	2
Whole peppercorns	25 to 28
Whole bay leaf (optional)	1
Whole mustard seed (optional)	1 to 3 teaspoons

Pickpocket: See **Shepherd's purse.**

Picotee: See **Carnation.**

PIE PLANT: See RHUBARB.

PIGEON BERRY: See POKE.

PIGEON GRASS: See VERVAIN.

PIGEONWEED: See VERVAIN.

PIGNOLIA NUTS: See PINE NUTS.

PIGWEED: See LAMB'S-QUARTERS, AMARANTH, and KNOTWEED.

PILEWORT: See AMARANTH, BUTTERCUP and LESSER CELANDINE.

PILI NUT: See ELEMI.

PILL-BEARING SPURGE: See SPURGE.

PILOSELLA: See MOUSE EAR.

PIMBINA: See CRAMPBARK.

PIMENTO OR PIMENTA: See ALLSPICE.

PIMIENTO; also correctly spelled PIMENTO:
   Pimiento is a sweet red pepper (*Capsicum annuum* var. *annuum Grossum* Group). It is usually thought of as being canned in oil or pickled in a brine or vinegar. Everyone is familiar with pimiento stuffed into green olives. Also see CAPSICUM.

PIMPERNEL (*Pimpinella major*, formerly *magna*) [*Umbelliferae*]
   False pimpernel; Greater pimpernel; Pimpinella
   (*Pimpinella saxifraga*)
   Burnet saxifrage; Small pimpernel:
   Both of these primarily European plants are closely related to the common anise, *Pimpinella anisum*. They have been used in a large number of herbal remedies for the treatment of an equally large number of common complaints. They are easily confused with burnet and scarlet pimpernel. See BURNET and SCARLET PIMPERNEL.

PIMPINELLA; PIMPINELLE: See BURNET.

PIN CHERRY: See WILD CHERRY.

PIN CLOVER: See STORKSBILL.

PIN GRASS: See STORKSBILL.

PINE FIR (*Abies alba*) [*Pinaceae*]

Fir needles oil; Pine fir; Silver fir; Silver spruce; Templin oil; White fir; White spruce

(*Abies sachalinensis*)

Japanese fir; Japanese fir needle oil; Japanese pine needle oil; Pine fir; Sachalin fir; Shin-yo-yu

(*Abies sachalinensis*, var. *mauriana*)

Mayr Sakhalin fir

(*Abies sibirica*)

European fir; Pine fir; Siberian fir; Siberian fir oil; Siberian pine needle oil:

Oils from the needles and twigs of these trees are used in concocting flavorings used for confections. They are also used extensively in perfumery, especially for room deodorants. Templin oil is made from the cones of *Abies alba*. GRAS. Hemlock oil is also sometimes sold as fir needle oil. See HEMLOCK (*Tsuga canadensis*).

PINE NUTS (*Pinus edulis*) [*Pinaceae*]

Piñon pine; Pinyon pine; Nut pine; Two-leaved nut pine

(*Pinus gerardiana*)

Chilghoza pine; Gerald's pine; Nepal nut pine

(*Pinus pinea*)

Italian stone pine; Umbrella pine

(*Pinus quadrifolia*)

Parry pinyon pine:

Pine nuts are used throughout the world. Some have a marked turpentine taste; others do not. In the United States pine nuts are also known as Indian nuts. *Pinus edulis* and *Pinus quadrifolia* (found in the southwestern United States) are the source of piñon nuts. *Pinus pinea* (found in southern Europe) is the source of pignolia nuts. *Pinus gerardiana* is the species found in the Himalayan area.

PINE OIL (*Pinus palustris*) [*Pinaceae*]

Georgia pine; Longleaf pine; Longleaf yellow pine; Pitch pine; Southern yellow pine:

Oils obtained by steam distillation of the wood are used in flavoring formulations for confections, but they are used mostly by the perfume industry. GRAS. This species is also the primary source of American gum turpentine.

PINE-SAP: See **INDIAN-PIPE.**

PINEAPPLE WEED: See **CAMOMILE.**

PINEAPPLE-SCENTED SAGE: See **SAGE.**

PINK PEPPERCORNS: See **PEPPER TREE.**

PINKROOT (*Spigelia marilandica*) [*Loganiaceae*]

Carolina pink; Indian pink; Star bloom; Worm grass:

The root of pinkroot has been used in herbal medicine as an anthelmintic, however, it can be extremely dangerous. It produces a very rapid heart rate and also has narcotic effects. Large amounts can be fatal.

PINKWEED: See **KNOTWEED.**

PIÑON NUTS: See **PINE NUTS.**

PIÑON PINE: See **PINE NUTS.**

PINYON PINE: See **PINE NUTS.**

PIPE PLANT: See **INDIAN-PIPE.**

PIPEL: See **PEPPER.**

PIPRAGE: See **BARBERRY.**

PIPSISSEWA (*Chimaphila umbellata*) [*Pyrolaceae*]

Bitter wintergreen; Ground holly; King's cure; Prince's pine; Rheumatism weed:

The leaves of this plant are described as being diuretic, astringent, and irritant. It was used formerly in the treatment of scrofula, nephritis, and cystitis. The word is supposed to be taken from the Cree Indian pipisisikew meaning "it reduces stone in the bladder to particles." Presently, extracts from the leaves are used in making flavoring formulations for beverages and candies. GRAS

PIQUE SEASONING:
This proprietary seasoning was a meat-free liquid compound made of vegetable protein derivatives, water, salt, yeast, vegetable extract, spices, and vegetable fat. It is no longer available. Prior to the mid-1940s it was widely used in cooking as a flavor enhancer, its sole purpose being to emphasize the natural richness of the food.

PIRUL: See **PEPPER TREE.**

PITCH PINE: See **PINE OIL.**

PITCHER PLANT (*Sarracenia purpurea*) [*Sarraceniaceae*]
Eve's cup; Flytrap; Huntsman's-cup; Indian-cup; Side-saddle flower; Smallpox plant; Southern pitcher plant; Sweet pitcher plant; Watercup:
This is a carnivorous plant native to eastern North America, growing in very moist or swampy areas. The American Indians believed that extracts of the roots would provide immunity to smallpox and lessen the severity of the disease. There are many natural and artificial hybrids grown as curiosities.

PITCHURIM BEAN: See **SASSAFRAS.**

PLANTAIN (*Plantago lanceolata*) [*Plantaginaceae*]
Buckhorn; Chimney-sweeps; English plantain; Headsman; Lance-leaf plantain; Narrow-leaved plantain; Ribgrass; Ribwort; Ripplegrass; Snake plantain; Soldier's herb
(*Plantago major*)
Broad-leaved plantain; Cart-track plantain; Common plantain; Dooryard plantain; Greater plantain; Round-leaved plantain; Way bread; White-man's foot
(*Plantago media*)
Gray ribwort; Hoary plantain
(*Plantago psyllium*)
Fleawort; Spanish psyllium:
All of these species of *Plantago*, which most consider nuisance weeds, have long been used in herbal remedies. Psyllium is the plantain seed which becomes mucilaginous when wet and is used as a mild laxative. *Plantago psyllium* is sometimes cultivated as a source of psyllium.

PLEURISY ROOT: See **INDIAN PAINTBRUSH.**

POCAN: See POKE.

POCKWOOD: See GUAIAC.

POET'S MARIGOLD: See MARIGOLD.

POISON ASH TREE: See FRINGE TREE.

POISON BLACK CHERRY: See BELLADONNA.

POISON DOGWOOD: See SUMAC.

POISON ELDER: See SUMAC.

POISON FLAG: See IRIS.

POISON HEMLOCK: See HEMLOCK (*Conium maculatum*).

POISON IVY: See SUMAC.

POISON OAK: See SUMAC.

POISON PARSLEY: See HEMLOCK (*Conium maculatum*).

POISON ROOT: See HEMLOCK (*Conium maculatum*).

POISON SNAKEROOT: See HEMLOCK (*Conium maculatum*).

POISON SUMAC: See SUMAC.

POISON TOBACCO: See HENBANE.

POISONBERRY: See NIGHTSHADE.

POISONOUS NIGHTSHADE: See NIGHTSHADE.

POKE (*Phytolacca americana*, formerly *P. decandra*) [*Phytolaccaceae*]
American nightshade; Coakum; Garget; Indian poke; Inkberry; Pigeon berry; Pocan; Pokeroot; Pokeweed; Redweed; Scoke; Virginia poke:
There is considerable confusion concerning poke. Poke, an Algonquian Indian word, refers most commonly to *Phytolacca americana*, however it can also be *Veratrum viride* [Liliaceae], (see FALSE HELLEBORE), *Symplocarpus foetidus* [Araceae], (see SKUNK CABBAGE), and *Nicotiana rustica* [*Solanaceae*], which is

wild tobacco. To add to the confusion, there is *Phytolacca acinosa*, a species native to China and Japan but naturalized in India, that is also known as Indian poke. Another species native to Japan and China, *Phytolacca esculenta*, is considered an edible plant by *Hortus Third*.

In areas of the United Sates, such as northeastern Oklahoma and parts of Arkansas, there are those people who look forward to the springtime when they can have "poke salad" which they claim to be "very beneficial" to their health. Whereas to most people, "salad" is made with raw greens, "poke salad" shoots and greens *must* be cooked, the cooking water changed and discarded several times. Poke salad advocates will say, "Everybody knows the water is poison!" There are many documented deaths from eating improperly prepared "poke salad." The entire plant should be considered highly toxic. If one feels a springtime need for the "beneficial effects," there are much safer laxative foods that can be consumed.

The term garget refers to a disease of cattle or swine which consists of swelling of the throat, an inflammation of the udder of cows, or a distemper of hogs. Poultices of the powdered roots were used to treat these diseases.

Those with roots in Appalachia use a "poke" to carry groceries home from the store. See **APPALACHIAN TEA**.

POKEROOT: See **POKE**.

POKEWEED: See **POKE**.

POLECAT WEED: See **SKUNK CABBAGE**.

POLISH MYRTLE: See **MYRTLE**.

POLK: An incorrect spelling of poke. See **POKE**.

POLYPODY: See **WALL FERN**.

POMEGRANATE (*Punica granatum*) [*Punicaceae*]

Bark from the branches and roots of this tree, best known for its edible fruit, is used in flavoring formulations for confections and condiments. It has an agreeable acid flavor. Red dye is made from the flowers. In the Middle East fresh pomegranate juice or a paste made from the boiled fruit is added to meat dishes. The dried seeds, which are sprinkled on dishes primarily as a decoration, have a sour taste. Dried seeds are the Indian condiment "anardana." GRAS

POMPONA VANILLA: See **VANILLA**.

POND LILY: See **LOTUS**.

POOR MAN'S WEATHERGLASS: See SCARLET PIMPERNEL.

POOR-MAN'S CABBAGE: See KNOTWEED.

POPINAC: See CASSIE.

POPLAR (*Populus balsamifera*, formerly *candicans*) [*Salicaceae*]
  Balsam poplar; Hackmatack; Tacamahac
  (*Populus nigra*)
  Black poplar
  (*Populus alba*)
  Abele; Silver-leaved poplar; White poplar
  (*Populus tremuloides*)
  Quaking aspen; Quiverleaf; Trembling aspen:
    Extracts from the buds and bark of *Populus balsamifera* have a balsamic
odor and a cinnamon-like flavor. In the United States they are permitted
to be used in alcoholic beverage flavoring formulations only. The familiar
Lombardy poplar is a cultivar of the black poplar. Bark and buds of the
poplar should not be used in herbal remedies.

POPPADOM: See BALACHONG.

POPPY SEEDS (*Papaver somniferum*) [*Papaveraceae*]
    These are the ripened seeds of the opium poppy. Opium is obtained
from the unripened seed pods by excoriating the pods and then collecting
the exuded juices after they have dried. The ripened seeds do not contain
as much of the habit forming alkaloids as the unripened seed pods. Eating
the quantity of seeds found on two poppy seed rolls will not have any
noticeable effect on an individual, but it is enough to produce a positive
urine drug test the following day. The ripe seeds do contain an oil which
is used in many of the same ways as linseed oil. When used in quantity such
as in a filling for German baked goods, the seeds have a distinctive flavor.
Most are familiar with them as the gray, blackish-blue little seeds sprinkled
on rolls. In India poppy seeds are called khus-khus. The Food and Drug
Administration lists *Papaver somniferum* as GRAS, and it should be
remembered that by their definition this means when used in accordance
with acceptable manufacturing procedures. I was told a story about a little
German girl who was sent to the poppy field to pick the ripened pods.
Because she liked them so much, she ate as many as she could while she
picked, went home, went to sleep and slept for four days! L. Frank Baum
must have heard the same story before he wrote *The Wizard of Oz*.

PORTLAND ARROWROOT: See ARUM.

PORTUGUESE PAPRIKA: See PAPRIKA.

POT MARIGOLD: See MARIGOLD.

POT MARJORAM: See MARJORAM.

POULAC KETCHUP:

Poulac ketchup is a ketchup based upon elderberries. See KETCHUP.

POULTRY SEASONING:

Poultry seasoning is not, as some believe, a specific herb or spice. It is a mixture. This mixture as purchased in stores can be highly variable as to the kind and quality of ingredients and the proportions of the ingredients. A common brand lists thyme, sage, marjoram, rosemary, black pepper, and nutmeg as ingredients. Most blends have a large amount of sage and thyme. A poultry seasoning, especially when used for stuffings, is a matter of individual taste. If you prefer a certain proprietary mixture, use it. If you don't like it, add whatever ingredient you think is needed, or make your own from scratch. For a guide to proportions to start with see "Herb mixture for poultry stuffings" under MIXED SEASONINGS.

PRAHOC:

This is a flavoring sauce from southeast Asia. According to Tom Stobart (p. 112) it is made in the following manner:

The heads are cut off small fish and they are put in baskets, well-trampled and then washed by repeated dunking in water. This gets rid of the scales and entrails. The water is then pressed out between banana leaves under heavy stones and the fish mixed with salt (one part salt to ten of fish), dried for a day in the strong sun, pounded and packed in earthenware jars to ferment. Every day over a period of about a month, the juice that comes to the top is taken off. This is prahoc sauce.

PRAIRIE ANEMONE: See PASQUE FLOWER.

PRAIRIE DOCK: See CUP PLANT.

PRAIRIE GRUB: See HOP TREE.

PRAIRIE HYSSOP: See BASIL.

PRAIRIE TEA: See CASCARILLA BARK.

PRAIRIE-SMOKE: See PASQUE FLOWER.

PRAYER-BEADS: See LICORICE.

PRETZEL SALT: See SALT.

PRICKLY ASH: See ANGELICA TREE and ANISE-PEPPER.

PRICKLY ASH TREE (*Zanthoxylum americanum*) [*Rutaceae*]
   Northern prickly ash; Toothache tree
   (*Zanthoxylum clava-herculis*)
      Hercules'-club; Pepperwood; Sea ash; Southern prickly ash:
      The bark of these trees contains xanthoxylin (zanthoxylin), a simple
bitter, that is, a bitter that has no significant medicinal effect other than
its taste. It is used in beverage, candy and baked goods flavoring formulations.
Extracts of the bark were said to relieve toothaches. Extracts of the bark
are GRAS.

PRICKLY COMFREY: See COMFREY.

PRICKLY CUSTARD APPLE: See CUSTARD APPLE.

PRICKLY JUNIPER: See CADE OIL.

PRIDE TREE: See CHINABERRY.

PRIDE-OF-CHINA: See CHINABERRY.

PRIDE-OF-INDIA: See CHINABERRY.

PRIDE-OF-THE-MEADOW: See HERB CHRISTOPHER.

PRIEST'S CROWN: See DANDELION.

PRIM: See PRIVET.

PRIMROSE: See COWSLIP and EVENING PRIMROSE.

PRIMWORT: See PRIVET.

PRINCE'S FEATHER: See AMARANTH.

PRINCE'S PINE: See PIPSISSEWA.

PRIVET (*Ligustrum vulgare*) [*Oleaceae*]
   Prim; Primwort; Privy:
   This is the common privet hedge. Leaves and bark have been used in herbal remedies. The shiny black berries are very poisonous. Children have died from eating them.

PRIVY: See PRIVET.

PROSTRATE COLEUS: See MARJORAM.

PSYLLIUM: See PLANTAIN.

PUBLIC HOUSE PLANT: See EUROPEAN SNAKEROOT.

PUDDING GRASS: See PENNYROYAL.

PUFFBALL: See DANDELION.

PULSATILLA: See PASQUE FLOWER.

PUMPKIN PINE: See WHITE PINE.

PURGING BUCKTHORN: See CASCARA.

PURPLE ANGELICA: See ANGELICA.

PURPLE AVENS: See WATER AVENS.

PURPLE BETONY: See WOOD BETONY.

PURPLE BONESET: See JOE-PYE WEED.

PURPLE CONEFLOWER (*Echinacea*, various species) [*Compositae*]
   Black Samson; Echinacea; Kansas niggerhead; Missouri snakeroot; Rudbeckia (erroneous); **Sampson root:**
   This plant was used by the Plains Indians to treat a wide variety of ailments. Extracts of the roots are reputed to have anti-inflammatory properties. *Rudbeckia* species are not the purple coneflower but the yellow coneflower, the most common of which is the black-eyed Susan. Some of the *Echinacea* species were formerly called *Rudbeckia* species, however, the two genera have now been separated.

PURPLE FOXGLOVE: See FOXGLOVE.

PURPLE GOATSBEARD: See GOATSBEARD.

PURPLE LEPTANDRA: See CULVER'S-PHYSIC.

PURPLE LOOSESTRIFE: See LOOSESTRIFE.

PURPLE MEDIC: See ALFALFA.

PURPLE OSIER: See WILLOW.

PURPLE SAGE: See SAGE.

PURPLE WILLOW: See WILLOW.

PURPLE WILLOW-HERB: See LOOSESTRIFE.

PURSLANE (*Portulaca oleracea*) [*Portulacaceae*]

Continental parsley; Kitchen-garden purslane; Pusley:

Purslane, originally from India, was widely grown in England in the Middle Ages for use as a salad leaf. It has reappeared in recent years and is often available in Greek or Cypriot food stores where it is called continental parsley. The tender tips of the leaves may be eaten raw, as a salad, alone or with other leaves. It is popular in mixed salads in France and in the Middle East and Arab countries. It can be cooked like spinach. In Greece it is cooked with eggs as a type of omelette. A few fresh young leaves are often included in light soups. Its sharp flavor blends well with bland ingredients such as cream cheese, and finely chopped leaves can be used in dips. The wild form of the plant is rather weedy and is not cultivated. The variety *sativa* is more erect and has thicker, more succulent leaves. This is the one cultivated as a salad green or herb.

PURVAIN: See BLUE VERVAIN.

PUSLEY: See PURSLANE.

PUSSY WILLOW: See WILLOW.

PUSSY-TOES: See EVERLASTING.

PYRETHRUM (*Chrysanthemum cinerariifolium*, formerly *Pyrethrum cinerariifolium*) [*Compositae*]

Dalmatia pyrethrum; Dalmatian insect flower; Dalmatian insect powder; Pellitory

(*Chrysanthemum coccineum*, formerly *Pyrethrum carneum*, *P. coccineum* and *P. hybridum*)

Painted daisy; Pellitory; Persian insect flower; Persian insect powder:

The dried flower heads of these plants are the source of the insecticide, pyrethrum. *Chrysanthemum cinerariifolium* is the primary commercial source. Pyrethrum can also refer to pellitory (see **Pellitory**) and to feverfew (see **Feverfew**).

Q

QAT: See ABYSSINIAN TEA.

QUACK GRASS: See COUCH GRASS.

QUAKING ASPEN: See POPLAR.

QUASSIA (*Quassia amara*, formerly *Simaruba amara*) [*Simarubaceae*]
   Bitter ash; Bitterwood; Surinam quassia:
   This tree grows primarily in Panama, Venezuela, Guiana, and northern Brazil. A bitter infusion, made from the wood, was formerly used by some brewers as a substitute for hops. It was used in apértifs and as a general cure-all. Formerly, this was listed by the FDA as being restricted to alcoholic beverages only, but the most recent listing is GRAS.

QUATRE ÉPICE: See FOUR SPICES.

QUEBRACHO (*Aspidosperma quebrachoblano*, formerly *Schinopsis lorentzii* or *Quebrachia lorentzii*) [*Apocynaceae*]
   Aspidosperma:
   Extracts of the bark of this South American tree have been called a "tonic aromatic." It is used in flavoring formulations for beverages, confections and baked goods. It is also used by the tanning and dyeing industries, in medicine as an emetic and in the treatment of cardiac-related shortness of breath. GRAS

QUEEN'S DELIGHT (*Stillingia sylvatica*) [*Euphorbiaceae*]
   Cockup hat; Marcory; Queen's root; Silverleaf; Stillingia; Yaw root:
   The dried roots of this plant were used in medicine during the Middle Ages to treat the symptoms of acute mercurial poisoning that occurred after

251

treating syphilis with mercury compounds, a treatment which hastened the patient's demise rather than curing the disease. Acute mercurial poisoning causes a painful sloughing of the mucous membranes of the mouth. *Stillingia sylvatica* contains an alkaloid which greatly stimulates the secretion of saliva so the treatment probably gave a little relief. This same alkaloid is also a cathartic and emetic. The fresh plant juices are very acrid and irritating if taken internally.

The name marcory comes from the Latin derived word marcor, meaning a state of withering or wasting of flesh.

QUEEN'S ROOT: See QUEEN'S DELIGHT.

QUEEN'S-LACE: See DAUCUS.

QUEEN-ANNE'S-LACE: See DAUCUS.

QUEEN-OF-THE-MEADOW: See HERB CHRISTOPHER and JOE-PYE WEED.

QUEENSLAND ASTHMA WEED: See SPURGE.

QUICK GRASS: See COUCH GRASS.

QUICK-SET THORN: See HAWTHORN BERRIES.

QUICKBEAM: See ROWAN.

QUILLAI: See QUILLAJA.

QUILLAJA (*Quillaja saponaria*) [*Rosaceae*]
   Panama bark; Quillai; Quillay bark; Soapbark:
   Extracts of the bark have a bittersweet, aromatic flavor and are used in beverage flavoring formulations. The bark has detergent properties and has been used instead of soap to wash fine silks and woolens. It has been added to hair lotions to combat dandruff. Smelling the bark will produce sneezing in almost all individuals. It has been used in the treatment of the common cold and for reducing fevers. GRAS

QUILLAY BARK: See QUILLAJA.

QUININE (*Cinchona*, various species) [*Rubiaceae*]
   Fever bark tree; Jesuits' bark; Peruvian bark:
   Quinine is one of the many alkaloids obtained from the bark of these trees. It is odorless, but has a bitter taste. It is the ingredient in tonic water

that gives the bitter flavor, and it has many medical uses including the treatment of malaria. The FDA permits extracts of *Cinchona* bark to be used in beverages only, and the concentration of cinchona alkaloids may not be more than eighty-three parts per million in the finished beverage.

QUINSY BERRY: See BLACK CURRANT.

QUINSY WORT: See WOODRUFF.

QUITCH GRASS: See COUCH GRASS.

QUIVERLEAF: See POPLAR.

R

RABBIT'S ROOT: See SARSAPARILLA.

RACCOON BERRY: See MAYAPPLE.

RAGGED CUP: See CUP PLANT.

RAGGED LADY: See NIGELLA.

RAGWEED: See SWEET GOLDENROD.

RAGWORT (*Senecia jacobaea*) [*Compositae*]
European ragwort; Tansy ragwort:
This plant, which is closely related to the ornamental dusty-miller (*Senecio cineraria*), appears in lists of plants used in herbal remedies. It should not be used. It is poisonous to man and cattle, causing liver damage.

RAINBOW WEED: See LOOSESTRIFE.

RAISIN TREE: See RED CURRANT.

RAMPION (*Campanula rapunculus*) [*Campanulaceae*]
The leaves and roots of the young plants are eaten raw in salads.

RAMSONS: See GARLIC.

RANSOMS: See GARLIC.

RAPESEED (*Brassica napus*) [*Cruciferae*]
Colza:

The rapeseed or rape plant is closely related to the mustards and to turnips. The ground seeds are sometimes used as an adulterant in ground and prepared mustards. Rape oil, colza oil or rapeseed oil is a nondrying or semi-drying oil obtained from rapeseed and turnip seeds. It is used as a lubricant, as a lamp oil, and, occasionally, in foods.

RASPBERRY: See BRAMBLES.

RATAFIA:

Ratafia usually means a fruit- or herb-flavored liqueur. In England, however, it can mean either a bitter almond flavored liqueur or a sweet cookie flavored strongly with bitter almond.

RATTLEROOT: See BLACK COHOSH.

RATTLESNAKE PLANTAIN (*Goodyera pubescens*) [*Orchidaceae*]

Adder's violet; Downy rattlesnake orchid; Downy rattlesnake plantain; Latticeleaf; Net-leaf plantain; Networt; Rattlesnake weed; Scrofula weed; Spotted plantain; Water plantain:

Extracts of the roots and leaves of this plant were applied externally to treat all sorts of skin problems from insect bites to the open sores of scrofula.

RATTLESNAKE ROOT: See BLAZING-STAR; LION'S-FOOT and TRILLIUM.

RATTLESNAKE VIOLET: See ADDER'S-TONGUE.

RATTLESNAKE WEED: See ERYNGO and RATTLESNAKE PLANTAIN.

RATTLESNAKE-MASTER: See ERYNGO and BLAZING-STAR.

RATTLETOP: See BLACK COHOSH.

RATTLEWEED: See WILD INDIGO and BLACK COHOSH.

RAYLESS MAYWEED: See CAMOMILE.

RED ALDER: See ALDER.

RED BANEBERRY: See HERB CHRISTOPHER.

RED BAY: See BAY LEAF and MAGNOLIA.

RED BEARBERRY: See UVA-URSI.

RED BRYONY: See BRYONY.

RED CENTAURY: See GENTIAN.

RED CHICKWEED: See SCARLET PIMPERNEL.

RED CLOVER: See CLOVER.

RED CLUSTER PEPPER: See CAPSICUM.

RED COCKSCOMB: See AMARANTH.

RED COUCHGRASS: See RED SEDGE.

RED CURRANT (*Ribes rubrum*) [*Saxifragaceae*]
Garden currant; Garnetberry; Northern red currant; Raisin tree; Wineberry:

The red currant is widely cultivated in Europe, seldom in the United States. In Europe they are eaten fresh, made into sauces, jellies, and wines. It is a shame it is so difficult to find them in the United States. They are delicious.

RED ELM: See SLIPPERY ELM.

RED EYEBRIGHT (*Euphrasia officinalis*) [*Scrophulariaceae*]
Euphrasy; Eye-bright:

This plant is commonly found in meadows and pastures in Europe and western Asia. It has been used in herbal remedies for colds and hay fever.

RED GUM: See STORAX.

RED HAW: See HAWTHORN BERRIES.

RED IRONBARK: See EUCALYPTUS.

RED JAMAICA SARSAPARILLA: See SARSAPARILLA.

RED JASMINE: See JASMINE.

RED LAUREL: See MAGNOLIA.

RED LEG: See KNOTWEED.

RED MALLEE: See EUCALYPTUS.

RED MAPLE (*Acer rubrum*) [*Aceraceae*]
Scarlet maple; Soft maple; Swamp maple:
Extracts of the bark of the red maple were used in American Indian remedies.

RED PAINT ROOT: See YARROW.

RED PEPPER: See CAPSICUM.

RED PEPPERCORNS: See PEPPER TREE.

RED PIMPERNEL: See SCARLET PIMPERNEL.

RED PUCCOON: See YARROW.

RED RIVER SNAKEROOT: See SERPENTARIA.

RED ROBIN: See HERB ROBERT.

RED ROOT: See CINQUEFOIL, NEW JERSEY TEA, and YARROW.

RED SANDALWOOD: See SANDALWOOD.

RED SAUNDERS: See SANDALWOOD.

RED SEASONING SAUCE: See HOISIN SAUCE.

RED SEDGE (*Carex arenaria*) [*Cyperaceae*]
German sarsaparilla; Red couchgrass; Sand sedge; Sea sedge:
There are about 2000 species of *Carex*, all known as sedges. Some are good forage crops, some are grown as ornamentals, especially in rock gardens, and all, because of their rhizome root structure, are good for erosion control. *Carex arenaria* is native to northern Europe and its roots have been used in herbal remedies. It is of questionable safety and may cause kidney problems.

RED SORREL: See SORREL.

RED SQUILL: See SQUILL.

RED VEGETABLE SAUCE: See HOISIN SAUCE.

RED WILLOW: See KINNIKINICK.

RED-BEAN VINE: See LICORICE.

RED-BERRIED ELDER: See ELDER.

RED-STEM FILAREE: See STORKSBILL.

RED-TOPPED SAGE: See SAGE.

REDBERRY: See GINSENG.

REDWEED: See POKE.

RESEDA: See HENNA.

RESIN-WEED: See GUM PLANT.

REST-HARROW (*Ononis spinosa*) [*Leguminosae*]
Cammock; Petty whin; Stayplough:
This is a common European plant. Long ago the tender shoots were pickled and eaten with meats. It has also been used in herbal remedies.

RHATANY (*Krameria triandra*) [*Polygalaceae*]
Krameria; Peruvian rhatany
(*Krameria argentia*)
Brazilian rhatany:
Extracts of the roots are bitter and astringent. They are used in flavoring formulations for beverages, confections, and baked goods. They have been used in medicine for the treatment of diarrhea and hemorrhages and locally for treatment of fissures and cracked skin. GRAS

RHEUMATISM ROOT: See WILD YAM and TWIN LEAF.

RHEUMATISM WEED: See PIPSISSEWA.

RHUBARB (*Rheum rhabarbarum*) [*Polygonaceae*]
Garden rhubarb; Pie plant; Wine plant:
The above plant is the rhubarb with which most are familiar. It is used to make pies, tarts, jams, and occasionally wine. Only the tender young

stalks should be used, since the leaves contain enough oxalic acid to be quite toxic. There seems to be some confusion as to the use of rhubarb root. The Food and Drug Administration restricts the use as a flavoring substance of "garden rhubarb root, *Rheum rhaponticum*," to "in alcoholic beverages only." *Hortus Third* states that the name *Rheum rhaponticum* has been misapplied to the garden rhubarb root, *Rheum rhabarbarum*. The FDA has no restrictions on the use of rhubarb root from "*Rheum officinale, R. palmatum*, or other spp. (excepting *R. rhaponticum*) or hybrids of *Rheum* grown in China." Rhubarb root from *Rheum palmatum*, known as Chinese rhubarb and Turkey rhubarb, is listed in herbal medicine books as a treatment for constipation and diarrhea. It is probably best to use only the stalks for rhubarb pie and leave the roots in the ground.

RHUBARB ROOT: See RHUBARB.

RHUBARB SORREL: See SORREL.

RIBGRASS: See PLANTAIN.

RIBWORT: See PLANTAIN.

RICHWEED: See CITRONELLA and BLACK COHOSH.

RIPPLEGRASS: See PLANTAIN.

RIVER PEPPERMINT: See EUCALYPTUS.

RIVER TEA TREE: See CAJEPUT.

RIVER WHITE GUM: See EUCALYPTUS.

ROANOKE-BELLS: See COWSLIP.

ROB ELDER: See ELDER.

ROCAMBOLE: See GARLIC.

ROCK BRAKE: See WALL FERN.

ROCK CINQUEFOIL: See CINQUEFOIL.

ROCK MAPLE: See SUGAR MAPLE.

ROCK PARSLEY: See PARSLEY.

ROCK POLYPOD: See WALL FERN.

ROCK ROSE (*Helianthemum canadense*) [*Cistaceae*]
Frost plant; Frostwort; Sun rose:
   Contrary to its name, *Helianthemum canadense* is not hardy in the
northern part of the United States but prefers dry, sunny locations in the
southeastern United States. It has astringent properties and has been used
in herbal remedies for the skin. If taken internally, it is emetic.

ROCK SALT: See SALT.

ROCK SAMPHIRE: See SAMPHIRE.

ROCKBERRY: See UVA-URSI.

ROCKET (*Eruca vesicaria*, subspecies *sativa*) [*Cruciferae*]
   **Arugula; Rocket-gentle; Rocket-salad; Roka; Roman rocket;
   Roquette; Ruchetta; Rugola; Rugula; Tira**
(*Barbarea vulgaris*) [*Cruciferae*]
   Herb Barbara; Rocket; Upland cress; Winter cress; Yellow rocket
(*Barbarea verna*)
   American cress; Scurvy grass; Winter cress
(*Hesperis matronalis*) [*Cruciferae*]
   **Damask violet; Dame's rocket; Dame's violet; Sweet rocket; Vesper
   flower**
(*Lepidium sativum*) [*Cruciferae*]
   Garden cress; Pepper cress; Upland cress
(*Sisymbrium irio*) [*Cruciferae*]
   London rocket
(*Sisymbrium orientale*) [*Cruciferae*]
   Eastern rocket
(*Diplotaxis tenuifolia*) [*Cruciferae*]
   Wall rocket:
   Rocket (*Eruca vesicaria*) was a very popular salad green in Elizabethan
England. It is native to southern Europe and is widely cultivated in that
area for use as a salad green. It is eaten alone or mixed with other greens.
It has a peppery flavor. *Barbarea vulgaris*, also known as rocket, is an edible
cress sometimes used in salads, as a seasoning, or as a garnish, however it
is considered by most to be a pesky weed. London rocket grew wild on

London bomb sites, and Eastern rocket grows wild in the Middle East. Wall rocket is found in southern France where it is used as a flavoring herb in salads. *Barbarea verna* was used for the treatment of scurvy. Scurvy grass can also be *Cochlearia officinalis* [*Cruciferae*], which is closely related to horseradish. *Cochlearia officinalis* is also known as spoonwort and scrubby grass.

ROCKET-GENTLE: See ROCKET.

ROCKET-SALAD: See ROCKET.

ROCKY MOUNTAIN GRAPE: See OREGON GRAPE.

ROCOTO: See CAPSICUM.

RODDEN: See ROWAN.

ROGATION FLOWER: See MILKWORT.

ROKA (*Trichilia emetica*) [*Meliaceae*]
    This is a tropical tree of Africa and Arabia. The seeds yield an oil which is used as an ointment and an emetic. Also see ROCKET.

ROMAN BAY: See BAY LEAF.

ROMAN CAMOMILE: See CAMOMILE.

ROMAN CASSIE: See CASSIE.

ROMAN CORIANDER: See NIGELLA.

ROMAN MOTHERWORT: See LION'S-TAIL.

ROMAN ROCKET: See ROCKET.

ROOF HOUSELEEK: See HOUSELEEK.

ROOT BEER:
    Root beer is a carbonated soft drink made from extracts of various plant roots, such as sarsaparilla and sassafras. Root beer flavoring, or root beer concentrate, can contain both natural and artificial substances as found in the following label list of ingredients: "caramel color, water, corn syrup, wild cherry bark extractives and other natural extractives, methyl salicylate

and other esters, vanillin and other aldehydes, eugenol and other ethers, gum acacia and gum tragacanth."

ROQUETTE: See ROCKET.

ROSARY PEA: See LICORICE.

ROSE (*Rosa*, various species) [*Rosaceae*]

The rose has long been used in perfumery, as a flavoring agent, and as a home remedy. Attar of roses is an oil extracted from the petals. Rose absolute, rose Bulgarian and true Otto oil are all rose oils extracted from various parts of the rose plant and differ primarily in their physical characteristics, such as color, viscosity, etc. They are all used in much the same way in perfumery and for flavorings. Rose hips are the fleshy seed pod, usually from wild varieties. They have a tart flavor and are a popular ingredient in teas. They are also used to make jellies. Dried flower petals and rose buds are often included in herbal teas. GRAS

ROSE ABSOLUTE: See ROSE.

ROSE APPLE

(*Syzygium jambos*, formerly *Eugenia jambosa*) [*Myrtaceae*]

Java plum; Malabar plum:

This oriental tree is very closely related to the ordinary clove. It bears a fruit with a rose-like perfume. The fruit is dry, crisp, and rather insipid when raw, but is highly prized for making jams and flavoring confections.

ROSE BULGARIAN: See ROSE.

ROSE GERANIUM: See GERANIUM.

ROSE HIPS: See ROSE.

ROSE LAUREL: See MOUNTAIN LAUREL.

ROSE MALLOW: See ABELMOSK.

ROSE PERIWINKLE: See PERIWINKLE.

ROSE PINK: See GENTIAN.

ROSE-OF-SHARON (*Hibiscus syriacus*) [*Malvaceae*] or (*Hypericum calycinum*) [*Hypericaceae*]

Rose-of-Sharon is a common name for both of the above plants. *Hibiscus syriacus* is also sometimes called althaea. See ALTHAEA, HIBISCUS FLOWERS, and SAINT JOHN'S WORT.

ROSELLA (*Hibiscus sabdariffa*) [*Malvaceae*]
Flor de Jamaica; Guinea sorrel; Indian sorrel; Jamaica sorrel; Roselle:
This species of *Hibiscus* is native to tropical Asia and is grown for its fleshy red sepals which are used in India, Southeast Asia, Cuba, and Central America to make drinks and preserves. The flavor is described as slightly sour but pleasant. Its use in the United States is restricted to alcoholic beverage flavoring formulations only.

ROSELLE: See ROSELLA.

ROSEMARY (*Rosmarinus officinalis*) [*Labiatae*]
Old man:
Rosemary, an evergreen shrub with hard, spiky needle-like leaves, contains an essential oil, rosemary oil, which gives it an aromatic, refreshing fragrance. It is used to season chicken, lamb, pork, soups, sauces and fish stuffings or is scattered over salads. It is a perennial. It grows easily from seed planted indoors in January or February and set out in late spring in a dry sunny place, well drained and sheltered. In the northern part of the United States it will require winter protection. It is often grown as a hedge in southern California, especially along the coast where it is dry and rocky. The oil has been used as an ingredient in liniments. There is a legend that when Mary hung the infant Jesus' clothes on a rosemary bush, it flowered at once. It is said that rosemary never grows higher than Christ stood and that it only lives for 33 years. It has always been a symbol of good friendship and remembrance. Legend also claims that rosemary is good for nervous headaches, trembling, dizziness, and stomach disorders. It improves the memory, disinfects air and protects garments from moths. It is used as a hair conditioner. A sprig under the pillow chases the evil eye. GRAS

ROSIN:
Rosin is the hard, brittle resin remaining after oil of turpentine has been distilled from crude turpentine. Its use is restricted to alcoholic beverage flavorings only. Colophony is a resin from Colophon, a Greek city. Its use is similarly restricted.

ROSINWEED: See GUM PLANT and CUP PLANT.

ROUCOU: See ANNOTTO.

ROUGH AVENS: See WATER AVENS.

ROUND BUCHU: See BUCHU.

ROUND CARDAMOM: See CARDAMOM.

ROUND-LEAVED MINT: See MINT.

ROUND-LEAVED PLANTAIN: See PLANTAIN.

ROUND-LEAVED SUNDEW: See SUNDEW.

ROUNDWOOD: See ROWAN.

ROWAN (*Sorbus aucuparia*) [*Rosaceae*]
European mountain ash; Mountain ash; Quickbeam; Rodden; Sorb apple
(*Sorbus americana*)
American mountain ash; Dogberry; Missey-moosey; Roundwood:
The fruit of these trees, a berry-like, pea-sized, red pome, is made into a tart jelly which is served with meats, particularly venison. The mountain ash is not related to the common ash tree, *Fraximus* spp. [*Oleaceae*]. The mountain ash belongs to the rose family and is more closely related to the apple trees, *Malus* spp. [*Rosaceae*].

ROYAL FERN: See HERB CHRISTOPHER.

ROYAL FLOWERING FERN: See HERB CHRISTOPHER.

ROYAL JASMINE: See JASMINE.

RUCHETTA: See ROCKET.

RUDBECKIA: See PURPLE CONEFLOWER.

RUE (*Ruta graveolens, montana, bracteosa* and *calepensis*) [*Rutaceae*]
Garden rue; German rue; Herb-of-grace; Herb-of-repentance:
The bitter leaves of this plant have been recommended in old cook books for seasoning in salads and for use in beverages. Its sale is restricted and controlled in a large number of countries. In the United States the dried leaves, buds and stems from the top of the plant may be used in food in accordance with § 184.1(b)(2) Section 21, *Code of Federal Regulations*, at concentrations not to exceed two parts per million. Oil of rue is the natural

substance obtained by steam distillation of the fresh blossoming plants. It may be used as a flavoring agent and adjuvant in baked goods and baking mixes, frozen dairy desserts and mixes, and soft candy in amounts less than ten parts per million. In all other food categories the concentration must be less than four parts per million. The leaves contain a volatile oil which is an irritant poison. If taken internally, it produces widespread hemorrhagic effects. It was used in the past to induce abortions. Goat's rue, *Galega officinalis* [*Leguminosae*], contains toxic alkaloids and should not be used.

RUGOLA: See ROCKET.

RUGULA: See ROCKET.

RUM CHERRY: See WILD CHERRY.

RUNAWAY ROBIN: See GROUND IVY.

RUNNING BOX: See PARTRIDGEBERRY.

RUNNING MYRTLE: See PERIWINKLE.

RUNNING PINE: See HERB-IVY.

RUSH NUT: See GALINGALE.

RUSSIAN COMFREY: See COMFREY.

RUSSIAN MUSTARD: See MUSTARD.

RUSSIAN TARRAGON: See TARRAGON.

RUSSIAN VIOLET: See VIOLET.

RUSSIAN WORMSEED: See WORMSEED.

RUTLAND BEAUTY: See WILD MORNING-GLORY.

S

SAFFRON (*Crocus sativus*) [*Iridaceae*]

Saffron, the dried stigmas of the crocus flower, is so aromatic and pungent that a few strands will perfume an entire room. About 20,000 flowers must be hand stripped to provide a pound of the spice, which justifies the outrageous price. A favorite flavoring and coloring for food in medieval England, saffron was so valuable and expensive that the nobles who grew it kept the special yard under lock and key. The ancient Egyptians called it "The Blood of Thoth" and used it in religious ceremonies. They considered it a plant dedicated to the sun. Ladies of ancient Greece used it as a hair dye, the Babylonians as a perfume and cosmetic; the French, the Italians, and the Spanish use it as a flavoring in curries, sauces, and rice. Spanish saffron, the powdered dried stigmas, is neither as powerful nor as aromatic as the whole dried stigmas. Spanish saffron is what is sold in most American grocery stores. GRAS

American saffron is *Carthamus tinctorus* [*Compositae*], the safflower, also known as bastard saffron, dyer's saffron, and false saffron. It is the source of safflower oil. The tender shoots are edible and the flower heads are a source of yellow dye. Dried safflower flowers have a very bland taste. The quantity of safflower must be increased five times to produce the same color as saffron, but there is no noticeable taste. Safflower is not a substitute for saffron in a recipe.

Meadow saffron is *Colchicum autumnale* [*Liliaceae*], also known as autumn crocus, fall crocus, mysteria, naked ladies, and wonder bulb. *Colchicum autumnale* is the source of the drugs colchicum and colchicine. The entire plant is considered highly poisonous and very small amounts of the bulbs or seeds can cause death. Because it sends up its leaves in the spring and the flowers in the fall after the leaves have died back, *Colchicum autumnale* has been called naked ladies. There are other totally unrelated "naked ladies" found in the flower garden. There are eleven or more species of *Lycoris* [*Amaryllidaceae*] and also *Amaryllis belladonna* [*Amaryllidaceae*] which have the characteristics of sending up the flower after the leaves have died back.

"Saffron substitute" is dinitrocresol, a poisonous, yellow coal tar dye.

SAFFRON OF THE INDIES: See TURMERIC.

SAGACKHOMI: See UVA-URSI.

SAGE (*Salvia officinalis*) [*Labiatae*]

Dalmatia sage; Garden sage; Salvia

(*Salvia officinalis aureum*)

Golden sage

(*Salvia sclarea*)

Clary; Clary sage; Muscatel sage

(*Salvia fruticosa*, formerly *triloba*)

Greek sage

(*Salvia lavandulifolia* and *barrelieri*)

Spanish sage

(*Salvia leucantha*)

Mexican bush sage

(*Salvia clevelandii*)

Blue sage

(*Salvia dorisiana*)

British Honduran sage; Peach-scented sage

(*Salvia elegans*)

Pineapple-scented sage

(*Salvia leucophylla*)

Gray sage; Purple sage

(*Salvia lyrata*)

Cancerweed; Lyre-leaved sage; Wild sage

(Salvia pomifera)

Apple sage

(Salvia verbenacea)

Vervain sage; Wild clary

(Salvia viridis)

Bluebeard sage; Joseph sage; Red-topped sage:

Garden sage has grayish-green leaves which are used dried or fresh. It has a strongly aromatic flavor which tends to overpower other flavors. It is a hardy perennial, usually propagated by cuttings set in sand in the spring. It can be grown from seed sown in the spring and likes a dry, poor soil. There are numerous species of *Salvia* with sage-like aroma and flavor, many with subtle hints of other flavors. Legend claims that sage is useful as a hair conditioner and will darken gray hair. It increases longevity, diminishes grief, stops trembling, and cures snake bites. *Salvia officinalis*, *triloba* and *lavandulifolia* are GRAS.

Salvia lyrata is found in dry woodlands of the eastern United States. It is much more harsh and acrid than the other sages listed above. It is said the crushed leaves will remove warts.

SAGE OF BETHLEHEM: See MINT.

SAGE TREE *(Vitex agnus-castus)* *[Verbenaceae]*

Chaste tree; Chasteberry; Hemp tree; Monk's pepper tree; Indian-spice; Wild pepper:

This is an aromatic shrub or small tree native to southern Europe and naturalized in the southern United States. Although it has been used in herbal remedies, it is best used as an ornamental or for basketry.

SAIGON CINNAMON: See CINNAMON.

SAILOR'S TOBACCO: See MUGWORT.

SAINT ANTHONY'S TURNIP: See BUTTERCUP.

SAINT BARTHOLOMEW'S TEA: See MATÉ.

SAINT BENEDICT'S THISTLE: See BLESSED THISTLE.

SAINT CATHERINE'S FLOWER: See NIGELLA.

SAINT CHRISTOPHER'S HERB: See HERB CHRISTOPHER.

SAINT GEORGE'S HERB: See VALERIAN.

SAINT JAMES' WEED: See SHEPHERD'S PURSE.

SAINT JOHN'S BREAD: See CAROB.

SAINT JOHN'S HERB: See MUGWORT.

SAINT JOHN'S-WORT (*Hypericum perforatum*) [*Hypericaceae*]
   Amber; Goatweed; Johnswort; Klamath weed; Tipton weed
   (*Hypericum calycinum*)
   Aaron's beard; Creeping Saint John's wort; Gold flower; Rose-of-Sharon:
   Technically, any plant belonging to the genus *Hypericum* can be called Saint John's-wort or Saint Peter's-wort. The flowers and leaves are described as having an aromatic and resinous fragrance with a bitter taste. The flowering tips of the plant were used in the past in medicinal herbal infusions. In the United States extracts of *Hypericum* are restricted to use in alcoholic beverage flavoring formulations and then only if certified hypericin-free. Hypericin, when taken internally, will cause a photo-dermatitis in fair-skinned persons.

SAINT JOSEPH'S LILY: See LOTUS.

SAINT JOSEPHWORT: See BASIL.

SAINT LUCIE CHERRY: See MAHALEB.

SAINT MARTIN'S-HERB (*Sauvagesia erecta*) [*Violaceae*]
   Adima; Yaoba; Yerba de St. Martin:
   This is a tropical American plant. In Guiana it is called adima or yaoba, and the leaves are eaten like spinach. In Peru it is known as yerba de St. Martin, or St. Martin's herb and is used for "medicinal purposes."

SAINT MARY'S THISTLE: See MILK THISTLE.

SAINT PETER'S HERB: See SAMPHIRE.

SAINT PETER'S-WORT: See SAINT JOHN'S-WORT.

SAKHALIN FIR: See PINE FIR.

SALAD BURNET: See BURNET.

SALICIN WILLOW: See WILLOW.

SALLOW: See WILLOW.

SALMONBERRY: See BRAMBLES.

SALSA CRUDA: See MIXED SEASONINGS.

SALSIFY: See GOATSBEARD and COMFREY.

SALT:

Ordinary table salt is sodium chloride. Usually it has a chemical such as sodium silicoaluminate added to keep the salt free flowing. Iodized salt has potassium iodide added. Years ago this was very necessary as a goiter preventative in inland areas where the population had a diet very low in iodide containing minerals. Today this dietary deficiency is rarely seen. Ordinary table salt is perfectly satisfactory for most household use, however there are other types of salt available that may be preferred for special purposes or as a matter of personal preference.

In Europe there is considerable use of sea salt in cooking. Sea salt is usually coarser than table salt and is referred to in some cook books as coarse salt or Kosher salt. Malden salt is a sea salt from England. Bay salt is obtained by the evaporation of sea water in pits by natural heat from the sun. Sea salt, generally, is artificially evaporated. In some areas of Europe brine salt is available. This is obtained from deep wells containing salt water. It is evaporated and purified.

Rock salt is an unrefined mined salt. Some may be more pure than others. This is the salt used for freezing ice cream and melting ice on driveways. Pretzel salt is currently mined on the Gulf of Mexico, where there is a rare deposit of salt that forms large, flat crystals that are perfectly suited to coating pretzels. Popcorn salt is a very fine salt.

For making pickles, a coarse pure salt is preferred over ordinary table salt. Chemicals added to table salt to prevent caking may make the pickling juices cloudy, and iodized salt may make the pickles darken. In bread making, table salt may be added directly to the flour, but coarse salt should be dissolved in the liquids. Coarse salt does not dissolve well when added directly to the flour, and one may end up with hard chunks of salt in the bread and uneven salt distribution.

Sea salt is considered by many to be more healthful than ordinary table salt because it does contain other minerals. It is not as "salty" as table salt, and recipes may have to be adjusted accordingly.

SALTRHEUM WEED: See TURTLEHEAD.

SAMBAC: See JASMINE.

SAMBHAR POWDER:

Sambhar powder is a mixture of spices used in Indian cookery. It usually contains coriander, chili peppers, fenugreek, cumin, cinnamon, black pepper, and asafoetida. Sambhar is a city in the state of Rajasthan in northwestern India.

SAMPHIRE (*Crithmum maritimum*) [*Umbelliferae*]

Peter's cress; Rock samphire; Saint Peter's herb; Sea fennel:

This plant with fat succulent leaves grows along the European shores. The leaves are pickled or eaten fresh in salads. They can also be cooked as a vegetable. It should not be confused with golden samphire (*Inula crithmoides* [*Compositae*]) which is closely related to elecampane.

SAMPSON ROOT: See PURPLE CONEFLOWER.

SAMPSON'S SNAKEROOT: See GENTIAN.

SAN QI GINSENG: See GINSENG.

SAND SEDGE: See RED SEDGE.

SAND LEEK: See GARLIC.

SANDALWOOD (*Santalum*, various species) [*Santalaceae*]

East Indian sandalwood; White sandalwood; White saunders; Yellow sandalwood; Yellow saunders:

The heartwood of various species of the sandalwood tree yields a fragrant essential oil, "santene," that is used in perfumery and in compounding flavoring formulations for beverages, confections, baked goods and chewing gum. *Santalum alba*, white sandalwood, is known as true sandalwood or "santal." Yellow and East Indian sandalwood and yellow and white saunders are all species of the genus *Santalum*. *Santalum* is GRAS.

Red sandalwood or red saunders is *Pterocarpus santalinus* [*Leguminosae*]. Derivatives of red saunders wood are used as a dye, "santalum," and may be used in alcoholic beverage flavoring formulations only. "Santol" is a colorless crystalline compound derived from the red saunders. "*Sanatol*" is a proprietary disinfectant and antiseptic containing sulfuric acid and phenol esters. Any references that describe this as being the same as sandalwood should be disregarded. Nor should any of these be confused with "santonica," *Artemisia maritima*, Russian wormseed, whose poisonous active ingredient is called "santonin." Needless to say, none of these compounds has any legitimate use in the home kitchen.

West Indian sandalwood is *Amyris balsamifera*. See AMYRIS.

SANDARAC (*Tetraclinis articulata*, formerly *Callistris quadrivalvis*) [*Cupressaceae*]

Arar tree; Juniper resin; Sandarach:

The bark of the sandarac tree exudes a white, semi-transparent resin with a turpentine-like smell. It is used as incense and for making a pale varnish for light-colored woods. In dentistry it is used as a preservative varnish for dental casts. In the United States it is restricted for use in alcoholic beverage flavoring formulations only. It is also called juniper resin.

SANDARACH: See SANDARAC.

SANDBERRY: See UVA-URSI.

SANGREE: See SERPENTARIA.

SANGUINARIA: See YARROW.

SANGUINARY: See YARROW.

SANICLE (*Sanicula marilandica*) [*Umbelliferae*]

American sanicle; Black sanicle; Black snakeroot

(*Sanicula europaea*)

European sanicle; Wood sanicle:

Extracts of the roots of *Sanicula marilandica* and of the leaves of *Sanicula europaea* have been used in herbal remedies. They possess astringent and styptic properties.

SANSHO PEPPER; SAN-SHO: See ANISE-PEPPER.

SANTOLINA (*Santolina chamaecyparissus*) [*Compositae*]

Cypress; Lavender cotton:

Santolina was once used to treat stomach aches and as a vermifuge. The dried leaves and flowers were used as a moth repellant. Both the gray and green forms are used widely in landscaping.

SANTONICA: See WORMSEED.

SARSAPARILLA (*Smilax*, various species) [*Smilacaceae*]

Catbrier; Greenbrier; Costa Rica sarsaparilla; Guayaquil sarsaparilla; Lima sarsaparilla; Red Jamaica sarsaparilla; Virginian sarsaparilla

(*Smilax glauca*)

Sawbrier; Wild sarsaparilla

(*Smilax herbacea*)

Jacob's-ladder

(*Smilax medica*, formerly *aristolochiaefolia*)

Gray sarsaparilla; Mexican sarsaparilla; Vera Cruz sarsaparilla

(*Smilax regelii*)

Brown sarsaparilla; Honduras sarsaparilla

(*Smilax febrifuga*)

Ecuadorean sarsaparilla

(*Aralia nudicaulis*) [*Araliaceae*]

American sarsaparilla; Rabbit's root; Small spikenard; Wild licorice; Wild sarsaparilla

(*Hardenbergia violacea*) [*Leguminosae*]

Australian sarsaparilla; Coral pea; Vine lilac

(*Menispermum canadense*) [*Menispermaceae*]

American sarsaparilla; Moonseed; Texas sarsaparilla; Vine-maple; Yellow parilla

(*Schisandra coccinea*) [*Schisandraceae*]

Bay star vine; magnolia vine; Wild sarsaparilla:

The dried roots of many species of *Smilax*, a tropical American woody vine, yield an extract with a bitter licorice taste that is used in soft drinks, ice cream, candy and baked goods. The extract contains parillin, a substance which has the effect of slowing the heart rate. It has a diuretic effect and formerly was held in high esteem as a "tonic and blood purifier." It was included in compounds used to treat syphilis and chronic rheumatism. The exact species associated with Costa Rica, Guayaquil, Lima, red Jamaica, and Virginian sarsaparillas have not been properly identified. *Smilax aristolochiaefolia, regelii, febrifuga* and "undetermined *Smilax* spp. (Ecuadorean or Central American sarsaparilla)" are listed by the FDA as GRAS.

American or wild sarsaparilla (*Aralia nudicaulis*) [*Araliaceae*] and Australian sarsaparilla (*Hardenbergia violacea*, formerly *monophylla*) [*Leguminosae*] are both used as substitutes for sarsaparilla. *Schisandra coccinea*, although called wild sarsaparilla, is grown only as an ornamental for its decorative red berries.

The American sarsaparilla, *Menispermum canadense*, is a woody vine, native to the eastern United States, that grows in moist woods and along streams. It is cultivated as an ornamental foliage plant to cover arbors or walls. Extracts of the roots have been used in herbal remedies, however they contain quite toxic bitter alkaloids. It is closely related to *Chondrodendron tomentosum* [*Menispermaceae*], a source of curare. The fruit is also poisonous.

SASSAFRAS (*Sassafras variifolium*, formerly *albidum*) [*Lauraceae*]

Ague tree; Cinnamon wood; Saxifrax:

The bark of the roots of this native North American tree contains a lemon-scented oil with a spicy flavor. It was used in soft drinks and candies as a flavoring. This oil contains safrole, a substance banned in 1960 from use in foods by the FDA because it was found to cause liver cancer in laboratory mice. In 1976, the FDA clarified its ruling and stated that sassafras leaves and bark could not be sold for use in herbal teas unless certified safrole-free. The sale of Filé or Filé gumbo powder which contains only dried sassafras leaves has not been banned, and it is still available in the stores.

Filé or Filé gumbo powder is dried, powdered sassafras leaves or a mixture of dried sassafras leaves and dried okra. It sometimes contains coriander, allspice, and sage. The source of this creole seasoning is not positively known. Some feel that this powder was originated by the Choctaw Indians in Louisiana. Others feel that the sassafras leaf was used by early French settlers as a substitute for bay leaves. This latter seems more logical since the sassafras is botanically distantly related to *Laurus nobilis*, the source of bay leaves.

Sassafras bark should not be confused with "sassy-bark," the poisonous bark of the African tree, *Erythrophloeum guineense* [*Leguminosae*], used in African ritual ordeals.

Australian sassafras is the tree *Doryphora sassafras* [?]. Its leaves and bark have been used in medicines.

Brazilian sassafras is *Nectandra puchury* [*Lauraceae*]. The seeds of this tree are called pichurims, sassafras nuts or pitchurim beans. They are used in medicines and as a spice. Related to this tree is the greenheart tree or bebeeru (*Nectandra rodiaei*). The bark of this tree has been used as a substitute for quinine. Primarily, the *Nectandra* trees are used for timber.

California sassafras is *Umbellularia californica* [*Lauraceae*]. It is known also as California laurel, California bay, California olive, myrtle, Oregon myrtle, and pepperwood. The wood is valued highly for fine woodworking.

Cayenne sassafras is *Licanea guianensis* [*Rosaceae*]. It grows in South America.

Chilean sassafras is the same as Peruvian nutmeg. See NUTMEG. There is also a Brazilian sassafras oil which comes from the tree *Ocotea cyrubarum*

[*Lauraceae*]. Ocotea pretiosa is also known as Brazilian sassafras, and Ocotea cymbarum is known as Amazonian sassafras.

There is also "artificial sassafras oil" which is from the tree *Cinnamomum camphora* [*Lauraceae*], the camphor tree. Extracts of the wood are distilled to make camphor. Extracts of *Cinnamomum camphora* must be certified safrole free if they are to be used in flavorings. *Cinnamomum micranthum* is Chinese sassafras.

None of the other "sassafras" trees is listed by the FDA.

SASSAFRAS NUT: See SASSAFRAS.

SATAN'S APPLE: See MAYAPPLE.

SATIN FLOWER: See CHICKWEED.

SAUCE ALONE: See ALLIARIA.

SAUDI FRANKINCENSE: See OLIBANUM.

SAVIN JUNIPER: See SAVIN OIL.

SAVIN OIL: (*Juniperus sabina*) [*Cupressaceae*]
Savin juniper
(*Juniperus phoenicea*)
Phoenician juniper; Phoenician savin oil:

Savin oil, extracted from the needles and twigs, is an acrid volatile oil which was used medically for the treatment of menstrual problems, gout and rheumatism. It was also applied locally to ulcers and decaying teeth.

SAVORY (*Satureja hortensis*) [*Labiatae*]
Bean herb; Summer savory
(*Satureja montana*)
Winter savory:

Summer savory is an annual plant, while winter savory is a perennial. The flavor is like a very mild marjoram. Some say that the summer savory is a little milder than the winter. The leaves are used, fresh or dried, in beans, sauerkraut, sausages, stuffings, vegetables, soups, and roast lamb. It should be cooked with the food. Legend claims that savory makes the old feel young again, cures colic, clears eyesight, ends deafness, relieves toothaches, and soothes wasp and bee stings. GRAS

SAW PALMETTO (*Serenoa repens*, formerly *serrulata*) [*Palmae*]

Scrub palmetto:

The dried berries of the saw palmetto have been used to make a tea thought to be a general tonic and by some as an aphrodisiac.

SAWBRIER: See SARSAPARILLA.

SAXIFRAGE: See PIMPERNEL.

SAXIFRAX: See SASSAFRAS.

SCABISH: See EVENING PRIMROSE.

SCABWORT: See ELECAMPANE.

SCALLION: See SHALLOT.

SCALY BLAZING-STAR: See BLAZING-STAR.

SCALY DRAGON'S-CLAW: See CORALROOT.

SCAMMONY ROOT: See WILD JALAP.

SCARLET BERRY: See NIGHTSHADE.

SCARLET MAPLE: See RED MAPLE.

SCARLET PIMPERNEL (*Anagallis arvensis*) [*Primulaceae*]

Poor man's weatherglass; Red chickweed; Red pimpernel; Shepherd's weatherglass; Shepherd's-clock:

Scarlet pimpernel, considered by most as a weed, is native to Europe. It was brought to North America where it has become widely naturalized. It has been used in home remedies, but because of its central nervous system effects and its extreme diuretic and laxative properties, it should be considered a very dangerous herb. Even the fresh leaves rubbed against the skin can cause a dermatitis. It is called the poor man's weatherglass because the flowers will close with impending bad weather. Try instead *The Scarlet Pimpernel* by Baroness Orczy. It is delightfully refreshing.

SCARLET SUMAC: See SUMAC.

SCENTLESS CAMOMILE: See CAMOMILE.

SCENTLESS MAYWEED: See CAMOMILE.

SCHICHMI TOGARASHI: See SEVEN-FLAVOR SPICE.

SCHNITTLAUCH: See CHIVES.

SCOKE: See POKE.

SCOT'S PINE: See SCOTCH PINE.

SCOTCH BROOM: See BROOM.

SCOTCH CAMOMILE: See CAMOMILE.

SCOTCH FIR: See SCOTCH PINE.

SCOTCH HEATHER: See HEATHER.

SCOTCH LOVAGE: See LOVAGE.

SCOTCH PINE (*Pinus sylvestris*) [*Pinaceae*]
Baltic redwood; Norway pine; Scot's pine; Scotch fir:
The Scotch pine is known as Scot's pine in the United Kingdom, Norway pine in Scandinavia, and Baltic redwood on the European continent. Extracts of the needles and twigs have a strong pine-turpentine odor. They are used in flavoring formulations for beverages, candies, and baked goods. GRAS

SCOURING RUSH: See SHAVE GRASS.

SCREW PINE: See KEWRA.

SCROFULA PLANT: See FIGWORT.

SCROFULA WEED: See RATTLESNAKE PLANTAIN.

SCRUB PALMETTO: See SAW PALMETTO.

SCRUBBY GRASS: See ROCKET.

SCUBBY TREFOIL: See HOP TREE.

SCUTCH: See COUCH GRASS.

SCURVISH: See EVENING PRIMROSE.

SCURVY GRASS: See ROCKET and WATERCRESS.

SEA ASH: See PRICKLY ASH TREE.

SEA ERYNGIUM: See ERYNGO.

SEA FENNEL: See SAMPHIRE.

SEA HOLLY: See ERYNGO.

SEA HOLM: See ERYNGO.

SEA LOVAGE: See LOVAGE.

SEA ONION: See SQUILL.

SEA PARSLEY: See LOVAGE.

SEA SALT: See SALT.

SEA SEDGE: See RED SEDGE.

SEA SQUILL: See SQUILL.

SEALROOT: See SOLOMON'S-SEAL.

SEALWORT: See SOLOMON'S-SEAL.

SEIRON-NIKKEI:
    This is the Japanese name for cinnamon. See CINNAMON.

SELF-HEAL: See HERB CARPENTER.

SENECA SNAKEROOT: See MILKWORT.

SENEGA SNAKEROOT: See MILKWORT.

SENNA: See CASSIA.

SERAH POWDER: See LEMON GRASS.

SERPENT GARLIC: See GARLIC.

SERPENTARIA (*Aristolochia serpentaria*) [*Aristolochiaceae*]

Birthwort; Virginia snakeroot:

Extracts of the roots have an aromatic, spicy flavor, almost gingery. An alkaloid found in the roots, if taken in pure form, can cause respiratory paralysis. It is permitted to be used in alcoholic beverage flavoring formulations only. At one time, it was one of the most highly valued snakebite remedies. It was also supposed to help in childbirth by stimulating uterine contractions. There are about 200 other *Aristolochia* species, all known as birthworts, with common names of calico flower, Dutchman's-pipe, pelican flower, Red River snakeroot, sangree, snakeweed, and Texas snakeroot. All should be considered to be toxic plants.

SESAME (*Sesamum indicum,* formerly *orientale*) [*Pedaliaceae*]

Benne:

Sesame is best known as the little seeds with a nut-like flavor used on rolls and in crackers. The seeds are also the source of sesame oil which is used in cooking. With stir-fry dishes it will impart a slightly nutty flavor. Sesame seeds come in a variety of colors. The black and tan seeds are unhulled while the white are hulled. Ground sesame seeds are used in making the Turkish confection, halvah (a mixture of ground sesame seeds and nuts combined with honey). Some sources refer to ground sesame seeds as tahini. Tahini, however, is a sauce made from sesame seed oil mixed with spicy seasonings. It is used in various Middle Eastern dishes. GRAS

SETO FUUMI:

This is a Japanese seasoning compound consisting of dried seaweed, tuna, sesame seed, and monosodium glutamate.

SETWALL: See VALERIAN.

SEVEN FLAVOR SPICE:

This is a very hot Japanese spice mixture also known as *schichmi togarashi* or *togarashi*. The exact quantities of the various spices may vary according to the brand. Generally the mixture is:

4 tablespoons ground chilies
1 1/4 teaspoons whole poppy seeds
20 grams (3/4 ounce) sansho pepper (anise-pepper)
1 3/4 teaspoons whole black sesame seeds
3 1/2 teaspoons ground white sesame seeds
20 grams (3/4 ounce) ground dried tangerine peel
5 grams (1/8 ounce) whole mustard seeds

It should be used sparingly as a seasoning. The Japanese use it also as a condiment and as a dry dip.

SEVEN-SEAS SPICE:

This is a southeast Asian mixture which is used in marinades and as a seasoning. Generally, it contains:

2 ½ teaspoons ground cardamom
1 ¾ teaspoons ground cassia or cinnamon
1 teaspoon ground celery seeds
2 ½ teaspoons ground dried chilies
1 teaspoon ground cloves
2 ½ teaspoons ground cumin seeds
2 tablespoons ground coriander seeds

SEVENBARK: See **HYDRANGEA.**

SHALLOT (*Allium cepa, Aggregatum* Group, formerly *Allium ascalonicum*) [*Liliaceae*]

Eschalotte; Éschalote:

The shallot, according to French cooks, has a delicate flavor with a slight hint of garlic. It is used when a mild onion taste is desired. The term scallion originally referred to the shallot but now is used interchangeably with "green onion," any onion with a thick stem and almost bulbless root including the leek. The white part of a green onion, chopped finely, is an acceptable substitute for shallots. The mature bulb of the shallot is small with a light red skin. The shallot is used as both the mature bulb and as an immature green onion. GRAS

SHAVE GRASS (*Equisetum hyemale*) [*Equisetaceae*]

Bottlebrush; Horsetail; Horsetail grass; Horsetail rush; Mare's tail; Pewterwort; Scouring rush:

Members of *Equisetaceae* (horsetail family) are closely related to ferns. They have been used in herbal remedies but are quite dangerous and can cause poisoning. The siliceous stems can be used for polishing.

SHEEP LAUREL: See **MOUNTAIN LAUREL.**

SHEEP SORREL: See **SORREL.**

SHEEP-LICE: See **HOUND'S-TONGUE.**

SHEEPBERRY: See **BLACK HAW.**

SHELL FLOWER: See **TURTLEHEAD.**

SHEPHERD'S KNOT: See **CINQUEFOIL.**

SHEPHERD'S WEATHERGLASS: See SCARLET PIMPERNEL.

SHEPHERD'S-BAG: See SHEPHERD'S-PURSE.

SHEPHERD'S-CLOCK: See SCARLET PIMPERNEL.

SHEPHERD'S-HEART: See SHEPHERD'S-PURSE.

SHEPHERD'S-POUCH: See SHEPHERD'S-PURSE.

SHEPHERD'S-PURSE (*Capsella bursa-pastoris*) [*Cruciferae*]
Cocowort; Mother's heart; Pepper and salt; Pickpocket; Saint James' weed; Shepherd's-bag; Shepherd's-heart; Shepherd's-pouch; Toywort; Witch's pouches:
This is a non-cultivated member of the mustard family and is often found growing along roadsides. It has been used in herbal remedies.

SHIELD FERN: See WOOD FERN.

SHIITAKE MUSHROOMS: See DRIED MUSHROOMS.

SHIN-YO-YU: See PINE FIR.

SHINLEAF (*Pyrola elliptica*) [*Pyrolaceae*]
Wild lily-of-the-valley:
This woodland plant is native to North America and Japan. The leaves have mild astringent properties and have been used in herbal remedies.

SHISO ZOKU: See PERILLA.

SHOOTING STAR: See COWSLIP.

SHRIMP PASTE; SHRIMP SAUCE:
Shrimp paste or sauce is a concentrate of dried ground shrimp preserved in brine. It is very pungent and similar to anchovies in saltiness. It is used in Chinese cooking for flavoring fish, pork, chicken, fried rice, bean curd, and vegetables. It should be used sparingly.

SHRUBBY TREFOIL: See HOP TREE.

SHUNGIKU (*Chrysanthemum coronarium*) [*Compositae*]
Chop suey green; Cooking chrysanthemum; Crown daisy; Garland chrysanthemum:

This species of *Chrysanthemum* is grown in the Orient for the tender, young leaves which are used fresh in salads or soups and stir-fried dishes. In Japan the flower heads are also used similarly.

SIBERIAN FIR OIL: See PINE FIR.

SIBERIAN GINSENG: See GINSENG.

SIBERIAN PINE NEEDLE OIL: See PINE FIR.

SICILIAN SUMAC: See SUMAC.

SICKLEWORT: See HERB CARPENTER.

SIDE-FLOWERING SKULLCAP: See SKULLCAP.

SIDE-SADDLE FLOWER: See PITCHER PLANT.

SILKWEED: See MILKWEED.

SILKY DOGWOOD: See KINNIKINICK.

SILKY SWALLOW-WORT: See MILKWEED.

SILVER BIRCH: See WHITE BIRCH.

SILVER CINQUEFOIL: See CINQUEFOIL.

SILVER FIR: See PINE FIR.

SILVER LEAF: See QUEEN'S DELIGHT.

SILVER SPRUCE: See PINE FIR.

SILVER-LEAVED POPLAR: See POPLAR.

SILVERWEED: See CINQUEFOIL.

SIMAROUBA BARK (*Simarouba amara*) [*Simaroubaceae*]
    Extracts of this bark are restricted to use in alcoholic beverage flavorings only.

SIMPLER'S JOY: See BLUE VERVAIN and VERVAIN.

SKULLCAP (*Scutellaria* spp.) (*Scutellaria lateriflora*) [*Labiatae*]

Blue skullcap; Blue pimpernel; Helmet flower; Hoodwort; Mad-dog-weed; Side-flowering skullcap; Virginia skullcap:

Skullcap can be found as an ingredient in commercial herbal teas. It has a bitter flavor and is not aromatic. It has been used in the past as an herbal medicine, especially for nervous disorders and was thought to be effective against rabies. It is not listed by the FDA.

SKUNK CABBAGE (*Symplocarpus foetidus*) [*Araceae*]

Meadow cabbage; Poke; Polecat weed; Skunk weed; Swamp cabbage:

Since most believe that medicines must smell and taste bad, it is easy to understand why skunk cabbage has been used in herbal remedies. Inhaling the stench of the crushed leaves was believed to cure headaches. Extracts of the roots are emetic and slightly narcotic. See POKE.

SKUNK WEED: See SKUNK CABBAGE.

SLIPPER ROOT: See NERVEROOT.

SLIPPERY ELM (*Ulmus rubra*, formerly *U. fulva*) [*Ulmaceae*]

Indian elm; Moose elm; Red elm; Sweet elm:

The dried inner bark of this elm tree has been used in many herbal remedies.

SLIPPERY ROOT: See COMFREY.

SLOE (*Prunus spinosa*) [*Rosaceae*]

Blackthorn:

The sloe is a variety of plum and is most commonly used as a flavoring for gin and other beverages. GRAS

SMALL CELANDINE: See LESSER CELANDINE.

SMALL CORALROOT: See CORALROOT.

SMALL HEMLOCK: See FOOL'S PARSLEY.

SMALL PIMPERNEL: See PIMPERNEL.

SMALL SPIKENARD: See SARSAPARILLA.

SMALLAGE: See CELERY SEED.

SMALLPOX PLANT: See PITCHER PLANT.

SMARTWEED: See KNOTWEED.

SMOKE-OF-THE-EARTH: See FUMITORY.

SMOOTH ALDER: See ALDER.

SMOOTH SUMAC: See SUMAC.

SMOOTH SWEET CICELY: See CHERVIL.

SNAKE LEAF: See ADDER'S-TONGUE.

SNAKE LILY: See IRIS.

SNAKE PLANTAIN: See PLANTAIN.

SNAKEBERRY: See HERB CHRISTOPHER.

SNAKEBITE: See TRILLIUM.

SNAKEHEAD: See TURTLEHEAD.

SNAKEROOT: See CANADIAN SNAKEROOT, ERYNGO, KNOTWEED and SERPENTARIA.

SNAKEWEED: See SERPENTARIA and KNOTWEED.

SNAPPING HAZEL: See WITCH HAZEL.

SNEEZEWEED: See PELLITORY.

SNEEZEWORT: See PELLITORY.

SNOWBALL BUSH: See CRAMPBARK.

SNOWDROP TREE: See FRINGE TREE.

SNOWFLAKE: See WHITE DEAD NETTLE.

SNOWFLOWER: See FRINGE TREE.

SOAP PLANT (*Chlorogalum pomeridianum*) [*Liliaceae*]

Amole; Wild potato:

This lily is native to western North America from southern Oregon to northern Baja California. The bulbs will yield a lather that can be used like soap.

SOAP ROOT: See SOAPWORT.

SOAPBARK: See QUILLAJA.

SOAPWORT (*Saponaria officinalis*) [*Caryophyllaceae*]

Bouncing Bet; Bruisewort; Dog cloves; Fuller's herb; Old maid's pink; Soap root:

The juice of the soapwort will form a lather with water and was thought to be helpful in the treatment of dermatitis and other skin problems. Root extracts have a laxative effect and in large amounts can be dangerously purgative.

SOCOTRINE ALOE: See ALOE.

SOFIA: See LEMONGRASS.

SOFT MAPLE: See RED MAPLE.

SOFT PINE: See WHITE PINE.

SOJA BEAN: See SOY PASTE.

SOLDIER'S HERB: See PLANTAIN.

SOLDIER'S WOUNDWORT: See YARROW.

SOLDIER'S-CAP: See MONKSHOOD.

SOLDIERS: See LOOSESTRIFE.

SOLOMON'S-SEAL (*Polygonatum multiflorum*) [*Liliaceae*]

Dropberry; King-Solomon's-seal; Sealroot; Sealwort

(*Polygonatum odoratum*):

All of the *Polygonatum* species are known as Solomon's-seal or King-Solomon's-seal. Extracts of the root have been used in herbal remedies primarily for external application. *Polygonatum multiflorum* roots were used to make a tea which the American Indians said was good for "female complaints." *Polygonatum odoratum* root extracts were used by the Chinese to treat diabetes. The roots have both astringent and emetic properties.

SOLOMON'S-ZIGZAG: See SPIKENARD.

SOMALI TEA: See ABYSSINIAN TEA.

SOMALIAN MYRRH: See MYRRH.

SONORA GUM: See CAPERS.

SORB APPLE: See ROWAN.

SORREL (*Rumex* spp.) [*Polygonaceae*]
   Dock; Herb patience; Patience; Patience dock
   (*Rumex alpinus*)
   Alpine dock; Monk's dock; Monk's rhubarb; Mountain rhubarb
   (*Rumex acetocella*)
   American sorrel; Common sorrel; Red sorrel; Sheep sorrel
   (*Rumex acetosa*)
   European sorrel; Garden sorrel; Meadow sorrel; Sour dock; Sourgrass
   (*Rumex crispus*)
   Rhubarb sorrel; Curled dock; Narrow dock; Sour dock; Yellow dock
   (*Rumex obtusifolius*)
   Broad-leaved dock
   (*Rumex patientia*)
   Garden patience; Herb patience; Patience; Patience dock; Spinach dock; Monk's rhubarb
   (*Rumex scutatus*)
   Buckler-leaf sorrel; French sorrel; Garden sorrel
   (*Oxalis acetosella*) [*Oxalidaceae*]
   Alleluia; Cuckoo bread; European wood sorrel; Green sauce; Irish shamrock; Mountain sorrel; Sour trefoil; Stubwort; Three-leaved grass; White sorrel; Wood sorrel
   (*Oxalis pes-caprae*)
   Bermuda buttercup; Soursob

(*Oxalis spiralis*)

Chulco

(*Oxalis stricta*)

Upright yellow wood sorrel:

The various species of the genus *Rumex* have sour tasting leaves and bitter roots. Common European sorrel is *Rumex acetosa*. French sorrel is *Rumex scutatus* and is used in salads and cooked like spinach. *Rumex acetosella* is the American common sheep sorrel. It is edible but is seldom used. Yellow dock is used for medicinal tonics.

Sorrel should not be confused with the wood sorrel which belongs to the genus *Oxalis*. These plants contain large quantities of oxalic acid, which is poisonous if ingested in large enough quantities. Cattle grazing on these plants become ill. Eating any of the *Oxalis* plants is not recommended. Nor should the various docks be confused with the common pie plant, rhubarb, which is *Rheum rhabarbarum* [*Polygonaceae*]. Rosella is called Jamaica or Indian sorrel. It is restricted in its use. (See ROSELLA.) There is no FDA listing of *Rumex* or *Oxalis* in the CFR.

Polygonum bistorta [*Polygonaceae*] has also been called patience dock and sweet dock. See KNOTWEED.

SOUR DOCK: See SORREL.

SOUR TREFOIL: See SORREL.

SOURBERRY: See LEMON BERRY.

SOURGRASS: See SORREL.

SOURSOB: See SORREL.

SOURSOP: See CUSTARD APPLE.

SOUTHERN BLUE GUM: See EUCALYPTUS.

SOUTHERN MAIDENHAIR: See MAIDENHAIR FERN.

SOUTHERN PITCHER PLANT: See PITCHER PLANT.

SOUTHERN PRICKLY ASH: See PRICKLY ASH TREE.

SOUTHERN SNAKEROOT: See CANADIAN SNAKEROOT.

SOUTHERN YELLOW PINE: See PINE OIL.

SOUTHERNWOOD (*Artemisia abrotanum*) [*Compositae*]

Lad's love; Old man:

This species of *Artemisia* grows wild in Spain and southern Italy. The smell is very strong and somewhat unpleasant. It is said by some to be used as a flavoring for cakes in Italy. The French use it to repel fleas and to keep moths out of clothing.

SOUTHERNWOOD ROOT: See CARLINE THISTLE.

SOWBERRY: See BARBERRY.

SOWBREAD: See CYCLAMEN.

SOY JAM: See SOY PASTES.

SOY PASTES:

The ordinary soybean, *Glycine max* [*Leguminosae*], also known as soja bean and soya bean, is the source of soy pastes, jams, sauces, and oil.

Soy pastes can be either fermented or unfermented. Soy jam usually refers to the fermented type. The Japanese miso is a fermented type, made by cooking the beans, mixing them with koji (steamed rice treated with the fungus *Aspergillus oryzae*), salt, water, and yeast. The miso is then left to ferment for several months. Natto is also a fermented paste. The cooked beans are inoculated with *Bacillus natto*, which makes the end product a dark sticky paste. Tempeh is a fermented bean cake made in Indonesia. The fermentation process of each new batch is started by adding a portion of already fermented tempeh containing the mold *Rhizopus oligosporus*.

Unfermented bean pastes are known as tofu, or Chinese bean curd. It is a cheese-like product made from a milk-like soybean flour mixture. Sweet red bean paste used in confectionery is also an unfermented paste.

SOY SAUCE:

Generally, soy sauce is a thin dark sauce made from a mixture of flaked soy beans and roasted wheat, inoculated with *Aspergillus oryzae*, and then fermented up to a year. Salt is always added. It is filtered, pasteurized, and bottled.

Imported Chinese soy sauces are basically of three types: light, dark, and heavy. Light soy (made from soy bean extracts, flour, salt, and sugar) is light colored and delicate. It is used as a table condiment and in dishes such as clear soups where soy flavor but not color is desired. Dark soy is made from the same ingredients but also contains caramel. It is blacker, richer and thicker. It is used when both flavor and color are wanted. Heavy soy, made with molasses, is thick and viscous. It is used more for color than for taste in the thick, dark brown sweet-and-pungent sauces.

Japanese soy sauce, made with malt, is between the light and dark Chinese sauces. Tamari is a naturally fermented Japanese soy sauce obtained as a by-product when making miso. (See SOY PASTES.)

Most of the American commercial soy sauces are made quickly by chemical processing rather than natural fermentation. They are quite concentrated, salty and bitter in contrast to the imported sauces. They usually contain no sugar. Low-salt soy sauces are available.

SOYA BEAN: See SOY PASTE.

SOYBEAN: See SOY PASTE.

SPADIC: See COCA.

SPANISH BROOM: See GENET.

SPANISH CHERVIL: See CHERVIL.

SPANISH GARLIC: See GARLIC.

SPANISH HOPS: See MARJORAM.

SPANISH JASMINE: See JASMINE.

SPANISH JUICE: See LICORICE.

SPANISH LAVENDER: See LAVENDER.

SPANISH MARJORAM: See THYME.

SPANISH ORIGANUM: See THYME and ZA'ATAR.

SPANISH PAPRIKA: See PAPRIKA.

SPANISH PSYLLIUM: See PLANTAIN.

SPANISH SAFFRON: See SAFFRON.

SPANISH SAGE: See SAGE.

SPANISH TEA: See EPAZOTE.

SPANISH THYME: See THYME and COLEUS.

SPANISH-BUTTONS: See KNAPWEED.

SPEARMINT: See MINT.

SPECKLED ALDER: See ALDER.

SPEEDWELL: See VERONICA.

SPICE BIRCH: See SWEET BIRCH.

SPICEBERRY: See WINTERGREEN.

SPICEBUSH (*Lindera benzoin*) [*Lauraceae*]
Benjamin bush; Feverbush; Spicewood; Wild allspice:
The berries of this North American shrub were used by the early colonists as a substitute for allspice. Twigs and bark harvested in late winter can also be cooked with foods for seasoning. The leaves harvested in midsummer were used for making tea. It was reputed to have tonic and stimulant properties. The berries were used as a worm medicine, and oil from the seeds was used externally for rheumatism.

SPICEWOOD: See SPICEBUSH.

SPICY WINTERGREEN: See WINTERGREEN.

SPIGNET: See SPIKENARD.

SPIKE LAVENDER: See LAVENDER.

SPIKED ALOE: See AGAVE.

SPIKED LOOSESTRIFE: See LOOSESTRIFE.

SPIKED WILLOW-HERB: See LOOSESTRIFE.

SPIKENARD (*Nardostachys jatamansi*) [*Valerianaceae*]
Nard; Indian spikenard
(*Nardostachys chinensis*)
Chinese spikenard
(*Aralia racemosa*) [*Aralaceae*]
American spikenard; Indian root; Life-of-man; Petty morel; Spignet
(*Valeriana celtica* and *saliunca*) [*Valerianaceae*]

Celtic nard

(*Smilacina racemosa*) [*Smilacaceae*]

False spikenard; Solomon's-zigzag; Treacleberry

(*Hyptis suaveolens*) [*Labiatae*]

Bush tea plant; West Indian spikenard; Wild spikenard:

Spikenard is one of those plant names that can refer to a wide variety of plants. Nard was a fragrant oil or ointment used in ancient times. It is believed to have been made from the roots of *Nardostachys jatamansi* [*Valerianaceae*], a Himalayan plant. This species is also called Indian spikenard, which is used in Malayan cooking and Oriental medicines. American spikenard is *Aralia racemosa* [*Araliaceae*], which has a strong, pleasant fragrance and a bitter aromatic flavor. In the past it was used as a stimulant type of home remedy. It has diaphoretic properties. It is also known as life-of-man, petty morel, and spignet. Celtic nard is *Valeriana celtica* or *Valeriana saliunca* [*Valerianaceae*], closely related to *Nardostachys jatamansi*. These are Alpine plants used in perfumery or medicine. False spikenard can be either *Cymbopogon nardus* [*Gramineae*] (see LEMONGRASS) or *Smilacina racemosa* [*Smilacaceae*], a North American plant grown as an ornamental. West Indian spikenard is a kind of mint, *Hyptis suaveolens* [*Labiatae*]. *Lavandula spica* [*Labiatae*] is occasionally called spikenard. This plant is the source of spike oil. (See LAVENDER.)

SPIKENARD TREE: See ANGELICA TREE.

SPINACH DOCK: See SORREL.

SPINDLE TREE: See WAHOO.

SPLEEN AMARANTH: See AMARANTH.

SPONGE TREE: See CASSIE.

SPOONWOOD: See MOUNTAIN LAUREL and LINDEN FLOWERS.

SPOONWORT: See ROCKET.

SPOTTED ALDER: See WITCH HAZEL.

SPOTTED COMFREY: See LUNGMOSS.

SPOTTED COWBANE: See HEMLOCK (*Cicuta maculata*).

SPOTTED CRANESBILL: See GERANIUM.

SPOTTED GERANIUM: See GERANIUM.

SPOTTED GUM: See EUCALYPTUS.

SPOTTED HEMLOCK: See HEMLOCK (*Conium maculatum*).

SPOTTED KNOTWEED: See KNOTWEED.

SPOTTED LUNGWORT: See LUNGMOSS.

SPOTTED PLANTAIN: See RATTLESNAKE PLANTAIN.

SPOTTED THISTLE: See BLESSED THISTLE.

SPREADING DOGBANE: See DOGBANE.

SPRING WINTERGREEN: See WINTERGREEN.

SPRUCE (*Picea glauca*) [*Pinaceae*]

Alberta spruce; Black Hills spruce; Canadian spruce; Cat spruce; White spruce

(*Picea mariana*)

Black spruce; Bog spruce; Canadian black pine; Double spruce

(*Picea abies*)

Common spruce; Norway pine; Norway spruce

(*Picea jezoensis*)

Yeddo spruce; Yezo spruce:

Extracts of needles and twigs of all of these species are used in flavoring formulations. Oils from *Picea abies*, *glauca* and *mariana* are sold simply as spruce oils. The oil from *Picea abies* is also sold as fir needles oil. The needles of *Picea jezoensis* are often mixed with the needles of *Abies sachalinensis* to produce Japanese pine needle oil. Oil from hemlock (*Tsuga canadensis*) is also sold as spruce oil. *Picea glauca* and *Picea mariana* are GRAS. The other *Picea* species are not specifically listed.

SPUR FLOWER: See MARJORAM.

SPURGE (*Euphorbia* spp.) [*Euphorbiaceae*]

There are over 1,600 species of *Euphorbia* and at least three times that many common names, including the well-known Christmas poinsettia. All should be treated as poisonous plants. The milky juice of most of these plants may produce a severe dermatitis in susceptible individuals, much like that of poison ivy. Succulent species should not be planted along edges of stocked pools since exudates from broken roots may be fatal to the fish. The juices of some species are used for arrow poisons. See CAPER SPURGE.

Euphorbia hirta, commonly called asthma weed, catshair, pill-bearing spurge, and Queensland asthma weed, is a tropical species that has been used in herbal remedies for the treatment of asthma.

SPURGE FLAX: See DAPHNE.

SPURGE LAUREL: See DAPHNE.

SPURGE OLIVE: See DAPHNE.

SQUAW BALM: See PENNYROYAL.

SQUAW MINT: See PENNYROYAL.

SQUAW ROOT; SQUAWROOT: See BLUE COHOSH, BLACK COHOSH and TRILLIUM.

SQUAW TEA: See EPHEDRA.

SQUAW VINE: See PARTRIDGEBERRY.

SQUAWBERRY: See PARTRIDGEBERRY.

SQUAWBUSH: See CRAMPBARK.

SQUILL (*Urginea maritima*) [*Liliaceae*]
   Red squill; Sea onion; Sea squill; White squill:
   Urginea maritima is native to the Canary Islands, to the Mediterranean region east to Syria, and to South Africa. There seems to be some confusion as to the difference between red squill and white squill. Botanically, white squill and red squill are the same species. Some herbalists say that white squill is safe to use, but red squill is a rat poison. Extracts of the bulb were used in olden medicine for their digitalis-like and diuretic effects. Large doses are emetic. The combination of cardiac, emetic, and diuretic effects makes an effective rat poison.

SQUIRREL CORN: See FUMITORY.

SRI LANKA CINNAMON: See CINNAMON.

STAFF VINE: See NIGHTSHADE.

STAGBUSH: See BLACK HAW.

STAGGERWEED: See CORYDALIS, FUMITORY and LARKSPUR.

STAGHORN: See HERB-IVY.

STAR ANISE (*Illicium verum*) [*Illiciaceae*, formerly *Magnoliaceae*]
Badian anise; Chinese anise; Indian anise; Weihsion powder
(*Illicium anisatum*)
Chinese anise; Japanese anise tree; Japanese star anise:
The seed pods of *Illicium verum*, a magnolia-like tree, open to a star shape, giving the name to the spice. Each pod contains a single shiny brown, smooth seed. They are collected before full maturity and dried in the sun. The pods have a pleasant, anise-like aroma, and an agreeable, highly aromatic, sweet anise-like taste. It is a more pungent taste than ordinary anise, *Pimpinella anisum* [*Umbelliferae*]. It is available whole and powdered. Powdered star anise is called weihsion powder (Chinese cookery). In India, China and Japan the plant is burned to scent the houses. It is eaten after the meal to freshen the mouth and is also mixed with tea and liqueurs. Brought to Europe at the end of the 16th century, it was used in making Bordeaux anisette. Infusions of the pods were used as a laxative, however, too strong an infusion can have severe toxic, even fatal, effects.

Cut branches of *Illicium anisatum* are common Buddhist grave decorations in temple grounds in Japan.

The FDA lists only *Illicium verum* as being GRAS.

STAR BLOOM: See PINKROOT.

STAR GRASS (*Aletris farinosa*) [*Liliaceae*]
Ague grass; Ague root; Bitter grass; Colicroot; Crow corn; Mealy starwort; Star root; Unicorn root:
Preparations from the dried roots of this plant were used in herbal medicines. Consumption of the fresh root can cause dizziness, intestinal pain, vomiting, and diarrhea.

STAR OF JERUSALEM: See GOATSBEARD.

STAR OF THE EARTH: See BENNET.

STARCHWORT: See ARUM.

STARWORT: See CHICKWEED.

STAUNCHWORT: See KIDNEY VETCH.

STAVESACRE: See LARKSPUR.

STAYPLOUGH: See REST-HARROW.

STEMLESS GENTIAN: See GENTIAN.

STEP-MOTHER: See PANSY.

STICK-A-BACK: See BEDSTRAW.

STICKLEWORT: See AGRIMONY.

STICKY-HEADS: See GUM PLANT.

STICKY-WILLIE: See BEDSTRAW.

STIFF GENTIAN: See GENTIAN.

STILLINGIA: See QUEEN'S DELIGHT.

STINGING NETTLE: See NETTLE.

STINGLESS NETTLE: See WHITE DEAD NETTLE.

STINKING ASH: See HOP TREE.

STINKING BALM: See PENNYROYAL.

STINKING BENJAMIN: See TRILLIUM.

STINKING CAMOMILE: See CAMOMILE.

STINKING ELDER: See ELDER.

STINKING GUM: See ASAFOETIDA.

STINKING HELLEBORE: See HELLEBORE.

STINKING MAYWEED: See CAMOMILE.

STINKING NIGHTSHADE: See HENBANE.

STINKING PRAIRIE BUSH: See HOP TREE.

Stinkweed: See Jimsonweed.

Stinkwort: See Jimsonweed.

Stitchwort: See Chickweed.

Stone brake: See Wall fern.

Stone mint: See Dittany, common.

Stonecrop (*Sedum reflexum*) [*Crassulaceae*]

There are many *Sedum* species. A few have been used medicinally and a few are used as salad plants, flavoring for soups, cooked like spinach or pickled. Montagné states that cooked, it is rather tasteless. Some species of *Sedum* are extremely bitter. It is probably best to regard *Sedum* as an ornamental.

Stoneroot: See Citronella.

Storax (*Liquidambar orientalis*) [*Hamamelidaceae*]

Asian storax; Copalm; Gum tree; Levant storax; Liquidamber; Liquid storax; Oriental sweet gum; Styrax

(*Liquidambar styraciflua*)

American storax or styrax; American sweet gum; Bilsted; Copalm; Gum tree; Liquidamber; Liquid storax; Opossum tree; Red gum; Sweet gum; White gum:

Copalm, the balsamic, spicy exudate of these trees, is used in flavoring formulations for beverages, confections, and baked goods. The term storax may also refer to any member of the genus *Styrax*. See Benzoin. GRAS

Storkbill: See Herb Robert.

Storksbill (*Erodium cicutarium*) [*Geraniaceae*]

Alfilaria; Heron's-bill; Pin clover; Pin grass; Red-stem filaree; Wild musk:

This is a weedy plant, used as forage in California. It has astringent properties and has been used in herbal remedies.

Stramonium: See Jimsonweed.

Strawberry leaves (*Fragaria* species) [*Rosaceae*]

Strawberry leaves are listed as an ingredient of commercial herbal teas. The exact species is not known.

STRAWBERRY TREE: See ARBUTUS BERRY.

STRAWBERRY-BUSH: See WAHOO.

STRAWFLOWER: See EVERLASTING.

STRIPED ALDER: See WITCH HAZEL.

STUBWORT: See SORREL.

STYRAX: See STORAX and BENZOIN.

SUCCORY: See CHICORY.

SUDAN GUM-ARABIC: See ACACIA.

SUDANESE FRANKINCENSE: See OLIBANUM.

SUGAR APPLE: See CUSTARD APPLE.

SUGAR MAPLE (*Acer saccharum*) [*Aceraceae*]

Hard maple; Rock maple:

Sap of the sugar maple is reduced by boiling to a syrup or, further, to the crystalline sugar. The flavor of real maple syrup is quite distinctive, and although there are many imitations and substitutes available on the market, none seems to capture the delicious, subtle flavor of the genuine article.

SULFURWORT: See IMPERATORIA.

SUMAC (*Rhus coriaria*) [*Anacardiaceae*]

Elm-leaved sumac; Sicilian sumac; Tanner's sumac

(*Rhus glabra*)

Dwarf sumac; Mountain sumac; Scarlet sumac; Smooth sumac; Vinegar tree:

Rhus coriaria grows wild in the Middle East and other areas around the Mediterranean. Its use as a spice and a souring agent, in contrast to a dye or tanning agent, is mainly confined to Levantine or Arabic food. The deep-red hairy berries when dried are used in cooking mainly as a souring agent. It has a sour but fruity, astringent taste. The rough, deep reddish-purple powder made from the dried berries, which is added directly to the cooking pot, is available at Middle Eastern, Lebanese, or Jewish specialty stores. If whole berries are used, they should be crushed, steeped in hot water, and then squeezed. The extracted juice is used like lemon juice. The juice is used in salad dressings and as a marinade for meat, poultry, and fish, especially when these are to be grilled or barbecued. Sumac powder is used to flavor meat, fish, and vegetable stews, also chicken dishes. The taste blends well with yogurt.

The bark, leaves, and fruit of *Rhus glabra* were a common herbal remedy among several American Indian tribes. A tea made from the bark or leaves was reputed to cure everything from sore throat to gonorrhea.

Great care must be taken not to confuse these two species of *Rhus* with other species of *Rhus* which are quite poisonous. The most common poisonous *Rhus* species are *Rhus radicans*, known as poison ivy, poison oak, mercury, markry, and cow-itch, and *Rhus vernix*, known as poison sumac, swamp sumac, poison dogwood, and poison elder.

SUMBUL: See GALBANUM.

SUMMER HAW: See HAWTHORN BERRIES.

SUMMER SAVORY: See SAVORY.

SUMMERBERRY: See CRAMPBARK.

SUN ROSE: See ROCK ROSE.

SUNDEW (*Drosera rotundifolia*) [*Droseraceae*]
Daily-dew; Dew plant; Lustwort; Round-leaves sundew; Youthwort:

The leaves of the sundew are covered and fringed with gland-tipped hairs capable of slowly changing direction and of holding and digesting insects. All of the plants in the *Droseraceae* family are carnivorous. *Drosera rotundifolia* can be found in North America, Europe, and Asia. It has been used in herbal remedies, but as one can realize from the fact that it can digest insects, it contains very irritating substances and should be avoided. In European folk medicine the juice was used to remove warts and was thought to have aphrodisiac properties when taken internally, hence the name lustwort.

SURINAM QUASSIA: See QUASSIA.

SWALLOW-WORT: See MILKWEED.

SWAMP CABBAGE: See SKUNK CABBAGE.

SWAMP CANDLEBERRY: See BAYBERRY.

SWAMP CEDAR: See WHITE CEDAR.

SWAMP DOGWOOD: See HOP TREE.

SWAMP HAW: See APPALACHIAN TEA.

SWAMP HELLEBORE: See FALSE HELLEBORE.

SWAMP LAUREL: See MAGNOLIA.

SWAMP MAPLE: See RED MAPLE.

SWAMP SASSAFRAS: See MAGNOLIA.

SWAMP SUMAC: See SUMAC.

SWAMP TEA: See WILD ROSEMARY.

SWEATING PLANT: See THOROUGHWORT.

SWEDISH BEGONIA: See MARJORAM.

SWEDISH IVY: See MARJORAM.

SWEDISH MYRTLE: See MYRTLE.

SWEET ACACIA: See CASSIE.

SWEET ALMOND: See ALMOND.

SWEET BALM: See BALM.

SWEET BALSAM: See EVERLASTING.

SWEET BASIL: See BASIL.

SWEET BAY: See BAY LEAF and MAGNOLIA.

SWEET BIRCH (*Betula lenta*) [*Betulaceae*]
   Black birch; Cherry birch; Mahogany birch; Mountain mahogany;
   Spice birch:

Extracts from the buds and leaves of the black birch trees have a wintergreen-like flavor. It is now the main source of oil of wintergreen (methyl salicylate) and is used as described under wintergreen. See Wintergreen.

Sweet brake: See Wood fern.

Sweet bush: See Sweet fern.

Sweet calabash: See Passionflower.

Sweet calamus: See Calamus.

Sweet chervil: See Chervil.

Sweet cicely: See Chervil.

Sweet clover (*Melilotus officinalis*) [*Leguminosae*]

Bird's-foot trefoil; Garden balm; Hay flowers; King's clover; Lotus; Melilot; Melist; Sweet trefoil; Swiss melilot; Trefoil; Yellow melilot; Yellow sweet clover

(*Melilotus coerules*)

Blue melilot

(*Melilotus alba*)

Bukhara clover; Hubam clover; White melilot; White sweet clover:

Sweet clover is known by many names. The leaves, stems and flowers of sweet clover have a pleasant fragrance, especially when dried. They can be used to flavor marinades. Blue melilot, grown in Switzerland at the eastern end of Lake Zurich, is used, along with other herbs, to flavor the local Schabzeiger cheese. Swiss melilot (as sweet clover is called in some parts of Europe) has also at times been called costmary. It is said that if the cavity of a tame rabbit is stuffed with a handful of leaves and flowers of sweet clover before roasting, the roasted rabbit will have more of the flavor of a wild rabbit. It is interesting to note that although the FDA lists clover, *Trifolium* spp., as GRAS, there is no mention of the very closely related sweet clover, *Melilotus* spp. in any of their listings.

Sweet coltsfoot: See Coltsfoot.

Sweet cumin: See Anise.

Sweet dock: See Knotweed.

Sweet elder: See Elder.

Sweet elm: See Slippery elm.

Sweet false camomile: See Camomile.

Sweet fern (*Comptonia peregrina*) [*Myricaceae*]
Fern bush; Fern gale; Meadow fern; Sweet bush:
Sweet fern is not a fern but a deciduous shrub of the eastern United States and Canada. It has fern-like leaves and grows to about five feet in height. Extracts of the leaves have astringent properties, and the American Indians would use infusions of the leaves to treat poison ivy.

Sweet flag: See Calamus.

Sweet gale: See Bog myrtle.

Sweet goldenrod (*Solidago odora*) [*Compositae*]
Anise-scented goldenrod; Blue Mountain tea; Bohea-tea; Common goldenrod; Woundweed
(*Solidago nemoralis*)
Dyer's weed; Field goldenrod; Gray goldenrod; Yellow goldenrod
(*Solidago virgaurea*)
European goldenrod
(*Solidago canadensis*)
Aaron's rod; Goldenrod; Woundwort:
The leaves of *Solidago odora* have an odor of anise when bruised. It is used to make Blue Mountain tea which has questionable medicinal effects. The other three species of *Solidago* have also been used in herbal remedies. *Solidago canadensis* grows only west of the Rocky Mountains. Aaron's rod usually refers to the houseleek. See Houseleek.

Goldenrod has often been falsely blamed for causing hay fever. The ragweeds, *Ambrosia* spp. [*Compositae*], are the common cause of hay fever.

Bohea-tea is actually a coarse, black, low-priced tea from the *Woo-ye* (*w* being pronounced like *b*) hills in Fukien, China.

Sweet grass: See Woodruff and Calamus.

Sweet gum: See Storax.

Sweet haw: See Black haw.

SWEET HORSEMINT: See DITTANY, COMMON.

SWEET JARVIL: See CHERVIL.

SWEET JAVRIL: See CHERVIL.

SWEET JOE-PYE WEED: See JOE-PYE WEED.

SWEET LAUREL: See BAY LEAF.

SWEET MACE: See MARIGOLD.

SWEET MAGNOLIA: See MAGNOLIA.

SWEET MARIGOLD: See MARIGOLD.

SWEET MARJORAM: See MARJORAM.

SWEET MARY: See COSTMARY.

SWEET MYRRH: See OPOPANAX.

SWEET MYRTLE: See CALAMUS.

SWEET PEPPER: See CAPSICUM.

SWEET PITCHER PLANT: See PITCHER PLANT.

SWEET POTATO: See WILD YAM.

SWEET ROCKET: See ROCKET.

SWEET RUSH: See CALAMUS.

SWEET-SCENTED MYRRH: See CHERVIL.

SWEET SEDGE: See GALINGALE.

SWEET TREFOIL: See SWEET CLOVER.

SWEET VEGETABLE PASTE OR SAUCE: See HOISIN SAUCE.

SWEET VIBURNUM: See BLACK HAW.

SWEET VIOLET: See VIOLET.

SWEET WOODRUFF: See WOODRUFF.

SWEET-SCENTED GERANIUM: See GERANIUM.

SWEET-SCENTED LIFE EVERLASTING: See EVERLASTING.

SWEET-SCENTED MARIGOLD: See MARIGOLD.

SWEET-SCENTED POND LILY: See LOTUS.

SWEET-SCENTED WATER LILY: See LOTUS.

SWEET-SMELLING TREFOIL: See HEMP AGRIMONY.

SWEETCUP: See PASSIONFLOWER.

SWEETHEARTS: See BEDSTRAW.

SWEETROOT: See LICORICE.

SWEETSOP: See CUSTARD APPLE.

SWEETWEED: See ALTHAEA.

SWEETWOOD: See LICORICE and CINNAMON.

SWEETWOOD BARK: See CASCARILLA BARK.

SWINE CRESS: See HERB-IVY.

SWINE SNOUT: See DANDELION.

SWINEBREAD: See CYCLAMEN.

SWISS MELILOT: See SWEET CLOVER.

SWISS MOUNTAIN PINE: See DWARF PINE.

SWISS VIOLET: See VIOLET.

SYRIAN BEAD TREE: See CHINABERRY.

SYRIAN MALLOW: See ABELMOSK.

SZECHUAN PEPPER: See ANISE-PEPPER.

T

TABASCO SAUCE:

Tabasco is the registered trademark for the pepper sauce originated by the McIlhenny family before 1868 and still manufactured by the McIlhenny Company, New Iberia, Louisiana. It is made from special hot peppers which the company grows on Avery Island, Louisiana. The peppers are harvested by hand, ground to a pulp, and packed into oak barrels with salt. The pulp is left to mature for over three years before being mixed with distilled vinegar. The seeds and skin are strained out, and the thin fiery sauce is bottled. There are other brands of pepper sauce available. Also see CAPSICUM.

TABASCO-SAUCE PEPPER: See CAPSICUM.

TACAMAHAC: See POPLAR.

TACAMAHACA: See LINALOE.

TAHINI: See SESAME.

TAHITIAN VANILLA: See VANILLA.

TAILED CUBEBS: See CUBEB.

TAILED PEPPER: See CUBEB.

TALEWORT: See BORAGE.

TALL BLAZING-STAR: See BLAZING-STAR.

TALL BUTTERCUP: See BUTTERCUP.

TALL CROWFOOT: See BUTTERCUP.

TALL FIELD BUTTERCUP: See BUTTERCUP.

TALL NASTURTIUM: See NASTURTIUM.

TALL SPEEDWELL: See CULVER'S-PHYSIC.

TALL VERONICA: See CULVER'S-PHYSIC.

TALLOW SHRUB: See BAYBERRY.

TAMARACK: See LARCH.

TAMARI: See SOY SAUCE.

TAMARIND SEED (*Tamarindus indica*) [*Leguminosae*]
Tamarind seed refers to the entire dried fruit pod of the tamarind tree. The tamarind tree bears curved seed pods about nine inches in length which are dark brown when ripe. The pods contain up to ten dark brown seeds, most of which are removed before the pods are processed. The pods are partially dried and compressed into rectangular cakes of a sticky, fibrous dark brown pulp. The pods are also preserved in sugar, or they can be totally dried. Tamarind can be prepared for use in several ways. The pods can be soaked in hot water and the juice squeezed out, or the following method can be used: Steep the pulp in boiling water, allow it to cool, then gently rub it to a purée with the fingers. Sieve the purée and discard the seeds and fiber. Excess tamarind purée will keep for up to a week in the refrigerator, however because of the high acid content, it should not be stored in a metal container. Dried or semi-dried tamarind cakes can be safely stored in a cool place for many months if kept in an air-tight container.

Tamarind is used in Indian, Southeast Asian, and Caribbean cooking in much the same way as vinegars and lemon juice are used in European and American cooking. It is included in savory stews, curries, relishes, and spicy sauces. Because of its high pectin content, it is often included in sweet jams and jellies. In the Middle East tamarind teas are considered very refreshing drinks. It is often included in commercial flavoring formulations for fruit drinks, and it is an ingredient in Worcestershire sauce. GRAS

TANNER'S DOCK: See GINSENG.

TANNER'S SUMAC: See SUMAC.

TANSY:
Tansy can refer, correctly or incorrectly, to any one of a number of plants. It is best not to use tansy unless you are very familiar with exactly

which plant you have. Tansy may be *Tanacetum vulgare* [*Compositae*], also known as bitter buttons, golden-buttons, hindheal, and parsley fern, a common weed in the United States, which, besides tannic acid, contains a bitter, volatile oil and a very toxic ketone, thujone. These poisonous substances can cause paralysis of the muscles of respiration and swallowing, vomiting, abdominal pain, convulsions, and death. *Tanacetum vulgare*, if it is certified free of thujone, may only be used in alcoholic beverage flavoring formulations in the United States. *Tanacetum vulgare* was formerly called *Chrysanthemum vulgare* [*Compositae*], especially in Europe. One source states that the leaves of this plant are chopped and used fresh. Also that it is an ingredient in "drisheen" sausage. I have no idea what "drisheen" sausage is, except that it may be an error in copying the German word *Dreeschling* or *Drieschling*, an edible mushroom. If this is so, then it is most likely that *Tanacetum vulgare* is being confused with the plant *Chrysanthemum balsamita majus*, which was formerly called *Tanacetum balsamita*. This plant is best known as costmary. (See **COSTMARY**.) Tansy may also be *Artemisia vulgaris*. (See **MUGWORT**.)

TANSY RAGWORT: See **RAGWORT**.

TARE: See **BEARDED DARNEL**.

TARGET-LEAVED HIBISCUS: See **ABELMOSK**.

TARRAGON (*Artemisia dracunculus*) [*Compositae*]

Estragon; French tarragon; Russian tarragon:

The aroma of tarragon is intermediate between anise and bay leaf. It is a perennial plant which does not grow well in the United States so that only the dried herb, which is much inferior to the fresh, is generally available. *Woman's Home Companion Cook Book* describes tarragon in the following manner:

> Tarragon—Estragon: Young tops cooked with other herbs for greens; leaves used to flavor vinegar and in preserves; flavoring for salad dressings and fish sauces. Perennial. Hardy with protection. Produces no seed. Set out root cuttings in spring in a partly shady place. Cut back in fall and protect either by hilling up or by covering with litter held in place by branches.

Russian tarragon is the wild species, *dracunculus*, which accounts for it being described as having a coarser leaf and an inferior flavor to French tarragon. French tarragon is a sterile clone (hence no seeds) of the wild species and more correctly should be called *Artemisia dracunculus*, cultivar, "Sativa." Tarragon belongs to the same genus of plants as sagebrush (*Artemisia tridentata*), santonica (*Artemisia cina*), and *Artemisia absinthium*, used to make absinthe. Legend claims that tarragon cures toothaches and the bites of mad dogs. *Artemisia dracunculus* is GRAS.

TARWEED: See YERBA SANTA and GUM PLANT.

TASMANIAN BLUE GUM: See EUCALYPTUS.

TASTE POWDER: See MONOSODIUM GLUTAMATE.

TEA TREE: See CAJEPUT.

TEABERRY: See WINTERGREEN and APPALACHIAN TEA.

TEAMSTER'S TEA: See EPHEDRA.

TEJPAT: See CASSIA.

TEMPEH: See SOY PASTE.

TEMPLIN OIL: See PINE FIR.

TEN-FLAVORED SAUCE:
    This is a Chinese seasoning sauce similar to hoisin sauce, however, it is supposed to be spicier. See HOISIN SAUCE.

TETTERBERRY: See BRYONY.

TETTERWORT: See CELANDINE and YARROW.

TEXAS SARSAPARILLA: See SARSAPARILLA.

TEXAS SNAKEROOT: See SERPENTARIA.

TEXAS TARRAGON: See MARIGOLD.

TEXAS UMBRELLA TREE: See CHINABERRY.

THATCH SCREW PINE: See KEWRA.

THE-SON-BEFORE-THE-FATHERS: See COLTSFOOT.

THIMBLEBERRY: See BRAMBLES.

THORN APPLE: See HAWTHORN BERRIES and JIMSONWEED.

THOROUGHWORT (*Eupatorium perfoliatum*) [*Compositae*]
Agueweed; Boneset; Crosswort; Eupatorium; Feverwort; Indian sage; Sweating plant; Vegetable antimony; Wood boneset:

Plants of the genus *Eupatorium* are known as bonesets and have been used in many old medicinal remedies, especially for the reduction of fevers. They have diuretic, diaphoretic, and laxative properties.

THOUSAND-LEAF: See YARROW.

THOUSAND-SEAL: See YARROW.

THREE-LEAVED GRASS: See SORREL.

THREE-LEAVED HOP TREE: See HOP TREE.

THREE-LEAVED NIGHTSHADE: See TRILLIUM.

THROAT ROOT: See WATER AVENS.

THROW-WORT: See LION'S-TAIL.

THUJA: See WHITE CEDAR.

THUNDER PLANT: See HOUSELEEK.

THYME (*Thymus vulgaris*) [*Labiatae*]
Common thyme; Garden thyme
(*Thymus caespititius*, formerly *azoricus*, *micans*, or *serpyllum*)
Tiny thyme; Tufted thyme
(*Thymus capitatus*, formerly *Satureja capitata* or *Thymbra capitata*)
Conehead thyme; Corido thyme; Cretan thyme; Headed savory; Spanish origanum; Thyme of the ancients; Za'atar farsi
(*Thymus* x *citriodorus*, formerly *serpyllum*)
Lemon thyme
(*Thymus herba-barona*)
Caraway thyme
(*Thymus mastichina*)
Spanish thyme; Herb mastic; Mastic thyme; Spanish marjoram
(*Thymus praecox*, subsp. *articus*)
Creeping thyme; Mother-of-thyme

(*Thymus pulegioides*)

Mother-of-thyme; Pennsylvania Dutch tea thyme; Wild thyme

(*Thymus quinquecostatus*)

Japanese thyme:

There are 300 to 400 different species of thyme. Many thymes grown in American gardens are of confused identity and are often erroneously named. It is said that if a French chef could only have two herbs, he would pick bay leaf and thyme. It goes well in all meat dishes but does not combine well with fish, for which parsley is preferred. The dried herb should be used with a light hand since prolonged cooking increases the intensity of the flavor. It should always be cooked with the food for the best flavor. When crushed, the foliage of caraway thyme has the scent of caraway seeds. Thyme is a perennial, preferring a well-drained sunny spot. It can be grown from seed or propagated by planting the rooted sections of the creeping stems. The Romans used thyme as a remedy for melancholy spirits. The Irish say that mounds of thyme are much liked by the fairies who choose aromatic flower beds for their hours of dancing. Thyme is supposed to ease muscle cramps, nervous disorders, headache, and giddiness. It was used as an antiseptic and fumigant. It inspires courage, heals leprosy, and cures whooping cough! The FDA lists *Thymus vulgaris*, *Thymus serpyllum*, and *Thymus capitatus* as GRAS.

THYME OF THE ANCIENTS: See THYME.

TICKLEWEED: See FALSE HELLEBORE.

TICKWEED: See PENNYROYAL.

TIGER NUT: See GALINGALE.

TILIA FLOWERS: See LINDEN FLOWERS.

TINY THYME: See THYME.

TIPTON WEED: See SAINT JOHN'S-WORT.

TIRA: See ROCKET.

TOADFLAX (*Linaria vulgaris*) [*Scrophulariaceae*]

Butter and eggs; Flaxweed; Pennywort; Wild snapdragon; Yellow toadflax:

Although extracts of this plant have been used in herbal remedies, it should be regarded as a poisonous plant. Taken internally it can cause severe liver and kidney damage.

TOBACCO WOOD: See WITCH HAZEL.

TOGARASHI: See SEVEN FLAVOR SPICE.

TOLU BALSAM (*Myroxylon balsamum*) [*Leguminosae*]
Opobalsam:
Extracts from this tree have a sweet odor similar to hyacinths. They are used in flavoring formulations for beverages, confections, baked goods, and chewing gums. Also see PERUVIAN BALSAM. GRAS

TOMARSEED: See ANISE-PEPPER.

TONGA BEAN: See TONKA BEAN.

TONGUE-GRASS: See CHICKWEED.

TONKA BEANS (*Dipteryx odorata*, formerly *oppositiafolia*) [*Leguminosae*]
Tonga beans; Tonquin beans; Dutch tonka bean:
Tonka beans and flavorings made from them are not permitted to be sold in the United States. See VANILLA.

TONQUIN BEAN: See TONKA BEAN.

TONQUIN MUSK: See MUSK.

TOOTHACHE TREE: See PRICKLY ASH TREE.

TORMENTIL: See CINQUEFOIL.

TOUTE-ÉPICE: See ALLSPICE.

TOYWORT: See SHEPHERD'S-PURSE.

TRAGACANTH (*Astragalus gummifer*) [*Leguminosae*]
"Astragal"; Gum dragon
(*Astragalus glycyphyllous*)
Milk vetch:
Tragacanth is a gum substance obtained from several species of *Astragalus* but primarily from *Astragalus gummifer*. It is a mixture of bassorin, pectin, and starch, and when mixed with water, it swells and forms a gelatinous mass that is used in confections to give body. "Astragal" is an incorrect translation of the French "astragale." The correct English translation of

"astragale" is *Astragalus*. Astragal is an architectural term referring to a narrow half-round molding. Milk vetch (*Astragalus glycyphyllous*), a European herb, is reputed to increase milk production in goats. Many other species of this genus are considered poisonous. *Astragalus mollissimus*, native to the United States, commonly called a "loco weed," is poisonous because of its high selenium content. *Astragalus membranaceus*, also known as milk vetch and huang qi, is native to Asia. Its roots have been used in Chinese herbal remedies for hundreds of years.

Astragalus is the bone in the ankle that articulates with the lower ends of the tibia and fibula.

TRAILING BINDWEED: See WILD MORNING-GLORY.

TRAILING MAHONIA: See OREGON GRAPE.

TRASI: See BALACHONG.

TRAVELER'S JOY: See BLUE VERVAIN.

TREACLEBERRY: See SPIKENARD.

TREE CRANBERRY: See CRAMPBARK.

TREE OF LIFE: See GUAIAC and WHITE CEDAR.

TREE PRIMROSE: See EVENING PRIMROSE.

TREFOIL: See SWEET CLOVER and BUCKBEAN.

TREMBLING ASPEN: See POPLAR.

TRILLIUM (*Trillium* spp.) [*Liliaceae*]
Birthroot; Wake-robin
(*Trillium erectum*)
Brown Beth; Nose-bleed; Squawroot; Stinking Benjamin
(*Trillium pendulum*)
Bethroot; Coughroot; Ground lily; Indian balm; Indian shamrock; Jew's-harp plant; Lamb's quarter; Milk ipecac; Nodding wake-robin; Pariswort; Rattlesnake root; Snakebite; Three-leaved nightshade:

There are about thirty species of *Trillium*, all known as birthroot and wake-robin. The roots of almost all of them have been used in herbal remedies, however, *Trillium pendulum* seems to be the most popular species for that purpose. It has been used as both an external and internal remedy and was popular for "female problems."

TROPICAL ALMONDS: See ALMOND.

TROUT LILY: See ADDER'S-TONGUE.

TRUE GINGER: See GINGER.

TRUE IVY: See ENGLISH IVY.

TRUE LAVENDER: See LAVENDER.

TRUE OTTO OIL: See ROSE.

TRUFFLE OAK: See ENGLISH OAK.

TRUFFLES:

Truffles are highly aromatic edible fungi (genus *Tuber*) which usually grow about one foot underground in the vicinity of certain trees (usually oak) and herbs. Unlike other fungi they cannot be cultivated and can only be detected by specially trained dogs and pigs. These factors all contribute to their scarcity and resulting high prices. There are two types of truffles, the black or Perigord truffle and the Italian white truffle. The black truffle is coal black and about the size of a walnut. It is found in the Perigord region of southwest France and has a rich aroma and almost no flavor. It is most often eaten cooked. The Italian white truffle, or Piedmont truffle, is found in the Piedmont region of Italy and in some areas of North Africa. (North African truffles are of inferior quality.) It is usually larger than the black truffle, creamy colored, and almost potato-like in appearance. It has a very strong aroma and a more garlic-like flavor. White truffles are almost always eaten raw. They are sliced thinly and used in salads or as a garnish. Truffles are harvested in the late fall and can be purchased fresh in France and Italy. Elsewhere truffles can be purchased canned as small whole truffles, truffle pieces, truffle peelings or truffle juice. Canned truffles are very much inferior to the fresh truffle. When adding black truffles to a dish to perfume it, it is best to add the truffle to whatever it is intended to perfume and allow it to sit for several hours so that the perfume will permeate the food.

TRUMPET WEED: See JOE-PYE WEED.

TUBEROSE (*Polianthus tuberosa*) [*Amaryllidaceae*]:

The tuberose has an intense floral odor. Extracts of the flowers are extremely costly and are used primarily in expensive perfumes. Only on rare occasions are they included in flavoring formulations. GRAS

TUBEROUS WATER LILY: See LOTUS.

Tuberroot: See Indian paintbrush.

Tufted thyme: See Thyme.

Turk's-cap: See Monkshood.

Turkey aloe: See Aloe.

Turkey burrseed: See Burdock.

Turkey corn: See Corydalis and Fumitory.

Turkey rhubarb: See Rhubarb.

Turkey-claw: See Coralroot.

Turmeric (*Curcuma domestica,* formerly *longa*) [*Zingiberaceae*]
Saffron of the Indies:
This dried and ground root of a plant related to ginger is probably not appreciated as it should be because of the poor quality of what is sold in the grocery stores. There are different methods for curing the rhizomes. Generally, they are boiled, allowed to cool, then spread to dry for five to seven days. It takes about five pounds of fresh rhizomes to produce one pound of dried. Good quality ground turmeric is orange-yellow in color, has a characteristic gingery, pepper-like aroma, and a slightly aromatic, somewhat bitter taste. There is none of the pungency or hotness of ginger. Turmeric also contains a very powerful yellow dye, universally used in the Orient to color boiled rice. It is said that saffron can be used for the same purpose, but if sufficient saffron were used to provide the same intensity of color, the pungency would make the dish inedible. Turmeric is used in all curry powders and in most prepared mustards. It should not be confused with other plants such as *Hydrastris canadensis* [*Ranunculaceae*], which is also called turmeric because of the color of its root. See Goldenseal. GRAS
For crossword puzzle fans: The two words found in crossword puzzles meaning turmeric are olena and rea. Where the puzzle makers found them is a mystery to me.

Turmeric root: See Goldenseal.

Turnhoof: See Ground ivy.

Turnip-rooted chervil: See Chervil.

Turnip-rooted parsley: See Parsley.

Turtlebloom: See Turtlehead.

Turtlehead (*Chelone glabra*) [*Scrophulariaceae*]
Balmony; Saltrheum weed; Shell flower; Snakehead; Turtlebloom:
Native to North America, turtlehead grows mostly in swampy places and damp woods. The leaves have been used as an herbal remedy internally for "general debility" and externally to relieve itching of hemorrhoids.

Twin leaf (*Jeffersonia diphylla*) [*Berberidaceae*]
Ground squirrel pea; Helmet pod; Rheumatism root; Yellowroot:
Extracts of the roots have diuretic and emetic properties and have been used in herbal remedies. It is said that if applied externally as a poultice, it will relieve pain anywhere!

Twinberry: See Partridgeberry.

Twitch grass: See Couch grass.

Two-eyed berry: See Partridgeberry.

Two-leaved nut pine: See Pine nuts.

U

UMBILROOT: See NERVEROOT.

UMBRELLA PINE: See PINE NUTS.

UMBRELLA TREE: See KEWRA.

UPLAND CRANBERRY: See UVA-URSI.

UPLAND CRESS: See ROCKET.

UPLAND SPEEDWELL: See VERONICA.

UPRIGHT SEPTFOIL: See CINQUEFOIL.

UPRIGHT YELLOW WOOD SORREL: See SORREL.

UNGUENTINE CACTUS: See ALOE.

UNICORN ROOT: See STAR GRASS.

UVA-URSI (*Arctostaphylos uva-ursi*) [*Ericaceae*]
Arberry; Bearberry; Bear's grape; Creashak; Hog cranberry; Hogberry; Kinnikinick; Mealberry; Mountain box; Mountain cranberry; Red bearberry; Rockberry; Sagackhomi; Sandberry; Upland cranberry:

This is a very low-growing evergreen shrub best known as kinnikinick. The leaves were smoked, alone or mixed with tobacco, by the American Indians. It had an intoxicating or stupefying effect. The dried leaves were also used in many medical concoctions and as a tea. The leaves contain large amounts of arbutin, a chemical which does have some medical use but which

317

can also cause extreme gastric irritation, vomiting, and in large amounts, convulsions. In Scandinavian countries the leaves are used in tanning fine leather—a much better use than tanning the inside of one's gastrointestinal tract. Bears seem to find the berries quite tasty.

V

VALERIAN (*Valeriana officinalis*) [*Valerianaceae*]

All-heal; Cat's valerian; English valerian; Garden heliotrope; Garden valerian; German valerian; Great wild valerian; Saint George's herb; Setwall; Vandal root; Vermont valerian; Wild valerian

(*Valeriana fauriei*, formerly *officinalis*)

Japanese valerian; Kesso

(*Valeriana wallichii*)

Indian valerian:

Also see GREEK VALERIAN. Valerian refers to any number of plants belonging to the genus *Valeriana*. Extracts of the roots are used in flavoring formulations for beverages, confections, baked goods, and condiments and were an old treatment for hysteria and other nervous disorders. Japanese valerian was previously included in the *officinalis* species but is now placed in a separate species. *Valeriana officinalis* is GRAS.

VANDAL ROOT: See VALERIAN.

VANILLA (*Vanilla planifolia*) [*Orchidaceae*]

Bourbon vanilla; Mexican vanilla

(*Vanilla pompona*)

Guadeloupe vanilla; Pompona vanilla; Vanillon; West Indian vanilla

(*Vanilla tahitensis*)

Tahitian vanilla:

The vanilla orchid is native to Central America, but it has been transplanted to many parts of the world. Madagascar is one of the major producers today along with Mexico. Madagascar, according to Eugen Pauli, was once called Bourbon Island, and vanilla from there was called "Bourbon

319

vanilla." It is supposed to be of excellent quality. *Vanilla pompona* produces a shorter, thicker pod than *Vanilla planifolia* and is a secondary source of commercial vanilla.

Vanilla pods are gathered before they are completely ripe, plunged into boiling water, then, before they are quite dry, closed in tight containers where their aroma develops. The best quality pods, very smooth in flavor, are covered with a frost of crystals. Basically there are three kinds of pods sold: (1) Fine vanilla, pods eight to twelve inches long, the surface black, smooth and frosted. (2) Woody vanilla, the pods five to eight inches long, reddish-brown, the surface dry and dull and not much frosted. (3) Vanillons, four to five inches long, the pods thicker, flat and soft, rarely frosted, the scent stronger and a little bitter. It is this poorest-quality bean that is found in American grocery stores at outrageous prices. For commercial purposes of making pure vanilla extract, the harvested beans are ground without drying. They are cured in a brine and then dehydrated. Even the poorest-quality vanilla bean will give better vanilla flavor than commercial extracts.

The best vanilla flavor can be obtained in a number of different ways. Use the whole vanilla bean to stir the liquid to be flavored, rinse, and dry. Allow a small piece (1-inch) to be cooked in the sauce or pudding, remove at the end of cooking, rinse and dry. Let the vanilla bean stand in the liquid to be used in cakes, or if kept in a container with sugar, the sugar will have a vanilla flavor. (Most commercial "vanilla sugar" is flavored artificially with vanillin and does not have that true vanilla flavor.) A small amount of the pulp can be scraped out and added to the dish. The whole vanilla bean will last for a long, long time. Vanilla extract is made by soaking broken vanilla pods in alcohol. You can safely make your own by soaking vanilla pods in a small bottle filled with vodka, just adding more vodka to the beans as the extract is used. This will have a much stronger vanilla flavor than most of the vanilla extracts sold commercially so smaller quantities should be used for flavoring. GRAS

There are at least twenty different chemicals which contribute to the aroma of real vanilla. One of these is vanillin, which is readily obtained from other sources and is also easily synthesized.

Coumarin, a substance with a vanilla aroma, is extracted from tonka beans (*Dipteryx odoratum*, formerly *oppositiafolia*) [*Leguminosae*]. This substance has been banned for use as a food or food additive in the United States since 1954 because of its toxic effects upon the liver and other organs. It is sold in Mexico as "Mexican Vanilla" or "Mexican Coumarin" and is very cheap. It can easily be confused with vanilla extract made from Mexican vanilla, *Vanilla planifolia*, which is perfectly safe. Not all countries have as strict labeling laws as the United Sates. Artificial vanilla extract sold in the United States contains vanillin, and although the flavor leaves much to be desired, it is quite safe to use. The wood of the tonka bean tree is a very hard, durable wood known as camara wood.

Wild vanilla is *Trilisa odoratissima* [*Compositae*], also known as deer's-tongue, which grows in the southeast United States. The dried leaves are sometimes mixed with tobacco for a vanilla-like aroma. It is not used as a flavoring.

Vanilla planifolia and *tahitensis* are GRAS.

VANILLA SUGAR: See VANILLA.

VANILLIN: See VANILLA.

VANILLON: See VANILLA.

VARNISH TREE: See CANDLENUT.

VEGETABLE ANTIMONY: See THOROUGHWORT.

VEGETABLE SULFUR: See HERB-IVY.

VEGETABLE TALLOW: See BAYBERRY.

VEGETABLE-OYSTER: See GOATSBEARD.

VELVET PLANT: See MULLEIN.

VENICE TURPENTINE: See LARCH.

VENUS' HAIR: See NIGELLA.

VENUS'-SHOE: See NERVEROOT.

VENUS'S-HAIR-FERN: See MAIDENHAIR FERN.

VERA CRUZ SARSAPARILLA: See SARSAPARILLA.

VERBENA OIL: See LEMON VERBENA.

VERJUICE:

Verjuice is the juice of unripe fruit. It is seldom used today but once was a common souring agent. In England it was made from sour green apples, in France from sour green grapes.

VERMONT SNAKEROOT: See CANADIAN SNAKEROOT.

VERMONT VALERIAN: See VALERIAN.

VERONICA (*Veronica* spp.) [*Scrophulariaceae*]
Brooklime; Speedwell

(*Veronica officinalis*)

Common speedwell; Fluellen; Groundhele; Gypsy weed; Low speedwell; Paul's betony; Upland speedwell

(*Veronica chamaedrys*)

Angel's-eye; Bird's-eye; Germander speedwell

(*Veronica beccabunga*)

Beccabunga; European brooklime; Mouth-smart; Neckweed; Speedwell; Water pimpernel; Water purslain:

The *Veronica* plants have been used in numerous herbal remedies, however in general, they are not considered very safe. In the United States use of the bitter flowers of all *Veronica* species is restricted to flavoring formulations for alcoholic beverages.

VERVAIN (*Verbena officinalis*) [*Verbenaceae*]

Enchanter's plant; European vervain; Herb of the cross; Juno's tears; Pigeon's grass; Pigeonweed; Simpler's joy:

Vervain is often confused with lemon verbena (*Aloysia triphylla*, formerly *Lippia citriodora*) because they both belong to the same plant family, *Verbenaceae*. However, they belong to different genera and do not possess similar characteristics. The vervains have been used in the past to make medicinal teas and are not used as seasonings. Vervain was supposed to be particularly effective as an ingredient in love potions. In the United States *Verbena officinalis* is restricted to use in alcoholic beverage flavoring formulations.

VERVAIN SAGE: See SAGE.

VESPER FLOWER: See ROCKET.

VETIVER (*Vetiveria zizanioides*) [*Gramineae*]

Cuscus oil; Khas-khas; Khus-khus:

In Asian countries the fibrous roots of vetiver have been used to weave mats and screens. They have an earthy odor. Vetiver oil, also called khus-khus oil, corrupted to cuscus oil, is used in perfumery. Alcohol extracts from the plant have a pea, asparagus-like flavor and are used at times to enhance the flavor of asparagus. In India khus-khus means poppy seed and khas-khas means vetiver. Cous-cous is the African dish made from baobab leaves, millet flour, and meat. The use of vetiver in the United States is restricted to alcoholic beverage flavorings.

VE-TSIN: See MONOSODIUM GLUTAMATE.

"VICK'S" PLANT: See MARJORAM.

VINDALOO MIXTURE:

This is a paste-type mixture used to season curries and for marinades. It is very hot.

1 teaspoon whole cardamom seeds
1 3-inch piece cinnamon stick
1 teaspoon whole cloves
2 teaspoons whole cumin seeds
1 teaspoon whole fenugreek seeds
1 $1/2$ teaspoons whole black mustard seeds
1 teaspoon whole black peppercorns
3 teaspoons whole coriander seeds
10 cloves garlic, peeled and chopped
1-inch piece ginger finely chopped or $1/4$ teaspoon ground ginger
$1/2$ teaspoon ground turmeric
1 to 5 teaspoons ground dried chilies (to taste)
1 $1/2$ teaspoons salt
1 teaspoon brown sugar (optional)
2 $1/2$ to 4 fluid ounces vinegar
6 ounces onions, peeled, chopped, fried and puréed (optional)

Lightly roast the first ten ingredients together, then grind and add the remaining ingredients to make a paste.

VINE LILAC: See SARSAPARILLA.

VINE-MAPLE: See SARSAPARILLA.

VINEGAR TREE: See SUMAC.

VINEGARS:

Edible vinegars are a dilute solution of acetic acid (5%) extracted from wine, fermented fruits or grains, or other alcoholic fluids. The bacteria *Mycoderma aceti* has the ability to convert alcohol into acetic acid. The bacteria grows best at a temperature between 60°–85° F. and forms a gelatinous, sticky mass on the surface of the liquid called the vinegar mother. Vinegar can also be manufactured by purely chemical processes and in Europe is referred to as vinegar essence.

There are many ways by which to classify vinegars, but the most common way is by the alcoholic fluid from which they are derived.

(1) Wine vinegars: Wine vinegar should be clear and transparent, white if from white wine, pinkish if from red wine. It should always be

lighter in color than the wine from which it was made. It should have a definite acid taste and an aroma which recalls the wine from which it was made. Sherry vinegars are quite sweet.

(2) Cider vinegar: Cider vinegar was the common homemade vinegar in the United States since cider was readily available. The acid content, color, and flavor were quite variable because of the many varieties of apples, the alcohol content of the cider, and the conditions under which the vinegar mother was allowed to grow. These wide variations in cider vinegar are responsible for both the laudatory and derogatory comments about it by various cookbook authors. Some say it is much stronger than wine vinegar with a very sharp taste while others comment that it is very mild. It is interesting to note that one of the most widely sold "cider" vinegars in the United States is not a true cider vinegar but a vinegar distilled from grains and flavored with cider. In this manner the manufacturer can control the amount of acidity, keeping it at the recommended 5% best for food preservation.

(3) Malt vinegar: Malt vinegar is made from any alcoholic beverage made from malted barley. Most are strong, dark colored vinegars, however color does not always denote strength since they may be artificially colored with caramel. Vinegar made from beer usually has a slightly bitter taste.

(4) Distilled or White vinegar: This is made from a dilute solution of pure ethyl alcohol in water and should be perfectly colorless. It is best for pickling since it has a known acid content, is colorless, and has no flavorings to interfere with the spices used in the recipe.

(5) Rice vinegar: Rice vinegars are made from rice wines and have a sweet, delicate flavor which makes them preferred for Oriental sweet and sour dishes. Yamabukizu is a Japanese rice wine vinegar. It is used for seasoning rice. A substitution can be made by adding one tablespoon of sugar to each cup of distilled white vinegar.

(6) Aromatic vinegar: Aromatic vinegar is a mixture of one part of ethyl alcohol and seven parts of vinegar.

(7) Flavored vinegars: Almost anything from herbs to flower petals can be used to flavor vinegars. The only limitation is your own imagination. Fruit and flower vinegars are diluted with water and served as refreshing cold drinks. Raspberry vinegar is made by covering raspberries with vinegar, allowing them to stand for eight days, and then straining without pressure through a fine sieve. Rose vinegar is made by adding about 4 ounces (100 grams) of red rose petals to about 4 cups (1 liter) of vinegar and allowing it to stand for ten days. Lemon vinegar can be either a mixture of equal parts of vinegar and lemon juice, or an elaborate mixture of lemon balm, lemon basil, lemon thyme, lemon verbena, the roots of lemongrass, and lemon peel steeped in vinegar for several weeks. Generally, to make any herb vinegar, fill a clean glass jar 2/3 full of the fresh herb or herb mixture, cover with heated (not boiling) vinegar, cover the jar with a nonmetallic lid or plastic wrap (anchored with a rubber band), and store in a cool place for several

weeks, shaking or stirring occasionally. The vinegar then can be strained into a clean container. Be sure to use noncorrosive containers and lids.

VIOLET BLOOM: See **NIGHTSHADE.**

VIOLETS (*Viola odorata*) [*Violaceae*]

English violet; Florist's violet; Garden violet; Sweet violet

(*Viola calcarata*)

Swiss violet

(*Viola alba*)

Parma violet

(*Viola suavis*)

Russian violet:

The *odorata* species of violet is native to Europe and Asia. The flowers are candied, used as decorations, and can be eaten in small quantities. Any species of violet flower can be candied and used for decorative purposes, however eating of any species other than *Viola odorata* is not recommended. The *Viola* genus of plants, especially the pansy, contains an emetic. The Swiss violet (*Viola calcarata*), like the pansy, was restricted (in 1967) to use in alcoholic beverage flavoring formulations in the United States, however now both *Viola odorata* and *calcarata* are listed as GRAS. The *alba* and *suavis* species are not listed.

African violets are an entirely different plant belonging to the *Saintpaulia* genus [*Gesneriaceae*].

VIPER'S BUGLOSS (*Echium vulgare*) [*Boraginaceae*]

BLUE-DEVIL; BLUEWEED:

This plant is similar to borage and can be used in the same ways. It does not have as strong a cucumber flavor. Its blue flowers are edible and can be used as decorations. It is often a pernicious pasture weed.

VIRGIN ISLAND SPICE:

This is an aromatic mixture from the West Indies used with vegetables, cheese, and egg dishes. Generally, it contains:

1 teaspoon whole celery seeds
1 ¾ teaspoons crushed cloves
1 ½ teaspoons garlic powder
¾ teaspoon ground or crushed mace
¾ teaspoon grated nutmeg
2 teaspoons crushed dried parsley
2 teaspoons ground black pepper
¾ teaspoon coarse salt

VIRGIN'S BOWER (*Clematis virginiana*) [*Ranunculaceae*]

Devil's-darning-needle; Leather flower; Woodbine:

This species of *Clematis* has been used in herbal remedies, however some people may get a severe allergic dermatitis from handling the plant. It is said that inhaling the fumes from the bruised roots will relieve headaches.

VIRGINIA BLUEBELLS: See COWSLIP.

VIRGINIA COWSLIP: See COWSLIP.

VIRGINIA CREEPER (*Parthenocissus quinquefolia*) [*Vitaceae*]

American ivy; American woodbine; Creeper; False grapes; Five leaves; Five-leaved ivy; Wild woodbine; Wild woodvine; Woodbine; Woody climber:

The bark and twigs of Virginia creeper have been used as an herbal remedy by making them into a syrup for the treatment of coughs and colds.

VIRGINIA DOGWOOD: See DOGWOOD.

VIRGINIA MOUNTAIN MINT: See BASIL.

VIRGINIA POKE: See POKE.

VIRGINIA SARSAPARILLA: See SARSAPARILLA.

VIRGINIA SILK: See MILKWEED.

VIRGINIA SKULLCAP: See SKULLCAP.

VIRGINIA SNAKEROOT: See SERPENTARIA.

VIRGINIA THYME: See BASIL.

VOMITROOT: See LOBELIA.

VOMITWORT: See LOBELIA.

W

WADALEE-GUM TREE: See CATECHU.

WAFER ASH: See HOP TREE.

WAHOO (*Euonymus atropurpurea*) [*Celastraceae*]
   Arrow-wood; Bitter ash; Burning bush; Indian arrow; Spindle tree
   (*Euonymus americanus*)
   Bursting-heart; Strawberry-bush:
      Wahoo bark has been used in herbal remedies for its diuretic and cathartic effects, but it is also a cardiac stimulant with digitalis-like effects. It should be considered a poisonous plant. *Euonymus americanus* has similar properties and should be considered poisonous.

WAKE-ROBIN; WAKEROBIN: See TRILLIUM and INDIAN TURNIP.

WALDMEISTER: See WOODRUFF.

WALEWORT: See ELDER.

WALL FERN (*Polypodium vulgare*) [*Polypodiaceae*]
   Adder's fern; Brake fern; Brake rock; Brakeroot; Common polypody; European polypody; Female fern; Fern brake; Fern root; Rock brake; Rock polypod; Stone brake; Wall polypody:
      The roots of this fern have been used in herbal remedies especially for treatment of worms. It is a relatively strong purgative.

WALL PLANT: See PELLITORY.

WALL POLYPODY: See WALL FERN.

327

WALL ROCKET: See ROCKET.

WALLFLOWER: See DOGBANE.

WALLWORT: See ELDER and COMFREY.

WALNUT (*Juglans regia*) [*Juglandaceae*]
English walnut; Carpathian walnut; Caucasian walnut; Circassian walnut; Madeira nut; Persian walnut

(*Juglans nigra*)
Black walnut

(*Juglans cinerea*)
Butternut; Lemon walnut; Oil nut; White walnut:

Extracts of the leaves, husks, and nuts of the English walnut are widely used in flavorings for many types of foods. The black walnut is less commonly used because of its extremely thick and hard shell and its much stronger flavor. The black walnut, contrary to some popular thought, is not poisonous. This misconception has arisen from the fact that the tree roots give off a chemical which is toxic to tomatoes and some other home garden plants. This chemical is not toxic to grass, making the black walnut an excellent shade tree to plant in a lawn. Butternuts have a very hard, thick shell, but the tasty kernels are well worth the work of retrieving them. GRAS

WALNUT KETCHUP:
Walnut ketchup is a ketchup based on green walnuts (*Juglans regia*). It is also called Irish walnut ketchup. See KETCHUP. The following recipe, taken from Montagné (p. 1004), is an example of a recipe which seems to have lost something in the translation. Is the ³/₄ cup powdered spice supposed to be allspice? and is the ¹/₂ cup cayenne pepper an example of the cayenne pepper baked in a cake with flour?

Walnut Ketchup

Put in a tub, with 2 or 3 pounds of rock salt, about 4 pounds of green walnut shells, mix well and leave for 6 days, crushing the shells from time to time with a pestle. Leave the tub tilted to one side after each operation so that the juice which runs from the fruit can be poured off every day, until only the pulp remains. Put the juice to boil and skim it. As soon as it is skimmed add to this juice ³/₄ cup of ginger, ³/₄ cup of powdered spice, ¹/₂ cup of cayenne pepper and an equal quantity of cloves. Simmer for half an hour. Put into small bottles the juice and ingredients. Seal hermetically and keep in a very dry place. Leave for several months before using.

This recipe from *The New Pennsylvania Dutch Cook Book* by Ruth Hutchinson is an example of a probable copying error. Are the English walnuts green or are they the shelled mature nut? To prick a shelled walnut meat with a steel-tined fork seems rather absurd. Use of green nuts makes more sense, especially since the phrase "crush the walnuts to a pulp" is used. Pulp is hardly the word to describe crushed walnut meats. Paste would be more appropriate.

Walnut Catsup for Fish

1 cup English walnuts	$^1/_4$ teaspoon powdered cloves
2 cups water to cover	$^1/_4$ teaspoon nutmeg
2 tablespoons salt	Few grains cayenne pepper
2 cups vinegar	1 teaspoon minced onion
$^1/_2$ teaspoon white pepper	$^1/_4$ teaspoon celery seed
$^1/_4$ teaspoon powdered ginger	

Prick each walnut with a steel-tined fork, place in jar, cover with salted water. Allow walnuts to stand in brine for a week. Drain. Cover with vinegar that has been heated to the boiling point; let it stand for a few hours. Drain off the vinegar and save it. Crush the walnuts to a pulp, combine with the vinegar. Place minced onion in a small bag with the spices and drop it in saucepan with the walnuts and vinegar. Bring mixture to a boil. When it boils, turn down heat and simmer for 1 hour. Cool and bottle. Makes 1 pint.

WALPOLE TEA: See NEW JERSEY TEA.

WANDERING MILKWEED: See DOGBANE.

WART CRESS: See HERB-IVY.

WARTWORT: See EVERLASTING.

WASABI: See LADY'S-SMOCK.

WASHINGTON THORN: See HAWTHORN BERRIES.

WATER ASH: See HOP TREE.

WATER AVENS (*Geum rivale*) [*Rosaceae*]

Avens root; Cure-all; Chocolate root; Indian chocolate; Purple avens; Throat root

(*Geum virginianum*)

Rough avens:

Water avens has been used in herbal remedies, especially for respiratory congestion and to counteract nausea. Excessive amounts are said to produce unpleasant side effects. What is excessive and what the side effects are, I have not determined. Rough avens was used in the same manner as water avens.

WATER CABBAGE: See LOTUS.

WATER CROWFOOT: See BUTTERCUP.

WATER DRAGON: See MARIGOLD.

WATER ERYNGO: See ERYNGO.

WATER FERN: See HERB CHRISTOPHER.

WATER FLAG: See IRIS.

WATER HEMLOCK: See HEMLOCK (*Cicuta virosa*).

WATER LEMON: See PASSIONFLOWER.

WATER LILY: See LOTUS.

WATER MALLOW: See ABELMOSK.

WATER MAUDLIN: See HEMP AGRIMONY.

WATER MINT: See MINT.

WATER PARSLEY: See HEMLOCK (*Cicuta virosa*).

WATER PENNYROYAL: See GUTU COLA.

WATER PEPPER: See KNOTWEED.

WATER PIMPERNEL: See VERONICA.

WATER PLANTAIN: See RATTLESNAKE PLANTAIN.

WATER PURSLAIN: See VERONICA.

WATER SHAMROCK: See BUCKBEAN.

WATER SMARTWEED: See KNOTWEED.

WATER TREFOIL: See BUCKBEAN.

WATER YAM: See WILD YAM.

WATERCRESS (*Nasturtium officinale*) [*Cruciferae*]
Cress; Scurvy grass:
    The common salad green, watercress, should not be confused because of its botanical name with the common garden nasturtium which is *Tropaeolum majus* [*Tropaeolaceae*].

WATERCUP: See PITCHER PLANT.

WAX CLUSTER: See WINTERGREEN.

WAX MYRTLE: See BAYBERRY.

WAXBERRY: See BAYBERRY.

WAXEN WOAD: See BROOM.

WAY BREAD: See PLANTAIN.

WAYTHORN: See CASCARA.

WEATHER PLANT: See LICORICE.

WEATHER VINE: See LICORICE.

WEAVERS' BROOM: See GENET.

WEEPING SPRUCE: See HEMLOCK (*Tsuga canadensis*).

WEEPING TEA TREE: See CAJEPUT.

WEIHSION POWDER: See STAR ANISE.

WEST INDIAN BAY-LEAF OIL: See BAYBERRY.

WEST INDIAN BIRCH: See LINALOE.

WEST INDIAN BLACKTHORN: See CASSIE.

WEST INDIAN DOGWOOD: See JAMAICAN DOGWOOD.

WEST INDIAN ELEMI: See LINALOE.

WEST INDIAN LEMONGRASS: See LEMONGRASS.

WEST INDIAN LOTUSBERRY: See LOTUSBERRY.

WEST INDIAN ROSEWOOD: See AMYRIS.

WEST INDIAN SANDALWOOD: See AMYRIS.

WEST INDIAN SPIKENARD: See SPIKENARD.

WEST INDIAN VANILLA: See VANILLA.

WESTERN BALM: See PENNYROYAL.

WESTERN WALLFLOWER: See DOGBANE.

WEYMOUTH PINE: See WHITE PINE.

WHIG PLANT: See CAMOMILE.

WHINBERRY: See BLUEBERRY.

WHIPPOORWILL-SHOE: See NERVEROOT.

WHITE ARCHANGEL: See WHITE DEAD NETTLE.

WHITE BALSAM: See EVERLASTING.

WHITE BANEBERRY: See HERB CHRISTOPHER.

WHITE BAY: See MAGNOLIA.

WHITE BIRCH (*Betula pendula*, formerly *Betula alba*) [*Betulaceae*]
European white birch
(*Betula papyrifera*, formerly *Betula alba*)
Canoe birch; Paper birch; Silver birch:
Extracts of leaves, bark, and sap of the white birch have been used in many herbal remedies to treat everything from acne to gout.

WHITE BRYONY: See BRYONY.

WHITE CANKERWEED: See LION'S-FOOT.

WHITE CEDAR (*Thuja occidentalis*) [*Cupressaceae*]
American cedar; Arborvitae; Eastern arborvitae; Northern white cedar; Swamp cedar; Thuja; Tree of life; White cedar wood oil; Yellow cedar:

Oil extracts of the fresh leaves and twigs have a strong camphor-like odor reminiscent of sage. The oil contains a very toxic ketone—thujone. The oil is used widely in perfumery, especially in room deodorants. Thujone-free oil, also called cedar leaf oil, is used in confectionery flavoring formulations. This should not be confused with the cedar oil from *Juniper oxycedrus*, which was used by the ancients for embalming bodies and preserving books (See Cade oil) or with cedarwood oil from *Juniperus virginianum*, the eastern red cedar.

WHITE CEDARWOOD OIL: See WHITE CEDAR.

WHITE CHERVIL: See CHERVIL.

WHITE COHOSH: See HERB CHRISTOPHER.

WHITE DAISY: See HERB MARGARET.

WHITE DEAD NETTLE (*Lamium album*) [*Labiatae*]
Dead nettle; Dumb nettle; Snowflake; Stingless nettle; White archangel:

This is a common weed in England and Europe that has become naturalized in the eastern part of North America. It is strongly aromatic and is said to be used in soups and even eaten as a vegetable, although cattle will not eat it. It is an ingredient in herbal remedies.

WHITE EGYPTIAN LOTUS: See LOTUS.

WHITE ENDIVE: See DANDELION.

WHITE FIR: See PINE FIR.

WHITE FRINGE: See FRINGE TREE.

WHITE GOOSEFOOT: See LAMB'S-QUARTERS.

WHITE GUM: See EUCALYPTUS and STORAX.

WHITE HELLEBORE: See FALSE HELLEBORE.

White horehound: See Horehound.

White ironbark: See Eucalyptus.

White Jerusalem artichoke: See Artichoke.

White lettuce: See Lion's-foot.

White mallow: See Althaea.

White melilot: See Sweet clover.

White mustard: See Mustard.

White oak (*Quercus albus*) [*Fagaceae*]

The astringent extracts of wood chips of the white oak are used in flavoring formulations for alcoholic and non-alcoholic beverages, confections and baked goods. GRAS

White pepper: See Pepper.

White pine (*Pinus strobus*) [*Pinaceae*]

Canadian white pine; Deal pine; Eastern white pine; Pumpkin pine; Soft pine; Weymouth pine:

Extracts from the needles and bark are restricted to use in alcoholic beverage flavoring formulations only.

White pond lily: See Lotus.

White poplar: See Poplar.

White root: See Indian paintbrush.

White sandalwood: See Sandalwood.

White sanicle: See White snakeroot.

White saunders: See Sandalwood.

White snakeroot (*Eupatorium rugosum*) [*Compositae*]

White sanicle:

This plant causes "trembles" in livestock that eat it, and people who drink milk or eat butter or meat from these animals may also be poisoned by the plant. Humans affected thusly are said to have "milk sickness." It can be fatal.

WHITE SORREL: See **SORREL.**

WHITE SPRUCE: See **SPRUCE** and **PINE FIR.**

WHITE SQUILL: See **SQUILL.**

WHITE STONECROP: See **STONECROP.**

WHITE SWEET CLOVER: See **SWEET CLOVER.**

WHITE THORN: See **HAWTHORN BERRIES.**

WHITE WALNUT: See **WALNUT.**

WHITE WATER LILY: See **LOTUS.**

WHITE WEED: See **HERB MARGARET.**

WHITE WILLOW: See **WILLOW.**

WHITE YAM: See **WILD YAM.**

WHITE-LEAVED EVERLASTING: See **IMMORTELLE.**

WHITE-MAN'S-FOOT: See **PLANTAIN.**

WHITEWOOD: See **LINDEN FLOWERS.**

WHITLOW GRASS (*Draba verna*) [*Cruciferae*]
   Chickweed; Nailwort; Whitlowwort
   (*Paronychia* spp.) [*Caryophyllaceae*]
   Chickweed; Nailwort; Whitlowwort:
      Whitlow, felon, and paronychia all refer to the same thing—a pyogenic infection of the tissues in the region of the fingernail or toenail. Whitlow grass can refer to any plant used in herbal remedies to cure whitlows, but usually it is one of the above species. The cure was probably more from soaking in warm water than any anti-bacterial action of the plant. Also see **CHICKWEED.**

WHITLOWWORT: See **WHITLOW GRASS.**

WHITTEN TREE: See CRAMPBARK.

WHORLYWORT: See CULVER'S-PHYSIC.

WHORTLEBERRY: See BLUEBERRY.

WILD ALLSPICE: See SPICEBUSH.

WILD BASIL: See BASIL.

WILD BEET: See AMARANTH.

WILD BERGAMOT: See BERGAMOT.

WILD BLACK CHERRY: See WILD CHERRY.

WILD BLEEDING HEART: See CORYDALIS and FUMITORY.

WILD BRYONY: See BRYONY.

WILD CAMOMILE: See CAMOMILE.

WILD CAPSICUM: See CAPSICUM.

WILD CARROT: See DAUCUS.

WILD CHERRY (*Prunus serotina*) [*Rosaceae*]
Black cherry; Black choke; Chokecherry; Rum cherry; Wild black cherry
(*Prunus pennsylvanica*)
Bird cherry; Fire cherry; Pin cherry; Wild red cherry:
Extracts of the bark are used for flavorings, such as in root beer flavor. It has also been used in cough medicines. The cherries make excellent jellies. GRAS

WILD CINNAMON: See CANELLA.

WILD CLARY: See SAGE.

WILD CLOVE: See CLOVES.

WILD COMFREY: See COMFREY.

WILD CRANESBILL: See GERANIUM and HERB ROBERT.

WILD CROCUS: See PASQUE FLOWER.

WILD CUMIN: See CUMIN.

WILD ELDER: See ELDER.

WILD ENDIVE: See DANDELION.

WILD FENNEL: See NIGELLA.

WILD GARLIC: See GARLIC.

WILD GERANIUM: See GERANIUM.

WILD GINGER: See CANADIAN SNAKEROOT.

WILD GUAIAC and WILD GUAIACUM: See GUAIAC.

WILD HOPS: See BRYONY.

WILD HYDRANGEA: See HYDRANGEA.

WILD HYSSOP: See BASIL and BLUE VERVAIN.

WILD INDIGO (*Baptisia tinctoria*) [*Leguminosae*]
   American indigo; False indigo; Indigo broom; Rattleweed; Yellow broom; Yellow indigo:
   Baptisia tinctoria has been used in herbal remedies primarily for external use. It should be considered a poisonous plant if taken internally because of its strong emetic, purgative, and stimulant properties. It can be used as a dye plant.

WILD IRIS: See IRIS.

WILD JALAP (*Ipomoea pandurata*) [*Convolvulaceae*]
   Bindweed; Hog potato; Man-in-the-earth; Man-in-the-ground; Man-of-the-earth; Man root; Scammony root; Wild potato; Wild scammony; Wild sweet potato:
   The roots of this plant have strong cathartic effects though not quite as potent as jalap (*Ipomoea jalapa*). It is found in the eastern United States.

Podophyllum pelatum [Berberidaceae] is also known as wild jalap. See MAYAPPLE and JALAP.

WILD JESSAMINE: See JASMINE.

WILD LEEK: See GARLIC.

WILD LEMON: See MAYAPPLE.

WILD LICORICE: See LICORICE and SARSAPARILLA.

WILD LILY-OF-THE-VALLEY: See SHINLEAF.

WILD MACE: See MACE.

WILD MANDRAKE: See MAYAPPLE.

WILD MARJORAM: See MARJORAM.

WILD MORNING-GLORY (*Calystegia sepium*, formerly *Convolvulus sepium*) [*Convolvulaceae*]

Bindweed; Devil's vine; Great bindweed; Hedge bindweed; Hedge lily; Lady's nightcap; Rutland beauty; Trailing bindweed:

This common weed has been used in herbal remedies. It is a strong purgative.

WILD MUSK: See STORKSBILL.

WILD NARD: See EUROPEAN SNAKEROOT.

WILD ONION: See ONION.

WILD ONION SEED: See NIGELLA.

WILD OREGON GRAPE: See OREGON GRAPE.

WILD PANSY: See PANSY.

WILD PARSLEY: See LOVAGE.

WILD PARSNIP: See ANGELICA.

WILD PASSIONFLOWER: See PASSIONFLOWER.

WILD PENNYROYAL: See CORN MINT and PENNYROYAL.

WILD PEPPER: See DAPHNE and SAGE TREE.

WILD PIE PLANT: See GINSENG.

WILD POTATO: See WILD JALAP and SOAP PLANT.

WILD RAISIN: See APPALACHIAN TEA.

WILD RED CHERRY: See WILD CHERRY.

WILD RHUBARB: See GINSENG.

WILD ROSEMARY (*Ledum palustre*) [*Ericaceae*]
   Crystal tea; Marsh cistus; Moth herb; Narrow-leaved Labrador tea; Swamp tea:
   Wild rosemary is an entirely different plant from true rosemary which belongs to the mint family. Wild rosemary has a similar aroma, and a tea made from its dried leaves has been used as an herbal remedy. It is diaphoretic and diuretic and can be toxic in large amounts.

WILD SAGE: See SAGE.

WILD SARSAPARILLA: See SARSAPARILLA.

WILD SCAMMONY: See WILD JALAP.

WILD SNAPDRAGON: See TOADFLAX.

WILD SNOWBALL: See NEW JERSEY TEA.

WILD SPINACH: See GOOD-KING-HENRY.

WILD SUCCORY: See GENTIAN.

WILD SUNFLOWER: See ELECAMPANE.

WILD SWEET POTATO: See WILD JALAP.

WILD THYME: See THYME.

WILD TOBACCO: See LOBELIA and POKE.

WILD TURKEY PEA: See CORYDALIS and FUMITORY.

WILD TURNIP: See INDIAN TURNIP.

WILD VALERIAN: See VALERIAN.

WILD VANILLA: See VANILLA.

WILD VINE: See BRYONY.

WILD WHITE VINE: See BRYONY.

WILD WOODBINE: See VIRGINIA CREEPER.

WILD WOODVINE: See VIRGINIA CREEPER.

WILD YAM (*Dioscorea villosa*) [*Dioscoreaceae*]
   China root; Colic root; Devil's bones; Rheumatism root; Yuma
(*Dioscorea alata*)
   Water yam; White yam
(*Dioscorea batatas*)
   Chinese yam; Cinnamon vine
(*Dioscorea bulbifera*)
   Air potato
(*Dioscorea elephantipes*)
   Elephant's-foot; Hottentot-bread
(*Dioscorea trifida*)
   Cush-cush; Yampee:

   Wild yam (*Dioscorea villosa*), which grows in the eastern United States, is an old herbal remedy for "bilious colic." It is not used as food. The root has diuretic properties and is emetic in large amounts. *Dioscorea alata* roots are used as food in tropical Asia. *Dioscorea batatas* is used as food in Asia but is considered an ornamental vine in the United States. *Dioscorea bulbifera* has both edible and inedible forms. The edible forms are cultivated in Asia. *Dioscorea elephantipes* grows in South Africa and is known as the Hottentot's famine food. *Dioscorea trifida* is a South American and West Indian edible yam. There are a number of other edible species of *Dioscorea*.

   The yam should not be confused with the sweet potato, *Ipomoea batatas* [*Convolvulaceae*], of which two types are grown in the United States. The soft, sweet, orange-fleshed sweet potato is often inaccurately called a yam, especially in the South.

WILLOW (*Salix alba*) [*Salicaceae*]
   Salicin willow; White willow; Withe; Withy
(*Salix caprea*)
   Florist's willow; Goat willow; Pussy willow; Sallow
(*Salix nigra*)
   Black willow
(*Salix purpurea*)
   Basket willow; Purple osier; Purple willow:

Willow bark was known by the ancients for its powers to reduce fevers. In 1827, Leroux discovered the active ingredient, a bitter glycoside called salicin. It took until 1899 for Deser to introduce acetylsalicylic acid (aspirin) to medicine. The name aspirin comes from "spirsäure," the German word for salicylic acid. The synthetic production of salicylates has completely replaced the expensive compounds obtained from natural sources.

There are over 300 *Salix* species, some having higher concentrations of salicin than others. The above species contain larger quantities of salicin and are also known for their decorative and basket-making purposes.

WILLOW SAGE: See **LOOSESTRIFE.**

WIND FLOWER: See **PASQUE FLOWER.**

WIND ROOT: See **INDIAN PAINTBRUSH.**

WINDERMERE KETCHUP:

   Windermere ketchup is a mushroom ketchup with horseradish. See **MUSHROOM KETCHUP** and **KETCHUP.**

WINE PLANT: See **RHUBARB.**

WINEBERRY: See **RED CURRANT** and **BRAMBLES.**

WINGED EVERLASTING: See **EVERLASTING.**

WINGED PRICKLY ASH: See **ANISE-PEPPER.**

WINGSEED: See **HOP TREE.**

WINTER CLOVER: See **PARTRIDGEBERRY.**

WINTER CRESS: See **ROCKET.**

WINTER FERN: See HEMLOCK (*Conium maculatum*).

WINTER HELLEBORE: See HELLEBORE.

WINTER MARJORAM: See MARJORAM.

WINTER SAVORY: See SAVORY.

WINTER TARRAGON: See MARIGOLD.

WINTERBERRY: See APPALACHIAN TEA.

WINTERBLOOM: See WITCH HAZEL.

WINTERGREEN (*Gaultheria procumbens*) [*Ericaceae*]
Canada tea; Checkerberry; Deerberry; Ground berry; Hill Berry; Ivry-leaves; Mountain tea; Oil of gaultheria; Partridgeberry; Spiceberry; Spicy wintergreen; Spring wintergreen; Teaberry; Wax cluster:
Wintergreen is a small, creeping evergreen shrub common in eastern North America. It has white bell-shaped flowers, a bright-red berry-like fruit, and aromatic leaves which yield a volatile oil rich in methyl salicylate. Pure methyl salicylate is extremely irritating so that it is used medically only in salves and liniments for cutaneous counter-irritation. Like all salicylates (including aspirin), methyl salicylate is toxic and ingestion of the pure substance can be fatal. The amount of oil of wintergreen needed for flavoring is extremely small. The fruit of the wintergreen plant is known as teaberries or checkerberries. The fruit is edible and has only a very faint wintergreen flavor. See also PARTRIDGEBERRY.

WINTERLIEN: See FLAX.

WINTERSWEET: See MARJORAM.

WINTERWEED: See CHICKWEED.

WITCH HAZEL (*Hamamelis virginiana*) [*Hamamelidaceae*]
Snapping hazel; Spotted alder; Striped alder; Tobacco wood; Winterbloom:
Extracts from the bark and leaves of witch hazel have astringent properties and have long been used for treatment of numerous skin irritations. It is often an ingredient in aftershave preparations. It is usually sold in a

10% alcohol solution which also gives a cooling effect when applied to the skin.

John Lust in *The Herb Book* lists hazel nut and pistachio as other common names by which witch hazel is known. This leads to considerable confusion. The hazelnut (one word) or filbert is a member of the *Corylus* genus [*Betulaceae*] and the pistachio is *Pistachia vera* [*Anacardiaceae*].

WITCH'S POUCHES: See **SHEPHERD'S-PURSE.**

WITCHGRASS: See **COUCH GRASS.**

WITHE: See **WILLOW.**

WITHE-ROD: See **APPALACHIAN TEA.**

WITHY: See **WILLOW.**

WITLOOF: See **CHICORY.**

WOADWAXEN: See **BROOM.**

WOLF CLAW: See **HERB-IVY.**

WOLF'S BANE: See **ARNICA** and **MONKSHOOD.**

WOLFRAM KETCHUP:
Wolfram ketchup is a ketchup based on ale, anchovies and mushrooms. See **KETCHUP.**

WOLFSBANE: See **ARNICA** and **MONKSHOOD.**

WOMEN'S GINSENG: See **ANGELICA TREE.**

WONDER BULB: See **SAFFRON.**

WONDER TREE: See **CASTOR OIL PLANT.**

WONDER-OF-THE-WORLD: See **GINSENG.**

WOOD AVENS: See **BENNET.**

WOOD BETONY (*Stachys officinalis*, formerly *betonica*) [*Labiatae*]
   Common betony; Purple betony

(*Pedicularis canadensis*) [*Scrophulariaceae*]

Wood betony (*Stachys officinalis*) is a common ingredient in herbal teas. The tops are astringent and aromatic and the roots have emetic and cathartic properties. It is sometimes called common betony. Wood betony may also refer to *Pedicularis canadensis*, a lousewort. Also see Betony and Lousewort.

Wood boneset: See Thoroughwort.

Wood fern (*Dryopteris filix-mas*) [*Polypodiaceae*]

Aspidium; Bear's paw root; Knotty brake; Male fern; Shield fern; Sweet brake:

This North American and European woodland fern can be found in lists of herbal remedies used for getting rid of worms. It is extremely dangerous when taken internally, causing blindness and death.

Wood mushroom: See Dried mushrooms.

Wood sage: See Germander.

Wood sanicle: See Sanicle.

Wood sorrel: See Sorrel.

Wood vine: See Bryony.

Woodbine: See Honeysuckle, Jasmine, Virgin's bower and Virginia creeper.

Woodroof: See Woodruff.

Woodruff: (*Galium odoratum*) [*Rubiaceae*], formerly (*Asperula odorata*) [*Rubiaceae*]

Master of the wood; Mugwort; Quinsy wort; Sweet woodruff; Sweet grass; Waldmeister; Woodroof; Woodward:

This perennial plant native to Europe has a distinctive scented taste, and the leaves and flowers are used fresh or dried. Its main uses when dried are in "May Cup"—a traditional English drink—and in medicinal teas. It is infused in champagne, Bénédictine, and in punch. In German and Austrian cooking it is used in braised beef dishes and in wine, particularly German May wine. In the United States its use is restricted to alcoholic beverages only. L. P. De Gouy (*The Gold Cook Book*, p. 1008) describes woodruff as follows:

Woodruff—or Waldmeister, meaning "master of the forest" is grown in many American gardens as well as imported from Europe, and is chiefly used to perfume wine punch, champagne bowls, and similar beverages. Voodoo magic, woodruff holds in leaf and flower. It is commended as most excellent "to open obstructions of the liver and spleen." Nourishing and restorative, but, more to the modern whim: "Put into wine, woodruff makes a man merry."

Sweet grass is usually any grass of the genus *Glyceria* but may also refer to woodruff. Quinsy wort is more closely related. It is actually *Asperula cynanchica*, which was once used as a gargle. It is difficult to determine exactly what plant is referred to by "mugwort," but the mugwort used for flavoring of ale was probably woodruff and not *Artemisia vulgaris*.

WOODWARD: See **WOODRUFF.**

WOODWAXEN: See **BROOM.**

WOODY: See **NIGHTSHADE.**

WOODY CLIMBER: See **VIRGINIA CREEPER.**

WOODY NIGHTSHADE: See **NIGHTSHADE.**

WOOLMAT: See **HOUND'S-TONGUE.**

WOOLY BETONY: See **LAMB'S-EARS.**

WOOLY PARSNIP: See **MASTERWORT.**

WOOLY PLANTAIN: See **PLANTAIN.**

WOOLY SWEET CICELY: See **CHERVIL.**

WORCESTERSHIRE SAUCE:

The original Worcestershire sauce was supposedly made by two English druggists, Mr. Lea and Mr. Perrins, from a recipe obtained from a gentleman recently returned from India. The gentleman did not like the product and told the druggists they could keep it. The druggists found that after the sauce had been sitting around for several years, it had developed a different flavor. They began to make, age, bottle, and sell it as *Lea and Perrins Worcestershire Sauce*. The original Worcestershire sauce was aromatic, pungent, and sweet-sour, very dark brown and with 25% visible sediment. The precipitate was an essential feature, and you had to shake the bottle before using. Although Lea & Perrin's recipe was secret, the principal ingredients for the standard recipe (according to Adrian Bailey et al.) are walnut and mushroom catsup, vinegar, sherry and brandy, soy sauce, pork liver, salt, sugar, tamarinds, cayenne and black pepper, coriander, mace, anchovies, shallots and garlic and caramel. The tamarinds, anchovies, and pork liver are simmered in vinegar, the liquor of which is then strained and combined with other ingredients. The sauce then must mature for at least 6 months to bring out the full flavor before being pasteurized and bottled.

Although Lea and Perrins made the first Worcestershire sauce, it is not a registered trademark. There are other brands made. According to Lea and Perrins label, their sauce now contains: water, vinegar, molasses, corn sweeteners, anchovies, natural flavorings, tamarinds, fresh onions, salt, fresh garlic, eschalots, cloves and chile peppers. The sauce is aged for two years.

WORM GRASS: See **PINKROOT.**

WORMSEED:

Wormseed may refer either to the dried unexpanded flower heads of santonica, *Artemisia cina* [*Compositae*], also known as Levant or Russian wormseed and santonica, or to the seeds of certain goosefoots, especially *Chenopodium anthelminticum* [*Chenopodiaceae*]. It really doesn't matter. There are much more efficacious anthelmintics and vermifuges available. In the United States, if any *Artemisia* plant is used as a flavoring, the finished product must be certified thujone-free.

WORMWOOD:

Wormwood refers to any plant of the genus *Artemisia* [*Compositae*], including *Artemisia cina* (santonica) and *Artemisia absinthium* (known as green ginger and formerly used as a vermifuge but now used only in the making of absinthe). In the United States, if any *Artemisia* plant is used as a flavoring, the finished product must be certified thujone-free.

WOUNDWEED: See **SWEET GOLDENROD.**

WOUNDWORT:

A woundwort may refer to any plant with soft downy leaves that was used to dress wounds, but most commonly refers to mints of the genus *Stachys* [*Labiatae*]. See also **KIDNEY VETCH, HERB CARPENTER,** and **SWEET GOLDENROD.**

WRINKLED GIANT HYSSOP: See **ANISE HYSSOP.**

WYCOPY: See **LINDEN FLOWERS.**

WYMOTE: See **ALTHAEA.**

X Y Z

YAM: See WILD YAM.

YAMABUKIZU: See VINEGAR.

YAMPEE: See WILD YAM.

YAOBA: See SAINT MARTIN'S-HERB.

YARROW (*Achillea millefolium*) [*Compositae*]

**Herb carpenter; Iva; Milfoil; Musk yarrow; Noble yarrow; Nose-
bleed; Sanguinary; Soldier's woundwort; Thousand-leaf; Thousand-
seal:**

The leaves, seeds, and roots of this perennial, native to southern
England, were used as a "stimulant tonic." The French called it herb carpenter
because they used it to stop bleeding of small wounds. The young leaves
are eaten in salads and used as a garnish, replacing chervil in parts of Europe.
In the United States, it is used only in beverage flavorings and only then
if the finished beverage is certified thujone-free.

Iva and musk yarrow are better identified as *Achillea erba-rotta*
subspecies *moschata*, however, they can still refer to the *millefolium* species.

Yarrow may also refer to *Sanguinaria canadensis* [*Papaveraceae*], also
known as bloodroot, Indian paint, Indian plant, Indian red paint, pauson,
red paint root, red puccoon, red root, sanguinaria, and tetterwort, which
has been used in old herbal medicines. Extracts of the roots have sedative
properties, and large amounts can be fatal.

Nose-bleed can also refer to *Trillium erectum* [*Liliaceae*] (see TRILLIUM)
or to any number of plants in the arum family [*Araceae*] including Jack-in-
the-pulpit, which is a poisonous plant.

YAUPON: See CASSINA.

Yaw root: See Queen's delight.

Yeast Extract:
The liquid from fresh yeast is extracted, evaporated, and added to vegetable extracts. It is used as a seasoning.

Yeddo spruce: See Spruce.

Yellow adder's-tongue: See Adder's-tongue.

Yellow avens: See Bennet.

Yellow bedstraw: See Bedstraw.

Yellow broom: See Wild indigo.

Yellow camomile: See Camomile.

Yellow cedar: See White cedar.

Yellow cleavers: See Bedstraw.

Yellow dock: See Sorrel.

Yellow erythronium: See Adder's-tongue.

Yellow gentian: See Gentian.

Yellow ginseng: See Blue cohosh.

Yellow goatsbeard: See Goatsbeard.

Yellow goldenrod: See Sweet goldenrod.

Yellow gum: See Eucalyptus.

Yellow Indian-shoe: See Nerveroot.

Yellow indigo: See Wild indigo.

Yellow jasmine: See Jasmine.

Yellow jessamine: See Jasmine.

Yellow lady's-slipper: See Nerveroot.

YELLOW MELILOT: See SWEET CLOVER.

YELLOW MOCCASIN FLOWER: See NERVEROOT.

YELLOW NUT GRASS: See GALINGALE.

YELLOW NUT SEDGE: See GALINGALE.

YELLOW PARILLA: See SARSAPARILLA.

YELLOW PUCCOON: See GOLDENSEAL.

YELLOW ROCKET: See ROCKET.

YELLOW SANDALWOOD: See SANDALWOOD.

YELLOW SAUNDERS: See SANDALWOOD.

YELLOW SNAKELEAF: See ADDER'S-TONGUE.

YELLOW SNOWDROP: See ADDER'S-TONGUE.

YELLOW STARWORT: See ELECAMPANE.

YELLOW STONECROP: See STONECROP.

YELLOW SWEET CLOVER: See SWEET CLOVER.

YELLOW TOADFLAX: See TOADFLAX.

YELLOW-FRUITED THORN: See HAWTHORN BERRIES.

YELLOWBERRY: See BRAMBLES.

YELLOWROOT: See GOLDTHREAD, GOLDENSEAL, and TWIN LEAF.

YELLOWS: See NERVEROOT and BUTTERCUP.

YELLOWWEED: See BUTTERCUP.

YERBA BUENA (*Satureja douglasii*, formerly *Micromeria chamissonis douglasii*) [*Labiatae*]

A very strong wild mint found in California, it must be used very carefully. Only the smallest pinch is necessary. In Spanish it means "good herb." The island in San Francisco Bay probably got its name from the wild herb. It is very closely related to savory.

YERBA DE ST. MARTIN: See SAINT MARTIN'S-HERB.

YERBA MATÉ: See MATÉ.

YERBA SANTA (*Eriodictyon californicum*) [*Hydrophyllaceae*]
**Bear's weed; Consumptive's weed; Holy herb; Mountain balm;
Tarweed:**
Extracts from the aromatic leaves are used in flavoring formulations
for beverages, confections, and baked goods. It has also been used in herbal
remedies, supposedly curing everything from insect bites to halitosis. GRAS

YEW (*Taxus* spp.) [*Taxaceae*]
(*Taxus baccata*)
Chinwood; English yew:
There are eight different species of *Taxus* but innumerable cultivars.
Although plant extracts have been used in herbal remedies, they are all toxic
and should not be consumed in any form.

YEZO SPRUCE: See SPRUCE.

YLANG-YLANG (*Cananga odorata*) [*Annonaceae*]
Cananga; Ilang-ilang:
An aromatic oil with an intense floral, sweet odor and a bitter taste
is extracted from the flowers of this tropical tree. Primarily, it is used in
perfumery but occasionally as a flavoring in soft drinks or candies. GRAS

YOUNGBERRY: See BRAMBLES.

YOUTHWORT: See SUNDEW and MASTERWORT.

YUCCA (*Yucca brevifolia* and *schidigera*) [*Agavaceae*, formerly *Liliaceae*]
Joshua tree; Mohave yucca:
Extracts of these species of yucca are used in root beer flavorings. The
Mohave yucca is the *schidigera* species. GRAS

YUMA: See WILD YAM.

ZANZIBAR ALOE: See ALOE.

ZA'ATAR (*Origanum syriacum*) [*Labiatae*]
(*Satureja thymbra*) [*Labiatae*]
Za'atar rumi; Za'atar franji

(*Thymbra spicata*) [*Labiatae*]

ZA'ATAR HOMMAR; ZA'ATAR MIDBARI

(*Thymus capitatus*, formerly *Satureja capitata* or *Thymbra capitata*) [*Labiatae*]

Conehead thyme; Corido thyme; Headed savory; Thyme of the ancients; Spanish origanum; Za'atar farsi:

These are all herbs closely related to garden thyme (*Thymus vulgaris*) and have a thyme-like flavor, some being more harsh than others. They are found listed in Middle Eastern recipes.

ZARTAR: See ZATHAR.

ZATHAR:

This is said to be a Middle Eastern spice mixture made of equal parts of powdered sumac and thyme. Others say it is a blend of za'atar, sumac bark, and chick-peas or sesame seeds. In some instances it may be a misspelling of za'atar.

ZEDOARY (*Curcuma zedoaria*) [*Zingiberaceae*]:

The rhizomes of this plant, which is closely related to turmeric, have a gingery taste and are used in the same manner as turmeric. GRAS

ZIMT:

This is the German word for cinnamon. See CINNAMON.

ZULU NUT: See GALINGALE.

Special Note

Some plant families are known by more than one name. Listed below are the family names used and those not used.

Used in this book	Other names
Guttiferae	*Clusiaceae*
Compositae	*Asteraceae*
Cruciferae	*Brassicaceae*
Gramineae	*Poaceae*
Labiatae	*Lamiaceae*
Leguminosae	*Fabaceae*
Palmae	*Arecaceae*
Umbelliferae	*Apiaceae*

As a cross-reference, where family names have been changed or genus and species names have been changed, both are contained in the listings of family, genus, and species. The currently used names are indicated in the text.

If a genus and species name or family name are not verified they are marked with a ?.

Families

Aceraceae [Maple family]

Acer rubrum
  red maple
  scarlet maple
  soft maple
  swamp maple
Acer saccharum
  hard maple
  rock maple
  sugar maple
Acer spicatum
  mountain maple

Agavaceae [Agave family]

Agave americana
  agave
  American aloe
  century plant
  flowering aloe
  maguey
  spiked aloe
Dracaena draco
  dragon tree
  dragon's blood
Yucca brevifolia
  Joshua tree
  yucca
Yucca schidigera
  Mohave yucca

Alstroemeriaceae [Alstroemeria family]

Alstroemeria haemantha
  herb lily
Bomarea edulis
  white Jerusalem artichoke

Amaranthaceae [Amaranth family]

Amaranthus spp.
  amaranth
  Joseph's-coat
  lady bleeding
  love-lies-bleeding
  lovely bleeding
  pigwort
  pilewort
  prince's feather
  red cockscomb
  spleen amaranth
  wild beet

Amaryllidaceae [Amaryllis family]

Polianthus tuberosa
  tuberose

Anacardiaceae [Cashew family]

Mangifera indica
  amchur
  mango
Pistacia lentiscus
  Chios mastic tree
  mastic tree
Pistacia vera

green almond
pistachio
pistacia nut
Rhus coriaria
   elm-leaved sumac
   Sicilian sumac
   sumac
   tanner's sumac
Rhus glabra
   dwarf sumac
   mountain sumac
   scarlet sumac
   smooth sumac
   vinegar tree
Rhus integrifolia
   lemon berry
   lemonade berry
   lemonade sourberry
   sourberry
Rhus radicans
   cow-itch
   markry
   mercury
   poison ivy
   poison oak
Rhus vernix
   poison dogwood
   poison elder
   poison sumac
   swamp sumac
Schinus molle
   Australian pepper tree
   California pepper tree
   molle
   pepper tree
   Peruvian mastic tree
   Peruvian pepper tree
   pink peppercorns
   pirul
   red peppercorns
Schinus terebinthifolius
   Brazilian pepper tree
   Christmasberry tree
   Florida pepper tree

Annonaceae [Annona or custard apple family]
Annona muricata

guanabana
prickly custard apple
soursop
Annona reticulata
   American nutmeg
   bullock's heart
   custard apple
Annona squamosa
   custard apple
   Jamaica nutmeg
   sugar apple
   sweetsop
Asimina triloba
   pawpaw
Cananga odorata
   cananga
   ilang-ilang
   ylang-ylang

Apocynaceae [Dogbane family]
Apocynum androsaemifolium
   bitterroot
   catchfly
   dogbane
   flytrap
   honeybloom
   milk ipecac
   milkweed
   mountain hemp
   spreading dogbane
   wallflower
   wandering milkweed
   western wallflower
Aspidosperma quebrachoblano
   aspidosperma
   quebracho
Catharanthus roseus
   old-maid
   periwinkle
   Madagascar periwinkle
   rose periwinkle
Plumeria ruba
   frangipani flower
   nosegay
   red jasmine
Quebrachia lorentzii
   aspidosperma
   quebracho

Schinopsis lorentzii
  aspidosperma
  quebracho
Vinca major
  band plant
  blue-buttons
  greater periwinkle
  periwinkle
Vinca minor
  common periwinkle
  lesser periwinkle
  myrtle
  running myrtle
Vinca rosea
  old-maid
  periwinkle
  Madagascar periwinkle
  rose periwinkle

Aquifoliaceae [Holly family]

Ilex glabra
  Appalachian tea
  bitter gallberry
  Carolina tea
  gallberry
  inkberry
  winterberry
Ilex paraguayensis
  maté
  Paraguayan holly
  Paraguayan tea
  Saint Bartholomew's tea
  yerba maté
Ilex spp.
  holly
Ilex vomitoria
  black drink
  cassena
  cassene
  cassina
  cassine
  Indian black drink
  yaupon

Araceae [Arum family]

Acorus calamus
  calamus
  flagroot

  grass myrtle
  myrtle flag
  sweet calamus
  sweet flag
  sweet grass
  sweet myrtle
  sweet rush
Arisaema triphyllum
  bog-onion
  dragonroot
  Indian turnip
  Jack-in-the-pulpit
  wake-robin
  wild turnip
Arum maculatum
  Adam-and-Eve
  arum
  cocky baby
  cuckoopint
  cypress powder
  dragon root
  gaglee
  ladysmock
  Portland arrowroot
  starchwort
Symplocarpus foetidus
  meadow cabbage
  poke
  polecat weed
  skunk cabbage
  skunk weed
  swamp cabbage

Araliaceae [Ginseng family]

Aralia elata
  angelica tree
  Chinese angelica
  dang qui
  dong quai
  female ginseng
  Japanese angelica
  women's ginseng
Aralia chinensis
  angelica tree
  Chinese angelica
  dang qui
  dong quai
  female ginseng

Japanese angelica
women's ginseng
Aralia japonica
  angelica tree
  Chinese angelica
  dang qui
  dong quai
  female ginseng
  Japanese angelica
  women's ginseng
Aralia nudicaulis
  American sarsaparilla
  rabbit's foot
  small spikenard
  wild licorice
  wild sarsaparilla
Aralia racemosa
  American spikenard
  Indian root
  life-of-man
  petty morel
  spignet
  spikenard
Aralia sinensis
  angelica tree
  Chinese angelica
  dang qui
  dong quai
  female ginseng
  Japanese angelica
  women's ginseng
Aralia spinosa
  angelica tree
  devil's-walkingstick
  Hercules'-club
  prickly ash
  spikenard tree
Eleutherococcus senticosis
  Siberian ginseng
  Panax ginseng
  ginseng (Eastern Asia)
Hedera helix
  English ivy
  gum ivy
  true ivy
Panax ginseng
  ginseng (Eastern Asia)
  Asiatic ginseng
  Chinese ginseng

Korean ginseng
San Qi ginseng
wonder-of-the-world
Panax pseudoginseng
  ginseng (Eastern Asia)
  Asiatic ginseng
  Chinese ginseng
  Korean ginseng
  San Qi ginseng
  wonder-of-the-world
Panax quinquefolia
  ginseng (North America)
  American ginseng
  five-fingers
  five-leafed ginseng
  redberry
Panax schinseng
  ginseng (Eastern Asia)
  Asiatic ginseng
  Chinese ginseng
  Korean ginseng
  San Qi ginseng
  wonder-of-the-world

Aristolochiaceae [Birthwort family]

Aristolochia spp.
  birthwort
  calico flower
  Dutchman's pipe
  pelican flower
  Red River snakeroot
  sangree
  snakeweed
  Texas snakeroot
Aristolochia serpentaria
  birthwort
  serpentaria
  Virginia snakeroot
Asarum canadense
  asarabacca
  asarum
  black snakeroot
  Canadian snakeroot
  coltsfoot snakeroot
  false coltsfoot
  heart snakeroot
  Indian ginger
  southern snakeroot

Vermont snakeroot
wild ginger
Asarum europaeum
asarabacca
asarum
European snakeroot
hazelwort
public house plant
wild nard

Asclepiadaceae [Milkweed family]

Asclepias syriaca
cottonweed
milkweed
silkweed
silky swallow-wort
swallow-wort
Virginia silk
Asclepias tuberosa
butterfly weed
Canada root
chigger flower
flux root
Indian paintbrush
milkweed
orange swallow-wort
pleurisy root
tuberroot
white root
wind root

Balsaminaceae [Balsam family]

Impatiens balsamina
garden balsam

Berberidaceae [Barberry family]

Berberis vulgaris
barberry
European barberry
jaundice berry
pepperidge
piprage
sowberry
Caulophyllum thalictroides
beechdrops
blue cohosh
blue ginseng
papoose root

squaw root
yellow ginseng
Jeffersonia diphylla
ground squirrel pea
helmet pod
rheumatism root
twin leaf
yellowroot
Mahonia aquifolium
blue barberry
California barberry
holly barberry
holly mahonia
mountain grape
Oregon grape
Rocky Mountain grape
trailing mahonia
wild Oregon grape
Podophyllum pelatum
American mandrake
duck's foot
hog apple
Indian apple
mandrake
mayapple
raccoon berry
wild jalap
wild lemon
wild mandrake

Betulaceae [Birch family]

Alnus oregona
alder
Oregon alder
red alder
Alnus rubra
alder
Alnus rugosa
alder
hazel alder
smooth alder
speckled alder
Alnus serrulata
alder
Betula alba
canoe birch
European white birch
paper birch

silver birch
white birch
Betula lenta
  black birch
  cherry birch
  mahogany birch
  mountain mahogany
  spice birch
  sweet birch
Betula papyrifera
  canoe birch
  paper birch
  silver birch
  white birch
Betula pendula
  European white birch
  white birch

Bignoniaceae [Bignonia family]
Crescentia spp.
  calabash tree

Bixaceae [Indian plum family]
Bixa orellana
  achiote
  annotto
  annatto
  anatto
  arnatto
  bija
  bijol
  lipstick tree
  roucou

Bombacaceae [Bombax family]
Adansonia digitata
  baobab
  calabash tree
  dead-rat tree
  lalo
  monkey-bread tree

Boraginaceae [Borage family]
Borago officinalis
  beebread
  bee plant
  borage

burridge
cool-tankard
talewort
Cynoglossum officinalis
  beggar's-lice
  dog-bur
  dog's tongue
  gypsy flower
  hound's-tongue
  sheep-lice
  woolmat
Cynoglossum virginicum
  wild comfrey
Echium vulgare
  blue-devil
  blueweed
  viper's bugloss
Mertensia virginica
  bluebells
  cowslip
  lungwort
  Roanoke-bells
  Virginia bluebells
  Virginia cowslip
Pulmonaria officinalis
  beggar's basket
  blue lungwort
  Jerusalem cowslip
  Jerusalem sage
  lungmoss
  lungwort
  maple lungwort
  spotted comfrey
  spotted lungwort
Symphytum asperum
  prickly comfrey
Symphytum officinale
  blackwort
  boneset
  bruisewort
  comfrey
  consormol
  gum plant
  healing herb
  knitback
  knitbone
  salsify
  slippery root
  wallwort

Symphytum x uplandicum
  Russian comfrey

Burseraceae [Torchwood family]
Boswellia bhau-dajiana
  frankincense
Boswellia carterii
  frankincense
  olibanum
Boswellia frereana
  African elemi
  elemi frankincense
Boswellia papyrifera
  Sudanese frankincense
Boswellia sacra
  Saudi frankincense
Boswellia serrata
  Indian frankincense
  Indian olibanum
Bursera aloexylon
  linaloe
Bursera fagaroides
  linaloe
Bursera glabrifolia
  linaloe
Bursera penicillata
  linaloe
Bursera simarouba
  gumbo limbo
  incense tree
  West Indian birch
  West Indian elemi
Canarium, ? species
  pili nut
Canarium commune
  elemi
Canarium luzonicum
  elemi
Commiphora abyssinica
  Abyssinian myrrh
  Arabian myrrh
Commiphora erythaea, var. glabrescens
  bisabol myrrh
  opopanax
  sweet myrrh
Commiphora molmol
  Somalian myrrh
Commiphora madagascariensis

  Abyssinian myrrh
  Arabian myrrh
Commiphora myrrha
  common myrrh
  hirabol myrrh
Commiphora opobalsamum
  balm of Gilead

Buxaceae [Box family]
Buxus sempervirens
  box
  boxwood
  bush tree

Byttneriaceae [Byttneria family]
Theobroma cacao
  cacao
  chocolate
  cocoa

Cactaceae [Cactus family]
Lophophora williamsii
  devil's root
  dumpling cactus
  mescal buttons
  pellote
  peyote
  sacred mushroom

Campanulaceae [Bellflower family]
Campanula rapunculus
  rampion

Canellaceae [Canella family]
Canella winterana
  canella
  canella bark
  wild cinnamon
Canellaceum alba
  canella
  canella bark
  wild cinnamon

Capparidaceae [Caper family]
Capparis spinosa
  caper bush

capers
mountain pepper

Caprifoliaceae [Honeysuckle family]

Lonicera spp.
  honeysuckle
Sambucus caerulea
  blue elder
Sambucus canadensis
  American elder
  black elder
  elder flowers
  rob elder
  sweet elder
Sambucus ebulus
  blood elder
  danewort
  dwarf elder
  walewort
  wallwort
  wild elder
Sambucus nigra
  black elder
  black-berried European elder
  boor tree
  bore tree
  bounty
  elder
  elfhorn
  ellanwood
  European elder
  German elder
Sambucus pubens
  American red elder
  red-berried elder
  stinking elder
Sambucus racemosa
  European red elder
Viburnum cassinoides
  Appalachian tea
  Carolina tea
  swamp haw
  teaberry
  wild raisin
  withe-rod
Viburnum opulus
  crampbark
  cranberry bush

European cranberry bush
guelder rose
high bush cranberry
snowball bush
whitten tree
Viburnum prunifolium
  black haw
  nannyberry
  sheepberry
  stagbush
  sweet haw
  sweet viburnum
Viburnum trilobum
  crampbark
  cranberry bush
  cranberry tree
  grouseberry
  high bush cranberry
  pimbina
  squawbush
  summerberry
  tree cranberry

Caricaceae [Papaya family]

Carica papaya
  melon tree
  papaw
  papaya
  pawpaw

Caryophyllaceae [Pink family]

Dianthus caryophyllus
  carnation
  clove pink
  divine flower
  gillyflower
  picotee
Paronychia spp.
  chickweed
  nailwort
  whitlow grass
  whitlowwort
Saponaria officinalis
  bouncing Bet
  bruisewort
  dog cloves
  fuller's herb
  old maid's pink

soap root
soapwort
Stellaria media
  adder's mouth
  chickweed
  Indian chickweed
  satin flower
  starwort
  stitchwort
  tongue-grass
  winterweed

Celastraceae [Staff-tree family]

Catha edulis
  Abyssinian tea
  African tea
  Arabian tea
  cafta
  chat
  kat
  khat
  qat
  Somali tea
Euonymus americanum
  bursting heart
  strawberry-bush
Euonymus atropurpurea
  arrow-wood
  bitter ash
  burning bush
  Indian arrow
  spindle tree
  wahoo

Chenopodiaceae [Goosefoot family]

Chenopodium album
  lamb's-quarters
  pigweed
  white goosefoot
Chenopodium ambrosiodes
  American wormseed
  epazote
  goosefoot
  Mexican tea
  Spanish tea
  wormseed
Chenopodium bonus-henricus
  allgood

fat-hen
Good-King-Henry
goosefoot
mercury
wild spinach
Chenopodium botrys
  feather geranium
  Jerusalem oak

Cistaceae [Rockrose family]

Cistus creticus
  Cretan rockrose
  labdanum
  ladanum
Cistus incanus, subsp. creticus
  Cretan rockrose
  labdanum
  ladanum
Helianthemum canadense
  frost plant
  frostwort
  rock rose
  sun rose

Compositae [Sunflower family]

Achillea erba-rotta moschata
  iva
  musk yarrow
Achillea millefolium
  herb carpenter
  iva
  milfoil
  musk yarrow
  noble yarrow
  nose-bleed
  sanguinary
  soldier's woundwort
  thousand-leaf
  thousand-seal
  yarrow
Achillea ptarmica
  bastard pellitory
  sneezeweed
  sneezewort
Ambrosia spp.
  ragweed
Ammobium alatum
  winged everlasting

Anacyclus pyrethrum
  pellitory of Spain
  pyrethrum
Anaphalis spp.
  cottonweed
  cudweed
  everlasting
  Indian posey
  ladies' tobacco
  large-flowered everlasting
  life everlasting
  pearly everlasting
Antennaria spp.
  cat's foot
  everlasting
  ladies' tobacco
  mountain everlasting
  pussy-toes
Anthemis arvensis
  corn camomile
Anthemis cotula
  dog fennel
  stinking camomile
  stinking mayweed
  wild camomile
Anthemis montana
  camomile adulterant
Anthemis nobilis
  camomile
  English camomile
  garden camomile
  ground apple
  lawn camomile
  manzanilla
  May-then
  marigold
  Roman camomile
  Scotch camomile
  Whig plant
Anthemis tinctoria
  golden Marguerite
  ox-eye camomile
  yellow camomile
Arctium lappa
  bardana
  beggar's-buttons
  burdock
  burr seed
  clotbur

cockle buttons
cocklebur
cuckold
edible burdock
gobo
grass burdock
great bur
great burdock
hardock
hareburr
harlock
hurrburr
lappa
turkey burrseed
Arctium minus
  common burdock
Arnica cordifolia
  arnica
  mountain daisy
  mountain tobacco
  wolf's bane
Arnica montana
  arnica
  mountain daisy
  mountain tobacco
  wolf's bane
Artemisia abrotanum
  lad's love
  old man
  southernwood
Artemisia absinthium
  absinthe
  green ginger
  wormwood
Artemisia cina
  Levant wormseed
  Russian wormseed
  santonica
  wormseed
  wormwood
Artemisia dracunculus
  estragon
  French tarragon
  Russian tarragon
  tarragon
Artemisia gmelinii
  Russian wormseed
Artemisia moxa
  moxa

Artemisia pallens
  davana
Artemisia vulgaris
  felon herb
  Indian wormwood
  moxa
  mugwort
  sailor's tobacco
  Saint John's herb
Balsamita major
  alecost
  Bible leaf
  costmary
  mint geranium
  sweet Mary
  tansy
Bellis perennis
  English daisy
Calendula officinalis
  bull's eyes
  calendula
  holigold
  marigold
  Mary bud
  poet's marigold
  pot marigold
Carduus benedictus
  blessed thistle
  cardin
  holy thistle
  Saint Benedict's thistle
  spotted thistle
Carduus marianus
  holy thistle
  Mary thistle
  Saint Mary's thistle
Carlina acaulis
  carline thistle
  dwarf carline
  ground thistle
  southernwood root
Carthamus tinctorus
  American saffron
  bastard saffron
  dyer's saffron
  false saffron
  safflower
Centaurea cyanus
  bachelor's-button

bluebonnet
bluebottle
blue centaury
cornflower
cyani
Centaurea nigra
  black knapweed
  bullweed
  hardheads
  knobweed
  Spanish-buttons
Centaurea spp.
  knapweed
Chamaemelum nobile
  camomile
  English camomile
  garden camomile
  lawn camomile
  manzanilla
  May-then
  marigold
  Roman camomile
  Scotch camomile
  Whig plant
Chamomilla recutita
  German camomile
  Hungarian camomile
  sweet false camomile
  wild camomile
Chamomilla suaveolens
  pineapple weed
  rayless mayweed
Chrysanthemum balsamita majus
  alecost
  Bible leaf
  costmary
  mint geranium
  sweet Mary
  tansy
Chrysanthemum cinerariifolium
  Dalmatia pyrethrum
  Dalmatian insect flower
  Dalmatian insect powder
  pellitory
  pyrethrum
Chrysanthemum coccineum
  painted daisy
  pellitory
  Persian insect flower

Persian insect powder
pyrethrum
Chrysanthemum coronarium
chop suey green
cooking chrysanthemum
crown daisy
garland chrysanthemum
shungiku
Chrysanthemum leucanthemum
camomile adulterant
golden daisy
herb Margaret
Marguerite
maudlinwort
oxeye daisy
white daisy
white weed
Chrysanthemum parthenium
febrifuge plant
feverfew
pellitory
Chrysanthemum spp.
herb Margaret
Chrysanthemum vulgare
European tansy
tansy
Cichorium endivia
endive
Cichorium intybus
barbe-de-capuchin
Belgian endive
blue-sailors
chicory
coffeeweed
succory
witloof
Cnicus benedictus
blessed thistle
cardin
holy thistle
Saint Benedict's thistle
spotted thistle
Conyza canadensis
bitterweed
bloodstaunch
butterweed
colt's tail
erigeron
fleabane

herb Christopher
horseweed
mare's tail
Cynara cardunculus
cardoon
Cynara scolymus
artichoke
French artichoke
globe artichoke
Echinacea spp.
black Samson
echinacea
Kansas niggerhead
Missouri snakeroot
purple coneflower
rudbeckia (erroneous)
Sampson root
Erigeron canadensis
bitterweed
bloodstaunch
butterweed
colt's tail
erigeron
fleabane
herb Christopher
horseweed
mare's tail
Eupatorium cannabinum
hemp agrimony
sweet-smelling trefoil
water maudlin
Eupatorium perfoliatum
agueweed
boneset
crosswort
eupatorium
feverwort
Indian sage
sweating plant
thoroughwort
vegetable antimony
wood boneset
Eupatorium purpureum
gravel weed
gravelroot
green-stemmed Joe-Pye weed
Joe-Pye weed
kidney root
purple boneset

queen-of-the-meadow
sweet Joe-Pye weed
trumpet weed
Eupatorium rugosum
  white sanicle
  white snakeroot
Eupatorium triplinerve?
  ayapana
Gnaphalium spp.
  chafeweed
  cudweed
  dysentery weed
  everlasting
  field balsam
  Indian posey
  life everlasting
  low cudweed
  marsh cudweed
  mouse ear
  old field balsam
  sweet balsam
  sweet-scented life everlasting
  wartwort
  white balsam
Grindelia robusta
  August flower
  gum plant
  gumweed
  resin-weed
  rosinweed
  sticky-heads
  tarweed
Helenium autumnale
  sneezeweed
Helianthus tuberosus
  girasole
  Jerusalem artichoke
Helichrysum angustifolium
  cultivated curry plant
  immortelle
Helichrysum italicum
  curry plant
  white-leaved everlasting
Helichrysum italicum, subsp. siitalicum
  cultivated curry plant
Helichrysum orientale
  everlasting
  immortelle
Helichrysum serpyllifolium

Hottentot tea
Helipterum spp.
  everlasting
  strawflower
Hieracium pilosella
  felon herb
  hawkeye
  mouse bloodwort
  mouse ear
  pilosella
Inula helenium
  alant
  elecampane
  elfdock
  elfwort
  horse-elder
  horsehead
  horseheal
  inula
  scabwort
  wild sunflower
  yellow starwort
Leontopodium alpinum
  edelweiss
  lion's-foot
Liatris scariosa
  blazing-star
  blue blazing-star
  button snakeroot
  gay-feather
  large button snakeroot
  tall blazing-star
Liatris spicata
  blazing-star
  button snakeroot
  colic root
  dense button snakeroot
  devil's bit
  devil's bite
  gay-feather
  marsh blazing-star
Liatris squarrosa
  blazing-star
  button snakeroot
  gay-feather
  rattlesnake-master
  scaly blazing-star
Matricaria chamomilla
  German camomile

Hungarian camomile
sweet false camomile
wild camomile
Matricaria inodora
corn feverfew
scentless camomile
scentless mayweed
wild camomile
Matricaria matricarioides
pineapple weed
rayless mayweed
Matricaria perforata
corn feverfew
scentless camomile
scentless mayweed
wild camomile
Matricaria recutita
German camomile
Hungarian camomile
sweet false camomile
wild camomile
Ormensis mixta
Moroccan camomile
Ormensis multicaulis
Moroccan camomile
Petasites japonicus
fuki
Petasites spp.
butterbur
sweet coltsfoot
Prenanthes alba
canker root
cankerweed
lion's-foot
rattlesnake root
white cankerweed
white lettuce
Prenanthes serpentaria
lion's-foot
rattlesnake root
Pyrethrum carneum
painted daisy
pellitory
Persian insect flower
Persian insect powder
pyrethrum
Pyrethrum cinerariifolium
Dalmatia pyrethrum
Dalmatian insect flower

Dalmatian insect powder
pellitory
pyrethrum
Pyrethrum coccineum
painted daisy
pellitory
Persian insect flower
Persian insect powder
Pyrethrum hybridum
painted daisy
pellitory
Persian insect flower
Persian insect powder
pyrethrum
Santolina chamaecyparissus
lavender cotton
santolina
Saussurea costus
costus
Saussurea lappa
costus
Senecio jacobaea
European ragwort
ragwort
tansy ragwort
Silphium perfoliatum
compass plant
cup plant
Indian cup
Indian gum
prairie dock
ragged cup
rosinweed
Silybum marianum
holy thistle
Marythistle
milk thistle
Saint Mary's thistle
Solidago canadensis
Aaron's rod
goldenrod
woundwort
Solidago odora
anise-scented goldenrod
Blue Mountain tea
bohea-tea
common goldenrod
sweet goldenrod
woundweed

Solidago nemoralis
  dyer's weed
  field goldenrod
  gray goldenrod
  yellow goldenrod
Solidago virgaurea
  European goldenrod
Tagetes erecta
  African marigold
  Aztec marigold
  big marigold
  marigold
Tagetes lucida
  cloud plant
  hierba de las nubes
  marigold
  Mexican marigold mint
  Mexican tarragon
  mint marigold
  sweet mace
  sweet marigold
  sweet-scented marigold
  Texas tarragon
  winter tarragon
Tagetes patula
  French marigold
  marigold
Tanacetum balsamita
  alecost
  costmary
  tansy
Tanacetum vulgare
  button bitters
  golden-buttons
  hindheal
  parsley fern
  tansy
Taraxacum officinale
  blowball
  cankerwort
  dandelion
  fairy clock
  lion's tooth
  pee-in-the-bed
  priest's crown
  puffball
  swine snout
  white endive
  wild endive

Tragopogon porrifolius
  goatsbeard
  oyster plant
  purple goatsbeard
  salsify
  vegetable-oyster
Tragopogon pratensis
  goatsbeard
  Jack-go-to-bed-at-noon
  John-go-to-bed-at-noon
  meadow salsify
  noon flower
  noonday flower
  noontide
  star of Jerusalem
  yellow goatsbeard
Trilisa odoratissima
  deer's-tongue
  wild vanilla
Tripleurospermum inodorum
  corn feverfew
  scentless camomile
  scentless mayweed
  wild camomile
Tripleurospermum recutita
  German camomile
  Hungarian camomile
  sweet false camomile
  wild camomile
Tussilago farfara
  ass's foot
  British tobacco
  bullsfoot
  butterbur
  coltsfoot
  cough wort
  flower velure
  foal's-foot
  hallfoot
  horsefoot
  horsehoof
  the-son-before-the-fathers
Vernonia spp.
  ironweed

Convolvulaceae [Morning-glory
  family]
Calystegia sepium

bindweed
devil's vine
great bindweed
hedge bindweed
hedge lily
lady's nightcap
Rutland beauty
trailing bindweed
wild morning-glory
Convolvulus sepium
bindweed
devil's vine
great bindweed
hedge bindweed
hedge lily
lady's nightcap
Rutland beauty
trailing bindweed
wild morning-glory
Ipomoea batatas
sweet potato
Ipomoea jalapa
jalap
Ipomoea pandurata
bindweed
hog potato
man-in-the-earth
man-in-the-ground
man-of-the-earth
man root
scammony root
wild jalap
wild potato
wild scammony
wild sweet-potato

Cornaceae [Dogwood family]
Cornus amomum
cornel
kinnikinick
red willow
silky dogwood
Cornus florida
boxwood
budwood
cornel
cornelian tree
dogtree

dogwood
false box
Florida cornel
Florida dogwood
flowering cornel
flowering dogwood
green ozier
Virginia dogwood

Crassulaceae [Orpine family]
Sedum album
white stonecrop
Sedum reflexum
stonecrop
yellow stonecrop
Sempervivum tectorum
Aaron's rod
bullock's eye
hen and chickens
houseleek
Jupiter's beard
Jupiter's eye
live-forever
old-man-and-woman
roof houseleek
thunder plant

Cruciferae [Mustard family]
Alliaria petiolata
alliaria
donkey's foot
garlic mustard
Jack-by-the-hedge
onion nettle
sauce alone
Armoracia rusticana
horseradish
Barbarea verna
American cress
scurvy grass
winter cress
Barbarea vulgaris
herb Barbara
rocket
upland cress
winter cress
yellow rocket
Brassica alba

white mustard
Brassica hirta
  white mustard
Brassica juncea
  brown mustard
  Russian mustard
  Sarepta mustard
Brassica juncea, var. crispifolia
  Indian mustard
  leaf mustard
  mustard greens
Brassica napus
  colza
  rapeseed
Brassica nigra
  black mustard
Capsella bursa-pastoris
  cocowort
  mother's heart
  pepper and salt
  pickpocket
  Saint James' weed
  shepherd's-bag
  shepherd's-heart
  shepherd's-pouch
  shepherd's-purse
  toywort
  witch's pouches
Cardamine amara
  bitter cress
  large bitter cress
Cardamine pennsylvanica
  bitter cress
Cardamine pratensis
  bitter cress
  cardamine
  cuckooflower
  lady's-smock
  Mayflower
  meadow cress
Cardamine yezoensis
  Japanese horseradish
  wasabi
Cochlearia armoracia
  horseradish
Cochlearia officinalis
  scrubby grass
  scurvy grass
  spoonwort

Diplotaxis tenuifolia
  wall rocket
Draba verna
  whitlow grass
Eruca vesicaria, subsp. sativa
  arugula
  rocket
  rocket-gentle
  rocket-salad
  roka
  Roman rocket
  roquette
  ruchetta
  rugola
  rugula
  tira
Hesperis matronalis
  dame's rocket
  dame's violet
  sweet rocket
  vesper flower
Lepidium sativum
  garden cress
  pepper grass
  upland cress
Nasturtium officinale
  cress
  scurvy grass
  watercress
Raphanus sativus, Cv. Longipinnatus
  Chinese radish
  daikon
Senebiera coronopus
  herb-ivy
  swine cress
  wart cress
Sinapis alba
  white mustard
Sisymbrium alliaria
  alliaria
  donkey's foot
  garlic mustard
  Jack-by-the-hedge
  onion nettle
  sauce alone
Sisymbrium irio
  London rocket
Sisymbrium orientale
  eastern rocket

Sisymbrium spp.
  hedge mustard
  herb Sophia

Cupressaceae [Cypress family]
Callistris quadrivalvis
  arar tree
  juniper resin
  sandarac
  sandarach
Juniperus communis
  juniper
  juniper berry
Juniperus oxycedrus
  cade oil
  juniper tar
  oil of cadeberry
  prickly juniper
Juniperus phoenicea
  Phoenician juniper
  Phoenician savin oil
Juniperus sabina
  savin juniper
  savin oil
Tetraclinis articulata
  arar tree
  juniper resin
  sandarac
  sandarach
Thuja occidentalis
  American cedar
  arborvitae
  cedar leaf oil
  eastern arborvitae
  northern white-cedar
  swamp cedar
  thuja
  tree of life
  white cedar
  white cedarwood oil
  yellow cedar

Curcurbitaceae [Gourd family]
Bryonia alba
  bryony
  tetterberry
  white bryony
  wild bryony

  wild hops
  wild vine
  wood vine
Bryonia dioica
  bryony
  devil's turnip
  red bryony
  wild hops
  wild vine
  wild white vine

Cyperaceae [Sedge family]
Carex arenaria
  German sarsaparilla
  red couchgrass
  red sedge
  sand sedge
  sea sedge
Cyperus esculentis
  nut grass
  nut sedge
  yellow nut grass
  yellow nut sedge
Cyperus esculentis, var. sativus
  chufa
  earth almond
  rush nut
  tiger nut
  Zulu nut
Cyperus longus
  galangale
  galingale
  sweet sedge

Dioscoreaceae [Yam family]
Dioscorea alata
  water yam
  white yam
Dioscorea batatas
  Chinese yam
  cinnamon vine
Dioscorea bulbifera
  air potato
Dioscorea elephantipes
  elephant's-foot
  Hottentot-bread
Dioscorea trifolia
  cush-cush

yampee
Dioscorea villosa
  China root
  colic root
  devil's bones
  rheumatism root
  wild yam
  yuma

Droseraceae [Sundew family]
Drosera rotundifolia
  daily-dew
  dew plant
  lustwort
  round-leaved sundew
  sundew
  youthwort

Ebenaceae [Ebony family]
Diospyrus lotus
  date plum
  European lotus

Ephedraceae [Ephedra family]
Ephedra spp.
  Brigham Young weed
  desert herb
  desert tea
  ephedra
  joint fir
  Mormon tea
  squaw tea
  teamster's tea
Ephedra sinica
  ma huang

Equisetaceae [Horsetail family]
Equisetum hyemale
  bottlebrush
  horsetail
  horsetail grass
  horsetail rush
  mare's tail
  pewterwort
  scouring rush
  shave grass

Ericaceae [Heath family]
Arbutus unedo
  arbutus berry
  cane apples
  strawberry tree
Arctostaphylos manzanita
  manzanita
Arctostaphylos uva-ursi
  arberry
  bear's grape
  bearberry
  creashak
  hog cranberry
  hogberry
  kinnikinick
  mealberry
  mountain box
  mountain cranberry
  red bearberry
  rockberry
  sagackhomi
  sandberry
  upland cranberry
  uva-ursi
Calluna vulgaris
  heather
  ling
  Scotch heather
Erica vulgaris
  heather
  ling
  Scotch heather
Gaultheria procumbens
  Canada tea
  checkerberry
  deerberry
  ground berry
  hill berry
  ivry-leaves
  mountain tea
  oil of gaultheria
  partridge berry
  spiceberry
  spicy wintergreen
  spring wintergreen
  teaberry
  wax cluster
  wintergreen

Kalmia latifolia
  American laurel
  calico bush
  ivy
  ivybush
  lambkill
  laurel
  mountain ivy
  mountain laurel
  rose laurel
  sheep laurel
  spoonwood
Ledum groenlandicum
  Labrador tea
Ledum palustre
  crystal tea
  marsh cistus
  moth herb
  narrow-leaved Labrador tea
  swamp tea
  wild rosemary
Vaccinium spp.
  bilberry
  blueberry
  cowberry
  cranberry
  deerberry
  foxberry
  grouseberry
  huckleberry
  lingberry
  lingenberry
  lingonberry
  moorberry
  whinberry
  whortleberry

Erythroxylaceae [Coca family]
Erythroxylum coca
  coca
  cocaine
  spadic

Euphorbiaceae [Spurge family]
Aleurites moluccana
  candleberry tree
  candlenut
  candlenut tree

  country walnut
  Indian walnut
  otaheite walnut
  varnish tree
Croton eluteria
  cascarilla bark
  sweetwood bark
Croton monanthogynus
  prairie tea
Croton tiglium
  croton oil
Euphorbia spp.
  spurge
Euphorbia antisyphilitica
  candelilla
Euphorbia hirta
  asthma weed
  catshair
  pill-bearing spurge
  Queensland asthma weed
Euphorbia lathyris
  caper spurge
  garden spurge
  mole plant
  myrtle spurge
Mercurialis annua
  mercury
  mercury herb
Mercurialis perennis
  dog's cole
  dog's mercury
  mercury
  perennial mercury
Ricinus communis
  bofareira
  castor bean
  castor oil plant
  Mexico seed
  oil plant
  palma Christi
  wonder tree
Stillingia sylvatica
  cockup hat
  marcory
  queen's delight
  queen's root
  silver leaf
  stillingia
  yaw root

Fagaceae [Beech family]

Castanea dentata
 American chestnut
 chestnut
Quercus albus
 white oak
Quercus robur
 English oak
 truffle oak
Quercus Suber
 cork oak

Fucaceae

Fucus vesiculosus
 bladderwrack
 kelp

Fumariaceae [Fumitory family]

Corydalis cava
 corydalis
 early fumitory
Corydalis formosa
 choice dielytra
 staggerweed
 turkey corn
 wild bleeding heart
 wild turkey pea
Dicentra canadensis
 squirrel corn
Dicentra cuculleria
 Dutchman's breeches
Dicentra eximia
 choice dielytra
 staggerweed
 turkey corn
 wild bleeding heart
 wild turkey pea
Dicentra spectabilis
 bleeding heart
Eschscholtzia californica
 California poppy
Fumaria officinalis
 earth smoke
 fumitory
 hedge fumitory
 smoke-of-the-earth

Gentianaceae [Gentian family]

Centaurium erythraea
 bitterherb
 centaury
 centaury gentian
 European centaury
 lesser centaury
 minor centaury
Centaurium umbellatum
 bitterherb
 centaury
 centaury gentian
 European centaury
 lesser centaury
 minor centaury
Erythraea centaurium
 bitterherb
 centaury
 centaury gentian
 European centaury
 lesser centaury
 minor centaury
Frasera caroliniensis
 American columbo or calumba
 American gentian
 green gentian
Gentiana acaulis
 stemless gentian
Gentiana catesbaei
 American gentian
 blue gentian
 Catesby's gentian
 Sampson's snakeroot
Gentiana crinita
 fringed gentian
Gentiana lutea
 bitter root
 bitterwort
 pale gentian
 yellow gentian
Gentiana quinquefolia
 gallweed
 stiff gentian
Gentiana spp.
 gentian
Gentianella quinquefolia
 gallweed
 stiff gentian
Gentianopsis crinita
 fringed gentian

Menyanthes trifoliata
  bean trefoil
  bog bean
  bog myrtle
  brook bean
  buckbean
  marsh clover
  marsh trefoil
  moonflower
  trefoil
  water shamrock
  water trefoil
Ophelia chirata or chirayita
  chirata
  chirayita
  chiretta
Sabatia angularis
  American centaury
  bitter-bloom
  bitter clover
  eyebright
  red centaury
  rose pink
  wild succory
Swertia chirata or chirayita
  chirata
  chirayita
  chiretta

Geraniaceae [Geranium family]

Erodium cicutarium
  alfilaria
  heron's-bill
  pin clover
  pin grass
  red-stem filaree
  storksbill
  wild musk
Geranium maculatum
  alumroot
  American cranesbill
  cranesbill
  crowfoot
  geranium
  spotted cranesbill
  spotted geranium
  wild cranesbill
  wild geranium

Geranium robertianum
  dragon's blood
  herb Robert
  red robin
  storkbill
  wild cranesbill
Geranium spp.
  cranesbill
Pelargonium citrosum
  orange-scented geranium
Pelargonium crispum
  lemon-scented geranium
Pelargonium fragrans
  nutmeg-scented geranium
Pelargonium graveolens
  rose geranium
  sweet-scented geranium
Pelargonium odoratissimum
  apple-scented geranium
Pelargonium tomentosum
  herb-scented geranium
  peppermint-scented geranium

Ginkgoaceae [Ginkgo family]

Ginkgo biloba
  ginkgo nut
  maidenhair tree

Gramineae [Grass family]

Agropyrum repens
  couch grass
  cutch
  dog grass
  durfa grass
  durfee grass
  quack grass
  quick grass
  quitch grass
  witchgrass
Cymbopogon citratus
  fever grass
  lemongrass
  serah powder
  West Indian lemongrass
Cymbopogon flexuosus
  East Indian lemongrass
Cymbopogon martinii, var. martinii
  East Indian geranium

motia
palmarosa
Cymbopogon martinii, var. sofia
 gingergrass
 sofia
Cymbopogon nardus
 citronella
 citronella grass
 false spikenard
 lemongrass
 nard grass
 oil grass
Cymbopogon pendulus
 Jammu lemongrass
Cymbopogon winterianus
 Java citronella
Hordeum vulgare
 barley
Lolium temulentum
 bearded darnel
 cheat
 tare
Vetiveria zizanioides
 cuscus oil
 khas-khas
 khus-khus
 vetiver

Guttiferae [Garcinia family]
Garcinia indica
 kokum
Garcinia mangostana
 mangosteen

Hamamelidaceae [Witch hazel family]
Hamamelis virginiana
 snapping hazel
 spotted alder
 striped alder
 tobacco wood
 winterbloom
 witch hazel
Liquidambar orientalis
 Asian storax
 copalm
 gum tree
 Levant storax
 liquidamber

liquid storax
Oriental sweet gum
storax
styrax
Liquidambar styraciflua
 American storax or styrax
 American sweet gum
 bilsted
 copalm
 liquidamber
 liquid storax
 gum tree
 opossum tree
 red gum
 storax
 sweet gum
 white gum

Hippocastanaceae [Horse chestnut family]
Aesculus hippocastanum
 buckeye
 horse chestnut

Hydrophyllaceae [Waterleaf family]
Eriodictyon californica
 bear's weed
 consumptive's weed
 holy herb
 mountain balm
 tarweed
 yerba santa

Hypericaceae [Hypericum family]
Hypericum spp.
 Saint John's-wort
 Saint Peter's-wort
Hypericum calycinum
 Aaron's beard
 creeping Saint John's-wort
 gold flower
 rose-of-Sharon
Hypericum perforatum
 amber
 goatweed
 Johnswort
 Klamath weed
 Saint John's-wort

Tipton weed

Illiciaceae [Illicium family]

Illicium anisatum
  Badian anise
  Chinese anise
  Indian anise
  Japanese anise tree
  Japanese star anise
Illicium verum
  star anise
  weihsion powder

Iridaceae [Iris family]

Crocus sativus
  saffron
Iris germanica, var. florentina
  flag
  Florentine iris
  German iris
  orris
  orris root
Iris versicolor
  blue flag
  flag lily
  fleur-de-lis
  flower-de-luce
  iris
  liver lily
  poison flag
  snake lily
  water flag
  wild iris

Juglandaceae [Walnut family]

Carya spp.
  hickory
Juglans cinerea
  butternut
  lemon walnut
  oil nut
  white walnut
Juglans nigra
  black walnut
Juglans regia
  Carpathian walnut
  Caucasian walnut
  Circassian walnut
  English walnut
  Madeira nut
  Persian walnut
  walnut

Labiatae [Mint family]

Acinos alpinus
  alpine basil thyme
Acinos arvensis
  basil thyme
Acinos thymoides
  basil thyme
Agastache foeniculum
  anise hyssop
  blue giant hyssop
  fennel giant hyssop
  fragrant giant hyssop
  giant hyssop
Agastache mexicana
  Mexican giant hyssop
Agastache rugosa
  Korean mint
  wrinkled giant hyssop
Calamintha acinos
  basil thyme
Calamintha alpina
  alpine basil thyme
Calamintha clinopodium
  wild basil
Calamintha glabella
  calamint
Cedronella canariensis
  balm of Gilead
  Canary balm
  false balm of Gilead
Cedronella triphylla
  balm of Gilead
  Canary balm
  false balm of Gilead
Clinopodium vulgare
  basil
  basilweed
  dog mint
  wild basil
Coleus amboinicus
  Cuban oregano
  Indian borage
  oregano

Spanish thyme
Collinsonia canadensis
citronella
hardback
hardhack
heal-all
horse balm
horse weed
knob grass
knob root
richweed
stoneroot
Cunila origanoides
American dittany
dittany, common
Maryland dittany
stone mint
sweet horsemint
Galeopsis tetrahit
bastard hemp
bee-nettle
dog-nettle
hemp dead nettle
hemp nettle
Glechoma hederacea
alehoof
cat's-foot
cat's-paw
creeping Charlie
field balm
gill tea
gill-over-the-ground
gillrun
ground ivy
hay maids
hedge maids
runaway robin
turnhoof
Hedeoma pulegioides
American pennyroyal
mock pennyroyal
mosquito plant
pudding grass
squaw balm
squaw mint
stinking balm
tickweed
Hyptis suaveolens
bush tea plant

West Indian spikenard
wild spikenard
Hyssopus officinalis
hyssop
Lamium album
dead nettle
dumb nettle
snowflake
stingless nettle
white archangel
white dead nettle
Lavandula augustifolia
English lavender
lavender
true lavender
Lavandula latifolia
spike lavender
Lavandula officinalis or vera
lavender
true lavender
Lavandula spica
spikenard
Lavandula stoechas
French lavender
Spanish lavender
Leonotis leonurus
lion's-ear
Leonurus cardiaca
lion's-ear
lion's-tail
motherwort
Roman motherwort
throw-wort
Marrubium vulgare
hoarehound
hoarhound
horehound
white horehound
Melissa majoranifolia
alpine basil thyme
Melissa officinalis
balm
balm mint
bee balm
blue balm
cure-all
dropsy plant
garden balm
lemon balm

melissa
sweet balm
Mentha aquatica
    bergamot
    water mint
Mentha arvensis
    corn mint
    field mint
    hakka
    Japanese mint
    wild pennyroyal
Mentha canadensis
    corn mint
    field mint
    hakka
    Japanese mint
    wild pennyroyal
Mentha citrata
    Eau de Cologne mint
Mentha crispa
    crisp-leaved mint
    cross mint
    curled mint
Mentha longifolia
    horsemint
Mentha officinalis
    julep mint
Mentha x piperita
    brandy mint
    lamb mint
    peppermint
Mentha pulegium
    European pennyroyal
    lurk-in-the-ditch
    pennyroyal
Mentha rotundifolia
    round-leaved mint
Mentha spicata
    lamb mint
    Our Lady's mint
    sage of Bethlehem
    spearmint
Mentha suaveolens
    applemint
Mentha sylvestre
    European horsemint
Mentha x villosa alopecuroides
    Bowles mint
Micromeria chamissonis douglasii

yerba buena
Monarda didyma
    bee balm
    bergamot
    blue balm
    high balm
    horsemint
    low balm
    mountain balm
    mountain mint
    Oswego tea
    wild bergamot
Monarda fistulosa
    bee balm
    bergamot
    blue balm
    high balm
    horsemint
    low balm
    mountain balm
    mountain mint
    Oswego tea
    wild bergamot
Monarda punctata
    dotted mint
    horsemint
    Oswego tea
    wild bergamot
Monardella lanceolata
    pennyroyal
Monardella odoratissima
    western balm
    wild pennyroyal
Monardella villosa
    coyote mint
    horsemint
    pennyroyal
Nepeta cataria
    catmint
    catnep
    catnip
    catrup
    catswort
    field balm
Nepeta hederacea
    alehoof
    cat's-foot
    cat's-paw
    creeping Charlie

field balm
gill
gill-over-the-ground
gillrun
ground ivy
hay maids
hedge maids
runaway robin
turnhoof
Ocimum basilicum
   basil
   bush basil
   lemon-scented basil
   monk's basil
   Saint Josephwort
   sweet basil
Ocimum citriodora
   lemon-scented basil
Ocimum minimum
   bush basil
   dwarf basil
Ocimum sanctum
   Indian holy basil
Origanum dictamnus
   dittany of Crete
   Greek oregano
   Spanish hops
Origanum majorana
   knotted marjoram
   origane
   orégano dolce
   sweet marjoram
Origanum onites
   Italian oregano
   marjoram
   origane des champs
   pot marjoram
   wild marjoram
Origanum syriacum
   za'atar
Origanum syriacum var. syriacum
   hyssop
   oregano
Origanum vulgare
   marjoram
   mountain mint
   origane des champs
   pot marjoram
   wild marjoram

winter marjoram
wintersweet
Perilla frutescens
   beef steak plant
   perilla
   shiso zoku
Phlomis fruticosa
   Jerusalem sage
Phlomis lychnitis
   lampwick plant
Plectranthus spp.
   Cuban oregano
   prostrate coleus
   spur flower
   Swedish begonia
   Swedish ivy
   "Vick's" plant
Pogostemon cablin
   patchouly
Pogostemon heyneanus
   patchouly
Pogostemon patchouly
   patchouly
Prunella vulgaris
   all-heal
   blue curls
   brownwort
   carpenter's herb
   carpenter's weed
   heal-all
   herb carpenter
   Hercules woundwort
   hock-heal
   self-heal
   sicklewort
   woundwort
Pycnanthemum virginianum
   prairie hyssop
   Virginia mountain mint
   Virginia thyme
   wild basil
   wild hyssop
Rosmarinus officinalis
   old man
   rosemary
Salvia barrelieri
   Spanish sage
Salvia clevelandii
   blue sage

Salvia dorisiana
  British Honduran sage
  peach-scented sage
Salvia elegans
  pineapple-scented sage
Salvia fruticosa
  Greek sage
Salvia lavandulifolia
  Spanish sage
Salvia leucantha
  Mexican bush sage
Salvia leucophylla
  gray sage
  purple sage
Salvia lyrata
  cancerweed
  lyre-leaved sage
  wild sage
Salvia officinalis
  Dalmatia sage
  garden sage
  sage
  salvia
Salvia officinalis aureum
  golden sage
Salvia pomifera
  apple sage
Salvia sclarea
  clary
  clary sage
  muscatel sage
Salvia triloba
  Greek sage
Salvia verbenacea
  vervain sage
  wild clary
Salvia viridis
  Bluebeard sage
  Joseph sage
  red-topped sage
Satureja acinos
  basil thyme
Satureja alpina
  alpine basil thyme
Satureja capitata
  conehead thyme
  corido thyme
  Cretan thyme
  headed savory

Spanish origanum
thyme of the ancients
za'atar farsi
Satureja douglasii
  yerba buena
Satureja glabella
  calamint
Satureja hortensis
  bean herb
  summer savory
Satureja montana
  winter savory
Satureja thymbra
  za'atar franji
  za'atar rumi
Satureja spp.
  savory
Scutellaria spp.
  skullcap
Scutellaria lateriflora
  blue skullcap
  blue pimpernel
  helmet flower
  hoodwort
  mad-dog-weed
  side-flowering skullcap
  skullcap
  Virginia skullcap
Stachys affinis
  Chinese artichoke
  chorogi
  crosnes-du-Japon
  Japanese artichoke
  knotroot
Stachys betonica
  betony
  common betony
  purple betony
  wood betony
Stachys byzantina
  lamb's-ears
  woolly betony
Stachys officinalis
  betony
  common betony
  purple betony
  wood betony
Stachys spp.
  woundwort

Teucrium canadense
  American germander
  wood sage
Teucrium chamaedrys
  European germander
Teucrium germander
  betony
  germander
Teucrium marum
  cat thyme
  herb mastic
Thymbra capitata
  conehead thyme
  corido thyme
  Cretan thyme
  headed savory
  Spanish origanum
  thyme of the ancients
  za'atar farsi
Thymbra spicata
  za'atar hommar
  za'atar midbari
Thymus caespititius
  tiny thyme
  tufted thyme
Thymus capitatus
  conehead thyme
  corido thyme
  Cretan thyme
  headed savory
  Spanish origanum
  thyme of the ancients
  za'atar farsi
Thymus x citriodorus
  lemon thyme
Thymus herba-barona
  caraway thyme
Thymus mastichina
  herb mastic
  mastic thyme
  Spanish marjoram
  Spanish thyme
Thymus micans
  tiny thyme
  tufted thyme
Thymus praecox subsp. articus
  creeping thyme
  mother-of-thyme
Thymus pulegioides

mother-of-thyme
Pennsylvania Dutch tea thyme
wild thyme
Thymus quinquecostatus
  Japanese thyme
Thymus serpyllum
  lemon thyme
  tiny thyme
  tufted thyme
Thymus vulgaris
  common thyme
  garden thyme
  thyme
Trichostema dichotomum
  bastard pennyroyal

Lauraceae [Laurel family]
Aniba duckei
  bois de rose
  Brazilian rosewood
Aniba parviflora
  bois de rose
  Brazilian rosewood
Aniba roseodora
  bois de rose
  Brazilian rosewood
Cinnamomum burmanii
  Batavia cassia
  Batavia cinnamon
  Burma cinnamon
  Indonesian cassia
  Java cassia
  Korintje cassia
  Padang cassia
  Padang cinnamon
Cinnamomum camphora
  artificial sassafras oil
  camphor tree
Cinnamomum cassia
  cassia
  cassia-bark tree
  Chinese cinnamon
Cinnamomum cecidodaphne
  Nepalese tejpat
Cinnamomum culiliban
  lawang
Cinnamomum loureirii
  cassia-flower tree

cinnamon, U. S. P.
Cinnamomum micranthum
  Chinese sassafras
Cinnamomum tamala
  Indian cassia
  tejpat
Cinnamomum zeylanicum
  Ceylon cinnamon
  cinnamon
  Madagascar cinnamon
  Seychelles cinnamon
  Sri Lanka cinnamon
  sweetwood
  canela (Spanish)
  cannella (Italian)
  cannelle (French)
  jou-kuei (Chinese)
  koritsa (Russian)
  seiron-nikkei (Japanese)
  Zimt (German)
Cryptocarya moschata
  Brazilian nutmeg
Laurus nobilis
  bay leaf
  Grecian laurel
  Indian bay
  laurel
  Roman bay
  sweet bay
  sweet laurel
Lindera benzoin
  Benjamin bush
  feverbush
  spicebush
  spicewood
  wild allspice
Nectandra rodiaei
  bebeeru
  greenheart tree
Nectandra puchury
  Brazilian sassafras
  pichurim
  pitchurim bean
  sassafras nut
Ocotea caudata
  Cayenne rosewood
  linaloe cayenne bois de rose
Ocotea cymbarum
  Amazonian sassafras

Ocotea pretiosa
  Brazilian sassafras
Persea borbonia
  red bay
  sweet bay
Sassafras albidum
  ague tree
  cinnamon wood
  sassafras
  saxifrax
Sassafras variifolium
  ague tree
  cinnamon wood
  sassafras
  saxifrax
Umbellularia californica
  California bay
  California laurel
  California olive
  California sassafras
  myrtle
  Oregon myrtle
  pepperwood

Leguminosae [Pea family]

Abrus precatorius
  coral-bead plant
  crab's eye
  Indian licorice
  Jamaican wild licorice
  jequirity
  licorice vine
  love pea
  prayer-beads
  red-bean vine
  rosary pea
  weather plant
  weather vine
  wild licorice
Anthyllis vulneraria
  kidney vetch
  ladies' fingers
  lamb's toes
  staunchwort
  woundwort
Astragalus glycyphyllous
  milk vetch
Astragalus gummifer

astragal
gumdragon
tragacanth
Astragalus membranaceus
huang qi
milk vetch
Astragalus mollissimus
loco weed
Baptisia tinctoria
American indigo
false indigo
horsefly weed
indigo broom
rattleweed
wild indigo
yellow broom
yellow indigo
Cassia acutifolia
Alexandria senna
cassia tree
Indian senna
senna
Ceratonia siliqua
algarroba bean
carob
locust bean
Saint John's bread
Copaifera spp.
capivi
copaiba
copaiva
copayva
Cytisus scoparius
broom
Irish broom
link
Scotch broom
Dipteryx odoratum
Dutch tonka bean
tonga bean
tonka bean
Tonquin bean
Dipteryx oppositiafolia
Dutch tonka bean
tonga bean
tonka bean
Tonquin bean
Galega officinalis
goat's rue

Genista spp.
broom buds
Genista tinctoria
broom
dyer's broom
dyer's greenweed
dyer's greenwood
dyer's whin
furze
green broom
waxen woad
woadwaxen
woodwaxen
Glycine max
soja bean
soya bean
soybean
Glycyrrhiza glabra
Chinese sweet root
licorice
Spanish juice
sweetroot
sweetwood
Haematoxylon campechianum
bloodwood tree
campeachy wood
logwood
Hardenbergia monophylla
Australian sarsaparilla
coral pea
vine lilac
Hardenbergia violaceae
coral pea
vine lilac
Medicago sativa
alfalfa
buffalo herb
lucerne
purple medic
Melilotus alba
bukhara clover
hubam clover
white melilot
white sweet clover
Melilotus coerules
blue melilot
Melilotus officinalis
bird's-foot-trefoil
garden balm

hay flowers
king's clover
lotus
melilot
melist
sweet clover
sweet trefoil
Swiss melilot
trefoil
yellow melilot
yellow sweet clover
Myroxylon balsamum
opobalsam
tolu balsam
Myroxylon balsamum, var. pereirae
Peruvian balsam
Ononis spinosa
cammock
petty whin
rest-harrow
stayplough
Piscidia piscipula
fish fuddle
fish-poison tree
Jamaican dogwood
West Indian dogwood
Pterocarpus draco
dragon's blood
Pterocarpus marsupium
bija
Pterocarpus santalinus
red sandalwood
red saunders
Sophora secundiflora
frijolito
mescal bean
Spartium junceum
genet
Spanish broom
weavers' broom
Tamarindus indica
tamarind seed
Trifolium alpinum
mountain licorice
Trifolium pratense
red clover
Trifolium spp.
clover
Trigonella foenum-graecum

bird's foot
fenugreek
Greek hay
methi

Lichen

Roccella fuciformis
Angola weed
Sticta pulmonacea
lungmoss

Liliaceae [Lily family]

Aletris farinosa
ague grass
ague root
bitter grass
colicroot
crow corn
mealy starwort
star grass
star root
unicorn root
Allium ampeloprasum
great-headed garlic
Levant garlic
wild leek
Allium ascalonicum
eschalotte
shallot
éschalote
Allium cepa
onion
Allium cepa, Aggregatum group
eschalotte
shallot
éschalote
Allium fistulosum
stone leek
Welsh onion
Allium sativum, var. sativum
cultivated garlic
Allium sativum, var. ophioscorodon
giant garlic
rocambole
serpent garlic
Allium sativum, var. pekinense
Peking garlic
Allium schoenoprasum

chives
cive
Schnittlauch
Allium scorodoprasum
  giant garlic
  sand leek
  Spanish garlic
Allium tricoccum
  ramps
  wild leek
Allium tuberosum
  Chinese chives
  garlic chive
  Oriental garlic
Allium ursinum
  bear's garlic
  buckrams
  gypsy onion
  hog's garlic
  ramsons
  ransoms
Aloe barbadensis
  Barbados aloe
  Curaçao aloe
  medicinal aloe
  unguentine cactus
Aloe ferox
  cape aloe
Aloe perryi
  Bombay aloe
  Socotrine aloe
  Turkey aloe
  Zanzibar aloe
Aloe spp.
  aloe
Chamaelirium luteum
  blazing-star
  devil's-bit
  fairy-wand
  false unicorn root
  rattlesnake root
Chlorogalum pomeridianum
  amole
  soap plant
  wild potato
Colchicum autumnale
  autumn crocus
  fall crocus
  meadow saffron

mysteria
naked lady
wonder bulb
Convallaria majalis
  lily of the valley
  May bells
  May lily
Dracaena draco
  dragon's blood
Erythronium americanum
  adder's-tongue
  amberbell
  dog-tooth violet
  erythronium
  lamb's tongue
  rattlesnake violet
  snake leaf
  trout lily
  yellow adder's-tongue
  yellow erythronium
  yellow snakeleaf
  yellow snowdrop
Hyacinthus orientalis
  hyacinth
Lachenalia spp.
  cape cowslip
Polygonatum multiflorum
  dropberry
  King-Solomon's-seal
  sealroot
  sealwort
  Solomon's seal
Polygonatum odoratum
  dropberry
  King-Solomon's-seal
  sealroot
  sealwort
  Solomon's seal
Ruscus aculeatus
  box holly
  butcher's broom
  hornet holly
  Jew's myrtle
  knee holly
  little holly
Smilacina racemosa
  false spikenard
  Solomon's zigzag
  treacleberry

Smilax aristolochiaefolia
  gray sarsaparilla
  Mexican sarsaparilla
  Vera Cruz sarsaparilla
Smilax febrifuga
  Ecuadorean sarsaparilla
Smilax glauca
  sawbrier
  wild sarsaparilla
Smilax herbacea
  Jacob's-ladder
Smilax medica
  gray sarsaparilla
  Mexican sarsaparilla
  Vera Cruz sarsaparilla
Smilax regelii
  brown sarsaparilla
  Honduras sarsaparilla
Smilax spp.
  catbrier
  Costa Rica sarsaparilla
  greenbrier
  Guayaquil sarsaparilla
  Lima sarsaparilla
  red Jamaica sarsaparilla
  sarsaparilla
  Virginia sarsaparilla
Trillium spp.
  birthroot
  trillium
  wake-robin
Trillium erectum
  birthroot
  brown Beth
  nose-bleed
  squawroot
  stinking Benjamin
  trillium
Trillium pendulum
  bethroot
  birthroot
  coughroot
  ground lily
  Indian balm
  Indian shamrock
  Jew's-harp plant
  lamb's quarter
  milk ipecac
  nodding wake-robin

  pariswort
  rattlesnake root
  snakebite
  three-leaved nightshade
  trillium
Urginea maritima
  red squill
  sea onion
  sea squill
  squill
  white squill
Veratrum viride
  American hellebore
  American white hellebore
  blazing-star
  bugbane
  devil's bite
  earth gall
  false hellebore
  green hellebore
  Indian poke
  itchweed
  swamp hellebore
  tickleweed
  white hellebore
Yucca brevifolia
  Joshua tree
  yucca
Yucca schidigera
  Mohave yucca

Linaceae [Flax family]
Linum usitatissimum
  flax
  flax seed
  linseed
  lint bells
  winterlien

Lobeliaceae [Lobelia family]
Lobelia inflata
  bladderpod
  emetic herb
  emetic weed
  gagroot
  Indian tobacco
  lobelia
  vomitroot

vomitwort
wild tobacco

Loganiaceae [Logania family]

Gelsemium sempervirens
  Carolina jasmine
  Carolina jessamine
  evening trumpet flower
  gelsemin
  wild jessamine
  woodbine
  yellow jasmine
  yellow jessamine
Spigelia marilandica
  Carolina pink
  Indian pink
  pinkroot
  star bloom
  worm grass

Loranthaceae [Mistletoe family]

Phoradendron flavescens
  American mistletoe
  birdlime
  golden bough
  mistletoe
Phoradendron serotinum
  American mistletoe
  birdlime
  golden bough
  mistletoe
Viscum album
  all-heal
  birdlime
  devil's fuge
  European mistletoe
  mistletoe

Lycopodiaceae [Club moss family]

Lycopodium spp.
  club moss
  ground pine
  herb-ivy
Lycopodium clavatum
  club moss
  foxtail
  ground pine
  herb-ivy
  lycopod
  running pine
  staghorn
  vegetable sulfur
  wolf claw

Lythraceae [Loosestrife family]

Lawsonia inermis
  alcanna
  Egyptian privet
  henna
  Jamaica mignonette
  mignonette tree
  reseda
Lythrum salicaria
  long purples
  loosestrife
  milk willow-herb
  purple loosestrife
  purple willow-herb
  rainbow weed
  soldiers
  spiked loosestrife
  spiked willow-herb
  willow sage

Magnoliaceae [Magnolia family]

Illicium anisatum
  Badian anise
  Chinese anise
  Indian anise
Illicium verum
  star anise
Magnolia glauca
  beaver tree
  holly bay
  Indian bark
  magnolia
  red bay
  red laurel
  swamp laurel
  swamp sassafras
  sweet bay
  sweet magnolia
  white bay
Magnolia virginiana
  beaver tree
  holly bay

Indian bark
magnolia
red bay
red laurel
swamp laurel
swamp sassafras
sweet bay
sweet magnolia
white bay

Malpighiaceae [Malpighia family]
Byrsonima coriacea
  lotusberry
  West Indian lotusberry

Malvaceae [Mallow family]
Abelmoschus moschatus
  abelmosk
  abelmusk
  ambrette seed
  musk mallow
  muskseed
  rose mallow
  Syrian mallow
  target-leaved hibiscus
  water mallow
Althaea officinalis
  althaea
  marsh mallow
  mortification root
  sweet weed
  white mallow
  wymote
Hibiscus, ? species
  hibiscus flowers
Hibiscus abelmoschus
  abelmosk
  abelmusk
  ambrette
  musk mallow
  muskseed
  rose mallow
  Syrian mallow
  target-leaved hibiscus
  water mallow
Hibiscus sabdariffa
  flor de Jamaica
  Guinea sorrel

Indian sorrel
Jamaica sorrel
rosella
roselle
Hibiscus syriacus
  althaea
  rose-of-Sharon
Malva rotundifolia
  blue mallow
  cheese plant
  cheeses
  dwarf mallow
  low mallow
  mallow
Malva sylvestris
  cheese flower
  cheese plant
  cheeses
  country mallow
  high mallow
  mallow

Marantaceae [Arrowroot family]
Maranta arundinacea
  arrowroot
  obedience plant

Meliaceae [Mahogany family]
Melia azedarach
  Africa lilac
  azedarach
  bead tree
  Chinaberry
  China tree
  hagbush
  hoptree
  Indian lilac
  Japanese bead tree
  paradise tree
  Persian lilac
  pride tree
  pride-of-China
  pride-of-India
  Syrian bead tree
  Texas umbrella tree
Trichilia emetica
  roka

Menispermaceae [Moonseed family]

Jateorhiza calumba or palmata
  calumba
  columba
  columbo
Menispermum canadense
  American sarsaparilla
  moonseed
  Texas sarsaparilla
  vine-maple
  yellow parilla

Mimosaceae [Mimosa family]

Acacia catechu
  black catechu
  cutch
  khair
  Wadalee-gum tree
Acacia caven
  Roman cassie
Acacia dealbata
  mimosa
Acacia decurrens
  Australian mimosa
  black wattle
  mimosa
Acacia farnesiana
  cassie
  huisache
  opopanax
  popinac
  sponge tree
  sweet acacia
  West Indian blackthorn
Acacia senegal
  acacia
  Cape gum
  Egyptian thorn
  gum arabic
  Sudan gum-arabic

Monimiaceae [Monimia family]

Laurelia sempervirens
  Chilean sassafras
  Peruvian nutmeg
Peumus boldus
  boldo
  boldus

Moraceae [Fig family]

Humulus japonica
  Japanese hops
Humulus lupulus
  bine
  European hop
  hops
  lupulin

Moringaceae [Moringa family]

Moringa pterygosperma
  ben tree
  drumstick
  horseradish tree

Myricaceae [Bayberry family]

Comptonia peregrina
  fern bush
  fern gale
  meadow fern
  sweet bush
  sweet fern
Myrica cerifera
  bayberry wax
  candleberry
  tallow shrub
  vegetable tallow
  wax myrtle
  waxberry
Myrica gale
  bog myrtle
  meadow fern
  sweet gale
Myrica pennsylvanica
  bayberry
  candleberry
  swamp candleberry
  wax myrtle
  waxberry

Myristicaceae [Nutmeg family]

Myristica argentica
  Macassar mace
  Papua mace
Myristica fragrans
  Banda mace
  mace

nutmeg
Penang mace
Myristica malabarica
Bombay mace
wild mace

Myrtaceae [Myrtle family]
Caryophyllus aromaticus
cloves
Eucalyptus citriodora
citron-scented gum
lemon-scented gum
spotted gum
Eucalyptus cneorifolia
Kangaroo Island narrow-leaved
mallee
Eucalyptus dives
blue peppermint
broad-leaved peppermint
peppermint
Eucalyptus dumosa
congoo mallee
mallee
Eucalyptus elata
river peppermint
river white gum
Eucalyptus globulus
blue gum
eucalyptus
southern blue gum
Tasmanian blue gum
Eucalyptus goniocalyx
apple jack
bundy
long-leaved box
olive-barked box
Eucalyptus leucoxylon
white gum
white ironbark
yellow gum
Eucalyptus macarthurii
Camden woollybut
Paddy's river box
Eucalyptus oleosa
glossy-leaved red
mallee
red mallee
Eucalyptus polybractea

blue-leaved mallee
Eucalyptus radiata
gray peppermint
narrow-leaved peppermint
Eucalyptus sideroxylon
ironbark
mugga
red ironbark
Eucalyptus smithii
blackbutt peppermint
gully gum
gully peppermint
Eucalyptus viridis
green mallee
Eucalyptus spp.
eucalyptus
fever tree
Eugenia acris
wild clove
Eugenia aromatica
cloves
Eugenia caryophyllata
cloves
Eugenia jambosa
Java plum
Malabar plum
rose apple
Eugenia pimenta
allspice
clove pepper
Jamaica pepper
myrtle pepper
pimenta
toute-épice
Melaleuca alterniflora
tea tree
Melaleuca cajaputi
cajeput
cajuput
Melaleuca leucadendron
cajeput
cajuput
oil of cajeput
river tea tree
weeping tea tree
Melaleuca linariifolia
tea tree
Melaleuca minor
cajeput

cajuput
Melaleuca viridiflora
  cajeput
  cajuput
  niaouli
Myrtus communis
  dwarf myrtle
  German myrtle
  Greek myrtle
  myrtle
  Polish myrtle
  Swedish myrtle
Pimenta dioica
  allspice
  clove pepper
  Jamaica pepper
  myrtle pepper
  pimenta or pimento
  toute-épice
Pimenta officinalis
  allspice
  clove pepper
  Jamaica pepper
  myrtle pepper
  pimenta
  toute-épice
Pimenta racemosa
  bay
  bay-rum tree
  bay malagueta
  myrcia oil
  oil of bay
  West Indian bay-leaf oil
Syzygium acris
  wild clove
Syzygium aromaticum
  cloves
Syzygium Jambos
  Java plum
  Malabar plum
  rose apple

Nymphaeaceae [Water lily family]

Nymphaea caerulea
  blue African lotus
Nymphaea lotus
  white Egyptian lotus
Nymphaea odorata
  cow cabbage
  fragrant water lily
  pond lily
  Saint Joseph's lily
  sweet-scented pond lily
  sweet-scented water lily
  water cabbage
  water lily
  white pond lily
  white water lily
Nymphaea stellata
  East Indian lotus
  Indian lotus
Nymphaea tuberosa
  magnolia water lily
  tuberous water lily
Nymphaea spp.
  lotus

Oleaceae [Olive family]

Chionanthus virginicus
  fringe tree
  gray beard tree
  old man's beard
  poison ash tree
  snowdrop tree
  snowflower
  white fringe
Fraximus excelsior
  ash
  bird's tongue
  European ash
Jasminum auriculatum
  Indian jasmine
Jasminum grandiflorum
  Catalonian jasmine
  royal jasmine
  Spanish jasmine
Jasminum sambac
  Arabian jasmine
  sambac
Jasminum spp.
  jasmine
Ligustrum vulgare
  prim
  primwort
  privet
  privy

Onagraceae [Evening primrose family]

Oenothera biennis
  evening primrose
  fever plant
  field primrose
  German rampion
  king's cureall
  night willow-herb
  primrose
  scabish
  scurvish
  tree primrose

Orchidaceae [Orchid family]

Angraecum fragrans
  Bourbon tea
  faham tea
Corallorhiza odontorhiza
  autumn coralroot
  chicken-toes
  coralroot
  crawley-root
  dragon's-claw
  fever root
  late coralroot
  scaly dragon's-claw
  small coralroot
  turkey-claw
Cypripedium calceolus
  American valerian
  golden-slipper
  lady-slipper
  lady's-slipper
  moccasin flower
  nerveroot
  Noah's-ark
  slipper root
  umbilroot
  Venus'-shoe
  whippoorwill-shoe
  yellow Indian-shoe
  yellow lady's-slipper
  yellow moccasin flower
  yellows
Goodyera pubescens
  adder's violet
  downy rattlesnake orchid

  downy rattlesnake plantain
  latticeleaf
  net-leaf plantain
  networt
  rattlesnake plantain
  rattlesnake weed
  scrofula weed
  spotted plantain
  water plantain
Vanilla planifolia
  Bourbon vanilla
  Mexican vanilla
  vanilla
Vanilla pompona
  Guadeloupe vanilla
  Pompona vanilla
  West Indian vanilla
  vanillon
Vanilla tahitensis
  Tahitian vanilla

Orobranchaceae [Broomrape family]

Epifagus virginiana
  beechdrops

Osmundaceae [Flowering fern family]

Osmunda cinnamomea
  buckhorn
  cinnamon fern
  cinnamon-colored fern
  fiddleheads
Osmunda regalis
  bog onion
  buckhorn brake
  buckhorn
  buckhorn male fern
  flowering brake
  flowering fern
  hartshorn bush
  herb Christopher
  king's fern
  royal fern
  royal flowering fern
  Saint Christopher's herb
  water fern

Oxalidaceae [Oxalis family]

Oxalis acetosella

alleluia
cuckoo bread
European wood sorrel
green sauce
Irish shamrock
mountain sorrel
sour trefoil
stubwort
three-leaved grass
white sorrel
wood sorrel
Oxalis corniculata
  creeping oxalis
  creeping wood sorrel
  yellow sorrel
Oxalis pes-caprae
  Bermuda buttercup
  soursob
Oxalis spiralis
  chulco
Oxalis stricta
  upright yellow wood sorrel

Paeoniaceae [Peony family]
Paeonia officinalis
  peony

Palmae [Palm family]
Areca catechu
  areca nut
  betel nut palm
Cocos nucifera
  coconut
Copernicia cerifera
  carnauba palm
  carnauba wax
Copernicia prunifera
  carnauba palm
  carnauba wax
Daemonorops draco
  dragon's blood
Serenoa repens
  saw palmetto
  scrub palmetto
Serenoa serrulata
  saw palmetto
  scrub palmetto

Pandanaceae [Screw pine family]
Pandanus fascicularis
  keora
  kewda
  kewra
  Nicobar breadfruit
  padang
  pandang
  screw pine
  umbrella tree
Pandanus odoratissimus
  keora
  kewda
  kewra
  Nicobar breadfruit
  padang
  pandang
  screw pine
  umbrella tree
Pandanus tectorus
  kewra
  pandanus palm
  thatch screw pine

Papaveraceae [Poppy family]
Chelidonium majus
  celandine
  garden celandine
  great celandine
  tetterwort
Papaver somniferum
  opium poppy
  poppy
Sanguinaria canadensis
  bloodroot
  Indian paint
  Indian plant
  Indian red paint
  pauson
  red paint root
  red puccoon
  red root
  sanguinaria
  tetterwort
  yarrow

Parmeliaceae [a lichen family]
Cetraria islandica

eryngo-leaved liverwort
Iceland moss

Passifloraceae [Passionflower family]

Passiflora incarnata
  apricot vine
  maypop
  passionflower
  wild passionflower
Passiflora maliformis
  conch apple
  sweet calabash
  sweetcup
Passiflora murucuja
  Dutchman's laudanum
Passiflora spp.
  granadilla
  passionflower
  passionfruit
  water lemon

Pedaliaceae [Pedalium family]

Sesamum indicum
  benne plant
  sesame
Sesamum orientale
  benne plant
  sesame

Phytolaccaceae [Pokeweed family]

Phytolacca acinosa
  Indian poke
  poke
Phytolacca americana
  American nightshade
  coakum
  garget
  inkberry
  pigeon berry
  pocan
  poke
  pokeroot
  pokeweed
  redweed
  scoke
  Virginia poke
Phytolacca esculenta
  poke

Pinaceae [Pine family]

Abies alba
  fir needles oil
  pine fir
  silver fir
  silver spruce
  templin oil
  white fir
  white spruce
Abies balsamea
  balm of Gilead
  balsam fir needle oil
  Canada balsam
Abies sachalinensis
  fir needles oil
  Japanese fir
  Japanese fir needle oil
  Japanese pine needle oil
  pine fir
  Sakhalin fir
Abies sachalinensis, var. mayriana
  Mayr Sakhalin fir
Abies sibirica
  European fir
  fir needles oil
  pine fir
  Siberian fir
  Siberian fir oil
  Siberian fir needle oil
  Siberian pine needle oil
Larix decidua
  European larch
  larch
  Venice turpentine
Larix europaea
  European larch
  larch
  Venice turpentine
Larix laricina
  American larch
  black larch
  hackamatack
  larch
  tamarack
Picea abies
  common spruce
  Norway pine
  Norway spruce

Picea glauca
  Alberta spruce
  Black Hills spruce
  Canadian spruce
  cat spruce
  white spruce
Picea jezoensis
  yeddo spruce
  yezo spruce
Picea mariana
  black spruce
  bog spruce
  Canadian black pine
  double spruce
Pinus edulis
  nut pine
  pinyon pine
  piñon nuts
  two-leaved nut pine
Pinus gerardiana
  Chilghoza pine
  Gerald's pine
  Nepal nut pine
Pinus mugo
  dwarf pine
  mountain pine
  Mugo pine
  Swiss mountain pine
Pinus palustris
  Georgia pine
  longleaf pine
  longleaf yellow pine
  pine oil
  pitch pine
  southern yellow pine
Pinus pinea
  Italian stone pine
  pignolia nuts
  stone pine
  umbrella pine
Pinus quadrifolia
  Parry pinyon pine
  piñon nuts
Pinus strobus
  Canadian white pine
  deal pine
  eastern white pine
  pumpkin pine
  soft pine

  Weymouth pine
  white pine
Pinus sylvestris
  Baltic redwood
  Norway pine
  Scot's pine
  Scotch fir
  Scotch pine
Tsuga canadensis
  Canadian hemlock
  Canada-pitch pine
  eastern hemlock
  hemlock
  hemlock gum tree
  hemlock pitch tree
  hemlock spruce
  weeping spruce

Piperaceae [Pepper family]

Piper angustifolium
  matico
Piper betle
  betel
  betle pepper
  pan leaves
Piper clusii
  ashanti pepper
  Guinea pepper
Piper cubeba
  cubeb
  Java pepper
  tailed cubebs
  tailed pepper
Piper longum
  long pepper
  pipel
Piper methysticum
  kava-kava
Piper nigrum
  green peppercorns
  white pepper
  black pepper
  pepper

Plantaginaceae [Plantain family]

Plantago coronopus
  hartshorn plantain
  herb-ivy

Plantago lanceolata
buckhorn
chimney-sweeps
English plantain
headsman
lance-leaf plantain
narrow-leaved plantain
plantain
ribgrass
ribwort
ripplegrass
snake plantain
soldier's herb
Plantago major
broad-leaved plantain
cart-track plantain
common plantain
dooryard plantain
greater plantain
round-leaved plantain
way bread
white-man's-foot
Plantago media
hoary plantain
gray ribwort
wooly plantain
Plantago psyllium
fleawort
Spanish psyllium

Polemoniaceae [Phlox family]

Polemonium caeruleum
charity
Greek valerian
Jacob's ladder

Polygalaceae [Milkwort family]

Krameria argentia
Brazilian rhatany
Krameria triandra
krameria
Peruvian rhatany
rhatany
Polygala amara
bitter milkwort
dwarf milkwort
European bitter polygala
European senega snakeroot

evergreen snakeroot
flowering wintergreen
fringed polygala
little pollom
milkwort
Polygala senega
milkwort
seneca snakeroot
Polygala vulgaris
European seneka
European milkwort
gang flower
milkwort
rogation flower
senega snakeroot

Polygonaceae [Buckwheat family]

Polygonum spp.
fleece flower
knotweed
smartweed
Polygonum aviculare
beggarweed
bird knotgrass
birdweed
cow grass
crawlgrass
doorweed
fleece flower
knotweed
ninety-knot
pigweed
smartweed
Polygonum bistorta
bistort
dragonwort
Easter giant
patience dock
poor-man's-cabbage
red leg
snake root
snakeweed
sweet dock
Polygonum hydropiper
water pepper
Polygonum multiflorum
fo-ti
ho shou wu

Polygonum persicaria
  doorweed
  heartease
  heartweed
  lady's thumb
  pinkweed
  red leg
  spotted knotweed
Polygonum punctatum
  water smartweed
Rheum palmatum
  Chinese rhubarb
  Turkey rhubarb
Rheum rhabarbarum
  garden rhubarb
  pie plant
  rhubarb
  wine plant
Rumex acetosa
  European sorrel
  garden sorrel
  meadow sorrel
  sour dock
  sourgrass
Rumex acetocella
  American sorrel
  red sorrel
  sheep sorrel
  sorrel, common
  garden sorrel
  sour dock
Rumex alpinus
  Alpine dock
  monk's rhubarb
  mountain rhubarb
Rumex crispus
  curled dock
  narrow dock
  rhubarb sorrel
  sour dock
  yellow dock
Rumex hymenosepalus
  canaigre
  tanner's dock
  wild pie plant
  wild rhubarb
Rumex obtusifolius
  broad-leaved dock
Rumex patientia

garden patience
herb patience
monk's rhubarb
patience
patience dock
spinach dock
Rumex scutatus
  buckler-leaf sorrel
  French sorrel
  garden sorrel
Rumex spp.
  dock
  rhubarb sorrel
  sorrel

Polypodiaceae [Polypody family]
Adiantum capillus-veneris
  dudder grass
  maidenhair fern
  southern maidenhair
  Venus's-hair-fern
Dryopteris filix-mas
  aspidium
  bear's paw root
  knotty brake
  male fern
  shield fern
  sweet brake
  wood fern
Polypodium vulgare
  adder's fern
  brake fern
  brake rock
  brake root
  common polypody
  European polypody
  female fern
  fern brake
  fern root
  rock brake
  rock polypod
  stone brake
  wall fern
  wall polypody

Portulacaceae [Purslane family]
Portulaca oleracea, var. sativa
  continental parsley

kitchen-garden purslane
purslane
pusley

Primulaceae [Primrose family]

Anagallis arvensis
  poor man's weatherglass
  red chickweed
  red pimpernel
  scarlet pimpernel
  shepherd's weatherglass
  shepherd's-clock
Cyclamen spp.
  Alpine violet
  cyclamen
  groundbread
  Persian violet
  sowbread
  swinebread
Dodecatheon spp.
  American cowslip
  shooting star
Primula officinalis
  butter rose
  cowslip
  English cowslip
  primrose
Primula veris
  butter rose
  cowslip
  English cowslip
  keyflower
  palsywort
  primrose
Primula vulgaris
  English primrose

Punicaceae [Pomegranate family]

Punica granatum
  pomegranate

Pyrolaceae [Wintergreen family]

Chimaphila umbellata
  bitter wintergreen
  ground holly
  king's cure
  pipsissewa
  prince's pine

rheumatism weed
Monotropa uniflora
  birdnest
  convulsion root
  corpse plant
  fairy smoke
  fit plant
  fitsroot
  ghost flower
  Indian-pipe
  pine-sap
  pipe plant
Pyrola elliptica
  shinleaf
  wild lily-of-the-valley

Ranunculaceae [Crowfoot or buttercup family]

Aconitum napellus
  aconite
  bear's-foot
  friar's-cap
  helmet flower
  monkshood
  mousebane
  soldier's-cap
  turk's-cap
  wolfsbane
Actaea spp.
  baneberry
  cohosh
  doll's-eyes
  herb Christopher
  necklaceweed
  red baneberry
  snakeberry
  white baneberry
  white cohosh
Anemone nuttalliana
  hartshorn plant
  lion's-beard
  pasque flower
  prairie-smoke
  wild crocus
Anemone patens
  Easter flower
  meadow anemone
  pasque flower

prairie anemone
pulsatilla
wild crocus
wind flower
Anemone pulsatilla
  Easter flower
  meadow anemone
  pasque flower
  prairie anemone
  pulsatilla
  wild crocus
  wind flower
Aquilegia vulgaris
  columbine
  European crowfoot
  garden columbine
Caltha palustris
  American cowslip
  kingcup
  marsh marigold
  may-blob
  meadow bouts
  meadow-bright
  palsywort
  water dragon
Cimicifuga racemosa
  black cohosh
  black snakeroot
  bugbane
  bugwort
  rattleroot
  rattletop
  rattleweed
  richweed
  squawroot
Clematis virginiana
  devil's-darning-needle
  leather flower
  virgin's bower
  woodbine
Consolida regalis
  branching larkspur
  knight's spur
  lark heel
  lark's claw
  larkspur
  staggerweed
  stavesacre
Coptis trifolia

cankerroot
goldthread
mouthroot
yellowroot
Delphinium consolida
  branching larkspur
  Knight's spur
  lark heel
  lark's claw
  larkspur
  staggerweed
  stavesacre
Helleborus foetidus
  bearsfoot
  fetid hellebore
  hellebore
  oxheal
  stinking hellebore
Helleborus niger
  black hellebore
  Christmas rose
  hellebore
Helleborus viridis
  green hellebore
  hellebore
  winter hellebore
Hepatica americana
  herb trinity
  liverwort
Hepatica nobilis
  herb trinity
  liverwort
Hydrastis canadensis
  eye balm
  eye root
  goldenseal
  ground raspberry
  Indian plant
  Indian turmeric
  jaundice root
  orangeroot
  turmeric root
  yellow puccoon
  yellowroot
Nigella damascena
  Damascene nigella
  love-in-a-mist
  ragged lady
  Saint Catherine's flower

Venus' hair
wild fennel
Nigella sativa
  black caraway
  black cumin
  devil-in-the-bush
  fennel flower
  kalonji
  nigella
  nutmeg flower
  Roman coriander
  wild onion seed
Pulsatilla amoena
  Easter flower
  meadow anemone
  pasque flower
  prairie anemone
  pulsatilla
  wild crocus
  wind flower
Pulsatilla patens
  Easter flower
  meadow anemone
  pasque flower
  prairie anemone
  pulsatilla
  wild crocus
  wind flower
Pulsatilla vulgaris
  Easter flower
  meadow anemone
  pasque flower
  prairie anemone
  pulsatilla
  wild crocus
  wind flower
Ranunculus acris
  bachelor's buttons
  blisterweed
  burrwort
  buttercup
  crowfoot
  crowfoot buttercup
  globe amaranth
  gold cup
  meadow crowfoot
  meadowbloom
  tall buttercup
  tall crowfoot

  tall field buttercup
  yellows
  yellowweed
Ranunculus bulbosus
  acrid crowfoot
  bulbous buttercup
  bulbous crowfoot
  buttercup
  crowfoot
  crowfoot buttercup
  cuckoo buds
  frogwort
  king's cup
  meadowbloom
  pilewort
  Saint Anthony's turnip
Ranunculus ficaria
  lesser celandine
  pilewort
  small celandine
Ranunculus sceleratus
  buttercup
  celery-leaved buttercup
  crowfoot
  cursed crowfoot
  marsh crowfoot
  water crowfoot

Rhamnaceae [Buckthorn family]

Ceanothus americanus
  liberty tea
  mountain sweet
  New Jersey tea
  red root
  Walpole tea
  wild snowball
Rhamnus cathartica
  common buckthorn
  purging buckthorn
  waythorn
Rhamnus frangula
  alder buckthorn
  alder dogwood
  arrowwood
  black alder dogwood
  black alder tree
  black dogwood
  buckthorn

European black alder
European buckthorn
Persian berries
Rhamnus purshiana
  bearberry
  bearwood
  California buckthorn
  cascara
  cascara buckthorn
  cascara sagrada
  chittambark
  sacred bark
Zizyphus spp.
  jujube
  lotus

Rhodophyceae [Red algae family]
Chondrus crispus
  carrageen
  carragheen
  Irish moss
  pearl moss

Rosaceae [Rose family]
Agrimonia eupatoria
  agrimony
  church steeples
  cockeburr
  cocklebur
  harvest-lice
  sticklewort
Alchemilla arvensis
  field lady's-mantle
Alchemilla microcarpa
  parsley piert
Alchemilla vulgaris
  bear's-foot
  lady's-mantle
  lion's-foot
Aphanes arvensis
  field lady's-mantle
Aronia arbutifolia
  chokeberry
Brayera anthelminica
  cusso
  kousso
Crataegus spp.
  cockspur

cockspur thorn
English hawthorn
hawthorn berries
May bush
May tree
Mayblossom
quick-set thorn
red haw
summer haw
thorn apple
Washington thorn
white thorn
yellow-fruited thorn
Filipendula spp.
  herb Christopher
  meadowsweet
Filipendula ulmaria
  bridewort
  dolloff
  herb Christopher
  meadowsweet
  meadow queen
  meadow-wort
  pride-of-the-meadow
  queen-of-the-meadow
Filipendula vulgaris
  drop wort
  goatsbeard
Fragaria spp.
  strawberry
Fragaria vesca, cultivar Alpine
  Alpine strawberry
Geum rivale
  avens root
  chocolate root
  cure-all
  Indian chocolate
  purple avens
  throat root
  water avens
Geum urbanum
  avens
  bennet
  blessed herb
  cloveroot
  colewort
  European avens
  geum
  goldy stone

herb-bennet
herba benedicta
star of the earth
wood avens
yellow avens
Geum virginianum
rough avens
Hagenia abyssinica
cusso
kousso
Licanea guianensis
Cayenne sassafras
Potentilla anserina
cinquefoil
crampweed
goose tansy
goosegrass
moor grass
silver cinquefoil
silverweed
Potentilla canadensis
finger leaf
five fingers
five-finger grass
Potentilla erecta
red root
shepherd's knot
tormentil
upright septfoil
Potentilla reptans
European five-finger grass
Potentilla rupestris
prairie tea
rock cinquefoil
Poterium sanguisorba
burnet
garden burnet
pimpinella
pimpinelle
salad burnet
Prunus amygdala, var. amara
bitter almond
Prunus amygdala, var. dulcis
almond
Greek nuts
sweet almond
Prunus dulcis, var. amara
bitter almond
Prunus dulcis, var. dulcis

almond
Greek nuts
sweet almond
Prunus laurocerasus
cherry laurel
cherry-bay
English laurel
Prunus mahaleb
mahaleb
mahleb
mahlepi
perfumed cherry
Saint Lucie cherry
Prunus pennsylvanica
bird cherry
fire cherry
pin cherry
wild cherry
wild red cherry
Prunus persica
peach leaves
Prunus serotina
black cherry
black choke
chokecherry
rum cherry
wild black cherry
wild cherry
Prunus spinosa
blackthorn
sloe
Prunus virginiana
chokecherry
Quillaja saponaria
Panama bark
quillai
quillaja
quillay bark
soapbark
Rosa spp.
attar of roses
rose
rose absolute
rose Bulgarian
rose hips
true Otto oil
Rubus spp.
baked-apple berry
blackberry

blackcap
boysenberry
cloudberry
dewberry
framboise
Himalaya berry
kneshenka
loganberry
malka
nagoonberry
raspberry
salmonberry
thimbleberry
wineberry
yellowberry
youngberry
Sanguisorba minor
   burnet
   garden burnet
   pimpinella
   pimpinelle
   salad burnet
Sanguisorba officinalis
   burnet bloodwort
   great burnet
   Italian burnet
   Italian pimpernel
Sorbus americana
   American mountain ash
   dogberry
   missey-moosey
   roundwood
Sorbus aucuparia
   European mountain ash
   mountain ash
   quickbeam
   rodden
   rowan
   sorb apple

Rubiaceae [Madder family]

Asperula cynanchica
   quinsy wort
Asperula odorata
   mugwort
   quinsy wort
   master of the wood
   sweet grass

sweet woodruff
waldmeister
woodroof
woodruff
woodward
Cinchona spp.
   fever bark tree
   Jesuits' bark
   Peruvian bark
   quinine
Galium aparine
   bedstraw
   catchweed
   cleavers
   cleaverwort
   clivers
   coachweed
   goose grass
   gosling weed
   gripgrass
   hedge-bur
   love-man
   stick-a-back
   sticky-willie
   sweethearts
Galium lanceolatum or circaezans
   wild licorice
Galium odoratum
   mugwort
   quinsy wort
   master of the wood
   sweet grass
   sweet woodruff
   waldmeister
   woodroof
   woodruff
   woodward
Galium verum
   bedstraw
   cheese rennet
   curdwort
   lady's bedstraw
   maid's hair
   Our Lady's bedstraw
   yellow bedstraw
   yellow cleavers
Gardenia jasminoides
   cape jasmine
Ourouparia gambier

catechu
gambier
gambir
pale catechu
Rubia tinctorum
  madder
Uncaria gambier
  catechu
  gambier
  gambir
  pale catechu

Rutaceae [Rue or citrus family]
Agathosma betulina
  bookoo
  bucco
  buchu
  bucku
  mountain buchu
  round buchu
  short buchu
Agathosma crenulata
  crenate buchu
  long buchu
  oval buchu
Amyris balsamifera
  amyris
  West Indian rosewood
  West Indian sandalwood
Barosma betulina
  bookoo
  bucco
  buchu
  bucku
  mountain buchu
  round buchu
  short buchu
Barosma crenulata
  crenate buchu
  long buchu
  oval buchu
Boronia megastigma
  boronia
Chalcas koenigii
  curry leaf
  curry leaf tree
Cusparia trifoliata
  angostura bark

cusparia bark
Dictamnus albus
  bastard dittany
  burning-bush
  diptam
  dittany
  false dittany
  fraxinella
  gas-plant
Galipea cusparia
  angostura bark
  cusparia bark
Galipea officinalis
  angostura bark
  cusparia bark
Galipea trifoliata
  angostura bark
  cusparia bark
Murraya koenigii
  curry leaf
  curry-leaf tree
Ptelea trifoliata
  hop tree
  pickaway anise
  prairie grub
  scubby trefoil
  shrubby trefoil
  stinking ash
  stinking prairie bush
  swamp dogwood
  three-leaved hop tree
  wafer ash
  water ash
  wingseed
Ruta bracteosa
  garden rue
  German rue
  herb-of-grace
  herb-of-repentance
  rue
Ruta calepensis
  garden rue
  German rue
  herb-of-grace
  herb-of-repentance
  rue
Ruta graveolens
  garden rue
  German rue

herb-of-grace
herb-of-repentance
rue
Ruta montana
  garden rue
  German rue
  herb-of-grace
  herb-of-repentance
  rue
Zanthoxylum alatum
  Chinese pepper
  hua-chiao
  Szechuan pepper
  tomarseed
  winged prickly ash
Zanthoxylum americanum
  northern prickly ash
  prickly ash tree
  toothache tree
Zanthoxylum bodrunga
  mulilam
Zanthoxylum bungei
  Chinese pepper
  hua-chiao
  Szechuan pepper
Zanthoxylum clava-Herculis
  Hercules'-club
  pepperwood
  prickly ash
  sea ash
  southern prickly ash
Zanthoxylum mantchuricum
  inuzansho
  pepperbush
Zanthoxylum piperitum
  anise-pepper
  Chinese pepper
  Japanese pepper
  prickly ash
  sansho pepper
  Szechuan pepper
Zanthoxylum rhetsa
  mulilam
Zanthoxylum schinifolium
  inuzansho
  pepperbush
Zanthoxylum simulans
  Chinese pepper
  hua-chiao

Szechuan pepper

Salicaceae [Willow family]
Populus alba
  abele
  silver-leaved poplar
Populus balsamifera
  balm of Gilead
  balsam poplar
  hackmatack
  poplar
  tacamahac
Populus candicans
  balm of Gilead
  balsam poplar
  hackmatack
  poplar
  tacamahac
Populus x gileadensis
  balm of Gilead
Populus nigra
  black poplar
  lombardy poplar
  poplar
Populus tremuloides
  quaking aspen
  quiverleaf
  trembling aspen
Salix alba
  salicin willow
  white willow
  withe
  withy
Salix caprea
  florist's willow
  goat willow
  pussy willow
  sallow
Salix nigra
  black willow
Salix purpurea
  basket willow
  purple osier
  purple willow

Santalaceae [Sandalwood family]
Santalum spp.
  East Indian sandalwood

sandalwood
white sandalwood
white saunders
yellow sandalwood
yellow saunders

Sapindaceae [Soapberry family]

Paullinia cupana
  guarana

Sarraceniaceae [Pitcher plant family]

Sarracenia purpurea
  Eve's cup
  flytrap
  huntsman's-cup
  Indian-cup
  pitcher plant
  side-saddle flower
  smallpox plant
  southern pitcher plant
  sweet pitcher plant
  watercup

Saxifragaceae [Saxifrage family]

Hydrangea arborescens
  hills-of-snow
  hydrangea
  sevenbark
  wild hydrangea
Mitchella repens
  checkerberry
  deerberry
  hive vine
  one-berry
  partridgeberry
  running box
  squaw vine
  squawberry
  twinberry
  two-eyed berry
  winter clover
Ribes nigrum
  black currant
  European black currant
  niribine oil
  quinsy berry
Ribes rubrum
  garden currant

garnetberry
northern red currant
raisin tree
red currant
wineberry

Schisandraceae [Schisandra family]

Schisandra coccinea
  bay star vine
  magnolia vine
  wild sarsaparilla

Scrophulariaceae [Figwort family]

Agalinus pedicularia
  American foxglove
  bushy gerardia
  false foxglove
  fern-leaved false foxglove
  feverweed
  lousewort
Aureolaria pedicularia
  American foxglove
  bushy gerardia
  false foxglove
  fern-leaved false foxglove
  feverweed
  lousewort
Chelone glabra
  balmony
  saltrheum weed
  shell flower
  snakehead
  turtlebloom
  turtlehead
Digitalis lanata
  Grecian foxglove
Digitalis purpurea
  American foxglove
  common foxglove
  dead men's bells
  digitalis
  dog's finger
  fairy fingers
  fairy gloves
  finger flower
  folks' glove
  lion's mouth
  ladies' glove

purple foxglove
Digitalis spp.
  foxglove
Euphrasia officinalis
  euphrasy
  eye-bright
  red eyebright
Gerardia pedicularia
  American foxglove
  bushy gerardia
  false foxglove
  fern-leaved false foxglove
  feverweed
  lousewort
Gratiola officinalis
  hedge hyssop
Leptandra virginica
  Beaumont root
  blackroot
  Bowman's root
  Culver's-physic
  Culver's-root
  hini
  leptandra
  oxadoddy
  physic root
  purple leptandra
  tall speedwell
  tall veronica
  whorlywort
Limnophila stolonifera
  oregano
Linaria vulgaris
  butter and eggs
  flaxweed
  pennywort
  toadflax
  wild snapdragon
  yellow toadflax
Mimulus spp.
  monkey flowers
Pedicularis canadensis
  wood betony
Pedicularis spp.
  lousewort
Scrophularia marilandica
  carpenter's square
  figwort
  heal-all

kernelwort
knotty-rooted figwort
scrofula plant
Verbascum phlomoides
  mullein
  mullen
Verbascum thapsiforme
  mullein
  mullen
Verbascum thapsus
  flannel plant
  mullein
  mullen
  velvet plant
Veronica beccabunga
  beccabunga
  European brooklime
  mouth-smart
  neckweed
  speedwell
  water pimpernel
  water purslain
Veronica chamaedrys
  angel's-eye
  bird's-eye
  germander speedwell
Veronica officinalis
  fluellen
  groundhele
  gypsyweed
  low speedwell
  Paul's betony
  speedwell
  upland speedwell
Veronica spp.
  brooklime
  speedwell
  veronica
Veronica virginica
  Beaumont root
  blackroot
  Bowman's root
  Culver's-physic
  Culver's-root
  hini
  leptandra
  oxadoddy
  physic root
  purple leptandra

tall speedwell
tall veronica
whorlywort
Veronicastrum virginicum
  Beaumont root
  blackroot
  Bowman's root
  Culver's-physic
  Culver's-root
  hini
  leptandra
  oxadoddy
  physic root
  purple leptandra
  tall speedwell
  tall veronica
  whorlywort

Simaroubaceae [Quassia family]

Quassia amara
  bitter ash
  bitterwood
  quassia
  Surinam quassia
Simarouba amara
  bitter ash
  bitterwood
  quassia
  simarouba bark
  Surinam quassia

Solanaceae [Nightshade family]

Atropa belladonna
  belladonna
  black cherry
  deadly nightshade
  dwale
  poison black cherry
Capsicum annuum, var. annuum
  bell pepper
  capsicum pepper
  cayenne pepper
  cherry pepper
  chili pepper
  cluster pepper
  cone pepper
  green pepper
  long pepper

paprika
pequin
petines
pimento
pimiento
red cluster pepper
red pepper
sweet pepper
Capsicum annuum, var. glabriusculum
  bird pepper
  wild capsicum varieties
Capsicum baccatum
  Brown's pepper
Capsicum chinense
  Chinese pepper
Capsicum frutescens
  malagueta (Spanish)
  Tabasco pepper
  Tabasco-sauce pepper
Capsicum pubescens
  chile manzana
  rocoto
Capsicum tetragonum
  paprika
Datura stramonium
  common thorn apple
  devil's apple
  devil's trumpet
  Jamestown weed
  jimsonweed
  mad-apple
  nightshade
  Peru-apple
  stinkweed
  stinkwort
  stramonium
  thorn apple
Hyoscyamus niger
  black henbane
  devil's eye
  fetid nightshade
  henbane
  henbell
  hog bean
  Jupiter's bean
  poison tobacco
  stinking nightshade
Mandragora officinarum
  love apple

mandrake
satan's apple
Nicotiana rustica
poke
wild tobacco
Solanum dulcamara
bittersweet
bittersweet herb
bittersweet nightshade
bittersweet stems
bittersweet twigs
blue nightshade
deadly nightshade
felonwood
felonwort
fever twig
nightshade
nightshade vine
poisonous nightshade
scarlet berry
staff vine
violet bloom
woody
woody nightshade
Solanum nigrum
black nightshade
common nightshade
deadly nightshade
garden nightshade
poisonberry

Sterculiaceae [Sterculia family]

Cola acuminata
abata cola
caffeine nut
cola
cola nut
goora nut
guru nut
kola
Cola nitida
abata cola
caffeine nut
cola
cola nut
goora nut
guru nut
kola

Styracaceae [Storax family]

Styrax benzoin
benzoin
storax
styrax
Sumatra benzoin

Taxaceae [Yew family]

Taxus baccata
chinwood
English yew
Taxus spp.
yew
Torreya californica
California nutmeg
Torreya taxifolia
Florida stinking cedar

Thymelaeaceae [Mezereum family]

Daphne mezereum
February daphne
daphne
mezereon
mezereum
spurge flax
spurge laurel
spurge olive
wild pepper

Tiliaceae [Linden family]

Tilia spp.
lime flowers
linden
tilia flowers
Tilia americana
American linden tree
basswood
bast tree
lime tree
spoonwood
whitewood
wycopy
Tilia x europaea
European lime tree
European linden

Tropaeolaceae [Nasturtium family]

Tropaeolum majus
  capucine (French)
  garden nasturtium
  Indian cress
  nasturtium
  tall nasturtium

Turneraceae [Turnera family]

Turnera diffusa
  damiana
  hierba de la pastora

Ulmaceae [Elm family]

Ulmus fulva
  Indian elm
  moose elm
  red elm
  slippery elm
  sweet elm
Ulmus rubra
  Indian elm
  moose elm
  red elm
  slippery elm
  sweet elm

Umbelliferae [Parsley family]

Aegopodium podagraria
  ashweed
  bishop's weed
  goutweed
  ground ash
  ground elder
  herb Gerard
Aethusa cynapium
  dog poison
  fool's cicely
  fool's parsley
  small hemlock
Ammi copticum
  ajowan
  ajuan
  omum
Anethum graveolens
  anet
  dill
  dill weed
Anethum sowa

  Indian dill
Angelica archangelica
  angelica
  archangel
  archangelica
  European angelica
  wild parsnip
Angelica atropurpurea
  alexanders
  American angelica
  bellyache root
  great angelica
  masterwort
  purple angelica
Angelica keiskei
  Japanese angelica
Angelica ursina
  Japanese angelica
Angelica officinalis
  angelica
  archangel
  archangelica
  European angelica
  wild parsnip
Anthriscus cerefolium
  chervil
  cicely
  French parsley
  garden chervil
Anthriscus sylvestris
  cow chervil
  cow parsley
Apium graveolens
  celery seed
  smallage
Carum ajowan
  ajowan
  ajuan
  omum
Carum bulbocastanum?
  earth-nuts
Carum carvi
  caraway
Carum copticum
  ajowan
  ajuan
  omum
Chaerophyllum bulbosum
  parsnip chervil

turnip-rooted chervil
Chaerophyllum sylvestre
   European wild cicely
Cicuta maculata
   beaver-poison
   musquash root
   spotted cowbane
Cicuta virosa
   water hemlock
   water parsley
Conium maculatum
   California fern
   hemlock
   Nebraska fern
   poison parsley
   poison root
   poison snakeweed
   spotted hemlock
   winter fern
   poison hemlock
Coriandrum sativum
   Chinese parsley
   cilantro
   coriander
Crithmum maritimum
   Peter's cress
   rock samphire
   Saint Peter's herb
   samphire
   sea fennel
Cryptotaenia canadensis
   honewort
   Japanese parsley
   Japanese wild chervil
   mitsuba
   white chervil
Cryptotaenia japonica
   honewort
   Japanese parsley
   Japanese wild chervil
   mitsuba
   white chervil
Cuminum cyminum
   comino
   cumin
Daucus carota, var. carota
   daucus
   devil's-plague
   queen's-lace

   Queen-Anne's-lace
   wild carrot
Daucus carota, var. sativus
   carrot
Eryngium aquaticum
   water eryngo
Eryngium campestre
   field eryngo
   snakeroot
Eryngium foetidum
   cilantro
   culantro
   oregano de Cartagena
Eryngium maritimum
   eringo
   eryngo
   sea eryngium
   sea holly
   sea holm
Eryngium yuccifolium
   button snake-root
   corn snakeroot
   rattlesnake weed
   rattlesnake-master
Ferula assa-foetida
   asafetida
   asafoetida
   devil's dung
   food-of-the-gods
   giant fennel
   Persian gum
   stinking gum
Ferula communis
   common giant fennel
Ferula diversivittata
   muskroot
   sumbul
Ferula foetida
   asafoetida
Ferula galbaniflua
   galban
   galbanum
Ferula moschata
   muskroot
   sumbul
Ferula rubricaulis
   galban
   galbanum
Foeniculum vulgare

fennel
Foeniculum vulgare subsp. vulgare var.
  azoricum
  fennel
  Florence fennel
  giant fennel
Heracleum lanatum
  American cow parsnip
  cow cabbage
  cow parsnip
  hogweed
  madnep
  masterwort
  wooly parsnip
  youthwort
Heracleum sphondylium, subsp.
  montanum
  American cow parsnip
  cow cabbage
  cow parsnip
  hogweed
  madnep
  masterwort
  wooly parsnip
  youthwort
Hydrocotyle asiatica
  gotu cola
  gutu cola
  navelwort
  water pennyroyal
Imperatoria osthruthium
  hog's fennel
  imperatoria
  imperial masterwort
  masterwort
  sulfurwort
Laserpitium latifolium
  asafoetida
  herb frankincense
  laserwort
Levisticum officinale
  European lovage
  garden lovage
  Italian lovage
  lavose
  lovage
  love parsley
  sea parsley
  wild parsley

Ligusticum mutellina
  alpine lovage
Ligusticum scoticum
  northern lovage
  Scotch lovage
  sea lovage
Myrrhis odorata
  anise
  anise chervil
  British myrrh
  European sweet cicely
  fern-leaved chervil
  garden myrrh
  giant sweet chervil
  myrrh
  Spanish chervil
  sweet chervil
  sweet scented myrrh
Opopanax chironium
  Bisabol myrrh
  opopanax
  sweet myrrh
Osmorhiza claytonii
  hairy sweet cicely
  sweet jarvil
  sweet javril
  wooly sweet cicely
Osmorhiza longistylis
  aniseroot
  New England sweet cicely
  smooth sweet cicely
  sweet chervil
  sweet cicely
Petroselinum crispum
  garden parsley
  parsley
  rock parsley
  turnip-rooted parsley
Petroselinum sativum
  garden parsley
  parsley
  rock parsley
Peucedanum osthruthium
  hog's fennel
  imperatoria
  imperial masterwort
  masterwort
  sulfurwort
Pimpinella anisum

anise
aniseed
sweet cumin
Pimpinella magna
false pimpernel
greater pimpernel
pimpernel
pimpinella
Pimpinella major
false pimpernel
greater pimpernel
pimpernel
pimpinella
Pimpinella saxifraga
burnet saxifrage
pimpernel
pimpinella
saxifrage
small pimpernel
Sanicula marilandica
American sanicle
black sanicle
black snakeroot
sanicle
Sanicula europaea
European sanicle
wood sanicle
Smyrnium olusatrum
alexanders
allisanders
black lovage
horse parsley
Thaspium aureum
alexanders
meadow parsnip
Trachyspermum ammi
ajowan
ajuan
omum
Trachyspermum copticum
ajowan
ajuan
omum
Zizia aurea
golden alexanders

Urticaceae [Nettle family]
Parietaria officinalis

pellitory
pellitory of the wall
wall plant
Urtica dioica
nettle
stinging nettle

Usneaceae [a lichen family]
Evernia furfuracea
tree moss
Evernia prunastri
oak moss
Usnea barbata
tree moss

Valerianaceae [Valerian family]
Nardostachys chinensis
Chinese spikenard
Nardostachys jatamansi
nard
Indian spikenard
Valeriana celtica
celtic nard
Valeriana fauriei
Japanese valerian
kesso
valerian
Valeriana officinalis
all-heal
cat's valerian
English valerian
garden heliotrope
garden valerian
German valerian
great wild valerian
Japanese valerian
kesso
Saint George's herb
setwall
valerian
vandal root
Vermont valerian
wild valerian
Valeriana saliunca
celtic nard
Valeriana spp.
valerian
Valeriana wallichii

Indian valerian

Verbenaceae [Verbena or vervain family]

Aloysia triphylla
 herb Louisa
 lemon verbena
 verbena oil
Lantana achyranthifolia
 orégano
Lantana glandulosissima
 orégano silvestre
 orégano xiu
Lantana hispida
 oréganillo del monte
Lantana involucrata
 orégano
Lantana microcephala
 orégano xiu
Lantana trifolia
 orégano
Lantana velutina
 orégano xiu
Lippia abyssinica
 Gambian bush tea
Lippia affinis
 orégano
 orégano montes
Lippia citriodora
 herb Louisa
 lemon verbena
 verbena oil
Lippia formosa
 orégano
Lippia fragrans
 orégano
Lippia graveolens
 American oregano
 Mexican oregano
 Mexican sage
 orégano
 orégano cimarron
Lippia micromeria
 false thyme
 orégano
 orégano del pais
Lippia origanoides
 orégano

 orégano del pais
Lippia palmeri
 orégano
Lippia pseudo-thea
 Brazilian tea
 gervao
Lippia umbellata
 orégano montes
Verbena hastata
 American vervain
 blue vervain
 false vervain
 Indian hyssop
 purvain
 simpler's joy
 traveler's joy
 wild hyssop
Verbena officinalis
 enchanter's plant
 European vervain
 herb of the cross
 Juno's tears
 pigeon's grass
 pigeonweed
 simpler's joy
 vervain
Vitex agnus-castus
 chaste tree
 chasteberry
 hemp tree
 Indian-spice
 monk's pepper tree
 sage tree
 wild pepper

Violaceae [Violet family]

Sauvagesia erecta
 adima
 Saint Martin's herb
 yaoba
 yerba de Saint Martin
Viola alba
 Parma violet
Viola calcarata
 Swiss violet
Viola odorata
 English violet
 florist's violet

garden violet
sweet violet
Viola suavis
  Russian violet
Viola tricolor
  European wild pansy
  field pansy
  heartease
  herb trinity
  Johnny jumper
  Johnny-jump-up
  miniature pansy
  pansy
  step-mother
  wild pansy

Vitaceae [Grape family]
Parthenocissus quinquefolia
  American ivy
  American woodbine
  creeper
  false grapes
  five fingers
  five-leaved ivy
  Virginia creeper
  wild woodbine
  wild woodvine
  woodbine
  woody climber

Winteraceae [Winter's bark family]
Drimys aromatica
  pepper berries
  pepper tree
Drimys lanceolata
  pepper berries
  pepper tree

Zingiberaceae [Ginger family]
Alpinea galanga
  catarrh root
  Chinese ginger
  East India root
  galangal
  galingal
  greater galangal
  laos
  lenkuas

Alpinea officinalis
  Chinese ginger
  East India root
  galangal
  galingal
  kencur
  lesser galangal
Amomum cardamomum
  cardamom, small
Amomum compactum
  cardamom, small
  round cardamom
Curcuma domestica
  saffron of the Indies
Curcuma domestica
  turmeric
Curcuma longa
  saffron of the Indies
  turmeric
Curcuma zedoaria
  zedoary
Elettaria cardamomum
  cardamom, large
  Ceylon cardamom
  Malabar cardamom
Elettaria granum-paradise
  false cardamom
  grains of paradise
  Guinea grains
  paradise nuts
Elettaria melegueta
  Melegueta pepper
Kaempferia galangal
  galangal
  kentjur
Zingiber officinale
  Canton ginger
  ginger
  Jamaican ginger
  true ginger

Zygophyllaceae [Caltrop family]
Bulnesia sarmienti
  wild guaiac
  wild guaiacum
Guaiacum officinale
  guaiac
  guaiacum

guayacan
lignum vitae
pockwood
tree of life
Larrea tridentata
chaparral
creosote bush
greasewood
Sonora gumn

Unidentified Genera

Cinnamodendron corticosum or
*   macranthum*
Jamaica canella
Doryphora sassafras
   Australian sassafras
Lagaecia cuminoides
   wild cumin

Genera

Abelmoschus moschatus [Malvaceae]
abelmosk
abelmusk
ambrette seed
musk mallow
muskseed
Abies alba [Pinaceae]
fir needles oil
pine fir
silver fir
silver spruce
templin oil
white spruce
white fir
Abies balsamea [Pinaceae]
balm of Gilead
balsam fir needle oil
Canada balsam oil
Abies sachalinensis [Pinaceae]
fir needles oil
Japanese fir needle oil
Japanese pine needle oil
Japanese fir
pine fir
Sakhalin fir
shin-yo-yu
Abies sachalinensis var. *mayriana*
[Pinaceae]
Mayr Sakhalin fir
Abies sibirica [Pinaceae]
European fir
fir needles oil
pine fir

Siberian fir
Siberian fir needle oil
Siberian pine needle oil
Abrus precatorius [Leguminosae]
coral-bead plant
crab's eye
Indian licorice
Jamaican wild licorice
jequirity
licorice vine
love pea
prayer-beads
red-bean vine
rosary pea
weather plant
weather vine
wild licorice
Acacia catechu [Mimosaceae]
black catechu
cutch
khair
Wadalee-gum tree
Acacia caven [Mimosaceae]
Roman cassie
Acacia dealbata [Mimosaceae]
mimosa
Acacia decurrens [Mimosaceae]
Australian mimosa
black wattle
mimosa
Acacia farnesiana [Mimosaceae]
cassie
huisache

opopanax
popinac
sponge tree
sweet acacia
West Indian blackthorn
Acacia senegal [Mimosaceae]
acacia
Cape gum
gum arabic
Egyptian thorn
Sudan gum-arabic
Acer rubrum [Aceraceae]
red maple
scarlet maple
soft maple
swamp maple
Acer saccharum [Aceraceae]
hard maple
rock maple
sugar maple
Acer spicatum [Aceraceae]
mountain maple
Achillea erba-rotta subsp. *moschata*
[Compositae]
iva
musk yarrow
Achillea millefolium [Compositae]
herb carpenter
iva
milfoil
musk yarrow
noble yarrow
nose-bleed
sanguinary
soldier's woundwort
thousand leaf
thousand-seal
yarrow
Achillea ptarmica [Compositae]
bastard pellitory
sneezeweed
sneezewort
Acinos alpinus [Labiatae]
alpine basil thyme
Acinos arvensis [Labiatae]
basil thyme
Acinos thymoides [Labiatae]
basil thyme
Aconitum napellus [Ranunculaceae]

aconite
bear's-foot
friar's-cap
helmet flower
monkshood
mousebane
soldier's-cap
turk's-cap
wolfsbane
Acorus calamus [Araceae]
calamus
flagroot
grass myrtle
myrtle flag
sweet calamus
sweet flag
sweet grass
sweet myrtle
sweet rush
Actaea spp. *[Ranunculaceae]*
baneberry
cohosh
doll's-eyes
herb Christopher
necklaceweed
red baneberry
snakeberry
white baneberry
white cohosh
Adansonia digitata [Bombacaceae]
baobab
calabash tree
dead-rat tree
lalo
monkey-bread tree
Adiantum capillus-veneris [Polypodiaceae]
dudder grass
maidenhair fern
southern maidenhair
Venus's-hair-fern
Aegopodium podagraria [Umbelliferae]
ashweed
bishop's weed
goutweed
ground ash
ground elder
herb Gerard
Aesculus hippocastanum
[Hippocastanaceae]

buckeye
horse chestnut
Aethusa cynapium [Umbelliferae]
    dog poison
    fool's cicely
    fool's parsley
    small hemlock
Agalinus pedicularia [Scrophulariaceae]
    American foxglove
    bush gerardia
    false foxglove
    fern-leaved false foxglove
    feverweed
    lousewort
Agastache foeniculum [Labiatae]
    anise hyssop
    blue giant hyssop
    fennel giant hyssop
    fragrant giant hyssop
    giant hyssop
Agastache mexicana [Labiatae]
    Mexican giant hyssop
Agastache rugosa [Labiatae]
    Korean mint
    wrinkled giant hyssop
Agathosma betulina [Rutaceae]
    bookoo
    bucco
    buchu
    bucku
    mountain buchu
    round buchu
    short buchu
Agathosma crenulata [Rutaceae]
    crenate buchu
    long buchu
    oval buchu
Agave americana [Agavaceae]
    agave
    American aloe
    century plant
    flowering aloe
    maguey
    spiked aloe
Agrimonia eupatoria [Rosaceae]
    agrimony
    church steeples
    cockeburr
    cocklebur

harvest-lice
sticklewort
Agropyrum repens [Gramineae]
    couch grass
    cutch
    dog grass
    durfa grass
    durfee grass
    quack grass
    quick grass
    quitch grass
    witchgrass
Alchemilla arvensis [Rosaceae]
    field lady's-mantle
Alchemilla microcarpa [Rosaceae]
    parsley piert
Alchemilla vulgaris [Rosaceae]
    bear's-foot
    lady's-mantle
    lion's-foot
Aletris farinosa [Liliaceae]
    ague grass
    ague root
    bitter grass
    colicroot
    crow corn
    mealy starwort
    star grass
    star root
    unicorn root
Aleurites moluccana [Euphorbiaceae]
    candleberry tree
    candlenut
    candlenut tree
    country walnut
    Indian walnut
    otaheite walnut
    varnish tree
Alliaria petiolata [Cruciferae]
    alliaria
    donkey's foot
    garlic mustard
    Jack-by-the-hedge
    onion nettle
    sauce alone
Allium ampeloprasum [Liliaceae]
    great-headed garlic
    Levant garlic
    wild leek

Allium ascalonicum [Liliaceae]
  eschalotte
  shallot
  éschalote
Allium cepa [Liliaceae]
  onion
Allium cepa, Aggregatum group
  [Liliaceae]
  eschalotte
  shallot
  éschalote
Allium fistulosum [Liliaceae]
  stone leek
  Welsh onion
Allium sativum [Liliaceae]
  garlic
Allium sativum, var. *ophioscorodon*
  [Liliaceae]
  giant garlic
  rocambole
  serpent garlic
Allium sativum var. *pekinense [Liliaceae]*
  Peking garlic
Allium schoenoprasum [Liliaceae]
  chives
  cive
  Schnittlauch
Allium scorodoprasum [Liliaceae]
  giant garlic
  sand leek
  Spanish garlic
Allium tricoccum [Liliaceae]
  ramps
  wild leek
Allium tuberosum [Liliaceae]
  Chinese chives
  garlic chive
  Oriental garlic
Allium ursinum [Liliaceae]
  bear's garlic
  buckrams
  gypsy onion
  hog's garlic
  ramsons
  ransoms
Alnus oregona [Betulaceae]
  alder
  Oregon alder
  red alder

Alnus rubra [Betulaceae]
  alder
Alnus rugosa [Betulaceae]
  alder
  hazel alder
  smooth alder
  speckled alder
Alnus serrulata [Betulaceae]
  alder
Aloe barbadensis [Liliaceae]
  Barbados aloe
  Curaçao aloe
  medicinal aloe
  unguentine cactus
Aloe ferox [Liliaceae]
  cape aloe
Aloe perryi [Liliaceae]
  Bombay aloe
  Socotrine aloe
  Turkey aloe
  Zanzibar aloe
Aloe spp. *[Liliaceae]*
  aloe
Aloysia triphylla [Verbenaceae]
  herb Louisa
  lemon verbena
  verbena oil
Alpinea galanga [Zingiberaceae]
  catarrh root
  Chinese ginger
  East India root
  galangal
  galingal
  greater galangal
  laos
  lenkuas
Alpinea officinarum [Zingiberaceae]
  Chinese ginger
  East India root
  galangal
  galingal
  kencur
  lesser galangal
Alstroemeria haemantha
  [Alstroemeriaceae]
  herb lily
Althaea officinalis [Malvaceae]
  althaea
  marsh mallow

mortification root
sweet weed
white mallow
wymote
Amaranthus spp. *[Amaranthaceae]*
amaranth
Joseph's-coat
lady bleeding
love-lies-bleeding
lovely bleeding
pigweed
pilewort
prince's feather
red cockscomb
spleen amaranth
wild beet
Ambrosia spp. *[Compositae]*
ragweed
Ammobium alatum [Compositae]
winged everlasting
Ammi copticum [Umbelliferae]
ajowan
ajuan
omum
Amomum cardamomum [Zingiberaceae]
cardamom, small
Amomum compactum [Zingiberaceae]
cardamom, small
round cardamom
Amyris balsamifera [Rutaceae]
amyris
West Indian rosewood
West Indian sandalwood
Anacyclus pyrethrum [Compositae]
pellitory of Spain
pyrethrum
Anagallis arvensis [Primulaceae]
poor man's weatherglass
red chickweed
red pimpernel
scarlet pimpernel
shepherd's weatherglass
shepherd's-purse
Anaphalis spp. *[Compositae]*
cottonweed
cudweed
everlasting
Indian posey
ladies' tobacco

large-flowered everlasting
life everlasting
pearly everlasting
Anemone nuttalliana [Ranunculaceae]
hartshorn plant
lion's-beard
pasque flower
prairie-smoke
wild crocus
Anemone patens [Ranunculaceae]
Easter flower
meadow anemone
pasque flower
prairie anemone
pulsatilla
wild crocus
wind flower
Anemone pulsatilla [Ranunculaceae]
Easter flower
meadow anemone
pasque flower
prairie anemone
pulsatilla
wild crocus
wind flower
Anethum graveolens [Umbelliferae]
anet
dill
dill weed
Anethum sowa [Umbelliferae]
Indian dill
Angelica archangelica [Umbelliferae]
angelica
archangel
archangelica
European angelica
wild parsnip
Angelica atropurpurea [Umbelliferae]
alexanders
American angelica
bellyache root
great angelica
masterwort
purple angelica
Angelica keiskei [Umbelliferae]
Japanese angelica
Angelica ursina [Umbelliferae]
Japanese angelica
Angelica officinalis [Umbelliferae]

angelica
archangel
archangelica
European angelica
wild parsnip
Angraecum fragrans [Orchidaceae]
    Bourbon tea
    faham tea
Aniba duckei [Lauraceae]
    bois de rose
    Brazilian rosewood
Aniba parviflora [Lauraceae]
    bois de rose
    Brazilian rosewood
Aniba roseodora [Lauraceae]
    bois de rose
Annona muricata [Annonaceae]
    guanabana
    prickly custard apple
    soursop
Annona reticulata [Annonaceae]
    American nutmeg
    bullock's heart
    custard apple
Annona squamosa [Annonaceae]
    custard apple
    Jamaica nutmeg
    sugar apple
    sweetsop
Antennaria spp. *[Compositae]*
    cat's foot
    everlasting
    ladies' tobacco
    mountain everlasting
    pussy-toes
Anthemis arvensis [Compositae]
    corn camomile
Anthemis cotula [Compositae]
    dog fennel
    stinking camomile
    stinking mayweed
    wild camomile
Anthemis montana [Compositae]
    camomile adulterant
Anthemis nobilis [Compositae]
    camomile
    English camomile
    garden camomile
    ground apple

lawn camomile
manzanilla
May-then
marigold
Roman camomile
Scotch camomile
Whig plant
Anthemis tinctoria [Compositae]
    golden Marguerite
    ox-eye camomile
    yellow camomile
Anthriscus cerefolium [Umbelliferae]
    chervil
    cicely
    French parsley
    garden chervil
Anthriscus sylvestris [Umbelliferae]
    cow chervil
    cow parsley
Anthyllis vulneraria [Leguminosae]
    kidney vetch
    ladies' fingers
    lamb's toes
    staunchwort
    woundwort
Aphanes arvensis [Rosaceae]
    field lady's-mantle
Apium graveolens [Umbelliferae]
    celery seed
    smallage
*Apocynum androsaemifolium
    [Apocynaceae]*
    bitterroot
    catchfly
    dogbane
    flytrap
    honeybloom
    milk ipecac
    milkweed
    mountain hemp
    spreading dogbane
    wallflower
    wandering milkweed
    western wallflower
Aquilegia vulgaris [Ranunculaceae]
    columbine
    European crowfoot
    garden columbine
Aralia chinensis [Araliaceae]

angelica tree
Chinese angelica
dang qui
dong quai
female ginseng
Japanese angelica
women's ginseng
Aralia elata [Araliaceae]
  angelica tree
  Chinese angelica
  dang qui
  dong quai
  female ginseng
  Japanese angelica
  women's ginseng
Aralia japonica [Araliaceae]
  angelica tree
  Chinese angelica
  dang qui
  dong quai
  female ginseng
  Japanese angelica
  women's ginseng
Aralia nudicaulis [Araliaceae]
  American sarsaparilla
  rabbit's foot
  small spikenard
  wild licorice
  wild sarsaparilla
Aralia racemosa [Araliaceae]
  American spikenard
  Indian root
  life-of-man
  petty morel
  spignet
  spikenard
Aralia sinensis [Araliaceae]
  angelica tree
  Chinese angelica
  dang qui
  dong quai
  female ginseng
  Japanese angelica
  women's ginseng
Aralia spinosa [Araliaceae]
  angelica tree
  devil's-walkingstick
  Hercules'-club
  prickly ash

spikenard tree
Arbutus unedo [Ericaceae]
  arbutus berry
  cane apples
  strawberry tree
Arctium lappa [Compositae]
  bardana
  beggar's-buttons
  burdock
  burr seed
  clotbur
  cockle buttons
  cocklebur
  cuckold
  edible burdock
  gobo
  grass burdock
  great bur
  great burdock
  hardock
  hareburr
  harlock
  hurrburr
  lappa
  turkey burrseed
Arctium minus [Compositae]
  common burdock
Arctostaphylos manzanita [Ericaceae]
  manzanita
Arctostaphylos uva-ursi [Ericaceae]
  arberry
  bear's grape
  bearberry
  creashak
  hog cranberry
  hogberry
  kinnikinick
  mealberry
  mountain box
  mountain cranberry
  red bearberry
  rockberry
  sagackhomi
  sandberry
  upland cranberry
  uva-ursi
Areca catechu [Palmae]
  areca nut
  betel nut palm

Arisaema triphyllum [Araceae]
  bog-onion
  dragonroot
  Indian turnip
  Jack-in-the-pulpit
  wakerobin
  wild turnip
Aristolochia spp. *[Aristolochiaceae]*
  birthwort
  calico flower
  Dutchman's-pipe
  pelican flower
  Red River snakeroot
  sangree
  snakeweed
  Texas snakeroot
Aristolochia serpentaria [Aristolochiaceae]
  birthwort
  serpentaria
  Virginia snakeroot
Armoracia rusticana [Cruciferae]
  horseradish
Arnica cordifolia [Compositae]
  arnica
  mountain daisy
  mountain tobacco
  wolf's bane
Arnica montana [Compositae]
  arnica
  mountain daisy
  mountain tobacco
  wolf's bane
Aronia arbutifolia [Rosaceae]
  chokeberry
Artemisia abrotanum [Compositae]
  lad's love
  old man
  southernwood
Artemisia absinthium [Compositae]
  absinthe
  green ginger
  wormwood
Artemisia cina [Compositae]
  Levant wormseed
  Russian wormseed
  santonica
  wormseed
  wormseed
Artemisia dracunculus [Compositae]

estragon
French tarragon
Russian tarragon
tarragon
Artemisia gmelinii [Compositae]
  Russian wormseed
Artemisia moxa [Compositae]
  moxa
Artemisia pallens [Compositae]
  davana
Artemisia vulgaris [Compositae]
  felon herb
  Indian wormwood
  moxa
  mugwort
  sailor's tobacco
  Saint John's herb
Arum maculatum [Araceae]
  Adam-and-Eve
  arum
  cocky baby
  cuckoopint
  cypress powder
  dragon root
  gaglee
  ladysmock
  Portland arrowroot
  starchwort
Asarum canadense [Aristolochiaceae]
  asarabacca
  asarum
  black snakeroot
  Canadian snakeroot
  coltsfoot snakeroot
  false snakeroot
  heart snakeroot
  Indian ginger
  southern snakeroot
  Vermont snakeroot
  wild ginger
Asarum europaeum [Aristolochiaceae]
  asarabacca
  asarum
  European snakeroot
  hazelwort
  public house plant
  wild nard
Asclepias syriaca [Asclepiadaceae]
  cottonweed

milkweed
silkweed
silky swallow-wort
swallow-wort
Virginia silk
Asclepias tuberosa [Asclepiadaceae]
  butterfly weed
  Canada root
  chigger flower
  flux root
  Indian paintbrush
  milkweed
  orange swallow-wort
  pleurisy root
  tuberroot
  white root
  wind root
Asimina triloba [Annonaceae]
  pawpaw
Asperula cynanchica [Rubiaceae]
  quinsy wort
Asperula odorata [Rubiaceae]
  master of the wood
  mugwort
  quinsy wort
  sweet grass
  sweet woodruff
  waldmeister
  woodroof
  woodruff
  woodward
Aspidosperma quebrachoblano
  [Apocynaceae]
  aspidosperma
  quebracho
Astragalus glycyphyllous [Leguminosae]
  milk vetch
Astragalus gummifer [Leguminosae]
  astragal
  gumdragon
  tragacanth
Astragalus membranaceus [Leguminosae]
  huang qi
  milk vetch
Astragalus mollissimus [Leguminosae]
  loco weed
Atropa belladonna [Solanaceae]
  belladonna
  black cherry

deadly nightshade
dwale
poison black cherry
Aureolaria pedicularia [Scrophulariaceae]
  American foxglove
  bushy gerardia
  false foxglove
  fern-leaved false foxglove
  feverweed
  lousewort
Balsamita major [Compositae]
  alecost
  Bible leaf
  costmary
  mint geranium
  sweet Mary
  tansy
Baptisia tinctoria [Leguminosae]
  American indigo
  false indigo
  horsefly weed
  indigo broom
  rattleweed
  wild indigo
  yellow broom
  yellow indigo
Barbarea verna [Cruciferae]
  American cress
  scurvy grass
  winter cress
Barbarea vulgaris [Cruciferae]
  herb Barbara
  rocket
  upland cress
  winter cress
  yellow rocket
Barosma betulina [Rutaceae]
  bookoo
  bucco
  buchu
  bucku
  mountain buchu
  round buchu
  short buchu
Barosma crenulata [Rutaceae]
  crenate buchu
  long buchu
  oval buchu
Bellis perennis [Compositae]

English daisy
Berberis vulgaris [Berberidaceae]
  barberry
  European barberry
  jaundice berry
  pepperidge
  piprage
  sowberry
Betula alba [Betulaceae]
  canoe birch
  European white birch
  paper birch
  silver birch
  white birch
Betula lenta [Betulaceae]
  black birch
  cherry birch
  mahogany birch
  mountain mahogany
  spice bush
  sweet birch
Betula papyrifera [Betulaceae]
  canoe birch
  paper birch
  silver birch
  white birch
Betula pendula [Betulaceae]
  European white birch
Bixa orellana [Bixaceae]
  achiote
  anatto
  annatto
  annotto
  arnatto
  bija
  bijol
  lipstick tree
  roucou
Bomarea edulis [Alstroemeriaceae]
  white Jerusalem artichoke
Borago officinalis [Boraginaceae]
  beebread
  bee plant
  borage
  burridge
  cool-tankard
  talewort
Boronia megastigma [Rutaceae]
  boronia

Boswellia bhau-dajiana [Burseraceae]
  frankincense
Boswellia carterii [Burseraceae]
  frankincense
  olibanum
Boswellia frereana [Burseraceae]
  African elemi
  elemi frankincense
Boswellia papyrifera [Burseraceae]
  Sudanese frankincense
Boswellia sacra [Burseraceae]
  Saudi frankincense
Boswellia serrata [Burseraceae]
  Indian frankincense
  Indian olibanum
Brassica alba [Cruciferae]
  white mustard
Brassica hirta [Cruciferae]
  white mustard
Brassica juncea [Cruciferae]
  brown mustard
  Russian mustard
  Sarepta mustard
Brassica juncea, var. *crispifolia*
  [Cruciferae]
  Indian mustard
  leaf mustard
  mustard greens
Brassica napus [Cruciferae]
  colza
  rapeseed
Brassica nigra [Cruciferae]
  black mustard
Brayera anthelminica [Rosaceae]
  cusso
  kousso
Bryonia alba [Curcurbitaceae]
  bryony
  tetterberry
  white bryony
  wild bryony
  wild hops
  wild vine
  wood vine
Bryonia dioica [Curcurbitaceae]
  bryony
  devil's turnip
  red bryony
  wild hops

wild vine
wild white vine
Bulnesia sarmienti [Zygophyllaceae]
  wild guaiac
  wild guaiacum
Bursera aloexylon [Burseraceae]
  linaloe
Bursera fagaroides [Burseraceae]
  linaloe
Bursera glabrifolia [Burseraceae]
  linaloe
Bursera penicillata [Burseraceae]
  linaloe
Bursera simarouba [Burseraceae]
  gumbo limbo
  incense tree
  West Indian birch
  West Indian elemi
Buxus sempervirens [Buxaceae]
  box
  boxwood
  bush tree
Byrsonima coriacea [Malpighiaceae]
  lotusberry
  West Indian lotusberry
Calamintha alpina [Labiatae]
  alpine basil thyme
Calamintha acinos [Labiatae]
  basil thyme
Calamintha clinopodium [Labiatae]
  wild basil
Calamintha glabella [Labiatae]
  calamint
Calendula officinalis [Compositae]
  bull's eyes
  calendula
  holigold
  marigold
  Mary bud
  poet's marigold
  pot marigold
Callistris quadrivalvis [Cupressaceae]
  arar tree
  juniper resin
  sandarac
  sandarach
Calluna vulgaris [Ericaceae]
  heather
  ling

  Scotch heather
Caltha palustris [Ranunculaceae]
  American cowslip
  kingcup
  marsh marigold
  may-blob
  meadow bouts
  meadow-bright
  palsywort
  water dragon
Calystegia sepium [Convolvulaceae]
  bindweed
  devil's vine
  great bindweed
  hedge bindweed
  hedge lily
  lady's nightcap
  Rutland beauty
  trailing bindweed
  wild morning-glory
Campanula rapunculus [Campanulaceae]
  rampion
Cananga odorata [Annonaceae]
  cananga
  ilang-ilang
  ylang-ylang
Canarium ? [Burseraceae]
  pili nut
Canarium commune [Burseraceae]
  elemi
Canarium luzonicum [Burseraceae]
  elemi
Canella winterana [Canellaceae]
  canella
  canella bark
  wild cinnamon
Canellaceum alba [Canellaceae]
  canella
  canella bark
  wild cinnamon
Capparis spinosa [Capparidaceae]
  caper bush
  capers
  mountain pepper
Capsella bursa-pastoris [Cruciferae]
  cocowort
  mother's heart
  pepper and salt
  pickpocket

Saint James' weed
shepherd's-bag
shepherd's-heart
shepherd's-pouch
shepherd's-purse
toywort
witch's pouches
Capsicum annuum, var. *annuum*
[Solanaceae]
bell pepper
capsicum pepper
cayenne pepper
cherry pepper
chili pepper
cluster pepper
cone pepper
green pepper
long pepper
paprika
pequin
petines
pimento
pimiento
red cluster pepper
red pepper
sweet pepper
Capsicum annuum, var. *glabriusculum*
[Solanaceae]
bird pepper
wild capsicum varieties
Capsicum baccatum [Solanaceae]
Brown's pepper
Capsicum chinense [Solanaceae]
Chinese pepper
Capsicum frutescens [Solanaceae]
malagueta (Spanish)
Tabasco pepper
Tabasco-sauce pepper
Capsicum pubescens [Solanaceae]
chile manzana
rocoto
Capsicum tetragonum [Solanaceae]
paprika
Cardamine amara [Cruciferae]
bitter cress
large bitter cress
Cardamine pennsylvanica [Cruciferae]
bitter cress
Cardamine pratensis [Cruciferae]

bitter cress
cardamine
cuckooflower
lady's-smock
Mayflower
meadow cress
Cardamine yezoensis [Cruciferae]
Japanese horseradish
wasabi
Carduus benedictus [Compositae]
blessed thistle
cardin
holy thistle
Saint Benedict's thistle
spotted thistle
Carduus marianus [Compositae]
holy thistle
Marythistle
milk thistle
Saint Mary's thistle
Carex arenaria [Cyperaceae]
German sarsaparilla
red couchgrass
red sedge
sand sedge
sea sedge
Carica papaya [Caricaceae]
melon tree
papaw
papaya
pawpaw
Carlina acaulis [Compositae]
carline thistle
dwarf carline
ground thistle
southernwood root
Carthamus tinctorus [Compositae]
American saffron
bastard saffron
dyer's saffron
false saffron
safflower
Carum ajowan [Umbelliferae]
ajowan
ajuan
omum
Carum bulbocastanum? [Umbelliferae]
earth-nuts
Carum carvi [Umbelliferae]

caraway
Carum copticum [Umbelliferae]
  ajowan
  ajuan
  omum
Carya spp. *[Juglandaceae]*
  hickory
Caryophyllus aromaticus [Myrtaceae]
  cloves
Cassia acutifolia [Leguminosae]
  Alexandria senna
  cassia tree
  Indian senna
  senna
Castanea dentata [Fagaceae]
  American chestnut
  chestnut
Catha edulis [Celastraceae]
  Abyssinian tea
  African tea
  Arabian tea
  cafta
  chat
  kat
  khat
  qat
  Somali tea
Catharanthus roseus [Apocynaceae]
  old-maid
  periwinkle
  Madagascar periwinkle
  rose periwinkle
Caulophyllum thalictroides [Berberidaceae]
  beechdrops
  blue cohosh
  blue ginseng
  papoose root
  squaw root
  yellow ginseng
Ceanothus americanus [Rhamnaceae]
  liberty tea
  mountain sweet
  New Jersey tea
  red root
  Walpole tea
  wild snowball
Cedronella canariensis [Labiatae]
  balm of Gilead
  Canary balm

false balm of Gilead
Centaurea cyanus [Compositae]
  bachelor's-button
  blue centaury
  bluebonnet
  bluebottle
  cornflower
  cyani
Centaurea nigra [Compositae]
  black knapweed
  bullweed
  hardheads
  knobweed
  Spanish-buttons
Centaurea spp. *[Compositae]*
  knapweed
Centaurium erythraea [Gentianaceae]
  bitterherb
  centaury
  centaury gentian
  European centaury
  lesser centaury
  minor centaury
Centaurium umbellatum [Gentianaceae]
  bitterherb
  centaury
  centaury gentian
  European centaury
  lesser centaury
  minor centaury
Ceratonia siliqua [Leguminosae]
  algarroba bean
  carob
  locust bean
  Saint John's bread
Cetraria islandica [Parmeliaceae]
  eryngo-leaved liverwort
  Iceland moss
Chaerophyllum bulbosum [Umbelliferae]
  parsnip chervil
  turnip-rooted chervil
Chaerophyllum sylvestre [Umbelliferae]
  European wild cicely
Chalcas koenigii [Rutaceae]
  curry leaf
  curry leaf tree
Chamaelirium luteum [Liliaceae]
  blazing-star
  devil's-bit

fairy-wand
false unicorn root
rattlesnake root

Chamaemelum nobile [Compositae]
camomile
English camomile
garden camomile
lawn camomile
manzanilla
May-then
marigold
Roman camomile
Scotch camomile
Whig plant

Chamomilla recutita [Compositae]
German camomile
Hungarian camomile
sweet false camomile
wild camomile

Chamomilla suaveolens [Compositae]
pineapple weed
rayless mayweed

Chelidonium majus [Papaveraceae]
celandine
garden celandine
great celandine
tetterwort

Chelone glabra [Scrophulariaceae]
balmony
saltrheum weed
shell flower
snakehead
turtlebloom
turtlehead

Chenopodium album [Chenopodiaceae]
lamb's-quarters
pigweed
white goosefoot

Chenopodium ambrosiodes
[Chenopodiaceae]
American wormseed
epazote
goosefoot
Jesuits' tea
Mexican tea
Spanish tea
wormseed

Chenopodium bonus-henricus
[Chenopodiaceae]
allgood
fat-hen
Good-King-Henry
goosefoot
mercury
wild spinach

Chenopodium botrys [Chenopodiaceae]
feather geranium
Jerusalem oak

Chimaphila umbellata [Pyrolaceae]
bitter wintergreen
ground holly
king's cure
pipsissewa
prince's pine
rheumatism weed

Chionanthus virginicus [Oleaceae]
gray beard tree
fringe tree
old man's beard
poison ash tree
snowdrop tree
snowflower
white fringe

Chlorogalum pomeridianum [Liliaceae]
amole
soap plant
wild potato

Chondrus crispus [Rhodophyceae]
carrageen
carragheen
Irish moss
pearl moss

Chrysanthemum balsamita majus
[Compositae]
alecost
Bible leaf
costmary
mint geranium
sweet Mary
tansy

Chrysanthemum cinerariifolium
[Compositae]
Dalmatia pyrethrum
Dalmatian insect flower
Dalmatian insect powder
pellitory

pyrethrum
Chrysanthemum coccineum [Compositae]
  painted daisy
  pellitory
  Persian insect flower
  Persian insect powder
  pyrethrum
Chrysanthemum coronarium [Compositae]
  chop suey green
  cooking chrysanthemum
  crown daisy
  garland chrysanthemum
  shungiku
Chrysanthemum leucanthemum
  [Compositae]
  camomile adulterant
  golden daisy
  herb Margaret
  Marguerite
  maudlinwort
  oxeye daisy
  white daisy
  white weed
Chrysanthemum parthenium [Compositae]
  febrifuge plant
  feverfew
  pellitory
Chrysanthemum spp. [Compositae]
  herb Margaret
Chrysanthemum vulgare [Compositae]
  European tansy
  tansy
Cichorium endivia [Compositae]
  endive
Cichorium intybus [Compositae]
  barbe-de-capuchin
  Belgian endive
  blue-sailors
  chicory
  coffeeweed
  succory
  witloof
Cicuta maculata [Umbelliferae]
  beaver-poison
  musquash root
  spotted cowbane
Cicuta virosa [Umbelliferae]
  water hemlock
  water parsley

Cimicifuga racemosa [Ranunculaceae]
  black cohosh
  black snakeroot
  bugbane
  bugwort
  rattleroot
  rattletop
  rattleweed
  richweed
  squawroot
Cinchona spp. [Rubiaceae]
  fever bark tree
  Jesuits' bark
  Peruvian bark
  quinine
Cinnamodendron corticosum or
  macranthum [?]
  Jamaica canella
Cinnamomum burmanii [Lauraceae]
  Batavia cinnamon
  Burma cinnamon
  Indonesian cassia
  Java cassia
  Korintje cassia
  Padang cassia
  Padang cinnamon
Cinnamomum camphora [Lauraceae]
  artificial sassafras oil
  camphor tree
Cinnamomum cassia [Lauraceae]
  cassia
  cassia-bark tree
  Chinese cinnamon
Cinnamomum cecidodaphne [Lauraceae]
  Nepalese tejpat
Cinnamomum culiliban [Lauraceae]
  lawang
Cinnamomum loureirii [Lauraceae]
  cassia-flower tree
  cinnamon, U. S. P.
Cinnamomum micranthum [Lauraceae]
  Chinese sassafras
Cinnamomum tamala [Lauraceae]
  tejpat
Cinnamomum zeylanicum [Lauraceae]
  Ceylon cinnamon
  cinnamon
  Madagascar cinnamon
  Seychelles cinnamon

Sri Lanka cinnamon
sweetwood
canela (Spanish)
cannella (Italian)
cannelle (French)
jou-kuei (Chinese)
koritsa (Russian)
seiron-nikkei (Japanese)
Zimt (German)
Cistus creticus [Cistaceae]
Cretan rockrose
labdanum
ladanum
Cistus incanus [Cistaceae]
Cretan rockrose
labdanum
ladanum
Clematis virginiana [Ranunculaceae]
devil's-darning-needle
leather flower
virgin's bower
woodbine
Clinopodium vulgare [Labiatae]
basil
basilweed
dog mint
wild basil
Cnicus benedicta [Compositae]
blessed thistle
cardin
holy thistle
Saint Benedict's thistle
spotted thistle
Cochlearia armoracia [Cruciferae]
horseradish
Cochlearia officinalis [Cruciferae]
scrubby grass
scurvy grass
spoonwort
Cocos nucifera [Palmae]
coconut
Cola acuminata [Sterculiaceae]
abata cola
caffeine nut
cola
cola nut
goora nut
guru nut
kola

Cola nitida [Sterculiaceae]
abata cola
caffeine nut
cola
cola nut
goora nut
guru nut
kola
Colchicum autumnale [Liliaceae]
autumn crocus
fall crocus
meadow saffron
mysteria
naked lady
wonder bulb
Coleus amboinicus [Labiatae]
Cuban oregano
Indian borage
oregano
Spanish thyme
Collinsonia canadensis [Labiatae]
citronella
hardback
hardhack
heal-all
horse balm
horse weed
knob grass
knob root
richweed
stoneroot
Commiphora abyssinica [Burseraceae]
Abyssinian myrrh
Arabian myrrh
Commiphora erythaea, var. *glabrescens*
[Burseraceae]
bisabol myrrh
opopanax
sweet myrrh
Commiphora madagascariensis
[Burseraceae]
Abyssinian myrrh
Arabian myrrh
Commiphora molmol [Burseraceae]
Somalian myrrh
Commiphora myrrha [Burseraceae]
common myrrh
hirabol myrrh
Commiphora opobalsamum [Burseraceae]

balm of Gilead
Comptonia peregrina [Myricaceae]
  fern bush
  fern gale
  meadow fern
  sweet bush
  sweet fern
Conium maculatum [Umbelliferae]
  California fern
  hemlock
  Nebraska fern
  poison hemlock
  poison parsley
  poison root
  poison snakeroot
  spotted hemlock
  winter fern
Consolida regalis [Ranunculaceae]
  branching larkspur
  knight's spur
  lark heel
  lark's claw
  larkspur
  staggerweed
  stavesacre
Convallaria majalis [Liliaceae]
  lily of the valley
  May bells
  May lily
Convolvulus sepia [Convolvulaceae]
  bindweed
  devil's vine
  great bindweed
  hedge bindweed
  hedge lily
  lady's nightcap
  Rutland beauty
  trailing bindweed
  wild morning-glory
Conyza canadensis [Compositae]
  bitterweed
  bloodstaunch
  butterweed
  colt's tail
  erigeron
  fleabane
  herb Christopher
  horseweed
  mare's tail

Copaifera spp. *[Leguminosae]*
  capivi
  copaiba
  copaiva
  copayva
Copernicia cerifera [Palmae]
  carnauba palm
  carnauba wax
Copernicia prunifera [Palmae]
  carnauba palm
  carnauba wax
Coptis trifolia [Ranunculaceae]
  cankerroot
  goldthread
  mouthroot
  yellowroot
Corallorhiza odontorhiza [Orchidaceae]
  autumn coralroot
  chicken-toes
  coralroot
  crawley-root
  dragon's-claw
  fever root
  late coralroot
  scaly dragon's-claw
  small coralroot
  turkey-claw
Coriandrum sativum [Umbelliferae]
  Chinese parsley
  cilantro
  coriander
Cornus amomum [Cornaceae]
  cornel
  kinnikinick
  red willow
  silky dogwood
Cornus florida [Cornaceae]
  boxwood
  budwood
  cornel
  cornelian tree
  dogtree
  dogwood
  false box
  Florida cornel
  Florida dogwood
  flowering cornel
  flowering dogwood
  green ozier

Virginia dogwood
Corydalis cava [Fumariaceae]
    corydalis
    early fumitory
Corydalis formosa [Fumariaceae]
    choice dielytra
    staggerweed
    turkey corn
    wild bleeding heart
    wild turkey pea
Crataegus spp. *[Rosaceae]*
    cockspur
    cockspur thorn
    English hawthorn
    hawthorn berries
    Mayblossom
    May bush
    May tree
    quick-set thorn
    red haw
    summer haw
    thorn apple
    Washington thorn
    white thorn
    yellow-fruited thorn
Crescentia spp. *[Bignoniaceae]*
    calabash tree
Crithmum maritimum [Umbelliferae]
    Peter's cress
    rock samphire
    Saint Peter's herb
    samphire
    sea fennel
Crocus sativus [Iridaceae]
    saffron
Croton eluteria [Euphorbiaceae]
    cascarilla bark
    sweetwood bark
Croton monanthogynus [Euphorbiaceae]
    prairie tea
Croton tiglium [Euphorbiaceae]
    croton oil
Cryptocarya moschata [Lauraceae]
    Brazilian nutmeg
Cryptotaenia canadensis [Umbelliferae]
    honewort
    Japanese parsley
    Japanese wild chervil
    mitsuba

    white chervil
Cryptotaenia japonica [Umbelliferae]
    honewort
    Japanese parsley
    Japanese wild chervil
    mitsuba
    white chervil
Cuminum cyminum [Umbelliferae]
    comino
    cumin
Cunila origanoides [Labiatae]
    American dittany
    dittany, common
    Maryland dittany
    stone mint
    sweet horsemint
Curcuma domestica [Zingiberaceae]
    saffron of the Indies
    turmeric
Curcuma longa [Zingiberaceae]
    saffron of the Indies
    turmeric
Curcuma zedoaria [Zingiberaceae]
    zedoary
Cusparia trifoliata [Rutaceae]
    angostura bark
    cusparia bark
Cyclamen spp. *[Primulaceae]*
    alpine violet
    cyclamen
    groundbread
    Persian violet
    sowbread
    swinebread
Cymbopogon citratus [Gramineae]
    fever grass
    lemongrass
    serah powder
    West Indian lemongrass
Cymbopogon flexuosus [Gramineae]
    East Indian lemongrass
Cymbopogon martinii var. *martinii*
    [Gramineae]
    East Indian geranium
    motia
    palmarosa
Cymbopogon martinii var. *sofia*
    [Gramineae]
    gingergrass

sofia
Cymbopogon nardus [Gramineae]
  citronella
  citronella grass
  false spikenard
  lemongrass
  nard grass
  oil grass
Cymbopogon pendulus [Gramineae]
  Jammu lemongrass
Cymbopogon winterianus [Gramineae]
  Java citronella
Cynara cardunculus [Compositae]
  cardoon
Cynara scolymus [Compositae]
  artichoke
  French artichoke
  globe artichoke
Cynoglossum officinale [Boraginaceae]
  beggar's-lice
  dog-bur
  dog's tongue
  gypsy flower
  hound's-tongue
  sheep-lice
  woolmat
Cynoglossum virginicum [Boraginaceae]
  wild comfrey
Cyperus esculentis [Cyperaceae]
  nut grass
  nut sedge
  yellow nut grass
  yellow nut sedge
Cyperus esculentis, var. *sativus*
  [Cyperaceae]
  chufa
  earth almond
  rush nut
  tiger nut
  Zulu nut
Cyperus longus [Cyperaceae]
  galangale
  galingale
  sweet sedge
Cypripedium calceolus [Orchidaceae]
  American valerian
  golden-slipper
  lady-slipper
  lady's-slipper

moccasin flower
nerveroot
Noah's-ark
slipper root
umbilroot
Venus'-shoe
whippoorwill-shoe
yellow Indian-shoe
yellow lady's-slipper
yellow moccasin flower
yellows
Cytisus scoparius [Leguminosae]
  broom
  Irish broom
  link
  Scotch broom
Daemonorops draco [Palmae]
  dragon's blood
Daphne mezereum [Thymelaeaceae]
  February daphne
  daphne
  mezereon
  mezereum
  spurge flax
  spurge laurel
  spurge olive
  wild pepper
Datura stramonium [Solanaceae]
  common thorn apple
  devil's apple
  devil's trumpet
  Jamestown weed
  jimsonweed
  mad-apple
  nightshade
  Peru-apple
  stinkweed
  stinkwort
  stramonium
  thorn apple
Daucus carota, var. *carota [Umbelliferae]*
  daucus
  devil's-plague
  queen's-lace
  Queen-Anne's-lace
  wild carrot
Daucus carota, var. *sativus*
  [Umbelliferae]
  carrot

Delphinium consolida [Ranunculaceae]
  branching larkspur
  knight's spur
  lark heel
  lark's claw
  larkspur
  staggerweed
  stavesacre
Dianthus caryophyllus [Caryophyllaceae]
  carnation
  clove pink
  divine flower
  gillyflower
  picotee
Dicentra canadensis [Fumariaceae]
  squirrel corn
Dicentra cuculleria [Fumariaceae]
  Dutchman's breeches
Dicentra eximia [Fumariaceae]
  choice dielytra
  staggerweed
  turkey corn
  wild bleeding heart
  Wild turkey pea
Dicentra spectabilis [Fumariaceae]
  bleeding heart
Dictamnus albus [Rutaceae]
  bastard dittany
  burning-bush
  diptam
  dittany
  false dittany
  fraxinella
  gas-plant
Digitalis lanata [Scrophulariaceae]
  Grecian foxglove
Digitalis purpurea [Scrophulariaceae]
  American foxglove
  common foxglove
  dead men's bells
  digitalis
  dog's finger
  fairy fingers
  fairy glove
  finger flower
  folks' glove
  lion's mouth
  ladies' glove
  purple foxglove

Digitalis spp. *[Scrophulariaceae]*
  foxglove
Dioscorea alata [Dioscoreaceae]
  water yam
  white yam
Dioscorea batatas [Dioscoreaceae]
  Chinese yam
  cinnamon vine
Dioscorea bulbifera [Dioscoreaceae]
  air potato
Dioscorea elephantipes [Dioscoreaceae]
  elephant's-foot
  Hottentot-bread
Dioscorea trifolia [Dioscoreaceae]
  cush-cush
  yampee
Dioscorea villosa [Dioscoreaceae]
  China root
  colic root
  devil's bones
  rheumatism root
  wild yam
  yuma
Diospyrus lotus [Ebenaceae]
  date plum
  European lotus
Diplotaxis tenuifolia [Cruciferae]
  wall rocket
Dipteryx odoratum [Leguminosae]
  Dutch tonka bean
  tonga bean
  tonka bean
  Tonquin bean
Dipteryx oppositiafolia [Leguminosae]
  Dutch tonka bean
  tonga bean
  tonka bean
  Tonquin bean
Dodecatheon spp. *[Primulaceae]*
  American cowslip
  shooting star
Doryphora sassafras [?]
  Australian sassafras
Draba verna [Cruciferae]
  whitlow grass
Dracaena draco [Agavaceae]
  dragon tree
  dragon's blood
Drimys aromatica [Winteraceae]

pepper berries
pepper tree
Drimys lanceolata [Winteraceae]
pepper berries
pepper tree
Drosera rotundifolia [Droseraceae]
daily-dew
dew plant
lustwort
round-leaved sundew
youthwort
Dryopteris filix-mas [Polypodiaceae]
aspidium
bear's paw root
knotty brake
shield fern
sweet brake
wood fern
Echinacea spp. *[Compositae]*
black Samson
echinacea
Kansas niggerhead
Missouri snakeroot
purple coneflower
rudbeckia (erroneous)
Sampson root
Echium vulgare [Boraginaceae]
blue-devil
blueweed
viper's bugloss
Elettaria cardamomum [Zingiberaceae]
cardamom, large
Ceylon cardamom
Malabar cardamom
Elettaria granum-paradise
[Zingiberaceae]
false cardamom
grains of paradise
Guinea grains
paradise nuts
Elettaria melegueta [Zingiberaceae]
Melegueta pepper
Eleutherococcus senticosis [Araliaceae]
Siberian ginseng
Ephedra spp. *[Ephedraceae]*
Brigham Young weed
desert herb
ephedra
joint fir

Mormon tea
squaw tea
teamster's tea
Ephedra sinica
ma huang
Epifagus virginiana [Orobranchaceae]
beechdrops
Equisetum hyemale [Equisetaceae]
bottlebrush
horsetail
horsetail grass
horsetail rush
mare's tail
pewterwort
scouring rush
shave grass
Erica vulgaris [Ericaceae]
heather
ling
Scotch heather
Erigeron canadensis [Compositae]
bitterweed
bloodstaunch
butterweed
colt's tail
erigeron
fleabane
herb Christopher
mare's tail
Eriodictyon californica [Hydrophyllaceae]
bear's weed
consumptive's weed
holy herb
mountain balm
tarweed
yerba santa
Erodium cicutarium [Geraniaceae]
alfilaria
heron's-bill
pin clover
pin grass
red-stem filaree
storksbill
wild musk
Eruca vesicaria, subspecies *sativa*
[Cruciferae]
arugula
rocket
rocket-gentle

roka
Roman rocket
rocket-salad
roquette
ruchetta
rugola
rugula
tira
Eryngium aquaticum [Umbelliferae]
water eryngo
Eryngium campestre [Umbelliferae]
field eryngo
Roman thistle
snakeroot
Eryngium foetida [Umbelliferae]
cilantro
culantro
orégano de Cartagena
Eryngium maritimum [Umbelliferae]
eringo
eryngo
sea eryngium
sea holly
sea holm
Eryngium yuccifolium [Umbelliferae]
button snake-root
corn snakeroot
rattlesnake weed
rattlesnake-master
Erythraea centaurium [Gentianaceae]
bitterherb
centaury
centaury gentian
European centaury
lesser centaury
minor centaury
Erythronium americanum [Liliaceae]
adder's-tongue
amberbell
dog-tooth violet
erythronium
lamb's tongue
rattlesnake violet
snake leaf
trout lily
yellow adder's-tongue
yellow erythronium
yellow snakeleaf
yellow snowdrop

Erythroxylum coca [Erythroxylaceae]
coca
cocaine
spadic
Eschscholtzia californica [Fumariaceae]
California poppy
Eucalyptus citriodora [Myrtaceae]
citron-scented gum
lemon-scented gum
spotted gum
Eucalyptus cneorifolia [Myrtaceae]
Kangaroo Island narrow-leaved
mallee
Eucalyptus dives [Myrtaceae]
blue peppermint
broad-leaved peppermint
peppermint
Eucalyptus dumosa [Myrtaceae]
congoo mallee
mallee
Eucalyptus elata [Myrtaceae]
river peppermint
river white gum
Eucalyptus globulus [Myrtaceae]
blue gum
eucalyptus
southern blue gum
Tasmanian blue gum
Eucalyptus goniocalyx [Myrtaceae]
apple jack
bundy
long-leaved box
olive-barked box
Eucalyptus leucoxylon [Myrtaceae]
white gum
white ironbark
yellow gum
Eucalyptus macarthurii [Myrtaceae]
Camden woollybut
Paddy's river box
Eucalyptus oleosa [Myrtaceae]
glossy-leaved red mallee
red mallee
Eucalyptus polybractea [Myrtaceae]
blue-leaved mallee
Eucalyptus radiata [Myrtaceae]
gray peppermint
narrow-leaved peppermint
Eucalyptus sideroxylon [Myrtaceae]

ironbark
mugga
red ironbark
Eucalyptus smithii [Myrtaceae]
blackbutt peppermint
gully gum
gully peppermint
Eucalyptus viridis [Myrtaceae]
green mallee
Eucalyptus spp. *[Myrtaceae]*
eucalyptus
fever tree
Eugenia acris [Myrtaceae]
wild clove
Eugenia aromatica [Myrtaceae]
cloves
Eugenia caryophyllata [Myrtaceae]
cloves
Eugenia jambosa [Myrtaceae]
Java plum
Malabar plum
rose apple
Eugenia pimenta [Myrtaceae]
allspice
clove pepper
Jamaica pepper
myrtle pepper
pimenta
toute-épice
Euonymus americanum [Celastraceae]
bursting-heart
strawberry-bush
Euonymus atropurpurea [Celastraceae]
arrow-wood
bitter ash
burning bush
Indian arrow
spindle tree
wahoo
Eupatorium cannabinum [Compositae]
hemp agrimony
sweet-smelling trefoil
water maudlin
Eupatorium perfoliatum [Compositae]
agueweed
boneset
crosswort
eupatorium
feverwort

Indian sage
sweating plant
thoroughwort
vegetable antimony
wood boneset
Eupatorium purpureum [Compositae]
gravel weed
gravelroot
green-stemmed Joe-Pye weed
Joe-Pye weed
kidney root
purple boneset
queen-of-the-meadow
sweet Joe-Pye weed
trumpet weed
Eupatorium rugosum [Compositae]
white sanicle
white snakeroot
Eupatorium triplinerve? [Compositae]
ayapana
Euphorbia antisyphilitica [Euphorbiaceae]
candelilla
Euphorbia hirta [Euphorbiaceae]
asthma weed
catshair
pill-bearing spurge
Queensland asthma weed
Euphorbia lathyris [Euphorbiaceae]
caper spurge
garden spurge
mole plant
myrtle spurge
Euphorbia spp. *[Euphorbiaceae]*
spurge
Euphrasia officinalis [Scrophulariaceae]
euphrasy
eye-bright
red eyebright
Evernia furfuracea [Usneaceae]
tree moss
Evernia prunastri [Usneaceae]
oak moss
Ferula assa-foetida [Umbelliferae]
asafetida
asafoetida
devil's dung
food-of-the-gods
giant fennel
Persian gum

stinking gum
Ferula communis [Umbelliferae]
  common giant fennel
Ferula diversivittata [Umbelliferae]
  muskroot
  sumbul
Ferula foetida [Umbelliferae]
  asafoetida
Ferula galbaniflua [Umbelliferae]
  galban
  galbanum
Ferula moschata [Umbelliferae]
  muskroot
  sumbul
Ferula rubricaulis [Umbelliferae]
  galban
  galbanum
Filipendula spp. *[Rosaceae]*
  herb Christopher
  meadowsweet
Filipendula ulmaria [Rosaceae]
  bridewort
  dolloff
  herb Christopher
  meadow queen
  meadow-wort
  meadowsweet
  meadsweet
  pride-of-the-meadow
  queen-of-the-meadow
Filipendula vulgaris [Rosaceae]
  drop wort
  goatsbeard
Foeniculum vulgare [Umbelliferae]
  fennel
Foeniculum vulgare subsp. *dulce* var.
  azoricum [Umbelliferae]
  Florence fennel
  giant fennel
Fragaria spp. *[Rosaceae]*
  strawberry
Fragaria vesca, cultivar *Alpine*
  [Rosaceae]
  Alpine strawberry
Frasera caroliniensis [Gentianaceae]
  American columbo or calumba
  American gentian
  green gentian
Fraximus excelsior [Oleaceae]

ash
  bird's tongue
  European ash
Fucus vesiculosus [Fucaceae]
  bladderwrack
  kelp
Fumaria officinalis [Fumariaceae]
  earth smoke
  fumitory
  hedge fumitory
  smoke-of-the-earth
Galega officinalis [Leguminosae]
  goat's rue
Galeopsis tetrahit [Labiatae]
  bastard hemp
  bee-nettle
  dog-nettle
  hemp dead nettle
  hemp nettle
Galipea cusparia [Rutaceae]
  angostura bark
  cusparia bark
Galipea officinalis [Rutaceae]
  angostura bark
  cusparia bark
Galipea trifoliata [Rutaceae]
  angostura bark
  cusparia bark
Galium aparine [Rubiaceae]
  bedstraw
  catchweed
  cleavers
  cleaverwort
  clivers
  coachweed
  goose grass
  gosling weed
  gripgrass
  hedge-bur
  love-man
  stick-a-back
  sticky-willie
  sweethearts
Galium circaezans [Rubiaceae]
  wild licorice
Galium lanceolatum [Rubiaceae]
  wild licorice
Galium odoratum [Rubiaceae]
  mugwort

quinsy wort
master of the wood
sweet grass
sweet woodruff
waldmeister
woodroof
woodruff
woodward
Galium verum [Rubiaceae]
bedstraw
curdwort
cheese rennet
lady's bedstraw
maid's hair
Our Lady's bedstraw
yellow bedstraw
yellow cleavers
Garcinia indica [Guttiferae]
kokum
Garcinia mangostana [Guttiferae]
mangosteen
Gardenia jasminoides [Rubiaceae]
cape jasmine
Gaultheria procumbens [Ericaceae]
Canada tea
checkerberry
deerberry
ground berry
hill berry
ivry-leaves
mountain tea
oil of gaultheria
partridge berry
spiceberry
spicy wintergreen
spring wintergreen
teaberry
wax cluster
wintergreen
Gelsemium sempervirens [Loganiaceae]
Carolina jasmine
Carolina jessamine
evening trumpet flower
gelsemin
wild jessamine
woodbine
yellow jasmine
yellow jessamine
Genista spp. [Leguminosae]

broom buds
Genista tinctoria [Leguminosae]
broom
dyer's broom
dyer's greenweed
dyer's greenwood
dyer's whin
furze
green broom
waxen woad
woadwaxen
woodwaxen
Gentiana acaulis [Gentianaceae]
stemless gentian
Gentiana catesbaei [Gentianaceae]
American gentian
blue gentian
Catesby's gentian
Sampson's snakeroot
Gentiana crinita [Gentianaceae]
fringed gentian
Gentiana lutea [Gentianaceae]
bitter root
bitterwort
pale gentian
yellow gentian
Gentiana quinquefolia [Gentianaceae]
gallweed
stiff gentian
Gentiana spp. [Gentianaceae]
gentian
Gentianella quinquefolia [Gentianaceae]
gallweed
stiff gentian
Gentianopsis crinita [Gentianaceae]
fringed gentian
Geranium maculatum [Geraniaceae]
alumroot
American cranesbill
cranesbill
crowfoot
geranium
spotted cranesbill
spotted geranium
wild cranesbill
wild geranium
Geranium robertianum [Geraniaceae]
dragon's blood
herb Robert

red robin
storkbill
wild cranesbill
Geranium spp. *[Geraniaceae]*
cranesbill
Gerardia pedicularia [Scrophulariaceae]
American foxglove
bushy gerardia
false foxglove
fern-leaved false foxglove
feverweed
lousewort
Geum rivale [Rosaceae]
avens root
chocolate root
cure-all
Indian chocolate
purple avens
throat root
water avens
Geum urbanum [Rosaceae]
avens
bennet
blessed herb
cloveroot
colewort
European avens
geum
goldy stone
herb-bennet
herba benedicta
star of the earth
wood avens
yellow avens
Geum virginianum [Rosaceae]
rough avens
Ginkgo biloba [Ginkgoaceae]
ginkgo nut
maidenhair tree
Glechoma hederacea [Labiatae]
alehoof
cat's-foot
cat's-paw
creeping Charlie
field balm
gill tea
gill-over-the-ground
gillrun
ground ivy

hay maids
hedge maids
runaway robin
turnhoof
Glycine max [Leguminosae]
soja bean
soya bean
soybean
Glycyrrhiza glabra [Leguminosae]
Chinese sweet root
licorice
Spanish juice
sweetroot
sweetwood
Gnaphalium spp. *[Compositae]*
chafeweed
cudweed
dysentery weed
everlasting
field balsam
Indian posey
life everlasting
low cudweed
marsh cudweed
mouse ear
old field balsam
sweet balsam
sweet-scented life everlasting
wartwort
white balsam
Goodyera pubescens [Orchidaceae]
adder's violet
downy rattlesnake orchid
downy rattlesnake plantain
latticeleaf
net-leaf plantain
networt
rattlesnake plantain
rattlesnake weed
scrofula weed
spotted plantain
water plantain
Gratiola officinalis [Scrophulariaceae]
hedge hyssop
Grindelia robusta [Compositae]
August flower
gum plant
gumweed
resin-weed

rosinweed
sticky-heads
tarweed
Guaiacum officinale [Zygophyllaceae]
 guaiac
 guaiacum
 guayacan
 lignum vitae
 pockwood
 tree of life
Haematoxylon campechianum
 [Leguminosae]
 bloodwood tree
 campeachy wood
 logwood
Hagenia abyssinica [Rosaceae]
 cusso
 kousso
Hamamelis virginiana [Hamamelidaceae]
 snapping hazel
 spotted alder
 striped alder
 tobacco wood
 winterbloom
 witch hazel
Hardenbergia monophylla [Leguminosae]
 Australian sarsaparilla
 coral pea
 vine lilac
Hardenbergia violaceae [Leguminosae]
 coral pea
 vine lilac
Hedeoma pulegioides [Labiatae]
 American pennyroyal
 mock pennyroyal
 mosquito plant
 pudding grass
 squaw balm
 squaw mint
 stinking balm
 tickweed
Hedera helix [Araliaceae]
 English ivy
 gum ivy
 true ivy
Helenium autumnale [Compositae]
 sneezeweed
Helianthemum canadense [Cistaceae]
 frost plant

frostwort
rock rose
sun rose
Helianthus tuberosus [Compositae]
 girasole
 Jerusalem artichoke
Helichrysum angustifolium [Compositae]
 curry plant (cultivated)
 immortelle
Helichrysum italicum [Compositae]
 curry plant
 white-leaved everlasting
Helichrysum italicum subsp. *siitalicum*
 [Compositae]
 curry plant (cultivated)
Helichrysum orientale [Compositae]
 everlasting
 immortelle
Helichrysum serpyllifolium [Compositae]
 Hottentot tea
Helipterum spp. *[Compositae]*
 everlasting
 strawflower
Helleborus foetidus [Ranunculaceae]
 bearsfoot
 fetid hellebore
 hellebore
 oxheal
 stinking hellebore
Helleborus niger [Ranunculaceae]
 black hellebore
 Christmas rose
 hellebore
Helleborus viridis [Ranunculaceae]
 green hellebore
 hellebore
 winter hellebore
Hepatica americana [Ranunculaceae]
 hepatica
 herb trinity
 liverwort
Hepatica nobilis [Ranunculaceae]
 hepatica
 herb trinity
 liverwort
Heracleum lanatum [Umbelliferae]
 American cow parsnip
 cow cabbage
 cow parsnip

hogweed
madnep
masterwort
wooly parsnip
youthwort
Heracleum sphondylium, subsp.
  montanum [Umbelliferae]
  American cow parsnip
  cow cabbage
  cow parsnip
  hogweed
  madnep
  masterwort
  wooly parsnip
  youthwort
Hesperis matronalis [Cruciferae]
  dame's rocket
  dame's violet
  sweet rocket
  vesper flower
Hibiscus ? [Malvaceae]
  hibiscus flowers
Hibiscus abelmoschus [Malvaceae]
  abelmosk
  abelmusk
  ambrette
  musk mallow
  muskseed
  rose mallow
  Syrian mallow
  target-leaved hibiscus
  water mallow
Hibiscus sabdariffa [Malvaceae]
  flor de Jamaica
  Guinea sorrel
  Indian sorrel
  Jamaica sorrel
  rosella
  roselle
Hibiscus syriacus [Malvaceae]
  althaea
  rose-of-Sharon
Hieracium pilosella [Compositae
  felon herb
  hawkweed
  mouse bloodwort
  mouse ear
  pilosella
Hordeum vulgare [Gramineae]

barley
Humulus japonica [Moraceae]
  Japanese hops
Humulus lupulus [Moraceae]
  bine
  European hop
  hops
  lupulin
Hyacinthus orientalis [Liliaceae]
  hyacinth
Hydrangea arborescens [Saxifragaceae]
  hills-of-snow
  hydrangea
  sevenbark
  wild hydrangea
Hydrastis canadensis [Ranunculaceae]
  eye balm
  eye root
  goldenseal
  ground raspberry
  Indian plant
  Indian turmeric
  jaundice root
  orangeroot
  turmeric root
  yellow puccoon
  yellowroot
Hydrocotyle asiatica [Umbelliferae]
  gotu cola
  gutu cola
  navelwort
  water pennywort
Hyoscyamus niger [Solanaceae]
  black henbane
  devil's eye
  fetid nightshade
  henbane
  henbell
  hog bean
  Jupiter's bean
  poison tobacco
  stinking nightshade
Hypericum calycinum [Hypericaceae]
  Aaron's beard
  creeping Saint John's-wort
  gold flower
  rose-of-Sharon
Hypericum perforatum [Hypericaceae]
  amber

goatweed
Johnswort
Klamath weed
Saint John's-wort
Tipton weed
Hypericum spp. *[Hypericaceae]*
  Saint John's-wort
  Saint Peter's-wort
Hyptis suaveolens [Labiatae]
  bush tea plant
  West Indian spikenard
  wild spikenard
Hyssopus officinalis [Labiatae]
  hyssop
Ilex glabra [Aquifoliaceae]
  Appalachian tea
  bitter gallberry
  Carolina tea
  gallberry
  inkberry
  winterberry
Ilex paraguayensis [Aquifoliaceae]
  maté
  Paraguayan holly
  Paraguayan tea
  Saint Bartholomew's tea
  yerba maté
Ilex spp. *[Aquifoliaceae]*
  holly
Ilex vomitoria [Aquifoliaceae]
  black drink
  cassena
  cassene
  cassina
  cassine
  Indian black drink
  yaupon
Illicium anisatum [Illiciaceae]
  Badian anise
  Chinese anise
  Indian anise
  Japanese anise tree
  Japanese star anise
  star anise
  weihsion powder
Impatiens balsamina [Balsaminaceae]
  garden balsam
Imperatoria osthruthium [Umbelliferae]
  hog's fennel

imperatoria
imperial masterwort
masterwort
sulfurwort
Inula helenium [Compositae]
  alant
  elecampane
  elfdock
  elfwort
  horse-elder
  horsehead
  horseheal
  inula
  scabwort
  wild sunflower
  yellow starwort
Ipomoea batatas [Convolvulaceae]
  sweet potato
Ipomoea jalapa [Convolvulaceae]
  jalap
Ipomoea pandurata [Convolvulaceae]
  bindweed
  hog potato
  man-in-the-earth
  man-in-the-ground
  man-of-the-earth
  man root
  scammony root
  wild jalap
  wild potato
  wild scammony
  wild sweet-potato
Iris germanica var. *florentina [Iridaceae]*
  flag
  Florentine iris
  German iris
  orris
  orris root
Iris versicolor [Iridaceae]
  blue flag
  flag lily
  fleur-de-lis
  flower-de-luce
  iris
  liver lily
  poison flag
  snake lily
  water flag
  wild iris

Jasminum auriculatum [Oleaceae]
  Indian jasmine
Jasminum grandiflorum [Oleaceae]
  Catalonian jasmine
  royal jasmine
  Spanish jasmine
Jasminum sambac [Oleaceae]
  Arabian jasmine
  sambac
Jasminum spp. [Oleaceae]
  jasmine
Jateorhiza calumba [Menispermaceae]
  calumba
  columba
  columbo
Jateorhiza palmata [Menispermaceae]
  calumba
  columba
  columbo
Jeffersonia diphylla [Berberidaceae]
  ground squirrel pea
  helmet pod
  rheumatism root
  twin leaf
  yellowroot
Juglans cinerea [Juglandaceae]
  butternut
  lemon walnut
  oil nut
  white walnut
Juglans nigra [Juglandaceae]
  black walnut
Juglans regia [Juglandaceae]
  Carpathian walnut
  Caucasian walnut
  Circassian walnut
  English walnut
  Madeira nut
  Persian walnut
  walnut
Juniperus communis [Cupressaceae]
  juniper
  juniper berry
Juniperus oxycedrus [Cupressaceae]
  cade oil
  juniper tar
  oil of cadeberry
  prickly juniper
Juniperus phoenicea [Cupressaceae]

Phoenician juniper
Phoenician savin oil
Juniperus sabina [Cupressaceae]
  savin juniper
  savin oil
Kaempferia galangal [Zingiberaceae]
  galangal
  kentjur
Kalmia latifolia [Ericaceae]
  American laurel
  calico bush
  ivy
  ivybush
  lambkill
  laurel
  mountain ivy
  mountain laurel
  rose laurel
  sheep laurel
  spoonwood
Krameria argentia [Polygalaceae]
  Brazilian rhatany
Krameria triandra [Polygalaceae]
  krameria
  Peruvian rhatany
  rhatany
Lachenalia spp. [Liliaceae]
  cape cowslip
Lagaecia cuminoides [?]
  wild cumin
Lamium album [Labiatae]
  dead nettle
  dumb nettle
  snowflake
  stingless nettle
  white archangel
  white dead nettle
Lantana achyranthifolia [Verbenaceae]
  orégano
Lantana glandulosissima [Verbenaceae]
  orégano silvestre
  orégano xiu
Lantana hispida [Verbenaceae]
  oréganillo del monte
Lantana involucrata [Verbenaceae]
  orégano
Lantana microcephala [Verbenaceae]
  orégano xiu
Lantana trifolia [Verbenaceae]

orégano
Lantana velutina [Verbenaceae]
  orégano xiu
Larix decidua [Pinaceae]
  European larch
  larch
  Venice turpentine
Larix decidua europaea [Pinaceae]
  European larch
  larch
  Venice turpentine
Larix laricina [Pinaceae]
  American larch
  black larch
  hackamatack
  larch
  tamarack
Larrea tridentata [Zygophyllaceae]
  chaparral
  creosote bush
  greasewood
  Sonora gum
Laserpitium latifolium [Umbelliferae]
  asafoetida
  herb frankincense
  laserwort
Laurelia sempervirens [Monimiaceae]
  Chilean sassafras
  Peruvian nutmeg
Laurus nobilis [Lauraceae]
  bay leaf
  Grecian laurel
  Indian bay
  laurel
  Roman bay
  sweet bay
  sweet laurel
Lavandula augustifolia [Labiatae]
  English lavender
  lavender
  true lavender
Lavandula latifolia [Labiatae]
  spike lavender
Lavandula officinalis [Labiatae]
  lavender
  true lavender
Lavandula spica [Labiatae]
  spikenard
Lavandula stoechas [Labiatae]

French lavender
Spanish lavender
Lavandula vera [Labiatae]
  lavender
  true lavender
Lawsonia inermis [Lythraceae]
  alcanna
  Egyptian privet
  henna
  Jamaica mignonette
  mignonette tree
  reseda
Ledum groenlandicum [Ericaceae]
  Labrador tea
Ledum palustre [Ericaceae]
  crystal tea
  marsh cistus
  moth herb
  narrow-leaved Labrador tea
  swamp tea
  wild rosemary
Leonotis leonurus [Labiatae]
  lion's-ear
Leontopodium alpinum [Compositae]
  edelweiss
  lion's-foot
Leonurus cardiaca [Labiatae]
  lion's-ear
  lion's-tail
  motherwort
  Roman motherwort
  throw-wort
Lepidium sativum [Cruciferae]
  garden cress
  pepper grass
  upland cress
Leptandra virginica [Scrophulariaceae]
  Beaumont root
  blackroot
  Bowman's root
  Culver's-physic
  Culver's-root
  hini
  leptandra
  oxadoddy
  physic root
  purple leptandra
  tall speedwell
  tall veronica

whorlywort
Levisticum officinale [Umbelliferae]
  European lovage
  garden lovage
  Italian lovage
  lavose
  lovage
  love parsley
  sea parsley
  wild parsley
Liatris scariosa [Compositae]
  blazing-star
  blue blazing-star
  button snakeroot
  gay-feather
  large button snakeroot
  tall blazing-star
Liatris spicata [Compositae]
  blazing-star
  button snakeroot
  colic root
  dense button snakeroot
  devil's bit
  devil's bite
  gay-feather
  marsh blazing-star
Liatris squarrosa [Compositae]
  blazing-star
  button snakeroot
  gay-feather
  rattlesnake-master
  scaly blazing-star
Licanea guianensis [Rosaceae]
  Cayenne sassafras
Ligusticum mutellina [Umbelliferae]
  alpine lovage
Ligusticum scoticum [Umbelliferae]
  northern lovage
  Scotch lovage
  sea lovage
Ligustrum vulgare [Oleaceae]
  prim
  primwort
  privet
  privy
Limnophila stolonifera [Scrophulariaceae]
  oregano
Linaria vulgaris [Scrophulariaceae]
  butter and eggs

flaxweed
pennywort
toadflax
wild snapdragon
yellow toadflax
Lindera benzoin [Lauraceae]
  Benjamin bush
  feverbush
  spicebush
  spicewood
  wild allspice
Linum usitatissimum [Linaceae]
  flax
  flax seed
  linseed
  lint bells
  winterlien
Lippia abyssinica [Verbenaceae]
  Gambian bush tea
Lippia affinis [Verbenaceae]
  orégano
  orégano montes
Lippia citriodora [Verbenaceae]
  herb Louisa
  lemon verbena
  verbena oil
Lippia formosa [Verbenaceae]
  orégano
Lippia fragrans [Verbenaceae]
  orégano
Lippia graveolens [Verbenaceae]
  American oregano
  Mexican oregano
  Mexican sage
  orégano
  orégano cimarron
Lippia micromeria [Verbenaceae]
  false thyme
  orégano
  orégano del pais
Lippia origanoides [Verbenaceae]
  orégano
  orégano del pais
Lippia palmeri [Verbenaceae]
  orégano
Lippia pseudo-thea [Verbenaceae]
  Brazilian tea
  gervao
Lippia umbellata [Verbenaceae]

orégano montes
Liquidambar orientalis [Hamamelidaceae]
   Asian storax
   copalm
   gum tree
   Levant storax
   liquidamber
   liquid storax
   Oriental sweet gum
   storax
   styrax
Liquidambar styraciflua
   [Hamamelidaceae]
   American storax or styrax
   American sweet gum
   bilsted
   copalm
   gum tree
   liquidamber
   liquid storax
   opossum tree
   red gum
   storax
   sweet gum
   white gum
Lobelia inflata [Lobeliaceae]
   bladderpod
   emetic herb
   emetic weed
   gagroot
   Indian tobacco
   lobelia
   vomitroot
   vomitwort
   wild tobacco
Lolium temulentum [Gramineae]
   bearded darnel
   cheat
   tare
Lonicera spp. [Caprifoliaceae]
   honeysuckle
Lophophora williamsii [Cactaceae]
   devil's root
   dumpling cactus
   mescal buttons
   pellote
   peyote
   sacred mushroom
Lycopodium clavatum [Lycopodiaceae]

club moss
foxtail
ground pine
herb-ivy
lycopod
running pine
staghorn
vegetable sulfur
wolf claw
Lycopodium spp. [Lycopodiaceae]
   club moss
   ground pine
   herb-ivy
Lythrum salicaria [Lythraceae]
   long purples
   loosestrife
   milk willow-herb
   purple loosestrife
   purple willow-herb
   rainbow weed
   soldiers
   spiked loosestrife
   spiked willow-herb
   willow sage
Magnolia glauca [Magnoliaceae]
   beaver tree
   holly bay
   Indian bark
   magnolia
   red bay
   red laurel
   swamp laurel
   swamp sassafras
   sweet bay
   sweet magnolia
   white bay
Magnolia virginiana [Magnoliaceae]
   beaver tree
   holly bay
   Indian bark
   magnolia
   red bay
   red laurel
   swamp laurel
   swamp sassafras
   sweet bay
   sweet magnolia
   white bay
Mahonia aquifolium [Berberidaceae]

blue barberry
California barberry
holly barberry
holly mahonia
mountain grape
Oregon grape
Rocky Mountain grape
trailing mahonia
wild Oregon grape
Malva rotundifolia [Malvaceae]
blue mallow
cheese plant
cheeses
dwarf mallow
low mallow
mallow
Malva sylvestris [Malvaceae]
cheese flower
cheese plant
cheeses
country mallow
high mallow
mallow
Mandragora officinarum [Solanaceae]
love apple
mandrake
satan's apple
Mangifera indica [Anacardiaceae]
amchur
mango
Maranta arundinacea [Marantaceae]
arrowroot
obedience plant
Marrubium vulgare [Labiatae]
hoarehound
hoarhound
horehound
white horehound
Matricaria chamomilla [Compositae]
German camomile
Hungarian camomile
sweet false camomile
wild camomile
Matricaria inodora [Compositae]
corn feverfew
scentless camomile
scentless mayweed
wild camomile
Matricaria matricarioides [Compositae]

pineapple weed
rayless mayweed
Matricaria perforata [Compositae]
corn feverfew
scentless camomile
scentless mayweed
wild camomile
Matricaria recutita [Compositae]
German camomile
Hungarian camomile
sweet false camomile
wild camomile
Medicago sativa [Leguminosae]
alfalfa
buffalo herb
lucerne
purple medic
Melaleuca alterniflora [Myrtaceae]
tea tree
Melaleuca cajaputi [Myrtaceae]
cajeput
cajuput
Melaleuca leucadendron [Myrtaceae]
cajeput
cajuput
oil of cajeput
river tea tree
weeping tea tree
Melaleuca linariifolia [Myrtaceae]
tea tree
Melaleuca minor [Myrtaceae]
cajeput
cajuput
Melaleuca viridiflora [Myrtaceae]
cajeput
cajuput
niaouli
Melia azedarach [Meliaceae]
azedarach
Africa lilac
bead tree
Chinaberry
China tree
hagbush
hoptree
Indian lilac
Japanese bead tree
paradise tree
Persian lilac

pride tree
pride-of-China
pride-of-India
Syrian bead tree
Texas umbrella tree
Melilotus alba [Leguminosae]
bukhara clover
hubam clover
white melilot
white sweet clover
Melilotus coerules [Leguminosae]
blue melilot
Melilotus officinalis [Leguminosae]
bird's-foot-trefoil
garden balm
hay flowers
king's clover
lotus
melilot
melist
sweet clover
sweet trefoil
Swiss melilot
trefoil
yellow melilot
yellow sweet clover
Melissa majoranifolia [Labiatae]
alpine basil thyme
Melissa officinalis [Labiatae]
balm
balm mint
bee balm
blue balm
cure-all
dropsy plant
garden balm
lemon balm
melissa
sweet balm
Menispermum canadense
[Menispermaceae]
American sarsaparilla
moonseed
Texas sarsaparilla
vine-maple
yellow parilla
Mentha aquatica [Labiatae]
bergamot
water mint

Mentha arvensis [Labiatae]
corn mint
field mint
hakka
Japanese mint
wild pennyroyal
Mentha canadensis [Labiatae]
corn mint
field mint
hakka
Japanese mint
wild pennyroyal
Mentha citrata [Labiatae]
Eau de Cologne mint
Mentha crispa [Labiatae]
crisp-leaved mint
cross mint
curled mint
Mentha longifolia [Labiatae]
horsemint
Mentha officinalis [Labiatae]
julep mint
Mentha x piperita [Labiatae]
brandy mint
lamb mint
peppermint
Mentha pulegium [Labiatae]
European pennyroyal
lurk-in-the-ditch
pennyroyal
Mentha rotundifolia [Labiatae]
round-leaved mint
Mentha spicata [Labiatae]
lamb mint
Our Lady's mint
sage of Bethlehem
spearmint
Mentha suaveolens [Labiatae]
applemint
Mentha sylvestre [Labiatae]
European horsemint
Mentha villosa alopecuroides [Labiatae]
Bowles mint
Menyanthes trifoliata [Gentianaceae]
bean trefoil
bog bean
bog myrtle
brook bean
buckbean

marsh clover
marsh trefoil
moonflower
trefoil
water shamrock
water trefoil
Mercurialis annua [Euphorbiaceae]
  mercury
  mercury herb
Mercurialis perennis [Euphorbiaceae]
  dog's cole
  dog's mercury
  mercury
  perennial mercury
Mertensia virginica [Boraginaceae]
  bluebells
  cowslip
  lungwort
  Roanoke-bells
  Virginia bluebells
  Virginia cowslip
Micromeria chamissonis douglasii
  [Labiatae]
  yerba buena
Mimulus spp. *[Scrophulariaceae]*
  monkey flowers
Mitchella repens [Saxifragaceae]
  checkerberry
  deerberry
  hive vine
  one-berry
  partridgeberry
  running box
  squaw vine
  squawberry
  twinberry
  two-eyed berry
  winter clover
Monarda didyma [Labiatae]
  bee balm
  bergamot
  blue balm
  high balm
  horsemint
  low balm
  mountain balm
  mountain mint
  Oswego tea
  wild bergamot

Monarda fistulosa [Labiatae]
  bee balm
  bergamot
  blue balm
  high balm
  horsemint
  low balm
  mountain balm
  mountain mint
  Oswego tea
  wild bergamot
Monarda punctata [Labiatae]
  dotted mint
  horsemint
  Oswego tea
  wild bergamot
Monardella lanceolata [Labiatae]
  pennyroyal
Monardella odoratissima [Labiatae]
  western balm
  wild pennyroyal
Monardella villosa [Labiatae]
  coyote mint
  horsemint
  pennyroyal
Monotropa uniflora [Pyrolaceae]
  birdnest
  convulsion root
  corpse plant
  fairy smoke
  fit plant
  fitsroot
  ghost flower
  Indian-pipe
  pine-sap
  pipe plant
Moringa pterygosperma [Moringaceae]
  ben tree
  drumstick
  horseradish tree
Murraya koenigii [Rutaceae]
  curry leaf
  curry-leaf tree
Myrica cerifera [Myricaceae]
  bayberry wax
  candleberry
  tallow shrub
  vegetable tallow
  wax myrtle

waxberry
Myrica gale [Myricaceae]
  bog myrtle
  meadow fern
  sweet gale
Myrica pennsylvanica [Myricaceae]
  bayberry
  candleberry
  wax myrtle
  swamp candleberry
  waxberry
Myristica argentica [Myristicaceae]
  Macassar mace
  Papua mace
Myristica fragrans [Myristicaceae]
  Banda mace
  mace
  nutmeg
  Penang mace
Myristica malabarica [Myristicaceae]
  Bombay mace
  wild mace
Myroxylon balsamum [Leguminosae]
  opobalsam
  tolu balsam
Myroxylon balsamum, var. pereirae
  [Leguminosae]
  Peruvian balsam
Myrrhis odorata [Umbelliferae]
  anise
  anise chervil
  British myrrh
  European sweet cicely
  fern-leaved chervil
  garden chervil
  giant sweet chervil
  myrrh
  Spanish chervil
  sweet chervil
  sweet scented myrrh
Myrtus communis [Myrtaceae]
  dwarf myrtle
  German myrtle
  Greek myrtle
  myrtle
  Polish myrtle
  Swedish myrtle
Nardostachys chinensis [Valerianaceae]
  Chinese spikenard

Nardostachys jatamansi [Valerianaceae]
  Indian spikenard
  nard
Nasturtium officinale [Cruciferae]
  cress
  scurvy grass
  watercress
Nectandra rodiaei [Lauraceae]
  bebeeru
  greenheart tree
Nectandra puchury [Lauraceae]
  Brazilian sassafras
  pichurim
  pitchurim bean
  sassafras nut
Nepeta cataria [Labiatae]
  catmint
  catnep
  catnip
  catrup
  catswort
  field balm
Nepeta hederacea [Labiatae]
  alehoof
  cat's-foot
  cat's-paw
  creeping Charlie
  field balm
  gill-over-the-ground
  gillrun
  ground ivy
  hay maids
  hedge maids
  runaway robin
  turnhoof
Nicotiana rustica [Solanaceae]
  poke
  wild tobacco
Nigella damascena [Ranunculaceae]
  Damascene nigella
  love-in-a-mist
  ragged lady
  Saint Catherine's flower
  Venus' hair
  wild fennel
Nigella sativa [Ranunculaceae]
  black caraway
  black cumin
  devil-in-the-bush

fennel flower
kalonji
nigella
nutmeg flower
Roman coriander
wild onion seed
Nymphaea caerulea [Nymphaeaceae]
blue African lotus
Nymphaea lotus [Nymphaeaceae]
white Egyptian lotus
Nymphaea odorata [Nymphaeaceae]
cow cabbage
fragrant water lily
pond lily
Saint Joseph's lily
sweet-scented pond lily
sweet-scented water lily
water cabbage
water lily
white pond lily
white water lily
Nymphaea stellata [Nymphaeaceae]
East Indian lotus
Indian lotus
Nymphaea tuberosa [Nymphaeaceae]
magnolia water lily
tuberous water lily
Nymphaea spp. [Nymphaeaceae]
lotus
Ocimum basilicum [Labiatae]
basil
bush basil
lemon-scented basil
monk's basil
Saint Josephwort
sweet basil
Ocimum citriodora [Labiatae]
lemon-scented basil
Ocimum minimum [Labiatae]
bush basil
dwarf basil
Ocimum sanctum [Labiatae]
Indian holy basil
Ocotea caudata [Lauraceae]
Cayenne rosewood
linaloe cayenne bois de rose
Ocotea cymbarum [Lauraceae]
Amazonian sassafras
Ocotea pretiosa [Lauraceae]

Brazilian sassafras
Oenothera biennis [Onagraceae]
evening primrose
fever plant
field primrose
German rampion
king's cureall
night willow-herb
primrose
scabish
scurvish
tree primrose
Ononis spinosa [Leguminosae]
cammock
petty whin
rest-harrow
stayplough
Ophelia chirata or *chirayita*
[Gentianaceae]
chirata
chirayita
chiretta
Opopanax chironium [Umbelliferae]
Bisabol myrrh
opopanax
sweet myrrh
Origanum dictamnus [Labiatae]
dittany of Crete
Greek oregano
Spanish hops
Origanum majorana [Labiatae]
knotted marjoram
origane
orégano dolce
sweet marjoram
Origanum onites [Labiatae]
Italian oregano
Origanum syriacum [Labiatae]
za'atar
Origanum syriacum, var. *syriacum*
[Labiatae]
hyssop
oregano
Origanum vulgare [Labiatae]
marjoram
mountain mint
origane des champs
pot marjoram
wild marjoram

winter marjoram
wintersweet
Ormensis mixta [Compositae]
  Moroccan camomile
Ormensis multicaulis [Compositae]
  Moroccan camomile
Osmorhiza claytonii [Umbelliferae]
  hairy sweet cicely
  sweet jarvil
  sweet javril
  wooly sweet cicely
Osmorhiza longistylis [Umbelliferae]
  aniseroot
  New England sweet cicely
  smooth sweet cicely
  sweet chervil
  sweet cicely
Osmunda cinnamomea [Osmundaceae]
  buckhorn
  cinnamon fern
  cinnamon-colored fern
  fiddleheads
Osmunda regalis [Osmundaceae]
  bog onion
  buckhorn
  buckhorn brake
  buckhorn male fern
  flowering brake
  flowering fern
  hartshorn bush
  herb Christopher
  king's fern
  royal fern
  royal flowering fern
  Saint Christopher's herb
  water fern
Ourouparia gambier [Rubiaceae]
  catechu
  gambier
  gambir
  pale catechu
Oxalis acetosella [Oxalidaceae]
  alleluia
  cuckoo bread
  European wood sorrel
  green sauce
  Irish shamrock
  mountain sorrel
  sour trefoil

stubwort
three-leaved grass
white sorrel
wood sorrel
Oxalis corniculata [Oxalidaceae]
  creeping oxalis
  creeping wood sorrel
  yellow sorrel
Oxalis pes-caprae [Oxalidaceae]
  Bermuda buttercup
  soursob
Oxalis spiralis [Oxalidaceae]
  chulco
Oxalis stricta [Oxalidaceae]
  upright yellow wood sorrel
Paeonia officinalis [Paeoniaceae]
  peony
Panax ginseng [Araliaceae]
  Asiatic ginseng
  Chinese ginseng
  ginseng (Eastern Asia)
  Korean ginseng
  San Qi ginseng
  wonder-of-the-world
Panax pseudoginseng [Araliaceae]
  Asiatic ginseng
  Chinese ginseng
  ginseng (Eastern Asia)
  Korean ginseng
  San Qi ginseng
  wonder-of-the-world
Panax quinquefolia [Araliaceae]
  American ginseng
  five-fingers
  five-leafed ginseng
  ginseng (North America)
  red berry
Panax schinseng
  Asiatic ginseng
  Chinese ginseng
  ginseng (Eastern Asia)
  Korean ginseng
  San Qi ginseng
  wonder-of-the-world
Pandanus fascicularis [Pandanaceae]
  keora
  kewda
  kewra
  Nicobar breadfruit

padang
pandang
screw pine
umbrella tree
Pandanus odoratissimus [Pandanaceae]
  keora
  kewda
  kewra
  Nicobar breadfruit
  padang
  pandang
  screw pine
  umbrella tree
Pandanus tectorus [Pandanaceae]
  kewra
  pandanus palm
  thatch screw pine
Papaver somniferum [Papaveraceae]
  opium poppy
  poppy
Parietaria officinalis [Urticaceae]
  pellitory
  pellitory of the wall
  wall plant
Paronychia spp. *[Caryophyllaceae]*
  chickweed
  nailwort
  whitlow grass
  whitlowwort
Parthenocissus quinquefolia [Vitaceae]
  American ivy
  American woodbine
  creeper
  false grape
  five leaves
  five-leaved ivy
  Virginia creeper
  wild woodbine
  wild woodvine
  woodbine
  woody creeper
Passiflora incarnata [Passifloraceae]
  apricot vine
  maypop
  passionflower
  wild passionflower
Passiflora maliformis [Passifloraceae]
  conch apple
  sweet calabash

  sweetcup
Passiflora murucuja [Passifloraceae]
  Dutchman's laudanum
Passiflora spp. *[Passifloraceae]*
  granadilla
  passionflower
  passionfruit
  water lemon
Paullinia cupana [Sapindaceae]
  guarana
Pedicularis canadensis [Scrophulariaceae]
  wood betony
Pedicularis spp. *[Scrophulariaceae]*
  lousewort
Pelargonium citrosum [Geraniaceae]
  orange-scented geranium
Pelargonium crispum [Geraniaceae]
  lemon-scented geranium
Pelargonium fragrans [Geraniaceae]
  nutmeg-scented geranium
Pelargonium graveolens [Geraniaceae]
  rose geranium
  sweet-scented geranium
Pelargonium odoratissimum [Geraniaceae]
  apple-scented geranium
Pelargonium tomentosum [Geraniaceae]
  herb-scented geranium
  peppermint-scented geranium
Perilla frutescens [Labiatae]
  beefsteak plant
  perilla
  shiso zoku
Persea borbonia [Lauraceae]
  red bay
  sweet bay
Petasites japonicus [Compositae]
  fuki
Petasites spp. *[Compositae]*
  butterbur
  sweet coltsfoot
Petroselinum crispum [Umbelliferae]
  garden parsley
  parsley
  rock parsley
  turnip-rooted parsley
Petroselinum sativum [Umbelliferae]
  garden parsley
  parsley
  rock parsley

Peucedanum osthruthium [Umbelliferae]
  hog's fennel
  imperatoria
  imperial masterwort
  masterwort
  sulfurwort
Peumus boldus [Monimiaceae]
  boldo
  boldus
Phlomis fruticosa [Labiatae]
  Jerusalem sage
Phlomis lychnitis [Labiatae]
  lampwick plant
Phoradendron flavescens [Loranthaceae]
  American mistletoe
  birdlime
  golden bough
  mistletoe
Phoradendron serotinum [Loranthaceae]
  American mistletoe
  birdlime
  golden bough
  mistletoe
Phytolacca acinosa [Phytolaccaceae]
  Indian poke
  poke
Phytolacca americana [Phytolaccaceae]
  American nightshade
  coakum
  garget
  inkberry
  pigeon berry
  pocan
  poke
  pokeroot
  pokeweed
  redweed
  scoke
  Virginia poke
Phytolacca esculenta [Phytolaccaceae]
  poke
Picea abies [Pinaceae]
  Common spruce
  Norway pine
  Norway spruce
Picea glauca [Pinaceae]
  Alberta spruce
  Black Hills spruce
  Canadian spruce

  cat spruce
  white spruce
Picea jezoensis [Pinaceae]
  yeddo spruce
  yezo spruce
Picea mariana [Pinaceae]
  black spruce
  Canadian black pine
  bog spruce
  double spruce
Pimenta dioica [Myrtaceae]
  allspice
  clove pepper
  Jamaica pepper
  myrtle pepper
  pimenta or pimento
  toute-épice
Pimenta officinalis [Myrtaceae]
  allspice
  clove pepper
  Jamaica pepper
  myrtle pepper
  pimenta
  toute-épice
Pimenta racemosa [Myrtaceae]
  bay
  bay malagueta
  bay-rum tree
  myrcia oil
  oil of bay
  West Indian bay-leaf oil
Pimpinella anisum [Umbelliferae]
  anise
  aniseed
  sweet cumin
Pimpinella magna [Umbelliferae]
  false pimpernel
  greater pimpernel
  pimpernel
  pimpinella
Pimpinella major [Umbelliferae]
  false pimpernel
  greater pimpernel
  pimpernel
  pimpinella
Pimpinella saxifraga [Umbelliferae]
  burnet saxifrage
  pimpernel
  pimpinella

saxifrage
small pimpernel
Pinus edulis [Pinaceae]
  nut pine
  pinyon pine
  piñon nuts
  two-leaved nut pine
Pinus gerardiana [Pinaceae]
  Chilghoza pine
  Gerald's pine
  Nepal nut pine
Pinus mugo [Pinaceae]
  dwarf pine
  mountain pine
  Mugo pine
  Swiss mountain pine
Pinus palustris [Pinaceae]
  Georgia pine
  longleaf pine
  longleaf yellow pine
  pine oil
  pitch pine
  southern yellow pine
Pinus pinea [Pinaceae]
  Italian stone pine
  pignolia nuts
  stone pine
  umbrella pine
Pinus quadrifolia [Pinaceae]
  Parry pinyon pine
  piñon nuts
Pinus strobus [Pinaceae]
  Canadian white pine
  deal pine
  Eastern white pine
  pumpkin pine
  soft pine
  Weymouth pine
  white pine
Pinus sylvestris [Pinaceae]
  Baltic redwood
  Norway pine
  Scot's pine
  Scotch fir
  Scotch pine
Piper angustifolium [Piperaceae]
  matico
Piper betle [Piperaceae]
  betel

betle pepper
pan leaves
Piper clusii [Piperaceae]
  ashanti pepper
  Guinea pepper
Piper cubeba [Piperaceae]
  cubeb
  Java pepper
  tailed cubebs
  tailed pepper
Piper longum [Piperaceae]
  long pepper
  pipel
Piper methysticum [Piperaceae]
  kava-kava
Piper nigra [Piperaceae]
  green peppercorns
  white pepper
  black pepper
  pepper
Piscidia piscipula [Leguminosae]
  fish fuddle
  fish-poison tree
  Jamaican dogwood
  West Indian dogwood
Pistacia lentiscus [Anacardiaceae]
  Chios mastic tree
  mastic tree
Pistacia vera [Anacardiaceae]
  green almond
  pistachio
  pistacia nut
Plantago coronopus [Plantaginaceae]
  hartshorn plantain
  herb-ivy
Plantago lanceolata [Plantaginaceae]
  buckhorn
  chimney-sweeps
  English plantain
  headsman
  lance-leaf plantain
  narrow-leaved plantain
  plantain
  ribgrass
  ribwort
  ripplegrass
  snake plantain
  soldier's herb
Plantago major [Plantaginaceae]

broad-leaved plantain
cart-track plantain
common plantain
dooryard plantain
greater plantain
round-leaved plantain
way bread
white-man's foot
Plantago media [Plantaginaceae]
hoary plantain
grey ribwort
wooly plantain
Plantago psyllium [Plantaginaceae]
fleawort
Spanish psyllium
Plectranthus spp. *[Labiatae]*
Cuban oregano
prostrate coleus
spur flower
Swedish begonia
Swedish ivy
"Vick's" plant
Plumeria ruba [Apocynaceae]
frangipani flower
nosegay
red jasmine
Podophyllum pelatum [Berberidaceae]
American mandrake
duck's foot
ground lemon
hog apple
Indian apple
mandrake
mayapple
raccoon berry
wild jalap
wild lemon
wild mandrake
Pogostemon cablin [Labiatae]
patchouly
Pogostemon heyneanus [Labiatae]
patchouly
Pogostemon patchouly [Labiatae]
patchouly
Polemonium caeruleum [Polemoniaceae]
charity
Greek valerian
Jacob's ladder
Polianthus tuberosa [Amaryllidaceae]

tuberose
Polygala amara [Polygalaceae]
bitter milkwort
dwarf milkwort
European bitter polygala
European senega snakeroot
evergreen snakeroot
flowering wintergreen
fringed polygala
little pollom
milkwort
Polygala senega [Polygalaceae]
milkwort
seneca snakeroot
Polygala vulgaris [Polygalaceae]
European seneka
European milkwort
gang flower
milkwort
rogation flower
senega snakeroot
Polygonatum multiflorum [Liliaceae]
dropberry
King Solomon's-seal
sealroot
sealwort
Solomon's-seal
Polygonatum odoratum [Liliaceae]
dropberry
King Solomon's-seal
sealroot
sealwort
Solomon's-seal
Polygonum spp. *[Polygonaceae]*
fleece flower
knotweed
smartweed
Polygonum aviculare [Polygonaceae]
beggarweed
bird knotgrass
birdweed
cow grass
crawlgrass
doorweed
fleece flower
knotweed
ninety-knot
pigweed
smartweed

Polygonum bistorta [Polygonaceae]
  bistort
  dragonwort
  Easter giant
  patience dock
  poor-man's-cabbage
  red leg
  snakeroot
  snakeweed
  sweet dock
Polygonum hydropiper [Polygonaceae]
  water pepper
Polygonum multiflorum [Polygonaceae]
  fo-ti
  ho shou wu
Polygonum persicaria [Polygonaceae]
  doorweed
  heartease
  heartweed
  lady's thumb
  pinkweed
  red leg
  spotted knotweed
Polygonum punctatum [Polygonaceae]
  water smartweed
Polypodium vulgare [Polypodiaceae]
  adder's fern
  brake fern
  brake rock
  brakeroot
  common polypody
  European polypody
  female fern
  fern brake
  fern root
  rock brake
  rock polypod
  stone brake
  wall fern
  wall polypody
Populus alba [Salicaceae]
  abele
  silver-leaved poplar
  white poplar
Populus balsamifera [Salicaceae]
  balm of Gilead
  balsam poplar
  hackmatack
  poplar

  tacamahac
Populus candicans [Salicaceae]
  balm of Gilead
  balsam poplar
  hackmatack
  poplar
  tacamahac
Populus x gileadensis [Salicaceae]
  balm of Gilead
Populus nigra [Salicaceae]
  black poplar
  lombardy poplar
  poplar
Populus tremuloides [Salicaceae]
  quaking aspen
  quiverleaf
  trembling aspen
Portulaca oleracea, var. sativa
  [Portulacaceae]
  continental parsley
  kitchen-garden purslane
  purslane
  pusley
Potentilla anserina [Rosaceae]
  cinquefoil
  crampweed
  goose tansy
  goosegrass
  moor grass
  silver cinquefoil
  silverweed
Potentilla canadensis [Rosaceae]
  finger leaf
  five fingers
  five-finger grass
Potentilla erecta [Rosaceae]
  shepherd's knot
  red root
  tormentil
  upright septfoil
Potentilla reptans [Rosaceae]
  European five-finger grass
Potentilla rupestris [Rosaceae]
  prairie tea
  rock cinquefoil
Poterium sanguisorba [Rosaceae]
  burnet
  garden burnet
  pimpinella

pimpinelle
salad burnet
Prenanthes alba [Compositae]
  canker root
  cankerweed
  lion's-foot
  rattlesnake root
  white cankerweed
  white lettuce
Prenanthes serpentaria [Compositae]
  lion's-foot
  rattlesnake root
Primula officinalis [Primulaceae]
  butter rose
  cowslip
  English primrose
  primrose
Primula veris [Primulaceae]
  butter rose
  cowslip
  English cowslip
  keyflower
  palsywort
  primrose
Primula vulgaris [Primulaceae]
  English primrose
Prunella vulgaris [Labiatae]
  all-heal
  blue curls
  brownwort
  carpenter's herb
  carpenter's weed
  heal-all
  herb carpenter
  Hercules woundwort
  hock-heal
  self-heal
  sicklewort
  woundwort
Prunus amygdala, var. *amara [Rosaceae]*
  bitter almond
Prunus amygdala, var. *dulcis [Rosaceae]*
  almond
  Greek nuts
  sweet almond
Prunus dulcis, var. *amara [Rosaceae]*
  bitter almond
Prunus dulcis, var. *dulcis [Rosaceae]*
  almond

Greek nuts
sweet almond
Prunus laurocerasus [Rosaceae]
  cherry laurel
  cherry-bay
  English laurel
Prunus mahaleb [Rosaceae]
  mahaleb
  mahleb
  mahlepi
  perfumed cherry
  Saint Lucie cherry
Prunus pennsylvanica [Rosaceae]
  bird cherry
  fire cherry
  pin cherry
  wild cherry
  wild red cherry
Prunus persica [Rosaceae]
  peach leaves
Prunus serotina [Rosaceae]
  black cherry
  black choke
  chokecherry
  rum cherry
  wild black cherry
  wild cherry
Prunus spinosa [Rosaceae]
  blackthorn
  sloe
Prunus virginiana [Rosaceae]
  chokecherry
Ptelea trifoliata [Rutaceae]
  hop tree
  pickaway anise
  prairie grub
  scubby trefoil
  shrubby trefoil
  stinking ash
  stinking prairie bush
  swamp dogwood
  three-leaved hop tree
  wafer ash
  water ash
  wingseed
Pterocarpus draco [Leguminosae]
  dragon's blood
Pterocarpus marsupium [Leguminosae]
  bija

Pterocarpus santalinus [Leguminosae]
  red sandalwood
  red saunders
Pulmonaria officinalis [Boraginaceae]
  beggar's basket
  blue lungwort
  Jerusalem cowslip
  Jerusalem sage
  lungmoss
  lungwort
  maple lungwort
  spotted comfrey
  spotted lungwort
Pulsatilla amoena [Ranunculaceae]
  Easter flower
  meadow anemone
  pasque flower
  prairie anemone
  pulsatilla
  wild crocus
  wind flower
Pulsatilla patens [Ranunculaceae]
  Easter flower
  meadow anemone
  pasque flower
  prairie anemone
  pulsatilla
  wild crocus
  wind flower
Pulsatilla vulgaris [Ranunculaceae]
  Easter flower
  meadow anemone
  pasque flower
  prairie anemone
  pulsatilla
  wild crocus
  wind flower
Punica granatum [Punicaceae]
  pomegranate
Pycnanthemum virginianum [Labiatae]
  prairie hyssop
  Virginia mountain mint
  Virginia thyme
  wild basil
  wild hyssop
Pyrethrum carneum [Compositae]
  painted daisy
  pellitory
  Persian insect flower

  Persian insect powder
  pyrethrum
Pyrethrum cinerariifolium [Compositae]
  Dalmatia pyrethrum
  Dalmatian insect flower
  Dalmatian insect powder
  pellitory
  pyrethrum
Pyrethrum coccineum [Compositae]
  painted daisy
  pellitory
  Persian insect flower
  Persian insect powder
  pyrethrum
Pyrethrum hybridum [Compositae]
  painted daisy
  pellitory
  Persian insect flower
  Persian insect powder
  pyrethrum
Pyrola elliptica [Pyrolaceae]
  shinleaf
  wild lily-of-the-valley
Quassia amara [Simaroubaceae]
  bitter ash
  bitterwood
  quassia
  Surinam quassia
Quebrachia lorentzii [Apocynaceae]
  aspidosperma
  quebracho
Quercus albus [Fagaceae]
  white oak
Quercus robur [Fagaceae]
  English oak
  truffle oak
Quercus suber [Fagaceae]
  cork oak
Quillaja saponaria [Rosaceae]
  Panama bark
  quillai
  quillaja
  quillay bark
  soapbark
Ranunculus acris [Ranunculaceae]
  bachelor's buttons
  blisterweed
  burrwort
  buttercup

crowfoot
crowfoot buttercup
globe amaranth
gold cup
meadow crowfoot
meadowbloom
tall buttercup
tall crowfoot
tall field buttercup
yellows
yellowweed
Ranunculus bulbosus [Ranunculaceae]
  acrid crowfoot
  bulbous buttercup
  bulbous crowfoot
  buttercup
  crowfoot
  cuckoo buds
  frogwort
  king's cup
  meadowbloom
  pilewort
  Saint Anthony's turnip
Ranunculus ficaria [Ranunculaceae]
  lesser celandine
  pilewort
  small celandine
Ranunculus sceleratus [Ranunculaceae]
  buttercup
  celery-leaved buttercup
  crowfoot
  cursed crowfoot
  marsh crowfoot
  water crowfoot
Raphanus sativus, Cv. *Longipinnatus*
  [Cruciferae]
  Chinese radish
  daikon
Rhamnus cathartica [Rhamnaceae]
  common buckthorn
  purging buckthorn
  waythorn
Rhamnus frangula [Rhamnaceae]
  alder buckthorn
  alder dogwood
  arrowwood
  black alder dogwood
  black alder tree
  black dogwood

buckthorn
European black alder
European buckthorn
Persian berries
Rhamnus purshiana [Rhamnaceae]
  bearberry
  bearwood
  California buckthorn
  cascara
  cascara buckthorn
  cascara sagrada
  chittambark
  sacred bark
Rheum palmatum [Polygonaceae]
  Chinese rhubarb
  rhubarb
  Turkey rhubarb
Rheum rhabarbarum [Polygonaceae]
  garden rhubarb
  pie plant
  rhubarb
  wine plant
Rhus coriaria [Anacardiaceae]
  elm-leaved sumac
  Sicilian sumac
  sumac
  tanner's sumac
Rhus glabra [Anacardiaceae]
  dwarf sumac
  mountain sumac
  scarlet sumac
  smooth sumac
  vinegar tree
Rhus integrifolia [Anacardiaceae]
  lemon berry
  lemonade berry
  lemonade sourberry
  sourberry
Rhus radicans [Anacardiaceae]
  cow-itch
  markry
  mercury
  poison ivy
  poison oak
Rhus vernix [Anacardiaceae]
  poison dogwood
  poison elder
  poison sumac
  swamp sumac

Ribes nigrum [Saxifragaceae]
  black currant
  European black currant
  niribine oil
  quinsy berry
Ribes rubrum [Saxifragaceae]
  garden currant
  garnetberry
  northern red currant
  raisin tree
  red currant
  wineberry
Ricinus communis [Euphorbiaceae]
  bofareira
  castor bean
  castor oil plant
  Mexico seed
  oil plant
  palma Christi
  wonder tree
Roccella fuciformis [Lichen]
  Angola weed
Rosa spp. [Rosaceae]
  attar of roses
  rose
  rose absolute
  rose Bulgarian
  rose hips
  true Otto oil
Rosmarinus officinalis [Labiatae]
  old man
  rosemary
Rubia tinctorum [Rubiaceae]
  madder
Rubus spp. [Rosaceae]
  baked-apple berry
  blackberry
  blackcap
  boysenberry
  cloudberry
  dewberry
  framboise
  Himalaya berry
  kneshenka
  loganberry
  malka
  nagoonberry
  raspberry
  salmonberry

thimbleberry
wineberry
yellowberry
youngberry
Rumex acetocella [Polygonaceae]
  American sorrel
  red sorrel
  sheep sorrel
  sorrel, common
Rumex acetosa [Polygonaceae]
  European sorrel
  garden sorrel
  meadow sorrel
  sour dock
  sourgrass
Rumex alpinus [Polygonaceae]
  Alpine dock
  monk's rhubarb
  mountain rhubarb
Rumex crispus [Polygonaceae]
  curled dock
  narrow dock
  rhubarb dock
  sour dock
  yellow dock
Rumex hymenosepalus [Polygonaceae]
  canaigre
  tanner's dock
  wild pieplant
  wild rhubarb
Rumex obtusifolius [Polygonaceae]
  broad-leaved dock
Rumex patientia [Polygonaceae]
  garden patience
  herb patience
  monk's rhubarb
  patience
  patience dock
  spinach dock
Rumex scutatus [Polygonaceae]
  buckler-leaf sorrel
  French sorrel
  garden sorrel
Rumex spp. [Polygonaceae]
  dock
  rhubarb sorrel
  sorrel
Ruscus aculeatus [Liliaceae]
  box holly

butcher's broom
hornet holly
Jew's myrtle
knee holly
little holly
Ruta bracteosa [Rutaceae]
 garden rue
 German rue
 herb-of-grace
 herb-of-repentance
 rue
Ruta calepensis [Rutaceae]
 garden rue
 German rue
 herb-of-grace
 herb-of-repentance
 rue
Ruta graveolens [Rutaceae]
 garden rue
 German rue
 herb-of-grace
 herb-of-repentance
 rue
Ruta montana [Rutaceae]
 garden rue
 German rue
 herb-of-grace
 herb-of-repentance
 rue
Sabatia angularis [Gentianaceae]
 American centaury
 bitter clover
 bitter-bloom
 eyebright
 red centaury
 rose pink
 wild succory
Salix alba [Salicaceae]
 salicin willow
 white willow
 withe
 withy
Salix caprea [Salicaceae]
 florist's willow
 goat willow
 pussy willow
 sallow
Salix nigra [Salicaceae]
 black willow

Salix purpurea [Salicaceae]
 basket willow
 purple osier
 purple willow
Salvia barrelieri [Labiatae]
 Spanish sage
Salvia clevelandii [Labiatae]
 blue sage
Salvia dorisiana [Labiatae]
 British Honduran sage
 peach-scented sage
Salvia elegans [Labiatae]
 pineapple-scented sage
Salvia fruticosa [Labiatae]
 Greek sage
Salvia lavandulifolia [Labiatae]
 Spanish sage
Salvia leucantha [Labiatae]
 Mexican bush sage
Salvia leucophylla [Labiatae]
 gray sage
 purple sage
Salvia lyrata [Labiatae]
 cancerweed
 lyre-leaved sage
 wild sage
Salvia officinalis [Labiatae]
 Dalmatia sage
 garden sage
 sage
 salvia
Salvia officinalis aureum [Labiatae]
 golden sage
Salvia pomifera [Labiatae]
 apple sage
Salvia sclarea [Labiatae]
 clary
 clary sage
 muscatel sage
Salvia triloba [Labiatae]
 Greek sage
Salvia verbenacea [Labiatae]
 vervain sage
 wild clary
Salvia viridis [Labiatae]
 Bluebeard sage
 Joseph sage
 red-topped sage
Sambucus caerulea [Caprifoliaceae]

blue elder
Sambucus canadensis [Caprifoliaceae]
  American elder
  black elder
  elder flowers
  rob elder
  sweet elder
Sambucus ebulus [Caprifoliaceae]
  blood elder
  danewort
  dwarf elder
  walewort
  wallwort
  wild elder
Sambucus nigra [Caprifoliaceae]
  black elder
  black-berried European elder
  boor tree
  bore tree
  bounty
  elder
  elfhorn
  ellanwood
  European elder
  German elder
Sambucus pubens [Caprifoliaceae]
  American red elder
  red-berried elder
  stinking elder
Sambucus racemosa [Caprifoliaceae]
  European red elder
Sanguinaria canadensis [Papaveraceae]
  bloodroot
  Indian paint
  Indian plant
  Indian red paint
  pauson
  red paint root
  red puccoon
  red root
  sanguinaria
  tetterwort
  yarrow
Sanguisorba minor [Rosaceae]
  burnet
  garden burnet
  pimpinella
  pimpinelle
  salad burnet

Sanguisorba officinalis [Rosaceae]
  burnet bloodwort
  great burnet
  Italian burnet
  Italian pimpernel
Sanicula europaea [Umbelliferae]
  European sanicle
  wood sanicle
Sanicula marilandica [Umbelliferae]
  American sanicle
  black sanicle
  black snakeroot
  sanicle
Santalum spp. [Santalaceae]
  East Indian sandalwood
  sandalwood
  white sandalwood
  white saunders
  yellow sandalwood
  yellow saunders
Santolina chamaecyparissus [Compositae]
  lavender cotton
  santolina
Saponaria officinalis [Caryophyllaceae]
  bouncing Bet
  bruisewort
  dog cloves
  fuller's herb
  old maid's pink
  soap root
  soapwort
Sarracenia purpurea [Sarraceniaceae]
  Eve's cup
  flytrap
  huntsman's-cup
  Indian-cup
  pitcher plant
  side-saddle flower
  smallpox plant
  southern pitcher plant
  sweet pitcher plant
  watercup
Sassafras albidum [Lauraceae]
  ague tree
  cinnamon wood
  sassafras
  saxifrax
Sassafras variifolium [Lauraceae]
  ague tree

cinnamon wood
sassafras
saxifrax
Satureja acinos [Labiatae]
  basil thyme
Satureja alpina [Labiatae]
  alpine basil thyme
Satureja capitata [Labiatae]
  conehead thyme
  corido thyme
  Cretan thyme
  headed savory
  Spanish thyme
  thyme of the ancients
  za'atar farsi
Satureja douglasii [Labiatae]
  yerba buena
Satureja glabella [Labiatae]
  calamint
Satureja hortensis [Labiatae]
  bean herb
  summer savory
Satureja montana [Labiatae]
  winter savory
Satureja thymbra [Labiatae]
  za'atar franji
  za'atar rumi
Satureja spp. *[Labiatae]*
  savory
Saussurea costus [Compositae]
  costus
Saussurea lappa [Compositae]
  costus
Sauvagesia erecta [Violaceae]
  adima
  Saint Martin's-herb
  yaoba
  yerba de Saint Martin
Schinopsis lorentzii [Apocynaceae]
  aspidosperma
  quebracho
Schinus molle [Anacardiaceae]
  Australian pepper tree
  California pepper tree
  molle
  pepper tree
  Peruvian mastic tree
  Peruvian pepper tree
  pink peppercorns

pirul
red peppercorns
Schinus terebinthifolius [Anacardiaceae]
  Brazilian pepper tree
  Christmasberry tree
  Florida pepper tree
Schisandra coccinea [Schisandraceae]
  bay star vine
  magnolia vine
  wild sarsaparilla
Scrophularia marilandica
  [Scrophulariaceae]
  carpenter's square
  figwort
  heal-all
  kernelwort
  knotty-rooted figwort
  scrofula plant
Scutellaria lateriflora [Labiatae]
  blue skullcap
  blue pimpernel
  helmet flower
  hoodwort
  mad-dog weed
  side-flowering skullcap
  skullcap
  Virginia skullcap
Scutellaria spp. *[Labiatae]*
  skullcap
Sedum album [Crassulaceae]
  white stonecrop
Sedum reflexum [Crassulaceae]
  stonecrop
  yellow stonecrop
Sempervivum tectorum [Crassulaceae]
  Aaron's rod
  bullock's eye
  hen and chickens
  houseleek
  Jupiter's beard
  Jupiter's eye
  live-forever
  old-man-and-woman
  roof houseleek
  thunder plant
Senebiera coronopus [Cruciferae]
  herb-ivy
  swine cress
  wart cress

Senecio jacobaea [Compositae]
European ragwort
ragwort
tansy ragwort
Serenoa repens [Palmae]
saw palmetto
scrub palmetto
Serenoa serrulata [Palmae]
saw palmetto
scrub palmetto
Sesamum indicum [Pedaliaceae]
benne plant
sesame
Sesamum orientale [Pedaliaceae]
benne plant
sesame
Silphium perfoliatum [Compositae]
compass plant
cup plant
Indian cup
Indian gum
prairie dock
ragged cup
rosinweed
Silybum marianum [Compositae]
holy thistle
Marythistle
milk thistle
Saint Mary's thistle
Simarouba amara [Simaroubaceae]
bitterwood
quassia
simarouba bark
Surinam quassia
bitter ash
Sinapis alba [Cruciferae]
white mustard
Sisymbrium alliaria [Cruciferae]
alliaria
donkey's foot
garlic mustard
Jack-by-the-hedge
onion nettle
sauce alone
Sisymbrium irio [Cruciferae]
London rocket
Sisymbrium orientale [Cruciferae]
eastern rocket
Sisymbrium spp. [Cruciferae]

hedge mustard
herb Sophia
Smilacina racemosa [Liliaceae]
false spikenard
Solomon's zigzag
treacleberry
Smilax aristolochiaefolia [Liliaceae]
gray sarsaparilla
Mexican sarsaparilla
Vera Cruz sarsaparilla
Smilax febrifuga [Liliaceae]
Ecuadorean sarsaparilla
Smilax glauca [Liliaceae]
sawbrier
wild sarsaparilla
Smilax herbacea [Liliaceae]
Jacob's-ladder
Smilax medica [Liliaceae]
gray sarsaparilla
Mexican sarsaparilla
Vera Cruz sarsaparilla
Smilax regelii [Liliaceae]
brown sarsaparilla
Honduras sarsaparilla
Smilax spp. [Liliaceae]
catbrier
Costa Rica sarsaparilla
greenbrier
Guayaquil sarsaparilla
Lima sarsaparilla
red Jamaica sarsaparilla
sarsaparilla
Virginia sarsaparilla
Smyrnium olusatrum [Umbelliferae]
alexanders
allisanders
black lovage
horse parsley
Solanum dulcamara [Solanaceae]
bittersweet
bittersweet herb
bittersweet nightshade
bittersweet stems
bittersweet twigs
blue nightshade
deadly nightshade
felonwood
felonwort
fever twig

nightshade
nightshade vine
poisonous nightshade
scarlet berry
staff vine
violet bloom
woody
woody nightshade
Solanum nigrum [Solanaceae]
  black nightshade
  common nightshade
  deadly nightshade
  garden nightshade
  poisonberry
Solidago canadensis [Compositae]
  Aaron's rod
  goldenrod
  woundwort
Solidago nemoralis [Compositae]
  dyer's weed
  field goldenrod
  gray goldenrod
  yellow goldenrod
Solidago odora [Compositae]
  anise-scented goldenrod
  Blue Mountain tea
  bohea-tea
  common goldenrod
  sweet goldenrod
  woundwort
Solidago virgaurea [Compositae]
  European goldenrod
Sophora secundiflora [Leguminosae]
  frijolito
  mescal bean
Sorbus americana [Rosaceae]
  American mountain ash
  dogberry
  missey-moosey
  roundwood
Sorbus aucuparia [Rosaceae]
  European mountain ash
  mountain ash
  quickbeam
  rodden
  rowan
  sorb apple
Spartium junceum [Leguminosae]
  genet

Spanish broom
weavers' broom
Spigelia marilandica [Loganiaceae]
  Carolina pink
  Indian pink
  pinkroot
  star bloom
  worm grass
Stachys affinis [Labiatae]
  Chinese artichoke
  chorogi
  crosnes-du-Japon
  Japanese artichoke
  knotroot
Stachys betonica [Labiatae]
  betony
  common betony
  purple betony
  wood betony
Stachys byzantina [Labiatae]
  lamb's-ears
  woolly betony
Stachys officinalis [Labiatae]
  betony
  common betony
  purple betony
  wood betony
Stachys spp. [Labiatae]
  woundwort
Stellaria media [Caryophyllaceae]
  adder's mouth
  chickweed
  Indian chickweed
  satin flower
  starwort
  stitchwort
  tongue-grass
  winterweed
Sticta pulmonacea [Lichen]
  lungmoss
Stillingia sylvatica [Euphorbiaceae]
  cockup hat
  marcory
  queen's delight
  queen's root
  silver leaf
  stillingia
  yaw root
Styrax benzoin [Styracaceae]

benzoin
storax
styrax
Swertia chirata or *chirayita*
   [Gentianaceae]
   chirata
   chirayita
   chiretta
Symphytum asperum [Boraginaceae]
   prickly comfrey
Symphytum officinale [Boraginaceae]
   blackwort
   boneset
   bruisewort
   comfrey
   consormol
   gum plant
   healing herb
   knitback
   knitbone
   salsify
   slippery root
   wallwort
Symphytum x *uplandicum [Boraginaceae]*
   Russian comfrey
Symplocarpus foetidus [Araceae]
   meadow cabbage
   poke
   polecat weed
   skunk cabbage
   skunk weed
   swamp cabbage
Syzygium acris [Myrtaceae]
   wild clove
Syzygium aromaticum [Myrtaceae]
   cloves
Syzygium jambos [Myrtaceae]
   Java plum
   Malabar plum
   rose apple
Tagetes erecta [Compositae]
   African marigold
   Aztec marigold
   big marigold
   marigold
Tagetes lucida [Compositae]
   cloud plant
   hierba de las nubes
   marigold

Mexican marigold mint
Mexican tarragon
mint marigold
sweet mace
sweet marigold
sweet-scented marigold
Texas tarragon
winter tarragon
Tagetes patula [Compositae]
   French marigold
   marigold
Tamarindus indica [Leguminosae]
   tamarind seed
Tanacetum balsamita [Compositae]
   alecost
   costmary
   tansy
Tanacetum vulgare [Compositae]
   button bitters
   golden buttons
   hindheal
   parsley fern
   tansy
Taraxacum officinale [Compositae]
   blowball
   cankerweed
   dandelion
   fairy clock
   lion's tooth
   pee-in-the-bed
   priest's crown
   puffball
   swine snout
   white endive
   wild endive
Taxus baccata [Taxaceae]
   chinwood
   English yew
Taxus spp. *[Taxaceae]*
   yew
Tetraclinis articulata [Cupressaceae]
   arar tree
   juniper resin
   sandarac
   sandarach
Teucrium canadense [Labiatae]
   American germander
   wood sage
Teucrium chamaedrys [Labiatae]

European germander
Teucrium germander [Labiatae]
  betony
  germander
Teucrium marum [Labiatae]
  cat thyme
  herb mastic
Thaspium aureum [Umbelliferae]
  alexanders
  meadow parsnip
Theobroma cacao [Byttneriaceae]
  cacao
  chocolate
  cocoa
Thuja occidentalis [Cupressaceae]
  American cedar
  arborvitae
  cedar leaf oil
  eastern arborvitae
  swamp cedar
  thuja
  tree of life
  white cedar
  white cedarwood oil
  yellow cedar
Thymbra capitata [Labiatae]
  conehead thyme
  corido thyme
  Cretan thyme
  headed savory
  Spanish origanum
  thyme of the ancients
  za'atar farsi
Thymbra spicata [Labiatae]
  za'atar hommar
  za'atar midbari
Thymus caespititius [Labiatae]
  tiny thyme
  tufted thyme
Thymus capitatus [Labiatae]
  conehead thyme
  corido thyme
  Cretan thyme
  headed savory
  Spanish origanum
  thyme of the ancients
  za'atar farsi
Thymus x citriodorus [Labiatae]
  lemon thyme

Thymus herba-barona [Labiatae]
  caraway thyme
Thymus mastichina [Labiatae]
  herb mastic
  mastic thyme
  Spanish marjoram
  Spanish thyme
Thymus micans [Labiatae]
  tiny thyme
  tufted thyme
Thymus praecox subsp. *articus*
  [Labiatae]
  creeping thyme
  mother-of-thyme
Thymus pulegioides [Labiatae]
  mother-of-thyme
  Pennsylvania Dutch tea thyme
  wild thyme
Thymus quinquecostatus [Labiatae]
  Japanese thyme
Thymus serpyllum [Labiatae]
  lemon thyme
  tiny thyme
  tufted thyme
Thymus vulgaris [Labiatae]
  garden thyme
  thyme
  thyme, common
Tilia spp. *[Tiliaceae]*
  lime flowers
  linden
  tilia flowers
Tilia americana [Tiliaceae]
  American linden tree
  basswood
  bast tree
  lime tree
  spoonwood
  whitewood
  wycopy
Tilia x *europaea [Tiliaceae]*
  European lime tree
  European linden
Torreya californica [Taxaceae]
  California nutmeg
Torreya taxifolia [Taxaceae]
  Florida stinking cedar
Trachyspermum ammi [Umbelliferae]
  ajowan

ajuan
omum
Trachyspermum copticum [Umbelliferae]
　ajowan
　ajuan
　omum
Tragopogon porrifolius [Compositae]
　goatsbeard
　oyster plant
　purple goatsbeard
　salsify
　vegetable-oyster
Tragopogon pratensis [Compositae]
　goatsbeard
　Jack-go-to-bed-at-noon
　John-go-to-bed-at-noon
　meadow salsify
　noon flower
　noonday flower
　noontide
　star of Jerusalem
　yellow goatsbeard
Trichilia emetica [Meliaceae]
　roka
Trichostema dichotomum [Labiatae]
　bastard pennyroyal
Trifolium alpinum [Leguminosae]
　mountain licorice
Trifolium pratense [Leguminosae]
　red clover
Trifolium spp. *[Leguminosae]*
　clover
Trigonella foenum-graecum
　[Leguminosae]
　bird's foot
　fenugreek
　Greek hay
　methi
Trilisa odoratissima [Compositae]
　deer's-tongue
　wild vanilla
Trillium erectum [Liliaceae]
　birthroot
　brown Beth
　nose-bleed
　squaw root
　Stinking Benjamin
　trillium
Trillium pendulum [Liliaceae]

bethroot
birthroot
coughroot
ground lily
Indian balm
Indian shamrock
Jew's-harp plant
lamb's quarter
milk ipecac
nodding wake-robin
pariswort
rattlesnake root
snakebite
three-leaved nightshade
trillium
Trillium spp. *[Liliaceae]*
　birthroot
　trillium
　wake-robin
Tripleurospermum inodorum [Compositae]
　corn feverfew
　scentless camomile
　scentless mayweed
　wild camomile
Tripleurospermum recutita [Compositae]
　German camomile
　Hungarian camomile
　sweet false camomile
　wild camomile
Tropaeolum majus [Tropaeolaceae]
　capucine (French)
　garden nasturtium
　Indian cress
　nasturtium
　tall nasturtium
Tsuga canadensis [Pinaceae]
　Canadian hemlock
　Canada-pitch tree
　eastern hemlock
　hemlock
　hemlock gum tree
　hemlock pitch tree
　hemlock spruce
　weeping spruce
Turnera diffusa [Turneraceae]
　damiana
　hierba de la pastora
Tussilago farfara [Compositae]
　ass's foot

British tobacco
bullsfoot
butterbur
coltsfoot
coughwort
flower velure
foal's-foot
hallfoot
horsefoot
horsehoof
the-son-before-the-fathers
Ulmus fulva [Ulmaceae]
  Indian elm
  moose elm
  red elm
  slippery elm
  sweet elm
Ulmus rubra [Ulmaceae]
  Indian elm
  moose elm
  red elm
  slippery elm
  sweet elm
Umbellularia californica [Lauraceae]
  California bay
  California laurel
  California olive
  California sassafras
  myrtle
  Oregon myrtle
  pepperwood
Uncaria gambier [Rubiaceae]
  catechu
  gambier
  gambir
  pale catechu
Urginea maritima [Liliaceae]
  red squill
  sea onion
  sea squill
  squill
  white squill
Urtica dioica [Urticaceae]
  nettle
  stinging nettle
Vaccinium spp. [Ericaceae]
  bilberry
  blueberry
  cowberry

cranberry
deerberry
foxberry
grouseberry
lingberry
lingenberry
lingonberry
moorberry
whinberry
whortleberry
Valeriana celtica [Valerianaceae]
  celtic nard
Valeriana fauriei [Valerianaceae]
  Japanese valerian
  kesso
  valerian
Valeriana officinalis [Valerianaceae]
  all-heal
  cat's valerian
  English valerian
  garden heliotrope
  garden valerian
  German valerian
  great wild valerian
  Japanese valerian
  kesso
  Saint George's herb
  setwall
  valerian
  vandal root
  Vermont valerian
  wild valerian
Valeriana saliunca [Valerianaceae]
  celtic nard
Valeriana spp. [Valerianaceae]
  valerian
Valeriana wallichii [Valerianaceae]
  Indian valerian
Usnea barbata [Usneaceae]
  tree moss
Vanilla planifolia [Orchidaceae]
  Bourbon vanilla
  Mexican vanilla
  vanilla
Vanilla pompona [Orchidaceae]
  Guadeloupe vanilla
  Pompona vanilla
  vanillon
  West Indian vanilla

Vanilla tahitensis [Orchidaceae]
  Tahitian vanilla
Veratrum viride [Liliaceae]
  American hellebore
  American white hellebore
  blazing-star
  bugbane
  devil's bite
  earth gall
  false hellebore
  green hellebore
  Indian poke
  itchweed
  swamp hellebore
  tickleweed
  white hellebore
Verbascum phlomoides [Scrophulariaceae]
  mullein
  mullen
Verbascum thapsiforme [Scrophulariaceae]
  mullein
  mullen
Verbascum thapsus [Scrophulariaceae]
  flannel plant
  mullein
  mullen
  velvet plant
Verbena hastata [Verbenaceae]
  American vervain
  blue vervain
  false vervain
  Indian hyssop
  purvain
  simpler's joy
  traveler's joy
  wild hyssop
Verbena officinalis [Verbenaceae]
  enchanter's plant
  European vervain
  herb of the cross
  Juno's tears
  pigeon's grass
  pigeonweed
  simpler's joy
  vervain
Vernonia spp. [Compositae]
  ironweed
Veronica beccabunga [Scrophulariaceae]
  beccabunga

  European brooklime
  mouth-smart
  neckweed
  speedwell
  water pimpernel
  water purslain
Veronica chamaedrys [Scrophulariaceae]
  angel's-eye
  bird's-eye
  germander speedwell
Veronica officinalis [Scrophulariaceae]
  fluellen
  groundhele
  gypsyweed
  low speedwell
  Paul's betony
  speedwell
  upland speedwell
Veronica spp. [Scrophulariaceae]
  brooklime
  speedwell
  veronica
Veronica virginicum [Scrophulariaceae]
  Beaumont root
  blackroot
  Bowman's-root
  Culver's-physic
  Culver's-root
  hini
  leptandra
  oxadoddy
  physic root
  purple leptandra
  tall speedwell
  tall veronica
  whorlywort
*Veronicastrum virginicum
  [Scrophulariaceae]*
  Beaumont root
  blackroot
  Bowman's-root
  Culver's-physic
  Culver's-root
  hini
  leptandra
  oxadoddy
  physic root
  purple leptandra
  tall speedwell

tall veronica
whorlywort
Vetiveria zizanioides [Gramineae]
  cuscus oil
  khas-khas
  khus-khus
  vetiver
Viburnum cassinoides [Caprifoliaceae]
  Appalachian tea
  Carolina tea
  swamp haw
  teaberry
  wild raisin
  withe-rod
Viburnum opulus [Caprifoliaceae]
  crampbark
  cranberry bush
  European cranberry bush
  guelder rose
  high bush cranberry
  snowball bush
  whitten tree
Viburnum prunifolium [Caprifoliaceae]
  black haw
  nannyberry
  sheepberry
  stagbush
  sweet haw
  sweet viburnum
Viburnum trilobum [Caprifoliaceae]
  crampbark
  cranberry bush
  cranberry tree
  grouseberry
  high bush cranberry
  pimbina
  squawbush
  summerberry
  tree cranberry
Vinca major [Apocynaceae]
  band plant
  blue-buttons
  greater periwinkle
  periwinkle
Vinca minor [Apocynaceae]
  common periwinkle
  lesser periwinkle
  myrtle
  running myrtle

Vinca rosea [Apocynaceae]
  old-maid
  periwinkle
  Madagascar periwinkle
  rose periwinkle
Viola alba [Violaceae]
  Parma violet
Viola calcarata [Violaceae]
  Swiss violet
Viola odorata [Violaceae]
  English violet
  florist's violet
  garden violet
  sweet violet
Viola suavis [Violaceae]
  Russian violet
Viola tricolor [Violaceae]
  European wild pansy
  field pansy
  heartease
  herb trinity
  Johnny jumper
  Johnny-jump-up
  miniature pansy
  pansy
  step-mother
  wild pansy
Viscum album [Loranthaceae]
  all-heal
  birdlime
  devil's fuge
  European mistletoe
  mistletoe
Vitex agnus-castus [Verbenaceae]
  chaste tree
  chasteberry
  hemp tree
  Indian-spice
  monk's pepper tree
  sage tree
  wild pepper
Yucca brevifolia [Agavaceae]
  Joshua tree
  yucca
Yucca schidigera [Agavaceae]
  Mohave yucca
Zanthoxylum alatum [Rutaceae]
  Chinese pepper
  hua-chiao

Szechuan pepper
tomarseed
winged prickly ash
Zanthoxylum americanum [Rutaceae]
  northern prickly ash
  prickly ash tree
  toothache tree
Zanthoxylum bodrunga [Rutaceae]
  mulilam
Zanthoxylum bungei [Rutaceae]
  Chinese pepper
  hua-chiao
  Szechuan pepper
Zanthoxylum clava-Herculis [Rutaceae]
  Hercules'-club
  pepperwood
  prickly ash
  sea ash
  southern prickly ash
Zanthoxylum mantchuricum [Rutaceae]
  inuzansho
  pepperbush
Zanthoxylum piperitum [Rutaceae]
  anise-pepper

Chinese pepper
Japanese pepper
prickly ash
sansho pepper
Szechuan pepper
Zanthoxylum rhetsa [Rutaceae]
  mulilam
Zanthoxylum schinifolium [Rutaceae]
  inuzansho
  pepperbush
Zanthoxylum simulans [Rutaceae]
  Chinese pepper
  hua-chiao
  Szechuan pepper
Zingiber officinale [Zingiberaceae]
  Canton ginger
  ginger
  Jamaican ginger
  true ginger
Zizia aurea [Umbelliferae]
  golden alexanders
Zizyphus spp. [Rhamnaceae]
  jujube
  lotus

Sources Consulted

Acton, Eliza. *Modern Cookery for Private Families, Reduced to a System of Easy Practice, in a Series of Carefully Tested Receipts, in Which the Principles of Baron Liebig and Other Eminent Writers Have Been as Much as Possible Applied and Explained.* London: Longmans, Green, Reader and Dyer, 1868.

Adams, Charlotte. *1001 Questions Answered About Cooking.* New York: Dodd, Mead & Company, 1963.

Anderson, Jean, and Hanna, Elaine. *The New Doubleday Cookbook.* Garden City: Doubleday & Company, Inc., 1985.

Arm & Hammer Book of Valuable Recipes, 75th ed., n.p., n.d.

Bailey, Adrian; Ortiz, Elizabeth Lambert; and Radecka, Helena. *Cooks' Ingredients.* New York: William Morrow and Company, Inc., 1980.

Bailey, L. H. *Manual of Cultivated Plants.* New York: The Macmillan Company, 1924.

Bailey, Liberty Hyde, and Bailey, Ethel Zoe, Compilers. *Hortus Third, A Concise Dictionary of Plants Cultivated in the United States and Canada.* Revised and expanded by the staff of the Liberty Hyde Bailey Hortorium at Cornell University. New York: Macmillan Publishing Company, 1976.

Beck, Simone; Bertholle, Louisette; and Child, Julia. *Mastering the Art of French Cooking.* New York: Alfred A. Knopf, 1965.

Berolzheimer, Ruth, ed. *The Encyclopedia of Cooking* or *Culinary Arts Institute Cookbook.* Chicago: Consolidated Book Publishers, 1940 to 1955. (The correct title of this book is unknown. Portions of the title page were missing.)

Betty Crocker's Picture Cook Book, 2nd ed. New York: McGraw-Hill Book Company, Inc., 1956.

Boxer, Arabella; Innes, Jocasta; Parry-Crooke, Charlotte; and Esson, Lewis. *Herbs, Spices and Flavorings*. First published in Great Britain in 1984 by Octopus Books Ltd. First published in the U.S.A. in 1984 by Crescent Books under the title *The Encyclopedia of Herbs, Spices and Flavorings*. New York: Crescent Books, distributed by Crown Publishers, Inc., 1988.

Brickell, C. D., ed. *International Code of Nomenclature for Cultivated Plants—1980*. Utrecht: Bohn, Scheltema & Holkema, 1980.

Child, Mrs. Lydia Maria. *The American Frugal Housewife*, 12th ed. Boston: Carter, Hendee, and Co., 1832.

Code of Federal Regulations, Section 21, Parts 1 to 199, Revised as of April 1, 1991.

Considine, Douglas M.; Considine, P. E.; and Considine, Glenn D., ed. *Foods and Food Production Encyclopedia*. New York: Van Nostrand Reinhold Company, 1982.

Cost, Bruce. *Ginger East to West*. Berkeley, CA: Aris Books/Harris Publishing Company, Inc., 1984.

Craker, Lyle E., and Simon, James E., ed. *Herbs, Spices, and Medicinal Plants: Recent Advances in Botany, Horticulture and Pharmacology*, Vol. 1. Phoenix, AZ: Oryx Press, 1986.

Craker, Lyle E., and Simon, James E., ed. *Herbs, Spices, and Medicinal Plants: Recent Advances in Botany, Horticulture and Pharmacology*, Vol. 2. Phoenix, AZ: Oryx Press, 1987.

Cunningham, Marion. *The Fannie Farmer Baking Book*. New York: Alfred A. Knopf, 1984.

David, Elizabeth. *English Bread and Yeast Cookery*. American Edition with notes by Karen Hess. New York: Penguin Books, 1982.

Day, Avanelle, and Stuckey, Lillie. *The Spice Cookbook*. New York: David White Company, 1964.

De Gouy, L. P. *The Cookery Book*. New York: Leisure League of America, 1936.

De Gouy, Louis P. *The Gold Cook Book*. New York: Galahad Books, 1948.

Dods, Matilda Lees. *My Mother's Cook Book. A Series of Practical Lessons in the Art of Cooking*. Edited by Henrietta De Condé Sherman. Chicago: Thompson & Thomas, 1902.

Dorland, W. A. Newman. *The American Illustrated Medical Dictionary*, 22nd Ed. Edited by Richard M. Hewitt, E. C. L. Miller and Arthur H. Sanford. Philadelphia: W. B. Saunders Company, 1954.

Editors of Sunset Books and *Sunset Magazine*. *Sunset Oriental Cook Book*. Menlo Park, CA: Lane Publishing Co., 1985.

Editors of Time-Life Books. *The Time-Life International Cookbook*. New York: Holt, Rinehart and Winston, 1977.

Farmer, Fannie Merritt. *The Original Boston Cooking-School Cook Book* (A facsimile of the 1st edition, 1896). New York: Weathervane Books, a division of Barre Publishing, New York. Distributed by Crown Publishing, Inc. by arrangement with Hugh Lantes Levin, Associates, 1973.

Fenaroli, Prof. Dr. Giovanni. *Fenaroli's Handbook of Flavor Ingredients*. Edited, translated and revised by Thomas E. Furia and Nicoló Bellanca. Cleveland: Chemical Rubber Co., 1971.

Fobel, Jim. *Jim Fobel's Old-Fashioned Baking Book*. New York: Ballantine Books, a division of Random House, Inc., 1987.

Foster, Steven. *Herbal Bounty! The Gentle Art of Herb Culture*. Layton, Utah: Gibbs M. Smith, Inc., 1984. Salt Lake City: Peregrine Smith Books, 1984.

Frederick, J. George. *The Pennsylvania Dutch and their Cookery*. New York: The Business Bourse, 1935.

Fulton, Margaret. *Encyclopedia of Food & Cookery*. London: Octopus Books Limited, 1985.

Gleason, Henry A. and Cronquist, Arthur. *Manual of Vascular Plants of Northeastern United States and Adjacent Canada*. New York: D. Van Nostrand Company, 1963.

Gray, Peter. *The Mistress Cook*. New York: Oxford University Press, 1956.

Hartwig, Daphne Metaxas. *More Make Your Own Groceries*. New York: The Bobbs-Merrill Co., Inc., 1983.

Hedrick, U. P., Ed. *Sturtevant's Edible Plants of the World*. New York: Dover Publications, Inc., 1972.

Hershey Foods Corporation. *Hershey's 1934 Cookbook*. n.p.: Western Publishing Company, Inc., 1934.

Hershey Foods Corporation. *Hershey's Chocolate Treasury*. New York: Golden Press, 1984.

Hill, Barbara. *The Cook's Book of Essential Information*. Kennewick, Washington: Sumner House Press, 1987.

Hillman, Howard. *Kitchen Science*. Boston: Houghton Mifflin Company, 1981.

Hutchinson, Ruth. *The New Pennsylvania Dutch Cook Book*. New York: Harper & Row, Publishers, Inc. 1958.

Hutson, Lucinda. *The Herb Garden Cookbook*. Austin: Texas Monthly Press Inc., 1987.

Jones, Lester W., ed. *A Treasury of Spices*. New York: American Spice Trade Association, 1956.

Kander, Mrs. Simon, and Schoenfeld, Mrs. Henry. *The "Settlement" Cook Book, 1903, The Way to a Man's Heart* (A facsimile of the edition originally published in 1903 under the auspices of "The Settlement," Milwaukee, Wisconsin). New York: Gramercy Publishing Company, 1987.

Kowalchik, Claire, and Hylton, William H. *Rodale's Illustrated Encyclopedia of Herbs*. Emmaus, PA: Rodale Press, 1987

Langenheim, Jean H., and Thimann, Kenneth V. *Botany: Plant Biology and Its Relation to Human Affairs*. New York: John Wiley & Sons, 1982.

Larkin Housewives' Cook Book. Buffalo: Larkin Co., n.d.

Lemmon, Robert S., and Johnson, Charles C. *Wild Flowers of North America*. Garden City: Hanover House, 1961.

Leslie, Eliza. *Directions for Cookery and Its Various Branches*. 31st ed. Introduction and suggested recipes by Louis Szathmáry. Philadelphia: Cary & Hart, 1848; reprint ed., New York: Arno Press, A New York Times Company, New York, 1973.

Lust, John. *The Herb Book*. New York: Bantam Books, 1987.

Mabey, Richard, Ed. *The New Age Herbalist*. New York: Macmillan Publishing Company, 1988.

McCully, Helen. *Nobody Ever Tells You These Things About Food and Drink*. New York: Holt, Rinehart and Winston, 1967.

McGee, Harold. *On Food and Cooking: The Science and Lore of the Kitchen*. New York: Charles Scribner's Sons, 1985.

Meier, Mrs. Lina, compiler and editor. *The Art of German Cooking and Baking*, 8th ed. Milwaukee: Wetzel Brothers Printing Co., 1946.

Miller, Gloria Bley. *The Thousand Recipe Chinese Cookbook*. New York: G. P. Putnam's Sons, 1983.

Mindell, Earl. *Earl Mindell's Herb Bible*. New York: Simon & Schuster, 1992.

Modern Priscilla Cook Book. Boston: The Priscilla Publishing Company, 1924.

Montagné, Prosper. *Larousse Gastronomique: The Encyclopedia of Food, Wine and Cookery.* Translated by Nina Froud, Patience Gray, Maud Murdock and Barbara Macrae Taylor. Edited by Charlotte Turgeon and Nina Froud. Paris: Augé, Gillon, Hollier-Larousse, Moreau et Cie (Librairie Larousse), 1938. New York: Crown Publishers, Inc., 1961.

Parry, John W. *Spices Vol. I, The Story of Spices, The Spices Described.* New York: Chemical Publishing Company, Inc., 1969.

Parry, John W. *Spices Vol. II, Morphology, Histology, Chemistry.* New York: Chemical Publishing Company, Inc., 1969.

Pauli, Eugen. *Classical Cooking the Modern Way.* Edited by Marjorie S. Arkwright. Translated by Peter C. March and Monroe S. Levine based on the 7th German and the 1st French editions. New York: Van Nostrand Reinhold Company Inc., 1979.

Perkins, Wilma Lord. *The All New Fannie Farmer Boston Cooking School Cookbook,* 10th ed. Boston: Little, Brown and Company, 1959.

Price, Mary and Vincent. *A Treasury of Great Recipes.* n.p.: Ampersand Press, Inc., 1965.

Rombauer, Irma S. *The Joy of Cooking.* New York: The Bobbs-Merrill Company, 1943.

Rosengarten, Frederic, Jr. *The Book of Spices.* Philadelphia: Livingston Publishing Co., 1969.

Smith, Beverly Sutherland. *The Book of Chocolates and Petits Fours.* Tucson, AZ: HP Books, 1986.

Smith, Jeff. *The Frugal Gourmet on Our Immigrant Ancestors.* New York: William Morrow and Company, Inc., 1990.

Stobart, Tom. *Herbs, Spices and Flavorings.* Woodstock, NY: Milton Peter Corp. in association with The Overlook Press, 1982.

Sultan, William J. *Practical Baking,* 3rd ed. Westport, CT: The AVI Publishing Co., Inc., 1976.

Teubner, Christian, and Wolter, Annette. *Back vergnügen wie noch nie.* Munich: Gräfe und Unzer GmbH, 1984.

Vogel, Virgil J. *American Indian Medicine.* Norman: University of Oklahoma Press, 1970.

Voss, E. G., ed. *International Code of Botanical Nomenclature.* Utrecht: Bohn, Scheltema & Holkema, 1983.

Washburn-Crosby's Gold Medal Cook Book. Minneapolis: Washburn-Crosby Co., 1910; reprint ed., Minneapolis: General Mills, Inc., 1983.

Wason, Betty. *Cooks, Gluttons & Gourmets A History of Cooking*. Garden City: Doubleday & Company, Inc., 1962.

Weiner, Michael A. *Earth Medicine—Earth Foods*. New York: Collier Books, 1972.

Woman's Home Companion Cook Book. Garden City: Garden City Publishing Co., Inc. by arrangement with The Crowell-Collier Publishing Co. and P. F. Collier and Son Corporation, 1946.